副理事长单位
Deputy Council Directors

理事单位
Council Members

EDITORIAL
主编寄语

时间 2019年4月1日　**地点** 安徽省黄山市徽州区西溪南村

中国的乡村振兴是一个需要通过实践研究来探索其实现路径和策略的宏大课题，涉及农民的生存与发展、农业效率和农产品品质的提升、宅基地产权登记与管理，以及生态和文化遗产保护等多方面的问题，目前尚无可以推而广之的模式。为此，北京大学建筑与景观设计学院团队已连续多年致力于乡村振兴的实践研究，并在安徽省黄山市徽州区建立了可以长期观察乡村生活的"望山生活"实验基地。图为学院师生在徽州区西溪南村开展实践研究的场景。

Date April 1, 2019　**Location** Xixinan Village, Huizhou District, Huangshan City, Anhui Province

Rural revitalization in China is an ambitious agenda which needs efforts of practice research to explore the paths and strategies, ranging from the survival and development of farmers, the enhancement of productivity, the quality improvement of agricultural products, the registration and management on homestead property right to ecological protection and cultural heritage conservation. However, it has not seen any solution that can be applicable to all the regions throughout the country. After years of practice research on rural revitalization, a team from the College of Architecture and Landscape of Peking University has been working on addressing such issues by founding the Wangshan Life Laboratory in Huizhou District of Huangshan City, Anhui Province, which studies rural localities through long-term field observation. In the photo, teachers and students of the college were in a field trip for practice research.

实践研究：创新知识和方法的范式

俞孔坚
哈佛大学设计学博士；美国艺术与科学院院士；北京大学建筑与景观设计学院教授

翻译 田乐 王胤瑜 田晓劼

摘要

通过回顾“北大－土人”实践研究的模式以及遇到的种种挑战，作者总结了三点思考：1）实践研究的意义在于在不断的尝试中积累经验，最终获得有用的知识和解决实际问题的方法；2）实践研究主体一般为院校教师、科研机构的研究员、学生，以及在实践一线的规划设计师，但国内现行的学术考核方式过度追求论文引用而非实践成就，甚至有着深厚研究传统的规划设计研究院也鲜有时间精力对实践中的问题进行深入探讨，以致模式套用成风；3）规划设计实践的充分市场化才是实践研究可持续发展的不竭动力。“原型研究”作为实践研究的一种，将有助于不断拓宽景观设计学科的发展路径，为设计师及相关领域的学者提供前瞻性的设计思路和更具韧性的工作方法，以适应充满不确定挑战的未来。

关键词

实践研究；规划设计；知识创新；范式；学科发展

https://doi.org/10.15302/J-LAF-1-010009
收稿时间 RECEIVED DATE / 2020-06-22
中图分类号 / TU984, TU986
文献标识码 / C

本文引用格式 / PLEASE CITE THIS ARTICLE AS

Yu, K. (2020). Practice Research: A Paradigm for the Innovation of Knowledge and Methodology. Landscape Architecture Frontiers, 8(4), 4-9. https://doi.org/10.15302/J-LAF-1-010009

2020年6月9日晚，一场中美国际线上研讨会持续了近两个小时。这是“实践研究”系列讨论的第一场，旨在揭示大学和规划设计机构如何通过研究，就具体实践问题实现理论、方法和技术创新，并促进相关应用与推广。

本次研讨会由麻省理工学院终身教授、著名景观和生态学者安妮·惠斯顿·斯本发起。她曾深入研究美国生态规划的开创者伊恩·L·麦克哈格在宾夕法尼亚大学和他本人创立的WMRT事务所进行的实践研究（包括其著名的创新性实践研究成果《设计结合自然》），以及两个机构间的互动关系。她亦非常好奇中国的相关实践研究如何进行，并为此于麻省理工学院设立了专门的研究课题，重点探讨过去20年间北京大学建筑与景观设计学院和土人设计的实践研究，以及这两个机构之间如何互动并进行知识创新，以解决中国城镇化过程中出现的紧迫问题。受斯本教授的启发，我回顾了“北大－土人”实践研究的模式以及遇到的种种挑战，由此总结了三点思考，与读者分享：

第一，为什么要做实践研究？当我们面对全新而陌生的问题，且缺乏成熟的解决方案或技术支持时，针对性研究便十分必要。例如，由于文化背景、社会制度及地域条件的不同，中国城镇化进程中出现的一系列城市问题，均难以从其他国家的经验和教训中直接找到可靠的预测模式和可借鉴的解决方案；同时，现存的理论方法繁多，但哪种方法更适用于当下中国所面临的具体问题亦不得而知。在某种意义上，这便是“摸着石头过河”——只有通过实践研究才能得到真正有用的知识和解决实际问题的方法，在不断的尝试中积累经验，最终解决问题。

第二，谁来做实践研究？一般而言，院校教师、科研机构的研究员、学生，以及在实践一线的规划设计师是实践研究的主体。但事实上，国内现行的学术考核方式并不鼓励实践研究，而是片面追求论文引用，对实践的理解偏差使得学者更倾向于做学究式的研究，从故纸堆里去寻找课题，热衷于申请由政府设立的所谓“纵向项目”，而较少考虑由企业资助的、用于解决实际问题的“横向项目”。在成果评定中，直接与社会实践相结合的研究课题或多或少会受到忽视。事实上，在“以文章论英雄”的大学里，从职位招聘开始就已经注定了实践研究的弱势地位，也奠定了院校的研究氛围：脱离实践的空泛研究不仅于解决当下的实际问题毫无益处，也使学生们在毕业后无法快速适应社会需求。长此以往，学科和专业的创新能力和解决问题的能力便每况愈下，学科也将失去其存在的意义。

在中国的城镇化和市场化的大潮到来之前，规划设计机构原本有着非常深厚的研究传统，为解决城乡发展过程中的症结开展了大量名副其实的研究，因此常被称为“规划设计研究院”。后来，越来越多的研究院所改制为公司，进入市场；与此同时，在巨变的社会经济环境中，新问题层出不穷，对知识创新和模式创新的需求也随之增加。然而，模式套用之风大行其道，诸如“一轴N廊N中心”“南扩、北控、东拓、西优”的盲目照搬充斥于大江南北各个城市的规划中，“跨江发展”“向海发展”成了套路，滨江大道、滨河大道蔚然成风。建筑与景观设计行业中千篇一律、自欺欺人的规划设计招投标、恶劣的低价竞标，以及近20年不变的低取费标准，导致规划设计人员鲜少能够投入足够的时间精力对实践中的问题进行深入研究，由此造成行业内劣币驱逐良币、从业者薪资和企业利润低下的状况，整体上使一个具有研究性的实践行业退化为“廉价劳动力”主导的生产性行业。在自然资源保护与城乡规划系统内，专业和行业难以适应国家行政机构的调整和国家需求的重大转变，亦暴露出过去数十年来实践研究的严重缺位。

PRACTICE RESEARCH: A PARADIGM FOR THE INNOVATION OF KNOWLEDGE AND METHODOLOGY

YU Kongjian
Doctor of Design at Graduate School of Design, Harvard University; Honorary Foreign Fellow of the American Academy of Arts and Sciences; Professor of College of Architecture and Landscape, Peking University

TRANSLATED BY Tina TIAN WANG Yinyu TIAN Xiaojie

ABSTRACT
In this article, the author concluded the patterns and challenges of practice research by Peking University-Turenscape into the answers to three questions: 1) By conducting practice research, people can gain the knowledge and methodologies to address authentic practice issues with constant attempts; 2) College faculties and students, researchers, and planners / designers are the agencies of practice research, but they are in dilemma because of the over pursuit for paper publication and citation in academic performance assessment, and the insufficient time and budget for research leading a fact that generic planning schemes and stereotypes are popularly employed; And 3) the healthy development and long-term promotion of practice research relies on the growth of the market-oriented industry. As one type of the practice research, "prototype study" offers a paradigm for the innovation of knowledge and methodology. Oriented to future challenges and uncertainties, it would help extend the horizon of Landscape Architecture, providing designers and scholars with prospective design insights and flexible working methods.

KEYWORDS
Practice Research; Planning and Design; Knowledge Innovation; Paradigm; Disciplinary Development

In the evening of June 9, 2020, a two-hour online China-US seminar took place as the first session of the Practice Research serial seminars, aiming to explore what planning and design colleges and institutions should do to encourage theoretical, methodological, and technological innovations on practical issues and promote associated applications.

This seminar was initiated by Anne Whiston Spirn, a tenured professor of MIT and a reputed landscape architect and ecologist. She has conducted extensive studies on the practice research carried out by Ian L. McHarg at the University of Pennsylvania and the WMRT Firm led by himself, including one of his most notable achievements of innovative practice research, *Design with Nature*. Meanwhile, she is curious about the practice research in China, and has started a program at MIT focusing on the work of the College of Architecture and Landscape of Peking University and Turenscape over the past two decades, and how the interaction between research and practice has promoted knowledge innovation to address the pressing issues of the urbanization in China. Inspired by Professor Spirn, my thoughts on the patterns and challenges of practice research by Peking University-Turenscape can be concluded into the answers to three questions:

First, why do we need practice research? Targeted practice research can help improve our understanding to new discourses and generate theoretical guidance or technical roadmaps to new challenges. For instance, issues arising midst the urbanization in China see few references of prediction patterns or solutions from other countries, given the regional differences in cultural contexts, social institution, and geographical conditions. Also, the applicability of the current wide-ranging theories and methods remains unknown to Chinese cases. In some sense, it requires the spirit of "crossing the river by feeling the stones"—Only by conducting practice research can we gain the knowledge and methodologies to address authentic practice issues with constant attempts.

Second, who does practice research? They can be college faculties and students, researchers, and planners / designers. However, the instructional evaluation of faculties of most Chinese design colleges measures the number of published papers and citations, rather than practice research, leading to a pedantic ecology where scholars are keen on studying the subjects commissioned by the government, instead of those sponsored by private enterprises coping with the problems in practice. In addition, the subjects on social topics are usually less studied. This "paper-first" instructional institution also defines the faculty structure of colleges and universities, neglecting practice research in curriculum design and teaching systems. The research that divorces from practice is bound to fail to solve actual problems, and such a college training would not guarantee the graduates to be prepared for real design tasks. This deteriorates the innovation capacity and problem-solving ability of design professionals and hinders the development of design disciplines to respond to contemporary missions.

In China, before the aggressive urbanization and market reform, many state-owned planning and design institutes had a good tradition of "practice as research" with authentic cases of urban-rural development; Afterwards, with the rapid changes of China's socio-economic environment, these institutes have finished their transformation into capital-driven firms, which have faced new challenges in knowledge and technical innovation and working-mode reform so as to fulfill the profession's contemporary tasks. However, generic planning schemes are popularly employed, and stereotypes like "axes-corridors-centers," "cross-river development," or "coastal growth" are prevailing across China. Worse, the fraudulent or vicious bidding and the low payment standard never raised for almost 20 years have hindered the industry's inputs in practice research. As a result, planning and design professionals have seen a degradation in research capacity and innovative intelligence, who now become nothing but "cheap labor force" for repetitive works, failing to respond to the new requirements of the state's institutional reforms in natural resource conservation and urban-rural planning.

第三，面对当前的不利状况，如何推动实践研究和知识创新？首先，我们希望高校及研究机构能够认识到实践研究的价值，并由此改变各种有损于实践研究积极性的“指挥棒”——事实上，此次新冠肺炎疫情已经以生命为代价，无情地揭示了中国实践研究的窘境，也迫使有关部门名义上取消了唯论文和引用率为导向的评价体系[1]；其次，少数有情怀的学者对社会问题异常敏感，且富有研究热情，他们利用自身影响力引领后辈积极开展实践研究，这些努力和尝试应该被鼓励；再次，随着市场机制逐步发挥作用，实践研究将使研究性规划设计机构具备持续的竞争优势，使他们可以有更高的取费用于长期创新和研发，用更高的薪酬吸引优秀人才，以形成市场选择下优胜劣汰的良性循环。正如恩格斯百余年前所言：社会一旦有技术上的需要，则这种需要就会比十所大学更能把科学推向前进[2]。因此，规划设计实践的充分市场化是实践研究最终获得重视和可持续发展的真正动力。

苟日新，日日新，又日新[3]。实践研究是面对动态的社会和自然挑战，不断创新思想、理论、方法和技术的必由途径，对于景观设计和城乡规划设计学科而言尤其如此。说到底，规划设计实践本身就是针对某一个或一组问题，寻求最优解的研究过程。而本期所探讨的“原型研究”作为一种创新知识和方法的范式，即为实践研究的一种。面向未来挑战的原型研究成果将不断拓宽景观设计学科的发展路径，为设计师及相关领域的学者提供更具前瞻性的设计思路和更有弹性的工作方法，以促使我们更好地适应充满不确定性挑战的未来。**LAF**

Third, how to promote practice research and knowledge innovation? First of all, colleges and research institutes should re-emphasize the importance of practice research for design disciplines, and then abolish the mechanisms impeding research enthusiasm—Alarmed by the cost of lives during COVID-19 pandemic and the problems exposed in this period, the "paper-first" evaluation system of college faculties has been called off by related departments[1]. Moreover, researchers who are enthusiastic for addressing social issues through design interventions and influencing younger scholars to put more efforts in practice research should be more rewarded. Also, the increasingly market-oriented industry is reshaping the climate in the fields of planning and design, where the institutes good at practice research would be more competitive in business and talent recruitment. As stated by Friedrich Engels over a century ago, one market demand works better than ten universities to stimulate technical progress[2]. Therefore, the healthy development and long-term promotion of practice research relies on the growth of the market-oriented industry.

As an ancient Chinese adage advises, if one can make things better for one day, he should make them better every day[3]. In face of the ever-changing social and natural challenges, practice research paves the path for innovations in theory, methodology, and technology. This is particularly true for Landscape Architecture and Urban and Rural Planning, because planning and design practices are essentially a research process to find out the optimal solutions. As one type of the practice research, "prototype study" discussed in this issue offers a paradigm for the innovation of knowledge and methodology. Oriented to future challenges and uncertainties, it would help extend the horizon of Landscape Architecture, providing designers and scholars with prospective design insights and flexible working methods. **LAF**

REFERENCES

[1] Ministry of Education of the People's Republic of China. (2020, February 20). Notice from the Ministry of Education and the Ministry of Science and Technology on Issuing "Several Opinions on Regulating the Use of Related Indicators of SCI Papers in Colleges and Universities to Establish Rational Evaluation Orientation". Retrieved from http://www.moe.gov.cn/srcsite/A16/moe_784/202002/t20200223_423334.html

[2] Lu, J. (2008). Interpretation of Marxism Literature. Beijing: China Social Sciences Press.

[3] Zeng, S. (2018). The Great Learning (Q. Liu, Tran.). Nanjing: Phoenix Science Press.

本文引用格式 / PLEASE CITE THIS ARTICLE AS

Zhang, Z., & Liu, X. (2020). Control and Uncertainty: Towards a Paradigm of Prototyping. Landscape Architecture Frontiers, 8(4), 10-25. https://doi.org/10.15302/J-LAF-1-020032

https://doi.org/10.15302/J-LAF-1-020032 收稿时间 RECEIVED DATE / 2020-05-30 中图分类号 / TU413.6, Q811.3 文献标识码 / A

控制与不确定性：对原型思维范式的展望

CONTROL AND UNCERTAINTY: TOWARDS A PARADIGM OF PROTOTYPING

张子豪
弗吉尼亚大学建筑学院构建环境博士候选人、景观系讲师

刘浔
弗吉尼亚大学建筑学院构建环境博士研究生、景观系教师

ZHANG Zihao*
PhD Candidate in Constructed Environment and Lecturer in Landscape Architecture, School of Architecture, University of Virginia

LIU Xun
PhD Student in Constructed Environment and Teaching Fellow in Landscape Architecture, School of Architecture, University of Virginia

*Corresponding Author
Address: Campbell Hall, School of Architecture, 110 Bayly Dr, Charlottesville, VA 22903, USA
Email: zz3ub@virginia.edu

摘要

本文探索了一种不同于模型设计的原型思维新范式。在将控制论与景观设计进行并置分析后发现，自20世纪至21世纪初，景观设计学科的发展规律反映了控制论在同一时期的发展进程。早期关于系统动力学的决定论和线性理解，逐渐被基于演生论和开放式的主张所取代。在演生论的框架下，笔者强调一类可被理解为原型的特殊模型不能被基于“建模 - 预测 - 控制”的传统框架所包容。原型并不像传统建模过程那样，用模型代表一个开放的生命系统，原型本身就可以被理解为一个独立的生命体系。原型思维可以取代模型设计，并展现出三方面的特质：1）原型本身即具有“生命力”，这是设计与创造力的根本；2）原型的真正意义在于其未被定义的状态，而不在于其可被定义的最直接的用途；3）这种未被定义的状态能够提供无限可能，并将人们与未来之间的关系从过去的偶然性和预测转变为期待与展望。

关键词

原型；景观；控制论；系统思维；不确定性；控制

ABSTRACT

This paper maps out a new paradigm of prototyping that acts as an alternative to the model-making paradigm. By juxtaposing the cybernetics movement with landscape design, the authors have mapped out a development in landscape discourse that mirrors the movement of cybernetics in the 20th century and early 21st century. The early deterministic and linear understanding of systems dynamics is replaced by an emergent and open-ended view. Taking on a framework of emergence, the authors highlight a special type of model that does not fit within the conventional model-predict-control framework. Rather than models that represent another living system, these models are living systems in themselves with autonomy and lives. This special type of model can be understood as prototypes. Prototyping replaces model-making and exhibits three distinctive qualities: 1) A prototype has a life of its own, which serves as the basis for design and creativity; 2) The real usefulness of a prototype lies in its undefined identity rather than its defined and direct application; And 3) the identified quality provides a wide range of possibilities, thus changing our relationship with the future from chance and prediction to anticipation and hope.

KEYWORDS

Prototype; Landscape; Cybernetics; Systems Thinking; Uncertainty; Control

编辑 田晓劼 **翻译** 张书瑞 张子豪 刘浔 田晓劼
EDITED BY TIAN Xiaojie **TRANSLATED BY** ZHANG Shurui ZHANG Zihao LIU Xun TIAN Xiaojie

1 引言：模型、控制与不确定性

“景观的非人类属性及其文化构建之间，以及人类对自然的敬畏和对其进行利用、管理与控制的冲动之间，总是存在着矛盾。”[1]景观设计师在对生命系统和物质进行设计时，经常会遇到意料之外的情况。那么，原型概念将如何帮助设计师应对设计中的不确定性？

牛津英语词典将“原型”（prototype）定义为“人或事物的第一个或主要类型；基于此本源可以模拟或衍生出其他事物；是一种典范（exemplar）或初型（archetype）”[2]。原型一词首先被普遍使用于工业设计和软件工程中，用来指代以概念测试为目的的第一台机器或第一个程序。原型概念具有双重属性：一方面，它是一种表明某一事物与另一事物之间存在着隐喻关系的模型；另一方面，原型还具有一种超越隐喻的真实感。原型的双重属性使其成为一种特殊的模型，通过它可以反思控制与不确定性之间的矛盾。

然而，由于西方文化中根深蒂固的“手段—目的链”思维方式（即以手段达到目的），原型理论在历史上被长期忽视。在西方哲学传统中，人们往往用一种理想形态（eidos）作为模型，并将其设为目标（telos）采取行动。正如法国哲学家弗朗索瓦·朱利安所说，“我们（西方人）将目光集中在构想出的模型上，并将其投射在现实世界中，以此来指导我们的行动；从这个意义上讲，我们选择去干预周遭世界并赋予现实以形式。”[3]这种思考模式将理论与实践区分开来：理论成为模型的基础，而实践则成为将模型变为现实的一系列行动。最重要的是，行动是否有效以及可否被测量，也受到这种思维习惯的深刻影响：人们习惯于评价工具和措施的功效性。由此可见，功效性决定了手段—目的链的思维逻辑。最后，尽管人们想把一个理想的模型投射在周遭世界中，并试图研究出各种方法来实现这一模型，但过程中总会出现无法预测的情况，影响计划的控制和实施。因此，所谓不确定性是指那些在构想出的模型中无法预测的状况[3]。

在当代的环境实践中，手段—目的链体现在方方面面。例如，在过去几年间，环境实践中出现了新一轮对建模的讨论。包括智慧城市在内的许多研究都提出要把传感网络融入环境中，从而产出更多数

1 Introduction: Model, Control, and Uncertainty

“There is always a tension in landscape between the reality and autonomy of the nonhuman and its cultural construction, between the human impulse to wonder at the wild and the compulsion to use, manage, and control.”[1] Designing with living systems and materials, landscape designers always have to deal with unexpected outcomes. What insights can the idea of prototype provide to address the issue of uncertainty?

Oxford English Dictionary defines the term of “prototype” as “[t]he first or primary type of a person or thing; an original on which something is modeled or from which it is derived; an exemplar, an archetype”[2]. The term was first popularized in industrial design and software engineering to denote the first machine or the first piece of program that was built to prove the concept. A prototype possesses a twofold quality: On the one hand, a prototype is a type of model, which has a kind of metaphorical relationship between one thing and another; On the other hand, a prototype also carries a sense of realism that is beyond a metaphor. This twofold quality makes prototype a special type of model that can transform people’s understanding of the tension between control and uncertainty.

However, rooted in the western means-end chain relationship, prototypes have always been overlooked theoretically and historically. In the western philosophical tradition, one envisages an ideal form (eidos) as a model, and then the model can serve as a goal (telos) and, at the same time, an end that calls for actions. As French Philosopher Francois Jullien puts forward that “with our eyes fixed on the model that we have conceived, which we project on the world and on which we base a plan to be executed, we choose to intervene in the world and give a form to reality.”[3] Based on this line of reasoning, theory can be differentiated from practice, the former being the basis for the model, and the latter being a set of operations that make the model turn into reality. Most importantly, with the means-end relationship, the idea of effectiveness and measure can be tied into this habitual reasoning. Once a range of possible tools and actions are at hand, their effectiveness will be evaluated. Efficacy becomes the concept that ties the “means” and the “end” together. Finally, although people want to project an ideal model on the world and develop means to achieve this end, unexpected circumstances will always rise to undermine the action and control regime of any plan. Thus uncertainty denotes those events that are outside the predictions allowed by the conceived model[3].

This means-end chain can be observed in every aspect of contemporary environmental practices. For example, the past few years have seen a new round of model-making in the

据，机器学习（ML）算法便能利用这些数据来构建人工智能（AI）系统，随后将AI系统（即模型）应用于信息物理系统之中，以管理各种环境过程（如雨洪控制[4]）。但是，这一建模框架受困于手段—目的链思维方式，因为在手段—目的链中，不确定性只被理解为模型与环境间必须要被消除的差异，而这种控制和不确定性间的矛盾只会一直横亘在人们与未来的关系之间。

在过去几十年间，景观理论与实践不断挑战着手段—目的链以及模型在环境设计实践中的作用[5]。这些景观实践强调了原型作为一种特殊模型的价值，而这种价值并不能用手段—目的链思维方式来解释。本文以景观实践为例，阐明原型在环境设计中的价值，即原型提供了一种新的方式来思考建模过程：建模不是为了消除不确定性，而在于探索更广泛的可能性。如此一来，人们与未来的关系也不再受困于控制与不确定性之间的矛盾，而是转变为一种期待与展望，这对于人类应对气候变化等诸多环境挑战而言至关重要。

鉴于模型和控制与不确定性之间的矛盾是控制论和系统论的核心议题，因此，在控制论和系统思维的发展过程中，重新研究如何诠释原型也就变得尤为重要。如将一系列景观作品和控制论的三次思潮进行对照，会发现早期控制论中的手段—目的链并不适用于当代系统性的景观设计；相反，景观设计可以为原型思维提供不同见解。

对原型的新的认知能够帮助解析控制论运动中的原型思维概念，并发掘了包括诺伯特·维纳的“蛾”和“臭虫”，以及约翰·冯·诺伊曼的细胞自动机在内的一系列“反馈生物”①。受手段—目的链思维方式的影响，这些可以作为控制论运动原型的反馈生物一直为人所忽视。基于此，这些控制论原型可与一个景观学科的案例——哈佛大学设计研究生院（GSD）的响应式环境及人工产品实验室（REAL）进行

environmental discourse. Myriad of research initiatives, such as smart cities, propose to embed sensing networks in the environment to produce more data. Then, the environmental data feeds into Machine Learning (ML) algorithms to build Artificial Intelligence (AI) systems. Finally, these AI systems, or models, are distributed in the cyberphysical systems to manage all kinds of environmental processes, such as stormwater control[4]. However, trapped in a means-end relationship, this framework only conceptualizes uncertainty as model-environment difference that needs to be reduced one way or another. In the means-end chain, human's relationship with the future always revolves around the tension between control and uncertainty.

Landscape theory and practice in the past decades have provided a body of work that challenges the means-end chain and the role of models in environmental practices[5]. These practices highlight the value of prototypes as a special type of model that does not fit within the means-end chain. This paper uses landscape practices to articulate the values of prototypes in the environmental discourse, and argues that with prototypes, model-making can be envisaged in such a way that is no longer on the line of reducing uncertainty but about providing a wide range of possibilities. Thus, our relationship with the future is transformed from the tension between control and uncertainty to anticipation and hope, which is crucial when humanities are faced with environmental challenges such as climate change.

Since the idea of model and the tension between control and uncertainty have always been central to the field of cybernetics and systems theory, it is crucial to re-examine how the idea of prototype was articulated in the development of cybernetics and systems thinking. Contrasting a body of landscape works and the three waves of cybernetics movement shows that the contemporary system-based landscape design framework does not fit within the means-end that is entailed by early cybernetic principles; Instead, landscape design can provide an alternative understanding of model-making on the line of prototyping.

This updated understanding can help parse out the concept of prototyping in the cybernetics movement and unearth a family of "cybernetic creatures,"① including Norbert Wiener's "the moth" and "the bedbug," and John von Neumann's cellular automaton, as prototypes in the cybernetics movement which has been overlooked within the means-end chain. These cybernetic prototypes can be juxtaposed with a case study in landscape design—a hydromorphology table experiment conducted at the Responsive Environments & Artifacts Lab

① Cybernetics研究的是动物和机器之间的控制与反馈机制，而控制只是其应用领域，单纯将cybernetics译为“控制论”并不准确且易造成歧义，因此本文将cybernetic creatures和cybernetic machine中的cybernetic译为“反馈”。

① Cybernetics studies the control and feedback mechanism between animals and machines, and control is only its application field. It is not accurate and easy to cause ambiguity to simply translate cybernetics as "控制论". Therefore, this paper translates cybernetics into "反馈" when it refers to cybernetic creatures and cybernetic machines.

的水文地貌沙床实验——进行并置分析。这一案例可以帮助总结出原型的三个特征，以重新理解环境实践中的不确定性。

2 背景：控制论与景观设计

控制论是自20世纪40年代以来在美国发展出的一个交叉学科研究领域。第二次世界大战后，包括工程师、数学家、人类学家和生态学家等在内的知识分子基于系统思维的新理论框架对机械系统和生物系统间的相互控制与交流进行了研究。控制论的核心焦点是如何通过反馈机制控制不同的系统，以减少不确定性。直到近几年，学者们才开始关注控制论原理对景观设计的影响[6][7]。有学者认为，某些控制论理念是在20世纪60年代通过生态科学和艺术等学科渗透到景观设计学科中来的。伊恩·麦克哈格和劳伦斯·哈普林是在控制论与景观设计之间建立联系的两位关键性人物[7]。但由于控制论的交叉学科属性，系统论思想早已盛行于各学科，因此控制论中的概念也早在20世纪便已经对学界产生了广泛影响。控制论最初提出的诸多概念（如反馈、耦合、自生系统论）已被纳入社会学、计算机科学、系统理论、生态学和人文学科，而这些学科都是景观设计师汲取灵感的土壤。因此，可以说自20世纪60年代以来，控制论以及控制与不确定性等议题已广为人知。本文通过介绍20世纪中叶以来控制论与景观设计理论和实践各自的发展历程，将重点论述原型思维对景观设计理论和实践的影响，从而帮助景观设计师重新思考不确定性这一议题。

凯瑟琳·海尔斯将控制论的发展概括为三次发生于不同学科领域的思潮[8]。第一次思潮（通常也被称为一阶控制论）是指1946 ~ 1953年间召开的关于控制论的“梅西会议”以及此后20年间的相关研究。维纳和冯·诺伊曼等早期控制论学者致力于研究稳态系统的反馈机制和控制策略。第一次思潮后期，包括玛格丽特·米德、格里高里·贝特森和海因茨·冯·福斯特等在内的人类学家和哲学家，开始对工程师在建模过程中扮演的观察者身份提出质疑，并提出二阶控制论的新

(REAL) of Harvard Graduate School of Design (GSD). With the cases, the case study can help map out three characteristics of prototypes that provide an alternative understanding of uncertainty in environmental practices.

2 Background: Cybernetics and Landscape Design

Cybernetics is an interdisciplinary field of study that started in the United States since the 1940s, when a team of post-war intellectuals, including engineers, mathematicians, anthropologists, and ecologists, converged on a new theoretical model based on systems thinking to understand control and communication between mechanical and biological systems. The core concern in the field is about how to control different systems through feedback mechanisms to mitigate uncertainty. It is only in recent years that scholars have started to pay attention to the influence of cybernetics principles on landscape design[6][7]. It is argued that cybernetics concepts instilled into the landscape discipline via ecological sciences and arts in the 1960s, and Ian McHarg and Lawrence Halprin were two prominent figures who established the link between cybernetics and landscape design[7]. However, because of the interdisciplinary nature of cybernetics, its concepts were instilled in every aspect of intellectual life in the 20th century as systems theory has prevailed across disciplines. Many ideas such as feedback, coupling, and autopoiesis that were initially developed in the field of cybernetics have been imported into disciplines such as Sociology, Computer Science, Systems Theory, Ecology, and Humanities, all of which are fields where landscape architects have been drawing inspirations. Thus, it can be simply recognized that, since the 1960s, cybernetics and the issue of control and uncertainty have been "in the air." This paper contrasts the cybernetics movement with landscape design theory and practice since the mid-20th century and highlights the idea of prototyping in both fields that help landscape architects rethink the issue of uncertainty.

Katherine Hayles schematized the development of cybernetics as three waves of research mobilizing among different fields of study[8]. The first wave of research, commonly known as first-order cybernetics, speaks to the Macy Conferences on cybernetics from 1946 to 1953 and the research in the following two decades. Early cyberneticians such as Wiener and von Neumann focused on the feedback mechanism and control strategies in homeostatic systems. Towards the end of the first wave of research, anthropologists and philosophers including Margret Mead, Gregory Bateson, and Heinz von Foerster problematized the role of engineers as observers in the model-making process, trying to propose a new framework,

框架——这一框架将观察者作为反馈系统的一部分（图1）。这种观念上的转变引发了20世纪60年代后期至70年代的第二次研究思潮。这期间，学者们致力于探寻观察者在建模过程中的作用，其中智利生物学家温贝托·曼图拉那和弗朗西斯科·瓦雷拉提出了“自生系统论”，以阐释系统如何利用物质和信息流维持自身属性[9]。之后，瓦雷拉开始涉足人工生命领域，并引发了于20世纪90年代初期兴起的第三次控制论思潮，其中的焦点议题是演生论与复杂性。通过人工生命实验这种多智能体模拟，学者们认为诸如“智能”和“意识”之类的复杂现象实际上可以被理解为分布式系统之间相互作用的结果。自20世纪90年代后期以来，第三次思潮开始不断挑战人类例外论，并引发了一系列后人类主义的思考[8]。

控制论的三次思潮的研究焦点可以与景观研究和实践进行比照（图2）。麦克哈格的生态学设计方法对于景观的控制可以视为一阶控制论的一种体现。工程师们通常通过控制熵来维持一个机械系统的稳态；在热力学中，熵是指系统向着无序状态发展的趋势；麦克哈格在其著作中大量使用熵的概念，并将其与生态适应性进行类比。在他看来，熵即不确定性，会对生态系统的完整性造成威胁。因此，他认为景观设计师应遵循理想的生态演替模型来控制景观变化，最终达到生态系统“演替顶级”的平衡状态[7]。然而，当代景观理论和实践注重开放性与演生，而麦克哈格设计框架中的环境决定论和对于生态过程的线性理解已遭到质疑。[10]

控制论的第二次思潮可以与大都会建筑事务所（OMA）的两个景观设计项目进行比照。其中一个是OMA于1982年参加的法国拉·维莱特公园设计竞赛作品，另一个是于20世纪90年代末参加的加拿大当斯

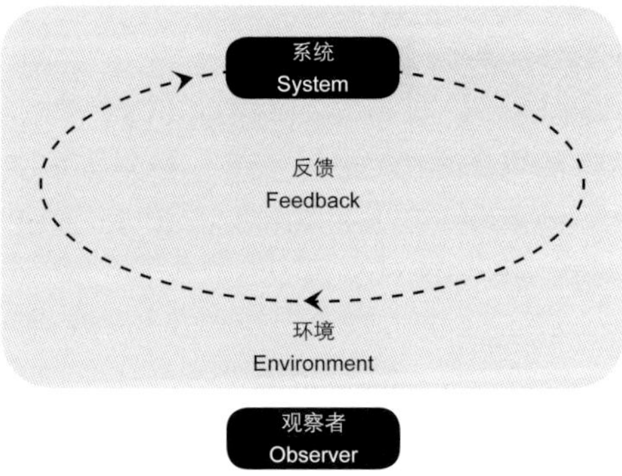

© 张子豪
1-1

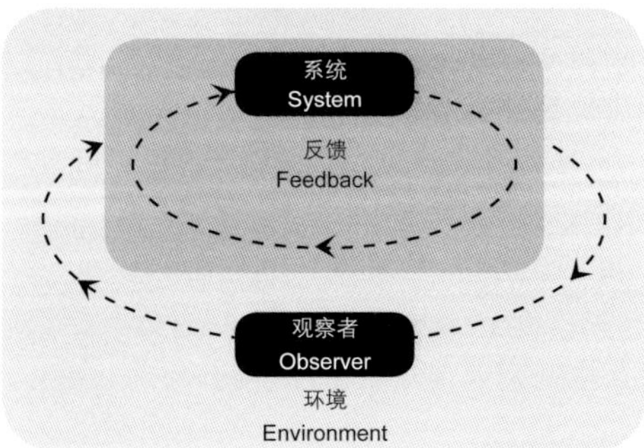

© 张子豪
1-2

known as second-order cybernetics, to include observers as part of the cybernetic system (Fig. 1). This conceptual shift gave rise to the second wave of research from the late 1960s to the 1970s, in which scholars focused on observing systems and their role in the model-making process. Chilean biologists Humberto Maturana and Francisco Varela introduced the term “autopoiesis” (self-production) to conceptualize how systems use the material and information flow to maintain their identities[9].Varela then ventured into the field of artificial life, thus connecting the third wave of cybernetics research in the early 1990s. The key concepts are emergence and complexity. Through the experiment of artificial life—a multi-agent simulation—scholars posit that complex phenomena such as intelligence and consciousness are, in fact, results of interactions between distributed systems. The third wave of research thus has challenged human exceptionalism and given rise to a range of posthumanist considerations since the late 1990s[8].

A body of landscape research and projects can be contrasted with the three waves of cybernetics in terms of their major concerns (Fig. 2). McHarg’s ecologically inspired design methodology can be understood as a version of landscape control through first-order cybernetics. To control a mechanical system, engineers usually manage the entropy to maintain the system’s homeostasis. In thermodynamics, entropy refers to the tendency of a system to move into disorder and chaos. McHarg used the concept of entropy extensively throughout his writing and always compared entropy with ecological fitness. For McHarg, entropy is another term for uncertainty, which poses a threat to the integrity of the ecosystem. Thus, landscape designers’ work is to control landscape change by following a set of ideal models of ecological successions and finally reach an equilibrium state as expressed in the “climax stage” of an ecosystem[7]. From a perspective of contemporary landscape theories and practices that focus on open-endedness and emergence, McHarg’s design framework has been critiqued for its inherent environmental determinism and linear understanding of ecological processes.[10]

The second wave of cybernetics can be contrasted with two landscape projects by OMA. The first one is the entry for the Parc de la Villette competition in 1982, and the second is the entry for Toronto’s Downsview Park competition in the late 1990s called “Tree City”[11][12]. The two projects can be understood as a seriation in which the designers deployed the tactic of “self-production” of the park system as design strategies, and the urban parks were understood as an autopoietic (self-producing) system that uses flows of material and information to reproduce their own organizations. An autopoietic system

1-1. 一阶控制论
1-2. 二阶控制论

1-1. First-order Cybernetics
1-2. Second-order Cybernetics

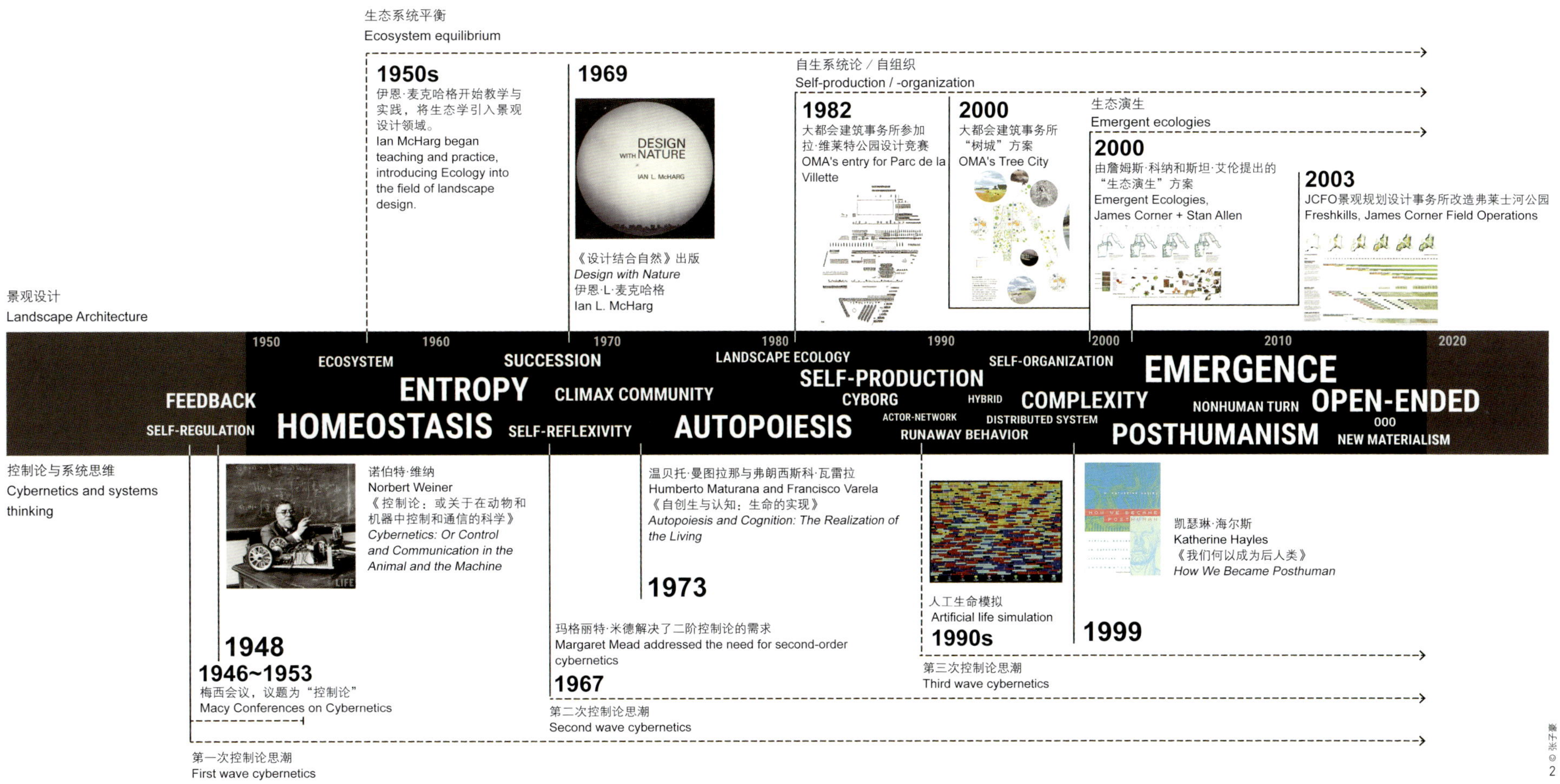

2

2\. 控制论与景观设计

2\. Cybernetics and Landscape Design

维尔公园设计竞赛作品"树城"[11][12]。这两个方案可被看作一个系列，它们都利用"自生系统"作为设计策略，将公园理解为一个自组织系统，即利用物质和信息不断复制自己的体系。所谓自生系统，是指系统通过其内部组织关系来处理信息物质流，从而维持自身特性。例如，在当斯维尔公园竞赛中，OMA用1 000条道路构成的路网和植物簇群作为空间框架，分割出大片未进行功能限定的区域，以满足公园未来发展需求。乍看之下，OMA的"树城"表现出一定的不确定性，因此是开放的。但是，这种灵活性是基于城市公园系统的自我生产，从而维持了另一个层面上的稳态，这种对稳态的控制可以由二阶控制论解释[13]。景观设计师、理论家克里斯蒂娜·希尔对OMA的设计持强烈的怀疑态度，她指出，尽管OMA的文案中描述了一个高度灵活的设计框架，但这个设计本质上还是一个传统的田园牧歌式的城市公园[14]。换言之，场地通过系统运转来维持其作为"田园式公园"的系统组织，几乎没有为景观演生和未知的发展可能预留任何空间。

由詹姆斯·科纳事务所、斯坦·艾伦与生态学家尼娜—玛丽·利斯特合作的参赛作品"生态演生"[15]可以和控制论的第三次思潮进行比照。第三次思潮注重开放性和演生，而该设计方案的框架将使场地通

maintains its identity by processing the flow of information and material using its components and relationships. For example, in the Downsview Park competition, OMA proposed a 1,000-path network and vegetal clusters separated by vast undesignated areas as a spatial framework to account for the future development of the park. It appears that OMA's Tree City exhibits some level of uncertainty, thus being open-ended. However, this flexibility is on the basis of self-production of the urban park as an autopoietic system, thus maintaining another level of homeostasis by legitimizing a control regime based on second-order cybernetics[13]. Landscape architect and theorist Kristina Hill was highly critical towards OMA's proposal, and she pointed out that despite the language which renders a flexible framework, OMA essentially proposed a traditional urban park with pastoral forms[14]. In other words, the site operates to maintain its system organization as a "pastoral park," leaving little room for the consideration of emergence and unfolding of how the landscape could become.

Another entry for the Downsview Park Emergent Ecologies[15] from the collaboration between James Corner Field Operations, Stan Allen, and ecologist Nina-Marie Lister can be contrasted with

过生态演生的方式实现长期发展。不同于其他入围方案将建设城市公园作为“最终目标”的分阶段式设计构想，“生态演生”将为期15年的最初阶段作为一种培育场地长期潜力的策略。这一设计将为建成后的场地发展提供多种可能性。换言之，该方案不是为了建造一个按照预期发展的、稳定的城市公园，而是意在把场地打造为一片潜力无穷的区域。该方案为人们预留了足够的想象空间，描绘了一个生机勃勃的场所，这是与“田园式城市公园”的本质区别[16]。

通过比较景观设计和控制论运动，可以看出三种不同的设计研究范式是如何阐释控制与不确定性的（图2）。在一阶控制论框架内，不确定性表现为模型与环境间的差异，要想消除这种差异则需要不断获取新知；另一方面，设计师通过采取合适的方法来获得更多的知识，并通过构建更复杂的模拟机制来缩小模型与环境间的差距，从而消除或控制不确定性。而在自生理论框架内（即第二次思潮），不确定性成为了一种信息流和物质流，以及系统维持自身特性的一种手段，这种控制手段只能通过二阶控制论来解读。而在开放和演生的框架内（即第三次思潮），不确定性成为了一种潜能，它不再是一个负面的概念，不再像麦克哈格所认为的熵那样需要加以规范和控制。相反，正是由于不确定性，未来才充满无限可能。

3 反馈生物与模拟实验

在演生和开放的理论框架内，原型发挥着重要作用，它能够帮助人们发掘不确定性中蕴含的潜力。作为一类特殊的模型，原型应该被置于控制论的发展进程中来理解，并分析这一概念在系统思维中的形成过程。在某种程度上，原型一直存在于控制论运动中，但其效用长

the third wave of cybernetics which focuses on open-endedness and emergence. The team also proposed a framework that allows for a long-term generation of the park based on emergent ecologies. Unlike other finalists which used phasing programs to build an urban park as an end point, Emergent Ecologies considered the initial 15-year phasing program as a strategy to cultivate the long-term potential of the site, providing multiple possibilities of how the site could be used after its construction. In other words, constructing a conceivable and stable urban park was not the goal of this proposal; instead, the aim was to prepare the Downsview site into a territory with a wide range of possibilities. The proposal leaves plenty of space to imagine a place that is wild and vibrant and is fundamentally different from a pastoral urban park[16].

Contrasting landscape design with the cybernetics movement highlights how control and uncertainty were conceptualized in three paradigms of design and research (Fig. 2). Within a first-order cybernetics framework, uncertainty represents the model-environment difference that needs to be reduced by gaining more knowledge about the phenomenon that we study. On the other side of this reasoning, designers can acquire knowledge by deploying proper means and close the gap between the model and the system by building more complex stimulation mechanisms, and uncertainty can be reduced and managed. Within the autopoiesis framework (second wave of cybernetics), uncertainty is instrumentalized as information and material flow that supports the system to maintain its own identity, thus legitimizing another kind of control regime that can only be articulated with second-order cybernetics. Within the framework of emergence and open-endedness (the third wave), uncertainty is transformed into potentiality. It is no longer a negative concept, like entropy in McHargian's terms, that needs to be regulated and controlled. Instead, because of the uncertainties, the future can be articulated to have a wide range of possibilities, thus becoming resourceful.

3 Cybernetic Creatures and Designers' Simulation

In the framework of emergence and open-endedness, prototypes act as an important component to help exploit the potential embedded in the uncertainty. Since a prototype can be understood as a special family of models, which should be situated in the history of cybernetics movement and analyze how it was conceptualized at large in systems thinking. In a way, prototypes have always existed in cybernetics movement, but the habitual means-end reasoning has limited their "usefulness." By analyzing a range of cybernetic creatures within the emergence

期受限于手段—目的链思维方式。通过在演生框架内分析一系列反馈生物，人们得以跳脱出手段—目的链的逻辑，转而重视原型思维。

3.1 “蛾”或“臭虫”、细胞自动机和人工生命

早期的控制论学者通过设计反馈机和模拟实验进行理论检验。其中一项重要成果是由维纳设计的反馈机，也被称为“蛾”或“臭虫”。在《人有人的用处》一书中，维纳详细讨论了如何通过制造反馈机来构建实体模型，以演示人类神经系统中姿态反馈和自愿反馈（或寻求目标时的反馈机制）两种机制间的相互作用[19]。维纳断言，这两种反馈机制存在于人类行为中，而神经系统疾病（如帕金森症和意向性颤抖）就是由于这些反馈机制过载崩溃而导致的。维纳进一步指出，在帕金森症中，自愿反馈会抑制和调节姿态反馈：患者在休息时会发生颤抖，而当他们执行任务（即寻求目标）时，颤抖便会减弱甚至消失。维纳系统通过设计一种装置来演示这两种反馈机制。

维纳和他的同事制作了一个叫做“蛾”或“臭虫”的装置，这个装置像一个小三轮车，有正趋光性（蛾）和负趋光性（臭虫），有两种可以相互调节的反馈机制。以“蛾”功能为例，小车前端装有两个光敏管，当有灯光时，电机便会将前轮转向有光的方向。但此动作将触发另一个负反馈电路，该负反馈电路会使前轮朝相反方向转动。因此，这个小车便会摇摆着移向光源（有目标的自愿反馈）。当没有灯光时，由于电位器和电机之间存在次级反馈，小车仍将摇摆着继续前进（姿势反馈）。而通过调节电路中的放大器使该反馈电路过载时，摇摆幅度会变大。因此，这个装置可以模拟帕金森症，其中的自愿反馈可抑制和调节姿势反馈（图3）。[17]

“蛾”可被看作反馈机制的实体示意模型，而反馈机制是第一次思潮期间梅西会议中的一个重要概念。然而，手段—目的链不能解释“蛾”的用途，因为当控制论学者制造它的时候并没有一个具体的

framework, it starts to articulate prototyping outside the means-end equation.

3.1 The Moth or the Bedbug, Cellular Automaton, and Artificial Life

Early cyberneticians built cybernetic machines and simulations as a way to test out their theoretical considerations. An important artifact was Wiener's cybernetic machine known as "the moth" or "the bedbug." In *The Human Use of Human Beings*, Wiener discussed in detail the process of making this "cybernetic robot" to build a working model of the interaction of two kinds of feedback mechanisms in the human nervous system: postural feedback and voluntary feedback (goal-seeking feedback)[19]. Wiener asserted that these two types of feedback mechanisms exist in human behavior and nervous system disorders, and Parkinsonism and intention tremors are the cases when these feedback mechanisms are overloaded and broken down. Wiener further posited that in Parkinsonism, voluntary feedback regulates postural feedback: the tremor happens when the patients are in rest, and when the patients perform a task (goal-seeking), the tremor subsides or even disappears. Wiener expected to conceptualize these theoretical explanations in action by building an apparatus that could act based on the two kinds of feedback mechanisms.

Wiener and his colleagues built a machine called "the moth" or "the bedbug." It was a three-wheeled cart with two major modes of action, positively photo-tropic (the moth) and negatively photo-tropic (the bedbug). This machine has two types of feedback mechanisms with one regulating the other. For example, to achieve the "the moth" function, the cart carries two photo-cells in the front, and when there is light, the motor will turn the wheel towards the direction of the light. This action will trigger a negative feedback circuit that turns the front wheel in the opposite direction. So, the cart will move towards the light in an oscillating pattern (voluntary feedback). If there is no light, the cart will keep oscillating because there is secondary feedback between the potentiometer and the motors (postural feedback). Moreover, when this feedback is overloaded by adjusting the amplifier in the circuit, the oscillation would grow bigger. This machine was argued to be an analog to Parkinsonism, in which the voluntary feedback suppresses the postural feedback (Fig. 3).[17]

"The moth" can be understood as a physical diagram of feedback mechanism, which was a key concept explored in the first wave of cybernetic research in the Macy Conferences era. However, its "usefulness" cannot be conceptualized within the means-end equation because when the cyberneticians built it, they did not have a specific goal in mind, such as solving a

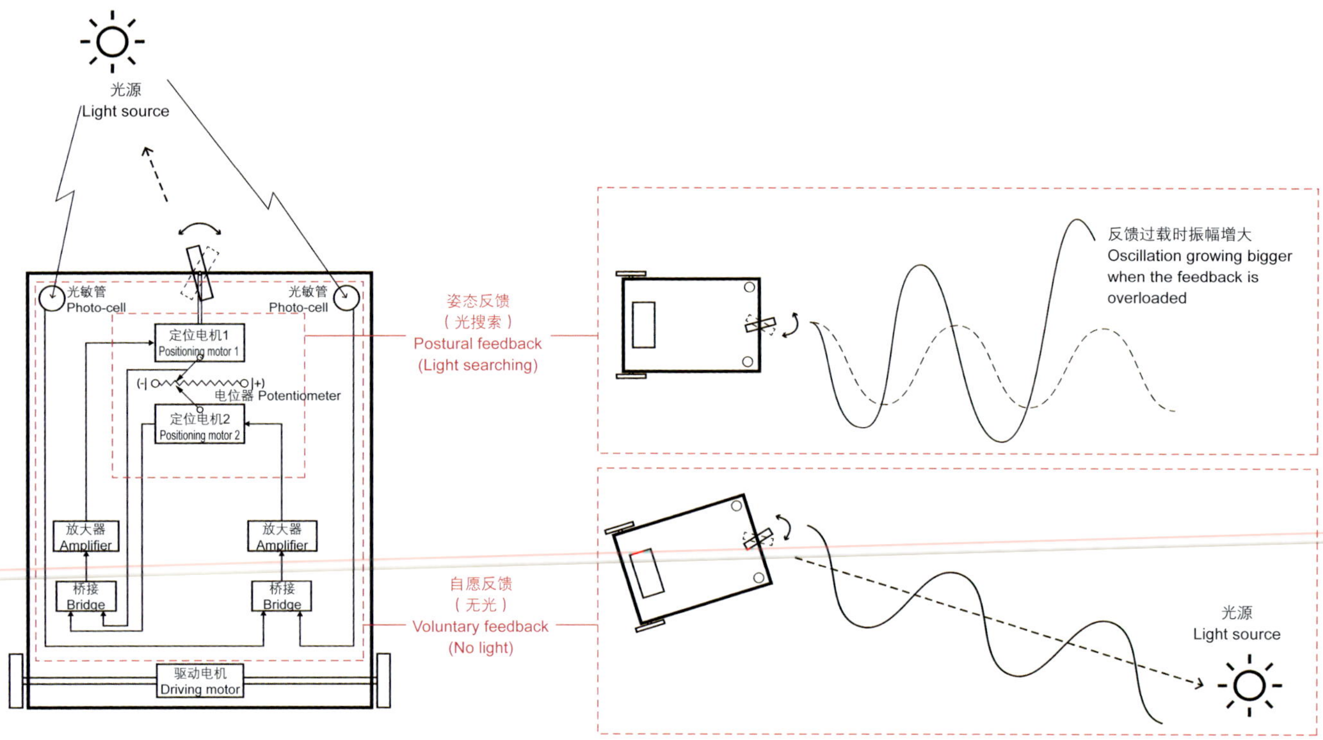

3

3. “蛾”或“臭虫”原型（改绘自参考文献[17]）

3. The prototype of "the moth" or "the bedbug" (Adaptation source: Ref. [17])

目标（比如要解决某个问题），所以“蛾”也并非达成目的的手段，学者们仅想通过它生动地演示控制论原理。在演生框架内，如果将“蛾”看作原型来理解，那么它的价值恰好在于其不确定性。由于它是反馈机制的一个抽象的示意模型，因此不同领域会对它产生不同的解读，而这种发散性思维正是创作和设计的基础。由此，“蛾”成为了一种存在于不同领域之间的临界物，帮助学者思考和讨论控制论原理，这对于早期控制论原理的普及有着重要作用。[18]

另外两个需并置讨论的例子分别是冯·诺伊曼的细胞自动机和人工生命实验。设计细胞自动机是为了研究“自我复制机”的逻辑需求。它可被看作一个二维网格，每一个单元格（细胞）都代表了一个有限状态自动机，在任何特定时间内，每一个单元格都处于一种有限状态之中，都可向相邻单元格传输信息。在冯·诺伊曼的模型中，每个单元格都有29种不同的状态，代表了29种信息传输规则。例如，若一个单元格在三个周期内都处于被激活状态，那么当它接收到来自相邻单元格的信息后，则会进入传输状态，并将信息传输至其上方单元格中。关于传输状态也有一些规则，例如，当处于基础状态的空单元格接收到信息时，空单元格便会进入被激活状态。如果两个单元格互

problem. Thus “the moth” is not a means to an end. Cyberneticians were simply interested to see the cybernetic principles in action. In the framework of emergence, “the moth” can be understood as a prototype, whose value lies in its uncertainty. Because it functions as an abstracted diagram of feedback mechanism, it can be interpreted differently among different fields, and the proliferation of meaning is the basis of creativity and design. It became a kind of boundary-object that facilitated the thinking and communication of cybernetic principles between scholars from different fields and played a critical role in popularizing the cybernetic principles in its early stage.[18]

The other two examples—von Neumann’s cellular automaton and artificial life experiment—can be discussed as a seriation. The cellular automaton was designed to provide insight into the logical requirements for self-replicating machines. It can be understood as a 2D grid, and each cell presents a finite-state automaton or machine, which can be in one of a finite number of states at any given time. Cells can transmit input to its adjacent cells. In von Neumann’s model, each cell has 29 different states, which can be understood as rules for transition signals. For example, if a cell is in the sensitized state for three cycles, and it receives an input from an adjacent cell, it will enter a transmission state that will pass the data to the cell to its north. There are also rules for transmission state. For example, when an input is given to a cell that is in the ground state (an empty cell), the cell will enter the sensitized state; if somehow two cells

相传输信息，那么信息就会被清空。当然，还有其他一些用来决定相邻细胞间互动的规则。[19]

人工生命实验比细胞自动机的机制更加复杂。生物学家受到自生系统论的启发，想要探索二阶控制论的广泛意义，以及自生系统如何脱离其原有轨迹并朝新的方向发展。其中一项著名实验是Tierra程序的编写，该程序可以基于简单的规则进行自我复制和变异，当程序将代码写入内存条时，会随机反转1和0形成一串新代码。假如新代码恰好是某个其他程序的机器代码，那么旧有程序就可以说是发生了变异。一旦计算机内存溢出，“淘汰”功能就会把旧有的或有缺陷的程序“杀死”。通过重复这一简单过程，一个电脑程序可以进化出五花八门的“数字物种”，形成各式各样的“生态系统”[20]。人工生命实验对于后人类主义的讨论起着重要作用，它证明了复杂行为（如人类的思考行为）不过是分布式系统（如神经网络）之间的相互作用产生的附带现象而已，而这样的认知也为海尔斯在内的后人类主义支持者挑战人类例外论提供了理论支持。[8]

这些反馈生物的范例没有明确定义，可被灵活解读，这些特性使它们成为了不同于当代环境设计实践（如适应性管理）中使用的预测性模型的原型。预测性模型具有隐喻性，用于反映某种现实中的现象，也与现实环境存在差异。因此，在预测性模型中，这种差异被视为威胁控制策略的不确定性。然而，原型却具有双重属性。一方面，和预测性模型一样，原型也具有隐喻性，即用一种事物来指代另一种事物——“蛾”即为反馈机制的示意模型；另一方面，原型来自于现实世界，故而具有现实性，可以不断衍生出其他事物。这种双重特性使原型成为一类特殊的模型，这种模型不用于预测或决策，而是为人们带来启发和洞见。

3.2 案例研究：水文地貌模拟沙床

在水力学模型的研究和工程实践中，大型物理河流模型通常用于模拟气象和雨洪事件,以及评估防洪措施的效果，如20世纪50年代由美国陆军工兵团建造的密西西比河流域模型和旧金山湾区模型[21]。另一方面，数字模型和模拟也广泛用于环境设计实践中，以预测系统行为并

transmit data to each other, then data disappear. Other rules guide how each cell interacts with its neighbors.[19]

The artificial life experiment is a more complex version of the cellular automaton. Inspired by autopoiesis theory, biologists wanted to explore the implication of second-order cybernetics and how self-production systems can spin off and evolve towards new directions. One famous experiment is called Tierra—A computer program designed to replicate and mutate based on simple rules. The self-replicating program would randomly flip ones and zeros on the computer memory when copying the data. If the new data happened to be machine code for another program, the original program mutated. A "reaper" function would "kill" old or defective programs when the computer memory became full. By repeating this simple process, a computer program could evolve into different "ecosystems" with a wide range of digital species[20]. The artificial life experiment had a high value in the discourse of posthumanism because it showed that complex behaviors, such as human thinking, were epiphenomenon of interactions between distributed systems, such as neural networks, and this realization allowed posthuman proponents, such as Hayles, to challenge human exceptionalism.[8]

The interpretation flexibility and undefined identity of these examples of cybernetic creatures make them prototypes, which are different from the predictive models used in contemporary environmental practices such as adaptive management. A predictive model entails a model-environment difference, as the model has a metaphorical quality, and it represents a phenomenon in reality. With predictive models, the gap between the model and the environment is conceptualized as uncertainty that can only be conceptualized as negative forces undermining control regimes. Nevertheless, a prototype has a twofold quality. On the one hand, like predictive models, a prototype has metaphorical quality, that is, it uses one thing to refer to another thing; "the moth" is a working diagram of feedback mechanisms. On the other hand, it has a sense of realism in it because it exists as part of reality so that other artifacts can be said to be derived from it. This twofold quality makes prototypes a special type of model that does not predict or determine, but inspire and anticipate.

3.2 A Case Study: Hydromorphology Table

In the scientific and engineering practice of physical hydraulic modeling, large physical river models are built to simulate weather and flood events and to evaluate the effect of flood control strategies. Precedents include large-scale hydraulic models built in the 1950s by the Army Corps of Engineers such as the Mississippi Basin Model and the San Francisco Bay Model[21]. On the other spectrum, digital models and simulations are also widely used

评估控制策略，如南佛罗里达州水管理模型[22]。物理模型和数字模型都是通过手段—目的的链来进行预测和控制。这些模型代表了某种理想状态，通过映射在环境中来指导环境改造。但正如朱利安所言，如果我们沿用手段—目的链思维方式来思考问题，总会遇到模型预测范围之外的意外情况，那么控制与不确定性之间的矛盾似乎永远无法调和。数字工具和运算方法的进步为景观设计师提供了有别于预测性模型和手段—目的链思维方式的新的原型。为了更好地阐述原型如何辅助设计思维，本文将介绍一系列基于水文地貌模拟沙床（以下简称“沙床”）的案例，以进一步说明原型的特性以及原型思维的价值。

哈佛GSD的REAL实验室基于Emriver径流模型建造了一个沙床②。Emriver径流模型这一常用于水文研究的模型被作为一种原型思维平台而引入景观设计学领域，以帮助设计师更好地了解水文地貌变化的过程，并辅助制定响应式设计策略。设计师可以通过4个进料器和一个水泵来控制沉积物和水流的输入，用以模拟水流和沉积物的变化。此外，设计师不仅能够通过调整变量来研究同一水文系统的迭代，也能在相同流量和沉积物输入的条件下测试不同系统的径流情况。除了Emriver模型本身自带的仪器外，REAL实验室的原型平台还配备了感应和监控设备（如在沙床上方安装的微软体感设备Kinect，以及位于沙床下游的超声波传感器），以收集实时数据。收集到的数据通过Grasshopper软件中的自定义插件实时传输到三维建模软件Rhinoceros中。

近年来，作为一种原型思维平台，沙床被广泛运用于研究和设计项目中，这些项目展现了构建自主系统的可能性，而自主系统能提出超越人类理解范畴的策略并创建“野生”场所[23]。例如，设计师雷夫·埃斯特拉达在“走向感知”项目中，测试了“感应—处理—制动”的响应式框架[24]。在一项设计实验中，埃斯特拉达提出了一种称为“调制

in environmental practices to predict system behaviors and evaluate control strategies, such as the South Florida Water Management Model[22]. These models, physical or digital, are all envisaged in the line with means-end relationships for prediction and control. The models begin as an ideal representation of the environment so that they can be projected and used to give form to reality. However, as pointed out by Jullien, following this line of reasoning, there will always be unexpected circumstances outside the scope of predictions that are allowed by the models. Thus, one is constantly challenged by the tension between control and uncertainty. Development in digital tools and computational methods has provided landscape architects with advanced techniques to build prototypes that challenge the predictive models and means-end reasoning. To better illustrate how prototyping helps with design thinking, this paper presents a series of case studies based on a hydromorphology table to demonstrate the qualities of prototypes and the value of prototyping.

The hydromorphology table was based on the Emriver stream table and was located at the REAL in Harvard GSD②. The Emriver stream tables, which were usually used by hydrologists, were introduced to the field of Landscape Architecture as a prototyping platform to help designers better understand hydro-morphological processes, and to facilitate the production of responsive design strategies. The inputs of both the sediments and water flow were controlled through 4 material feeders and a water pump to simulate water flows and behaviors of sediment. The table allowed for running iterations of the same hydromorphological system with measurable adjustments, as well as testing multiple systems with the same flow and sediment input. Besides the instruments provided by the Emriver, the prototype platform was also equipped with sensing and monitoring devices to gather real-time data, including a Microsoft Kinect above the table and ultrasonic sensors down the stream. The real-time data then were fed into Rhinoceros 3D through grasshopper plugins and customized interfaces.

As a prototyping platform, the hydromorphology table facilitates many research and design projects over the years, shedding light on the possibility of constructing autonomous systems that can devise strategies beyond human comprehension to create “wild” places[23]. For instance, designer Leif Estrada tested the sensing-processing-actuating responsive framework in the project Towards Sentience[24]. In one of the design experiments, the designer proposed an actuating system called “attuner” that consists of a matrix of acrylic dowels connected to servo motors. Every servo motor drives a dowel, the bottom of which sticks into the sediments. When the servo motors

② 了解更多关于Emriver径流模型及哈佛GSD REAL实验室沙床模型的信息，请访问Emriver径流模型及REAL实验室官方网站。

② For more information about Emriver stream table and the hydromorphology table at the REAL in Harvard GSD, please visit the websites of Emriver stream table and REAL.

器”的系统，该系统由连接到伺服马达的一组亚克力杆组成。每个亚克力杆均由伺服马达单独驱动，其底部插入沉积物中。当伺服马达转动时，会驱动亚克力杆上下移动来改变水流形态，从而在沙床的下游形成不同的地形。随后，通过沙床上方的Kinect传感器实时跟踪地形，形成数字高程模型，以识别出地势的高低。这些信息会反馈到制动系统，这样就能在高地上借由更多的沉积物来造陆，或引流更多的水体来侵蚀陆地。埃斯特拉达描述道，水文地貌模拟沙床构建的控制系统具有实时更新和反馈能力，而这种自主能力是人类无法企及的[25]。

在另一个示例中，设计师刘浔基于实体界面（TUI）的概念开发了一种混合仿真模型[26]。TUI逐渐取代了传统的图形用户界面（GUI），它结合了物理模型和数字模型的优势，现已被广泛用于增强物理模型性能以及物理模型的数据可视化，从而实现“比特和原子”的无缝耦合[27]。自定义程序使用从Kinect传感器感测到的高程数据来生成实时数字地形模型，该模型可在Rhino和其他软件中用于进行水流、植被分布、污染物和沉积物等不同类型的数值模拟（图4）。地形变化、景观

turn, they drive the dowels moving up and down to change the flow pattern, creating different landforms in the downstream of the table. The topography is then live tracked by the Kinect sensor above the table, forming a digital elevation model of the topography so that a series of high grounds and low grounds can be identified. This information then feeds back to the actuating system so that it could either build more land in a high ground by depositing more sand on it or erode the high ground away by directing more water towards it. The designer described that the cyborg system built with the hydromorphology table exhibited a level of live updates and feedback that was beyond human capacity[25].

In another example, designer Liu Xun developed a hybrid simulation based on the concept of the Tangible User Interface (TUI)[26]. TUI is increasingly accepted as an alternative paradigm to the conventional Graphic User Interface (GUI). It combines the benefits of physical and digital models in the same representation and is widely used to enhance the performance of physical models and visualize the unseen data beneath the physical model, creating a seamless coupling of “bits and atoms”[27]. The customized program uses the sensed elevation data from the Kinect sensor as input to generate a live digital terrain model, which can be used in Rhino and other softwares to conduct numerical simulations for different purposes such as water flow, vegetation distribution, pollution, and sedimentation (Fig 4). Topographic changes, landscape morphology, water streamline, and patterns of other simulated agents can be

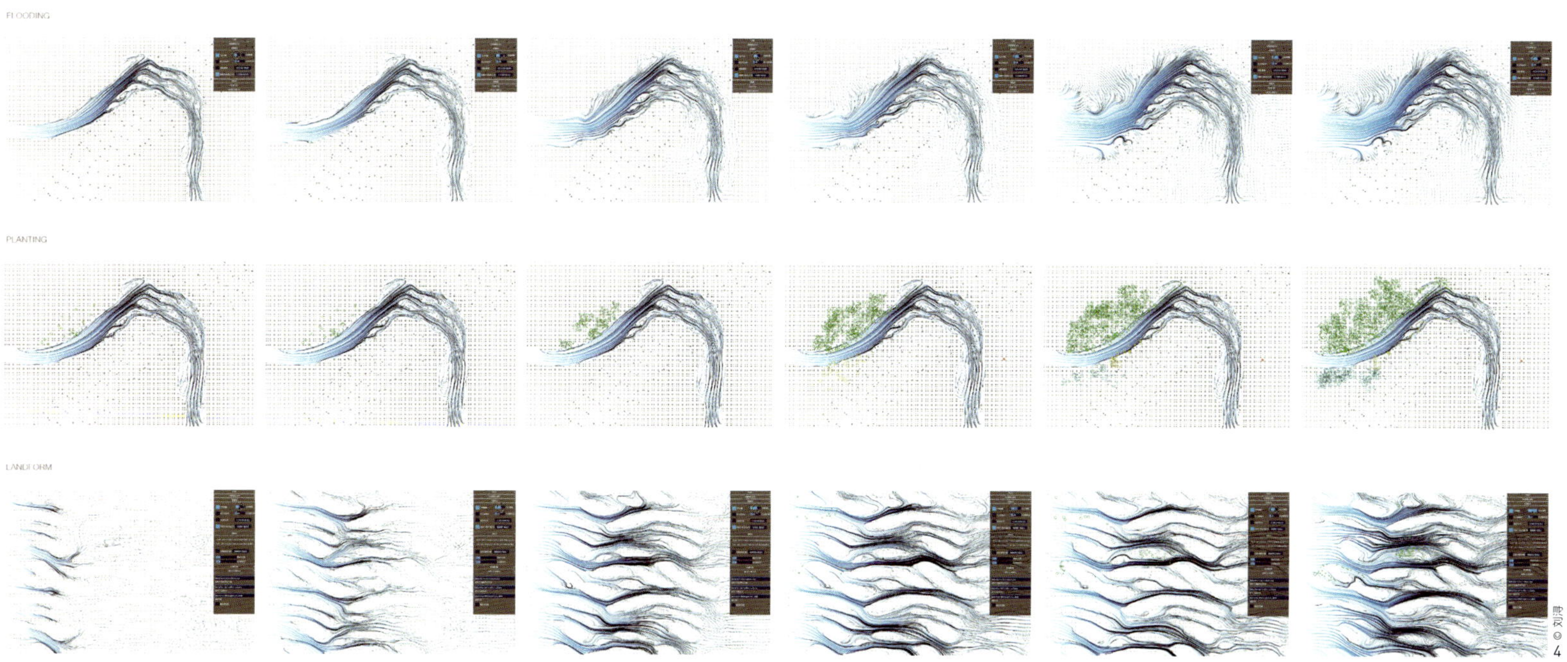

4. 自定义水文模拟和可视化程序

4. Customized digital hydrological simulation and visualization tool

形态、水流线，以及其他模拟图像都可通过短程投影仪投射到沙床上（图5）。如此，基本的地形分析与动态流体模拟被集成到同一个平台中，可以更好地实现地形数据的可视化，数字模拟和物理模拟也能通过反馈回路实现耦合。设计师可以依据沙床上的投影信息（如等高线和填方图）即时手动调整物理模型（图6~9）。

增强现实的沙床可成为景观设计师新的设计工具，也可被当作一种合作平台，帮助社区参与中的不同利益相关者进行沟通协商。该原型并非基于从设计构思到计算机模拟、再到材料处理和结果呈现的线性设计过程，而是开启了一种新的工作流程，其支持设计过程中的不同步骤同时或反复进行。本实验中讨论的实体交互概念超越了界面的接触，是指两种不同类型的模拟的协同与组合：数字模拟可用于验证物理模拟，物理模拟可用于检测数字模拟，两种模拟相互配合并彼此适应。通过运用增强现实技术将物理河流模拟与实时的数字河流模拟相整合，该原型使景观设计师可以直观地利用有形的材料进行设计，并同步获得计算模拟结果的校验。作为设计师与实体空间之间的动态界面，实体交互模型的变化性和不确定性对于理解水力形态过程的复杂性和动态过程非常重要。

需要特别指出的是，沙床模型并没有按照真实景观比例来建造，所以该原型不宜用来模拟特定地点的水文和生态系统。换句话说，如果以手段—目的链来理解沙床的概念，那么沙床必须按照真实环境的比例来建造，这样才能用于预测设计结果并决定相应策略（如密西西比河流域模型或南佛罗里州达水管理模型）。但是，围绕模型制作的讨论最终离不开如何用模型“精确”地表达环境的问题，这与模拟参数的不确定性有关。在建模中，造成不确定性的原因有很多，如结构的不确定性、算法的不确定性等。其中，参数的不确定性来自模型输入变量的可变性。对于沙床而言，设计人员可以通过调整介质的大小以及不同介质之间的比例改变河道“沉积物”的组成，进而调节水流的速度和流量。这些都是模型本身包含的变量，更改其中的任何变量都将对模拟结果产生显著影响。如果将沙床视为一个预测性模型，那么设计人员需要计算建模过程中的所有参数值，以最大程度地减少参数的不确定性。设计人员不仅必须选择合适的材料尺寸来模拟真实的景观环境，而且需要确定恰当的材料构成比例，更不用说计算缩放过程中涉及的物理变化，因为理论上除了水以外，所有事物都被缩小了。为了解决这个问题，设计人员必须找到另一种具有适当粘滞阻力的流体，以代表流体与要按比例缩放的固体颗粒之间的相互作用。由此可知，如果遵循手段—目的链来理解沙床，会不可避免地将它看作一种重构现实世界的理想模型，而这种想法会导致不确定性永远存在。最重要的是，这种基于手段—目的链框架

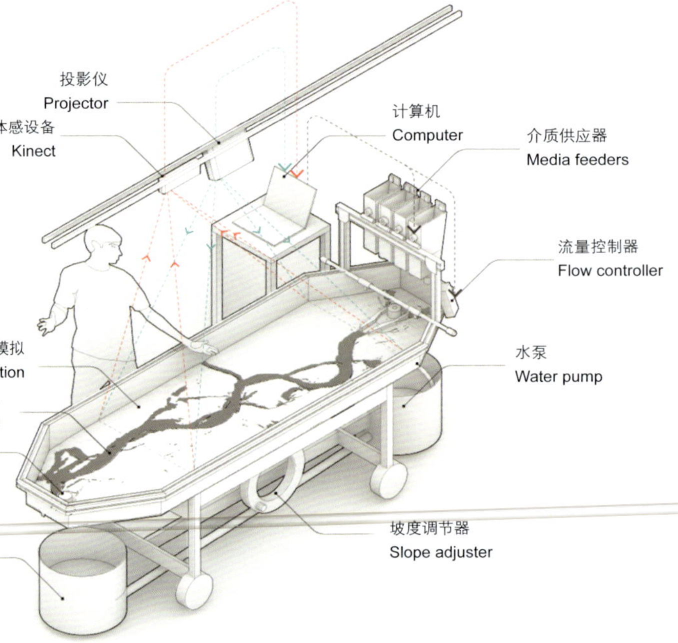

5. 增强现实沙床控制系统

5. Augmented hydromorphology table: control system

visualized in diagrammatic representations. These representations then can be projected back onto the hydromorphology table with a short-throw projector (Fig. 5). In such a way, basic terrain analysis is integrated into this platform together with dynamic fluid simulation to better visualize the invisible aspects of the topography, and the digital simulation and the physical simulation are coupled through a feedback loop. Designers can manually change the physical model according to the projected information, such as contour lines and cut-and-fill maps (Fig. 6 ~ 9).

This augmented hydromorphology modeling table can be used as a new design tool for landscape designers, as well as a cooperation platform for community engagement and communication between different stakeholders. Rather than developing design in a linear progression from idea to computer-simulated model, and material manipulation and result, this prototype inspires an alternative workflow that allows different steps in the design process to play concurrently or recursively. The concept of tangibility developed in this experiment is more than the tangibility of the interface, but the synthesis and composition of the two different types of simulation: numerical models being used to manipulate while validating physical models, and vice versa. Two kinds of simulations feed and adapt to each other. By integrating physical hydraulic simulation with the real-time computational fluvial simulation through augmented reality technologies, this prototype allows landscape architects to design intuitively with tangible material processes and simultaneously be

6. 增强现实沙床地形实验
7. 基于智能体的模拟。设计师能通过投影，直观感受设计干预对水文系统的影响。
8. 现实增强的地形分析
9. 软件操作界面

6. Augmented hydromorphology table: landform experiment
7. Agent-based simulation. Designers can observe the direct impact of design intervention on the hydrological systems through projected simulation.
8. Augmented topographical analysis
9. Software interface

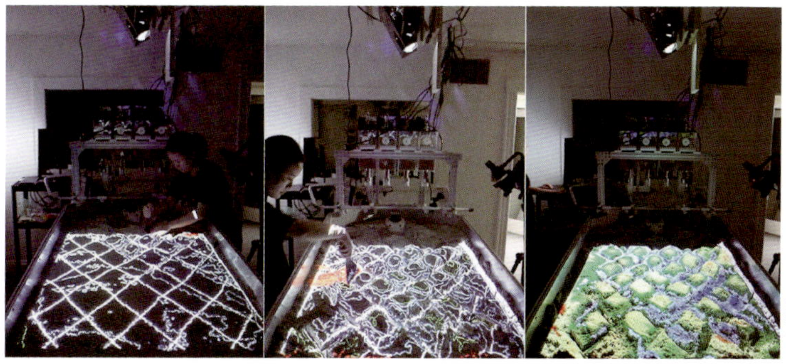

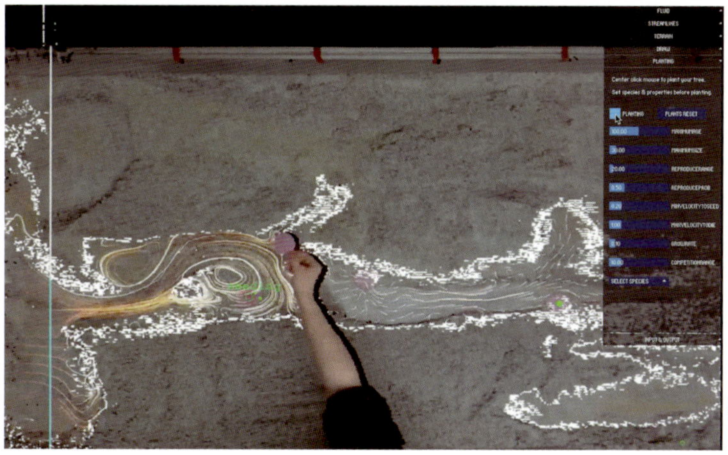

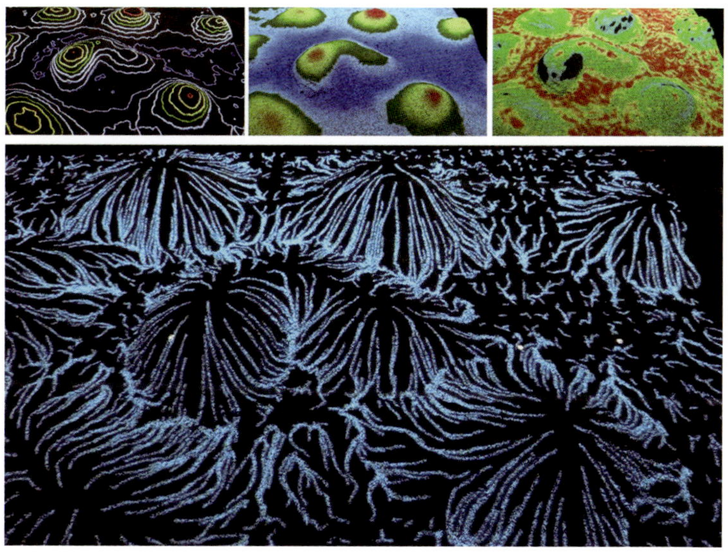

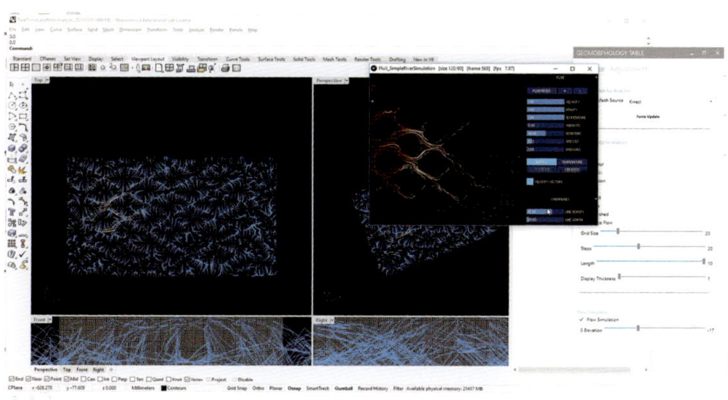

informed by computational simulation results. The dynamics and indeterminacy of the tangible model are important in terms of understanding the complexity and dynamic process of the hydro-morphological process. This prototype acts as a dynamic interface between designers and the physical world.

Particularly, this hydromorphology table as a prototype is not meant to replicate processes in a site-specific hydrological and ecological system. The presumed scale of the model is not built based on a mathematically scaled relationship with real landscape conditions. In other words, if the table is understood in the means-end relation, it can only exist as a scaled simulation of the real environment so that to predict and determine outcomes of different intervention strategies, like the Mississippi Basin Model or the South Florida Water Management Model. However, the discussion about model-making would eventually revolve around the question of how "accurate" the model is to represent the environment; that is, the parameter uncertainty involved in the simulation. In modeling practices, uncertainties come from various sources such as structural uncertainty and algorithmic uncertainty. Parameter uncertainty comes from the variability of input variables of the model. In the case of the hydromorphology table, the designer can change the composition of the "sediment" by adjusting the size of each material and the percentage of that material in the sediment mixture. The designer can also vary the flow of water in terms of speed and quantity. These are all implicit variables involved in the model itself, and changing any of them could easily alter the outcome of the simulation. If the table is treated as a predictive model, then the designer is challenged to minimize parameter uncertainties by figuring out the values of all the parameters in the modeling process. The designer has to select not only the correct size of the material to emulate the sediment on-site but also the composition of the material that best represents the sediment. Not to mention that the designer has to calculate the underlying physics involved in the scaling process itself, since everything but water is scaled down; and to counter this issue, the designer might have to switch to another type of fluid with the right viscosity that best represents the interaction between the fluid and the solid particles to scale. These examples only provide a glimpse of the line of reasoning that one inevitably takes if one follows the means-end equation and understands the hydromorphology table as a model of an ideal form to reconstruct the reality. In such conceptualization, uncertainty always exists. Most importantly, following the means-end equation, the discussion drifted away from the design practice and creativity. However, if designers understand the

下的讨论偏离了设计和创造性。然而，如果将沙床理解为一种原型，将它视作一个自成体系的环境，一种自主的、不断演化的系统，设计师就能探索更多的设计可能性（如响应式框架），从而避免陷入控制和不确定性的无解争取，景观的未来才能拥有更多的机遇。

4 结论与讨论

控制论运动和景观设计的比照揭示了自20世纪60年代以来的现代景观设计发展历程反映着控制论的三次思潮。不确定性概念起初被理解为模型与环境间必须要被消除的差异，而后来则被视为演生与机遇的来源。在演生论的框架下，原型被解读为一种特殊的模型，将其与预测性模型进行对比，会发现二者对于不确定性有着截然不同的理解思路。利用预测性模型思考问题，会不由自主地通过手段—目的链来理解不确定性，环境也因此被简化成了一种理想化模型，任何的行为都必须具有目的性，必须通过手段来实现一个最终目标。不同于预测性模型所追求的生命系统，原型本身就是一个独立自主的生命系统，不存在与现实环境的差异，因为原型正是环境的一部分。用原型思维取代建模思维后，不确定性也具有了新的含义——更多的机会与期待。在原型思维范式中，不确定性将激发演生行为，以及无限的可能性（图10）。

原型思维范式具有如下三个特点。首先，原型最初可能只用于测试某一原理或想法，但一旦被制造出来，便会成为现实的一部分，从而引发新一轮的观察与建模。这种迭代过程是设计和创造力的基础。其次，尽管原型可直接用于某些场景，但其真正的用途恰恰在于其未被限定用途——“蛾”、沙床等原型甚至没有专业名称——但正由于不确定性，原型才具有无限的潜力。最后，这种无定义的状态，以及原型所具有的不确定性和无限潜能将改变人们与未来之间的关系。LAF

hydromorphology table as a prototype, then their relationship with the future is in the line of emergence and opportunity. By regarding this model as its own environment, with its own autonomous and evolving processes, designers can explore a wide range of possibilities of intervention, such as the responsive framework, thus bypassing the discussion about control and uncertainty.

4 Conclusion and Discussion

Contrasting the cybernetics movement with landscape design reveals that the development in landscape discourse since the 1960s mirrors the movement of cybernetics. Uncertainty has transformed from the early understanding that the disconnection between the model and the environment has to be reduced to a contemporary understanding that uncertainty can be the source of emergence and opportunity. The framework of emergence highlights prototypes as a special type of model. Prototypes can be contrasted with predictive models as they entail two different lines of reasoning around the issue of uncertainty. With predictive models, we are forced to understand uncertainty within a means-end relationship that reduces the environment to a simplified representation or ideal image, and then make it a goal and an end, which calls for means to achieve it. Rather than predictive models that represent another living system, prototypes are living systems in themselves with autonomy and lives, and no longer entail a model-environment difference because they are part of the environment. Prototyping replaces model-making and helps establish a new relationship with uncertainty in the line of opportunity and anticipation. Uncertainty in the paradigm of prototyping can be understood as the source for emergent behaviors and a wide range of possibilities (Fig. 10).

There are three characteristics of the paradigm of prototyping. First, prototypes might start as a test of a principle or an idea, but when they are built, they take on a life of their own and become part of reality that triggers new rounds of observation and model-making. This iterative process is the basis for design and creativity. Second, prototypes may have some direct applications, but their true application lies in their undefined identity. “The moth” did not even have a proper name, and neither did the hydromorphology table. However, just because of this undefined identity, a prototype has the potential to become anything. Third, because of this undefined quality of prototypes, they are full of uncertainty, thus infinite possibility, and our relationship with the future has changed. LAF

10. 预测性模型与原型思维关系图

10. The relationship between predictive modeling and prototyping

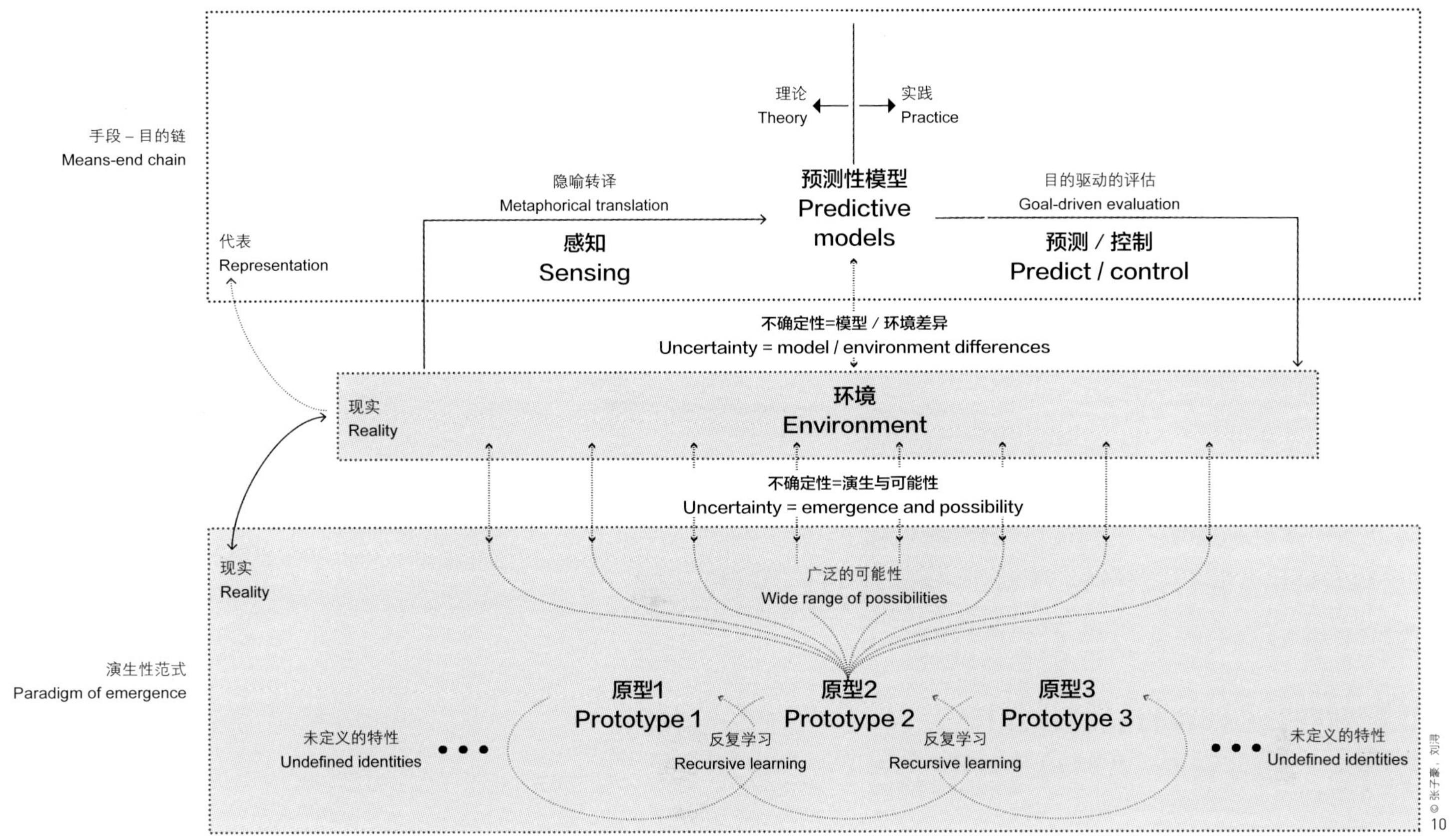

REFERENCES

[1] Spirn, A. W. (1995). Constructing Nature: The Legacy of Frederick Law Olmsted. In W. Cronon (Ed.), Uncommon Ground: Toward Reinventing Nature (pp. 91-113). New York: W.W. Norton and Company.

[2] Prototype. (2000). In Oxford English Dictionary. Oxford: Oxford University Press.

[3] Jullien, F. (2004). A Treatise on Efficacy: Between Western and Chinese Thinking (J. Lloyd, Tran.). Honolulu: University of Hawaii Press.

[4] Sadler, J. M., Goodall, J. L., Behl, M., Bowes, B. D., & Morsy, M. M. (2020). Exploring real-time control of stormwater systems for mitigating flood risk due to sea level rise. Journal of Hydrology, (583), 124571. https://doi.org/10.1016/j.jhydrol.2020.124571

[5] Fung, S. (1999). Mutuality and the Cultures of Landscape Architecture. In J. Corner (Ed.), Recovering landscape: Essays in contemporary landscape theory (pp. 141-151). Hudson: Princeton Architectural Press.

[6] Herrington, S. (2016). Landscape Theory in Design. London: Routledge.

[7] Lystra, M. (2014). McHarg's Entropy, Halprin's Chance: Representations of Cybernetic Change in 1960s Landscape Architecture. Studies in the History of Gardens and Designed Landscapes, 34(1), 71-84. https://doi.org/10.1080/14601176.2013.850313.

[8] Hayles, N. K. (1999). How We Became Posthuman: Virtual Bodies in Cybernetics, Literature, and Informatics. Chicago: University of Chicago Press.

[9] Maturana, H. R., & Varela, F. J. (1980). Autopoiesis and Cognition: The Realization of the Living. Heidelberg: Springer Netherlands. https://doi.org/10.1007/978-94-009-8947-4

[10] Steiner, F. R. (2008). The Ghost of Ian McHarg. Log, (13/14), 147-151.

[11] OMA Office Work Research. (n.d.). Parc de la Villette. Retrieved from https://oma.eu/projects/parc-de-la-villette

[12] OMA Office Work Research. (n.d.). The Downsview Park competition. Retrieved from https://oma.eu/projects/downsview-park

[13] Czerniak, J. (2001). Downsview Park Toronto. New York: Prestel.

[14] Hill, K. (2001). Urban Ecologies: Biodiversity and Urban Design. In J. Czerniak (Ed.), Downsview Park Toronto (pp. 90-101). New York: Prestel.

[15] Reed, C., & Lister, N. M. (2014). Ecology and Design: Parallel Genealogies. Places Journal. Retrieved from https://placesjournal.org/article/ecology-and-design-parallel-genealogies/

[16] Berrizbeitia, A. (2001). Scale of Undecidability. In J. Czerniak (Ed.), Downsview Park Toronto (pp. 117-125). New York: Prestel.

[17] Wiener, N. (1950). The Human Use of Human Beings: Cybernetics and Society. Boston: Houghton Mifflin.

[18] Star, S. L., & Griesemer, J. R. (2016). Institutional Ecology, 'Translations' and Boundary Objects: Amateurs and Professionals in Berkeley's Museum of Vertebrate Zoology, 1907-39. Social Studies of Science, 19(1989), 387-420.

[19] Von Neumann, J., & Burks, A. W. (1966). Theory of Self-Reproducing Automata. Urbana: University of Illinois Press

[20] Ray, T. S. (n.d.). Tierra. Retrieved from https://web.stanford.edu/class/sts129/Alife/html/Tierra.htm

[21] Cheramie, K. (2011). The Scale of Nature: Modeling the Mississippi River. Retrieved from https://placesjournal.org/article/the-scale-of-nature-modeling-the-mississippi-river/

[22] South Florida Water Management District. (n.d.). South Florida Water Management Model (SFWMM). Retrieved from https://www.sfwmd.gov/science-data/sfwmm-model

[23] Cantrell, B., Martin, L. J., & Ellis, E. C. (2017). Designing Autonomy: Opportunities for New Wildness in the Anthropocene. Trends in Ecology and Evolution, 32(3), 156-166. https://doi.org/10.1016/j.tree.2016.12.004

[24] Cantrell, B., & Holtzman, J. (2016). Responsive landscapes: Strategies for responsive technologies in landscape architecture. New York: Routledge.

[25] Estrada, L. (2018). Towards Sentience. In B. Cantrell & A. Mekies (Eds.), Codify: Parametric and Computational Design in Landscape Architecture (pp. 279-288). New York: Routledge.

[26] Liu, X. (2020). The Third Simulation: Augmented Reality Fluvial Modeling Tool. Journal of Digital Landscape Architecture, (5), 413-421. https://doi.org/doi:10.14627/537690042

[27] Ishii, H., & Ullmer, B. (1997). Tangible Bits: Towards Seamless Interfaces between People, Bits and Atoms. In Proceedings of the SIGCHI Conference on Human Factors in Computing Systems (pp. 234-241). Retrieve from: http://ebusiness.mit.edu/sponsors/common/LnchSemExecSum/ishii.pdf

本文引用格式 / PLEASE CITE THIS ARTICLE AS

Wei, F., & Huang, Z. (2020). Physical Experience and Space-Time Imagery—Research on the Prototype of Landscape Design by Understanding Site, Sight, and Insight. Landscape Architecture Frontiers, 8(4), 26-41. https://doi.org/10.15302/J-LAF-1-020031

身体经验与时空想象——基于场地、场景、场域的景观建构原型研究

PHYSICAL EXPERIENCE AND SPACE-TIME IMAGERY —RESEARCH ON THE PROTOTYPE OF LANDSCAPE DESIGN BY UNDERSTANDING SITE, SIGHT, AND INSIGHT

https://doi.org/10.15302/J-LAF-1-020031 收稿时间 RECEIVED DATE / 2020-06-05 中图分类号 / TU986 文献标识码 / A

摘要

当代景观作为抵抗环境同质化、提供丰富文化想象力的重要媒介，对身体体验的忽视更易造成人与环境之间的感知矛盾与割裂。本文提出将身体－时间－空间的关系原型作为研究基于差异性要素建构的场地、场景、场域三种设计维度的抽象话语，分别表征为物质建构、意义建构和场域建构；随后探讨了如何通过控制空间序列与内外向、阈的设置、文本与句法的建构、激发事件与社会想象力等具体施行路径的作用，构成物质空间中的推拉运动、意义空间中的侧显与完形、场域空间的统觉，从而加深人对景观空间的感知。本文以身体经验与时空想象为切入点，提取并梳理了不同维度的景观建构思维，认为合理的差异要素组织设计方式可以通过以上三元维度建立深刻且亲密的人地关系。

关键词

体验景观；原型；时间－空间；阈；社会互动；景观构建

ABSTRACT

Contemporary landscape is an important medium that resists the environmental homogeneity and diversifies the cultural imagery. The neglect of physical experience would intensify the perception contradiction and separation between people and the site. This paper proposes to use the prototype of the interactions between the body, time, and space to build an abstract discourse to study the design dimensions of site, sight, and insight based on different elements—the three dimensions are represented as perception, conception, and live. It then focuses on how to employ design methods (including the arrangement of spatial sequence and direction, the design of thresholds in the space, the creation of texts and syntaxes, and the stimulation of events and social imagery) to form the push-pull movement in the material space, the abschattung and gestalt of ideographic texts in the meaning space, and the apperception of the social field, so as to enhance people's perception of the landscape. This paper studies physical experience and space-time imagery to extract and deduce the thinking of landscape design within varied dimensions, and argues that a profound and intimate relationship between man and the site can be established by organizing different elements under the ternary system of site, sight, and insight.

KEYWORDS

Experiencing Landscape; Prototype; Space-Time; Threshold; Social Interaction; Landscape Design

基金项目

国家自然科学基金项目"基于复写理论的后工业景观重构方法及场所认知关联机制研究"（编号：51908035）
北京市社会科学基金项目"基于公共价值提升的北京工业遗存分级保护与景观重构利用研究"（编号：19YTC040）
中央高校基本科研业务费专项基金"城市剩余空间改造的景观介入方法及景观绩效研究"（编号：BLX201810）
上海市城市更新及其空间优化技术重点实验室开放课题"基于社会传感交叉验证的上海后工业景观'恢复性－抑制性'价值感知及分级重构优化研究"（编号：2020030301）

RESEARCH FUNDS

Research on Landscape Reconstruction and Place Perception Mechanism of Industrial Remains with Recommended Grade of Protection Based on Theory of Palimpsest, National Natural Science Foundation of China (No. 51908035)
Research on Classified Protection and Landscape Reconstruction of Industrial Remains in Beijing Based on the Promotion of Public Value, Beijing Social Science Fund Project (No. 19YTC040)
Research on Landscape Intervention and Landscape Performance of Urban Residual Spaces, Special Funds of Central Colleges Basic Scientific Research Business Expenses (No. BLX201810)
Research on Game Mechanism of "Restorative-Repressive" Value Perception and Classified Reconstruction Approach Optimization of Shanghai Post-Industrial Landscape Based on Cross Validation of Social Sensing Methods, Open Projects Fund of Shanghai Key Laboratory of Urban Renewal and Spatial Optimization Technology (No.2020030301)

编辑 田乐 **翻译** 田乐 张健
EDITED BY Tina TIAN **TRANSLATED BY** Tina TIAN Angus ZHANG

魏方*
北京林业大学园林学院讲师

黄子舰
清华大学美术学院博士候选人

WEI Fang
Lecturer at the School of Landscape Architeture, Beijing Forestry University

HUANG Zijian
PhD Candidate at Academy of Arts and Design, Tsinghua University

*通讯作者
地址：北京市海淀区清华东路35号北京林业大学学研中心A1410
邮编：100083
Email：weif13@bjfu.edu.cn

1 景观设计空间建构的深层结构与原型

当代景观设计已经从“平面描绘”转变为“场地作业”，由如绘的设计思维转向关注场地的特质并对其进行放大，以揭示场地当下与历史的状态。当代设计理论研究已不再囿于“手法”“构图”及“比例”，而强调如何引导认知主体的直接体验、如何提供场地适应性、灵活性及事件激发性，从而进一步明确相关实施路径。生命哲学、现象学、实用主义哲学、解释学、体验哲学等学科都强调了身体体验的重要性，将之作为引发人与外界的交互作用，以及理解与解释生命与存在的前提。[1]-[4]身体美学[5]观念的涌现展现出的回归生活的趋势、时空作用下认知主体的身体经验特质与规律，以及通过身体延伸走向本真生活的过程，被认为具有多种意象图式。

景观建构从物质空间限定、心理体验延伸，以及精神生活支撑三个方面完成人与场所的互动。景观中“深刻而亲密的关系模式”[6]存在于各种时空模式中，影响着社会的基本构成形态。景观空间能够化解社会焦虑，促进社会资源良性循环，也是提升社会成员效能感的有效路径。[7]在此过程中，众多学者探寻着美学范畴外的深层结构索引，即透过浅层的意义表征与行为互动来探寻感知更深层的存在意义——正如彼得·艾森曼援引艾弗拉姆·诺姆·乔姆斯基的语言学框架，探寻表面结构的知觉性结构和深层结构中的概念结构关系：艾森曼以人的空间感知和体验为锚点，基于谱记形式发生的深层结构体系寻求所谓更纯粹的自治状态，形成设计原型的表征，并作为后续创作来源的典型模式。[8]

2 差异要素组织下的身体－时间－空间潜藏体验维度

后现代语境中对场地信息的强调，使景观成为抵抗环境同质化、提供丰富文化想象力的重要媒介。而在时空压缩的背景下，多元纷杂的场地信息过于碎片化的状态更易造成时空分裂，后现代激进观念中

1 The Deep Structure and the Prototype of Spatial Construction in Landscape Architecture

Contemporary landscape architecture has gone beyond plane depiction towards site works, from creating picturesque landscapes towards exploring and magnifying the uniqueness of the site to narrate the present and the past. Contemporary design theories are no longer prospecting skills, composition or proportion of drawings; they rather emphasize how to guide the direct experience of the cognitive subject and how to enhance the site's adaptability, flexibility, and the generating of an event, in order to concretize the design. Disciplines such as Philosophy of Life, Phenomenology, Pragmatic Philosophy, Hermeneutics, and Experience Philosophy, emphasize the importance of physical experience and consider it a prerequisite for the interaction between the subject and the outside world, as well as for the understanding and explanation of life and existence.[1]-[4] The concept of somaesthetics[5] manifests the return to life, the characteristics and laws of the cognitive subject's physical spatio-temporal experience, and the process towards authentic life through body extension, all of which have multiple image schemas.

In landscape design, the interaction between the viewer and the site is constituted with physical space limitation, psychological experience extension, and spiritual life support. The deep and intimate mode of relationship in landscape[6] exists among the spatio-temporal patterns, referring to those forms and ideas that structure society in general. Landscapes can alleviate social anxiety, form virtuous circles of social resources, and enhance the sense of efficacy of community members.[7] In this process, scholars explore the index of the deep structure beyond the aesthetics, that is, comprehending the deeper connotation of existence through meaning representation of shallow space and interactive behavior—Just like how Peter Eisenman adopted the linguistic framework proposed by Avram Noam Chomsky to explain the relationship between the perceptual structure of the surface structure and the conceptual structure of the deep structure. By underlying people's spatial perception and experience, Eisenman seeks the so-called "pure form of autonomy" upon the system of deep structure interpreted with notational orders, to form the representation of the design prototype which serves as a typology to inspire design.[8]

2 The Dimension of Body-Time-Space Experience under the Organization of Different Elements

In the discourse of post-modern design, the emphasis on the site elements or components makes the landscape an important medium that denies the homogeneity of the environment and

对所有事物的通盘接受使人与环境之间产生感知矛盾与割裂。认知主体在认识世界过程中产生的虚妄与无意义感，其核心是缺少了对身体体验的强调。

吉尔·德勒兹的身体美学研究逻辑、莫里斯·梅洛—庞蒂的身体—知觉理论等，均开启了主体与空间互动关系的大门，再到约翰·迪克逊·亨特提出的以人为本、注重质量和体验感受的观点，学者日益关注设计与心理学之间的关系，一定程度上对抗了创造性思维被逻辑推理取代的状态，并实现了对人与环境的关联及内涵的重新重视。[2][9][10]人与物质环境属性相互作用并构成持续动态的进化，借由文化脉络形成一种秩序或序列构成原型特征，其空间秩序也被表征为身体—时间—空间的体验质量，这种人与物质空间环境的持续调和会形成一定时期内的稳定性，这为提取原型本质提供了可能。

古斯塔夫·西奥多·费希纳提出可衡量的感觉单位、感觉阈，以及最小可觉差异等概念，认为感知者的内部与外部世界不再有隔膜且呈现一定的互动规律[11]①（图1）。景观空间同样呈现了对复杂差异要素进行组织的需要，界限模糊的景观要素交织关系显示出审美价值与视觉张力，引导主体对场地形成完整的介入式认知——差异是种种生成之流，个体之间的差异也促成了景观空间的内在性、过程性与不确定性。体验本身基于异质要素的不同编排结果，实现历时的、可变的，塑造动态表征、场景整合、事件组织的空间。

差异性的表征与意义也体现在人与环境互动的不同维度，亨利·列斐伏尔[12]、爱德华·W·索亚[13]、约翰·迪克逊·亨特[10]都将空间分为不同的三元层级，论述了景观视野中设计师针对场地的感知、对景象的认知与社会观想的过程[10]。这种较为普遍的空间认知方式也辅助构建了景观空间价值研究的三个基点——物质建构（场地）、意义建

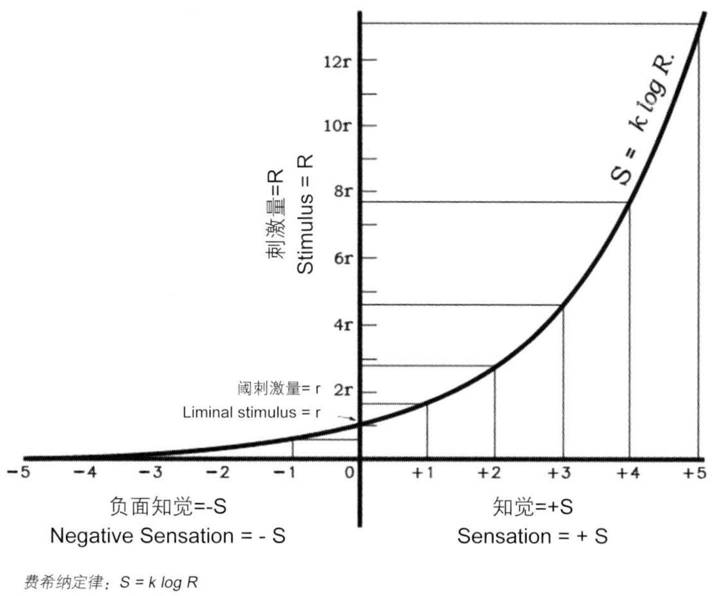

1

inspires cultural imagination. In a compressed spatio-temporal context, when the diversity and complexity of site elements fragments, it is more likely to cause space-time splits, and the overall acceptance of the elements in the post-modern radicalism results in the viewer's perception contradiction and separation with the site. The sense of illusion and meaninglessness what the cognitive subject would have in the process of understanding the world results from the lack of emphasis on physical experience.

Earlier efforts exploring the interactions between the subject and the space include Gilles Deleuze's research on body aesthetics and Maurice Merleau-Ponty's theory on body perception, and since John Dixon Hunt's emphasis on people-oriented spatial quality and experience, scholars have increasingly paid attention to the relationship between the design and Psychology. This, to a certain extent, confronts the shifting that creative thinking is being replaced with logical deduction, and re-emphasizes the connection and connotation between people and the environment.[2][9][10] The interaction between human and the attributes of the physical environment evolves continuously and dynamically, forming an order or a sequence of prototype characteristics by the cultural means. The spatial order is represented as an interactive experience quality of the body, time, and space. This continuous reconciliation of human and physical environment forms a stability in a certain period of time, which makes it possible to extract the essence of prototype.

By putting forward concepts such as measurable units of sensation, thresholds of sensation, and just noticeable difference, Gustav Theodor Fechner argued that to the viewer there is no longer a separation between the internal and external worlds, where the interaction follows certain patterns[11]① (Fig. 1). The landscape also reflects the need to organize the complex elements. The blur interweaving relationship of the landscape elements manifests the aesthetic quality and the visual tension, and leads the subject to form a complete interventional cognition of the site—the differences are the streams of generation, and differences between individuals also intensify the internality, process, and uncertainty of the landscape. The variety of experience depends on the different orchestrations of heterogeneous elements, realizing diachronic and variable spaces that define the dynamic representation, scene integration, and event organization.

The representation and meaning of the dissimilarity also reflect in various dimensions of the interaction between the subject and the environment. Henry Lefebvre[12], Edward W. Soja[13], and John Dixon Hunter[10] all defined the space into ternary levels, though upon different theories, discussing the

① 韦伯—费希纳定律可用于表明心理量和物理量之间的关系。这一定律从韦伯定律发展而来：德国生理学家恩斯特·海因里希·韦伯发现，同一刺激差别量必须达到一定比例，才能引起差别感觉。

① The Weber-Fechner Law is used to study the relation between the perceptional stimulus and physical stimulus. The law is stemmed from the Weber's Law, by German physiologist Ernst Heinrich Weber, which states that the just-noticeable difference between two stimuli is proportional to the magnitude of the stimuli.

1. 费希纳定律对感知的定量测度（改绘自参考文献[11]）

1. Fechner's Law offers a quantitative measure to perception [Adaptation source: Ref. [11]]

2. 景观空间三元关系是身体经验与时空想象的载体

2. The ternary relationship of landscape space shapes the place where physical experience and space-time imagery occur

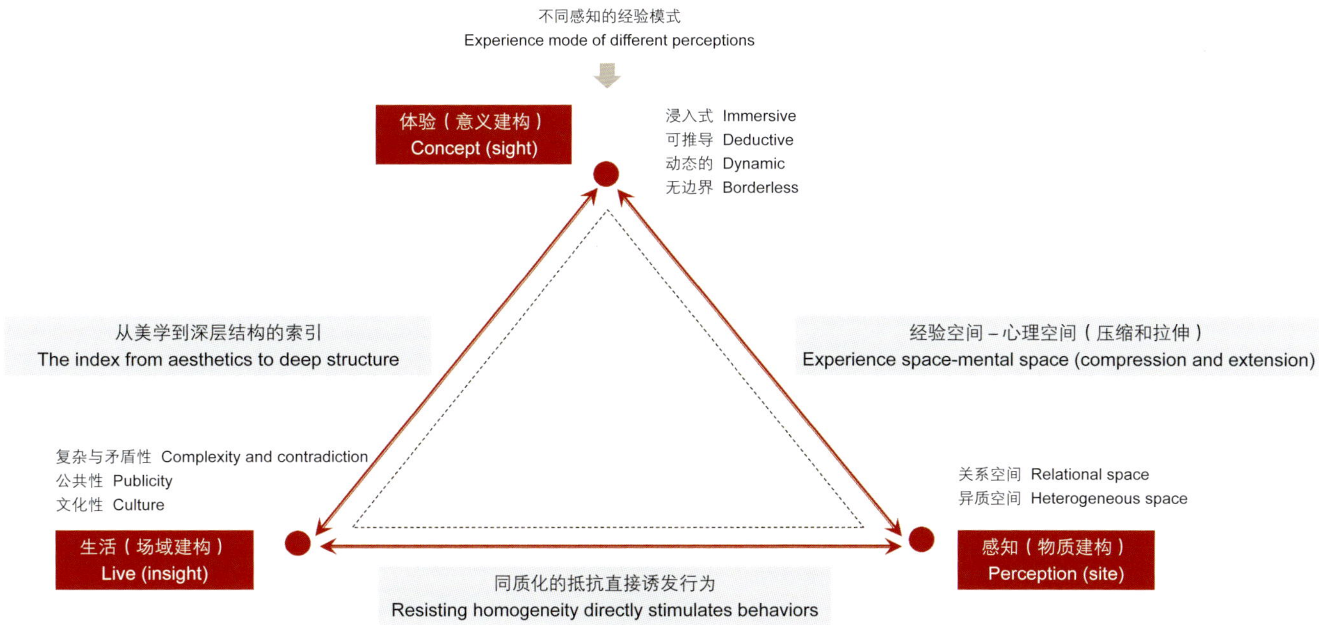

2 © 魏方，黄子舰

构（场景）、场域建构（场域）——从而建立新的空间情感与社会场域，形成流动性与体验情景的推动力，从而抵抗平面单一的"瞬时"体验过程，运用整个身体和所有感官更好地接近意义[14]，产生知觉和物质现象的交织，实现场地的增值[15]（图2）。

在这三个维度中，通过场地（物质空间）引发身体的推拉运动，场景（意义空间）中文本、句法的传递，以及场域空间中的情境构建、事件激发、社会效能提升，均体现了主体身体经验与时空想象在景观空间的可获得性与建构意义。在三元关系的发展与相互影响的过程中，景观空间分别在这三个维度中行使着主客体交互媒介、表意媒介与社会交换媒介的不同身份职能。

3 场地：物质空间中的推拉运动

物质空间中异质性元素的分布体现在时空层面[16]、文化与自然层面[17]，以及历史与考古层面[18]。梅洛–庞蒂及克里斯蒂安·诺伯格–舒尔茨探讨的身体图式和经验模式，作用于外部空间异质多元要素构建中的主体解读过程。物质空间中的行为可持续、停顿和逆转可以使

process in the designer's perception of the site, the cognition of sight, and the meditating and reconsidering of social insight[10]. This universal method of spatial cognition also assists in the building of the three basic points of the research on landscape space value, namely perception (site), conception (sight), and live (insight). This situates emotion and social fields in space, forms the flows and the impulse of experiencing the sight, and then resists the instantaneous, flattened experiencing process—using the whole body and all senses to approach the meaning[14], producing the interweaving of the perception and material phenomena and realizing the value-adding of the site[15] (Fig. 2).

In these three dimensions, the push-pull movement of the body in the site (material space), the convey of text and syntax in the sight (conceptive space), and the scenario construction, event impetus, and social efficacy improvement in the insight all emphasize the availability and constructive significance of the subject's physical experience and space-time imagery in the landscape. In such a triadic interplaying process, landscape performs different identities among the subject-object relationships, as agencies for interaction, ideography, and social exchange.

3 The Site: Push-Pull Movement in Material Space

The distribution of heterogeneous elements in the material space is amplified in the spatio-temporal level[16], the cultural and natural level[17], and the historical and archeological

连续、均质与抽象的心理空间产生压缩与拉伸。观者以知觉画面为线索构建对于场所的整体认知，以自发完成的蒙太奇方式实现意义的重建。在这一过程中，通过空间序列、空间方向，以及转换中的节点与阈②设置，充分建构了主体与外部环境的互动以及推拉运动的形成条件。主体视域在一种可指明的接受性感觉和自发性运动之间统一，形成运动中的动知觉与现象序列，并充实了空乏视域，使得场地内涵的在场与缺席形成交互关系。

3.1 序列与内外向空间

不同场地之间的要素链接定义了一种网络结构，以及引导运动产生的引力节点，促生了递进关系及序列空间中运动的可分性：运动以和谐及切分的节奏编排方式，结合方向感设定形成坐标系，其中除了对差异元素本身的关注，还包括了编排节奏中空间距离、路径组成的差异，异化的路径与非线性编辑引发时空的压缩、延伸或叠合互渗，强化了超序空间中的身体意识。景观空间的浸入式体验——主体在运动当中获得感知累积——延长了心理上的体验时间。运动和场所借由路径关联形成空间的流动性、固定性、生成性与推拉运动，突出特定空间片段中运动的具体特征，通过空间编排形成节点之间视觉与地形上的链接[19]。

在比利时海里纳利斯公园项目中，设计师通过在游览项目中融入第一次世界大战历史线索，并重新刻画场地表面，结合线路设置与相关设施排布串联起了场地内的战争遗迹。场地内弹坑周边低洼地积聚的雨水促生了新的植被群落类型，进而产生了新的生态斑块与场所记忆。设计按照战争时期军队的实际前进路线设置了一条“前线路线”，并利用色彩鲜艳的灌木林线界定这一沿线空间。观者可以同时感知到当代农业生产的场地文脉与旧时战场的氛围，当代农业与战争遗迹得以交互展现。[20]空间层次之间的关系处于动态震荡的状态，随着观者的注视而稳定，在整个过程中实现印象的叠加与整体空间结构的获取。受场地历史的持续影响，情景中的物质景观与抽象认知得以混合，在不断打破与整合中形成“视野融合”。主体的视觉目标与行走路线之间的关系形成了变化的张力，促进了主客体的合并融合，自身意识在可识别的差异中不断重新定位。在主体对有限的、非连续的、异质的空间信息进行感知的过程中，外部时间呈现均质线性的特征，内部时间又充满了压缩、延展、暂停与返回（图3）。

除了序列空间中的链接关系，彼得·拉茨基于空间的多重属性提出了一种设计观念，即区分“内向空间”与“外向空间”[21]。他认为德

level[18]. According to Merleau-Ponty and Christian Norberg-Schul's arguments, the body schema and empirical pattern act on the process when the subject interprets the construction of heterogeneous elements of external space. The continuity, pause, and reversal of the subject's behavior in the material space can compress or stretch the subject's mental space that is continuous, homogeneous, and abstract. The viewer uses the perceptual images as clues to construct the overall cognition of the place, so as to reconstruct the meaning through spontaneous montages. In this process, the design of spatial sequence and direction, as well as the nodes and thresholds② in the space transition, substantially defines the interaction between the subject and the space and the formation conditions of the push-pull movement. The unity of the subject's vision between the specifiable, receptive sensation with the spontaneous movement forms the kinesthetic and phenomenon sequence in the movement, fills in the vision vacancy, and establishes an interplaying relationship between the presence and absence of the connotation of the site.

3.1 The Sequence and the Introvert and Extrovert Space

The linkages of elements between different sites define a network structure and the tensional nodes within the conduct of the movement, which generates the progressive relationship and the separability of the movement in the sequence space: the rhythm of movement is choreographed by harmonization and syncopation in a coordinate of the sense of direction, which emphasizes not only the elements themselves, but also the spatial distance and the difference of path composition in rhythm choreography, the disparity of path and the non-linear editing, the spatio-temporal compression, extension, and overlapping or mutual penetration, augmenting the body consciousness in the hyperspace. The immersive experience of the landscape—when the subject accumulates his / her perception during the movement—prolongs the psychological experience. By establishing path relatedness, it leads to the fluidity, fixity, generativeness, and push-pull movement in the space, highlighting the characteristics of movement in a given space section, and forming visual and topographical linkages between the nodes through spatial arrangement[19].

In the project of the Herinnerings Park, Belgium, designers incorporated historical clues of World War I into viewers' touring experience by resurfacing the site and combining the war relics with the route setting and the arrangement of structure. New ecologies and new types of vegetation are spawned at the crater sites, where rainwater gathers in the deep spots, cultivating new memories of the site. Front-line pathways were designed along the actual front-lines during wartime and

② 在动知觉理论中，阈指空间中忽然产生变化的重要节点，是一种具有分隔及联系作用的中间状态。

② According to the theory of the Kinesthetic Sense, threshold refers to the just noticeable difference of the change of the space, and an immediate and abrupt nature that separates and connects the sides of it.

③ 马科斯・韦太默于1912年发表了《关于运动知觉的实验研究》一文，研究了所谓的"似动现象""频闪运动"，由此得出结论：事物的运动并非是其本身在运动，而是大脑皮质的完型组织作用所致。他借用了"生理短路"的物理学概念来解释兴奋的迅速传递。

③ In his publication Experimental Studies on the Perception of Movement in 1912, Max Wertheimer explored the so-called "phi phenomenon" and "stroboscopic motion" and concluded that the illusion of the apparent motion of an object is formed by human's gestalt organization in the visual cortex. He also explained the rapid neurotransmission of excitement with the concept of physiological short-circuit.

3 © Stoss Landscape Urbanism

3. 比利时海里纳利斯公园的行走序列体验

3. Sequential walking experience in Herinnerings Park, Belgium

国北杜伊斯堡公园通过建立外向空间的视觉联系链接了外部环境，这些视觉形象使场地具有相对侵入性的外部特征；同时，内向空间只有主体在内部进行游历时才可获取，但其外部信息也是构成场所质量的重要组成部分。鉴于内向空间与外向空间共同构成了认知主体在其中的身体体验，设计团队将全景图作为分析工具，来展现不同信息之间的联系，并评估要素信息的种类与密度（图4）。[21]

3.2 阈

空间连接与转换的整合性作用引发了"阈"的概念[22]。它基于空间序列内部发挥作用，主体由此获得双重空间结构信息，形成持续观察累积，拓展看待世界的方式，最终形成自成一体的感知体验：时间或空间仿佛混合进入主体心理的连贯维度之中[23]。韦太默试验③指出频闪实验中屏幕上的运动现象事实上是片段跳跃和不连续的，而观者最

were marked as brightly colored coppice-lines. The design "re-orients the visitor itinerary to the geographies of the war, and choreographs a series of ephemeral plantings and atmospheric effects that give presence to the battle fields within the context of working agricultural fields."[20] The relationship between varying spatial levels dynamically oscillates, which gets stabilized when the viewer gazes, forming a superposed image of the whole process and a perception of the overall spatial structure. Continuously affected within the historical ambience on the site, the physical landscape and the subject's abstract cognition intermingles, forming a "vision fusion" through such continuous breakings and integrations. The subject's walking route and his / her focal objects interact which forms a changing tension and promotes the merging of the subject and the object by constantly repositioning the self-consciousness during the perceiving of discernible differences. When the subject perceiving the space information that is limited, discontinuous, and heterogeneous, the external time is defined by the linear homogeneousness, while the internal time is shaped by the sense of compression, extension, pause, and return (Fig. 3).

In addition to the linkages in the sequence space, Peter Latz also proposed a pair of design concepts upon the multiple attributes of space: introvert space and extrovert space[21]. He believes that in the Duisburg-Nord Park in Germany visual connections with the panorama was established with extrovert space which draws attention to special features in the surroundings. Although the inward space can only be conceived when the subject situates and tours inside the park, the quality of the place is primarily shaped by its external information. In view of the fact that the introvert space and extrovert space together shape the physical experience of the cognitive subject, panorama was used as an analysis tool "to absorb information from the outside and signal information to the outside," and evaluate the type and density of the element information (Fig. 4).[21]

3.2 The Threshold

The integration effect of the connectivity and transition of the space introduces the concept of "threshold"[22]. It acts on the internal spatial sequence which makes the subject obtain the spatial structure information from both the inside and outside, form continuous accumulation of observation that expands the way of looking at the world, and finally shape the subject's own perception experience: time or space seems to be mixed into the coherence of the subject's mental world[23]. The Wertheimer Experiment③ verified that the apparent motion that arises when an object is viewed on the screen is formed with discontinuous image intervals, and the viewer finally perceives a continuous

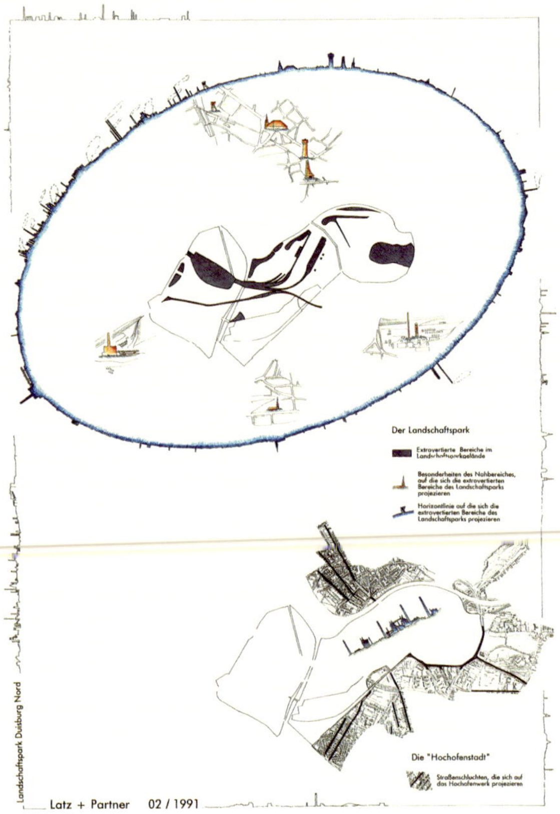

© Latz + Partner
4

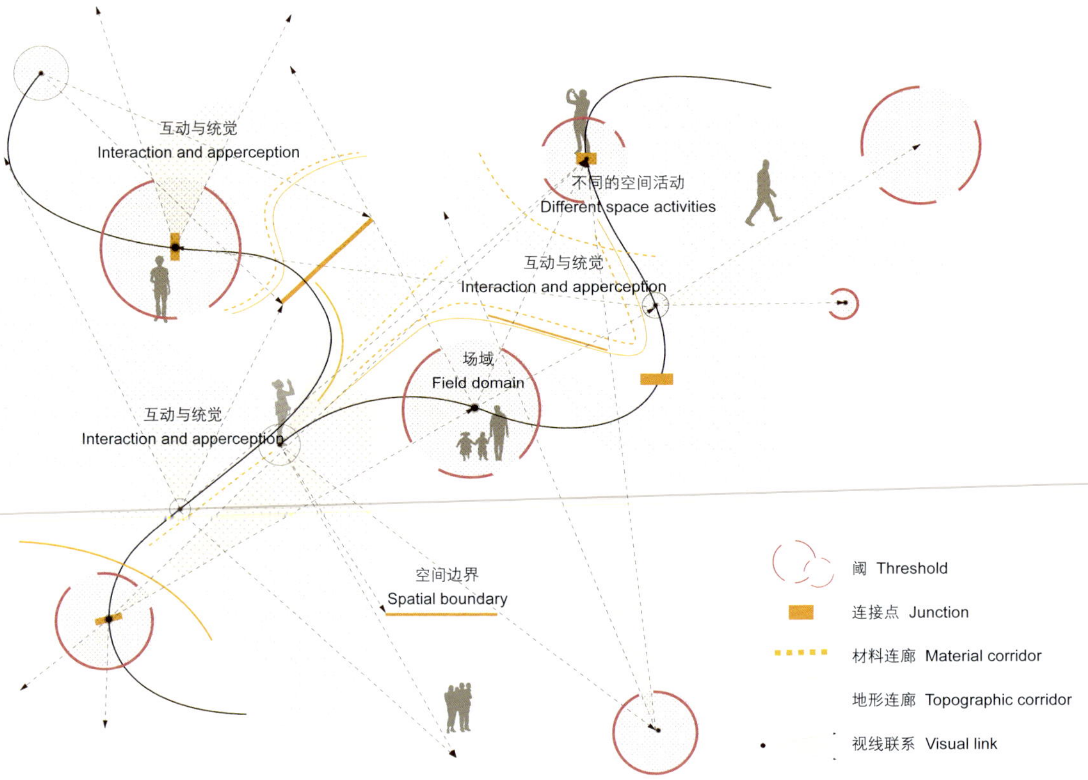

© 魏方，黄子彬
5

终获得连续的心理认知“阈”及“转换”空间，这其中包含主体已经产生和预知要发生的感知的层叠[24]。

阈的作用在于美学经验在时间持续作用中会呈现延迟，发生于主体感知与其知识经验的交换过程中[22]。当两个单独的景观画面具有分别的显性意义时，其间的状态和情感诱发也同时存在；主体在不断的运动状态之中感知世界，两处景观视觉之间的中间状态也是主体感知体验中的重要一环[25]。在预想的驱动下，主体体验过程中的感知速度被加速或放慢，感知到的空间丰富度得以提升；通过关系空间的制造，不连续碎片式信息得到有意义的连续解读，观者的空间性得到重要反馈与重塑。阈作为在运动状态下不同空间的转换处，标志着差异的连接，其中边界共享的视觉特征与对场地整体性的压缩式洞察使观者对世界的想象超越了纯粹的视觉印象，借由经验与想象，碎片式的空间要素得以完形（图5）。

在青海原子城爱国主义教育基地纪念园项目中，设计通过叙事结构的安排，在空间转换处呈现出阈界面的双重性质（图6），即主体在结构关系转换处可以分别获得上一段信息的留存与下一段信息的暗示。人在亲身介入空间的过程中，产生身体—空间—时间的组织与辩证关系，引发持续性的感知、思想和行为。设计通过设置阈限和地形变化来引导重力运动及推拉运动，并建立视觉关联，从而形成了空间深度；通过空间距离设置异化的路径与视觉通道，建立了迭代指示作

space through the “threshold” and “transition” in the cognition, where the subject’s perception cascade has occurred or to occur[24].

The function of the threshold lies in the phenomenon that one’s aesthetic experience delays in the exchange process between the perception and personal knowledge and experience[22]. When two separate landscape images become spatially distinct, they will become increasingly different, physically and emotionally; the subject perceives the world through constant movement, and the transitioning state between the two landscape visions is also constitutive to the subject’s perception experience[25]. Subject to one’s anticipation, the perception in the experience process is either accelerated or slowed down which increases the perceived spatial richness; the creation of relational space interprets the discontinuous information fragments into meaningful and continuous perceptions, during which the viewer’s spatiality is reacted and redefined. Threshold, as the turning point between different spaces in the state of motion, marks the connection of differences, and the visual characteristics of the sharing boundaries and the compressed insight into the integrity of the site enable the viewer’s imagination of the world to transcend

4. 德国北杜伊斯堡公园的内、外向空间信息的全景分析
5. 物质空间中引导推拉运动的阈与方向

4. In the Duisburg-Nord Park, Germany, panorama was used as an analysis tool of the information from both introvert space and extrovert space.
5. The threshold and direction leading the push-pull movement in material space

6. 中国青海原子城爱国主义教育基地纪念园项目中的空间转换——阈（底图来源：朱育帆工作室）

6. The interface of threshold in the design of the Memorial Park of Qinghai Atomic City Patriotism Education Base, China (Site plan source: Zhu Yufan Landscape Atelier)

6 © 魏方，黄子舰

用；通过将阈作为内部界框，主体对交互性双重系统的同时感知使得其在运动中不断切换关注重点，产生对空间理解的新意义，加之内在时间意识的控制形成滞留与前摄的连续性体验流，从而标记所有运动轨迹。

4 场景：意义的侧显与完形

景观依赖于主客观的集合形态，众多学者对现代主义的批判指出感知即智识，挑战了启蒙主义运动之后的科学观念[26]；景观是一种可以被阅读的文本，并且包含了多层意义及文学性[27]。将景观看作一个物体、将客体从对复杂现实的参与中进行分离的狭隘观念会影响主体的意识形态及审美。作为表意媒介，景观以多种方式表征场所被赋予的意义，形成无法被替换的、直接的身体经验及引人深思的可读观点。景观要素的碎片信息组合中包含不同的文本意义，并通过一定的句法结构使其得以表征和完形。

4.1 文本

在当代，多样与差异激活了地方的复原与整修。例如，历史文本和传统建筑的保留与纳入揭示了场地先前的历史沉淀，将场所置于时间与运动的某一历史节点，创造景观的开放性，多元并重和共同延展

the pure visual impression—Through experience and imagination, fragmented spatial elements can form a gestalt (Fig. 5).

Through the arrangement of narrative structure, the design of the Memorial Park of Qinghai Atomic City Patriotism Education Base presents the dual nature of the interface of threshold (Fig. 6) at the transitions of the space, where the subject can obtain both the persisting information from the previous space section and the hint from the next section. In the process of being in the space, the subject comes into an organizational and dialectical relationship between the body, space, and time, which triggers continuous perceptions, thoughts, and behaviors. The design guides the gravitational movement and push-pull movement by choreographing thresholds and terrain changes and establishing visual relationship to define the spatial depth; the disparity of path and visual channels is designed through the arrangement of spatial distance to instruct the iterative indicative function; by using thresholds as internal frames, the subject's simultaneous perception of the dual system of interaction makes the focal objects keep changing during the movement, continually reshaping one's understanding of the space; the control of the consciousness of the internal time forms the continuous experience flow of retention and protention, thus marking all the trajectories of movement.

4 The Sight: Abschattung and Gestalt of Meaning

Landscape is defined by the collective of subjective and objective forms. Scholars' critiques on Modernism point out that perception is intelligence which challenges the scientism after the Enlightenment[26]; landscape is an anatomy of message which consists of multiple speeches and literatures[27]. The idea that considers landscape an object and separates it from the complex context of the reality limits the subject's ideology and aesthetics. Being an ideographic medium, landscape represents the meaning of the site in a variety of ways, forming irreplaceable, direct physical experience and thought-provoking legible insights. The combinations of fragment information of landscape elements contain different textual massages that are represented as the gestalt with grammars and syntaxes.

4.1 The Text

In contemporary times, diversity and difference activate the restoration and renovation of the locality. For example, the preservation and integration of historical texts and historic buildings evince the site's existing sedimentation in history, placing the site at a certain historical segment in time and movement, and creating an openness for the landscape. Multiple

的关系使场地具有“谱性”，在“踪迹”④中得到自我证明，承载不同的场所意义与群体集体意义。景观要素的表意性可呈现为“意符”[28]，以超现实主义和蒙太奇的方法对冲突的非连接元素进行协调，并保持并置关系的模糊性，打破图像框架，使观者可以掌握再现景观的多样性。在德国柏林波茨坦广场项目中，理查德·韦勒探索了文化及人类学层面上的意义呈现过程。他通过拼贴和蒙太奇的方法描述了公园的5个层次，分别为地面形态、白天剧场、夜晚剧场、机器的极乐世界，以及生活的机器，以细微的踪迹揭示了场地的过往，展现了冷战时期柏林的历史状态，形成一种具有差异层次的混合视野（图7）[29]。

进行表意的媒介以多元要素、景象、尺度等形式集结在超链接中，实现时间性和概念性的延展。例如，通过对不同时期的历史痕迹进行共时呈现，各部分的区别一目了然，同时也共同构建了未来共同生长的可能，使之成为了一种互惠媒介。这种差异性的混合贯穿在继承场地与发展未来的过程中，部分层次承载了新置层次信息，而使差异之间具有更为密切的相关性；不同的表意媒介以交叠状态形成其间相互依存或相互制约的关系，通过组织使主体更倾向于将其作为整体的新的认知。当差异性的要素以整合、渲染、折叠、并置等方式呈现

equal emphasis and coextension bring spectral to the site, which proves itself in the trace④ and carries the meaning of individual sites and the collective. The ideography of the elements of the landscape can be presented as ideograms[28], which use the means of surrealism and montages to coordinate the non-connected conflicting elements, and maintain the ambiguity of the juxtaposition by breaking the image frame to enable the viewer to grasp the diversity of reproducing the landscape. In the design of the Potsdamer Platz in Berlin, Germany, Richard Weller explored the process of meaningful presentation from the cultural and anthropological perspectives. He described the 5 layers of the park by collage and montage means, namely the Earth Work, the Day Theater, the Night Theater, the Machine Elysium, and the Living Machines, where the viewer can find the subtle traces to disclose the past of the site—the historical state of Berlin during the Cold War—and form a visual mixture of different layers (Fig. 7)[29].

The ideographic medium is displayed in hyperlinks in multiple forms of elements, scenes, scales, etc. to achieve temporal and conceptual extension. For example, by simultaneously presenting the historical traces of different times, the difference between each part is obvious; meanwhile, they jointly build the possibility of future co-growth by acting as mutually beneficial media. This mixture of differences can be found through the process of inheriting the site's history and shaping its future, where the new information levels are integrated into existing levels, so that the differences are more closely interconnected; the different ideographic media, overlapping with each other, form a relationship of either interdependence or mutual restraint, where the organization of space leads the subject to the new perception of the space as a whole. When the elements of differences are presented in the

④ 在彼得·埃森曼的“踪迹操作”建筑作品中，他将踪迹——即建筑外在性——与建筑先在性和内在性相结合，并形成一个叠加的状态，在分析建筑的外在性过程中，文本与场地是图解建筑外在性的重要支撑条件。

④ Among Peter Eisenman's architectural work that appreciates tracing, he combined and overlapped all the traces—the exteriority of architecture—with the anteriority and interiority of architecture; he also makes texts and the site become constitutive to the diagraming of the exteriority of architecture.

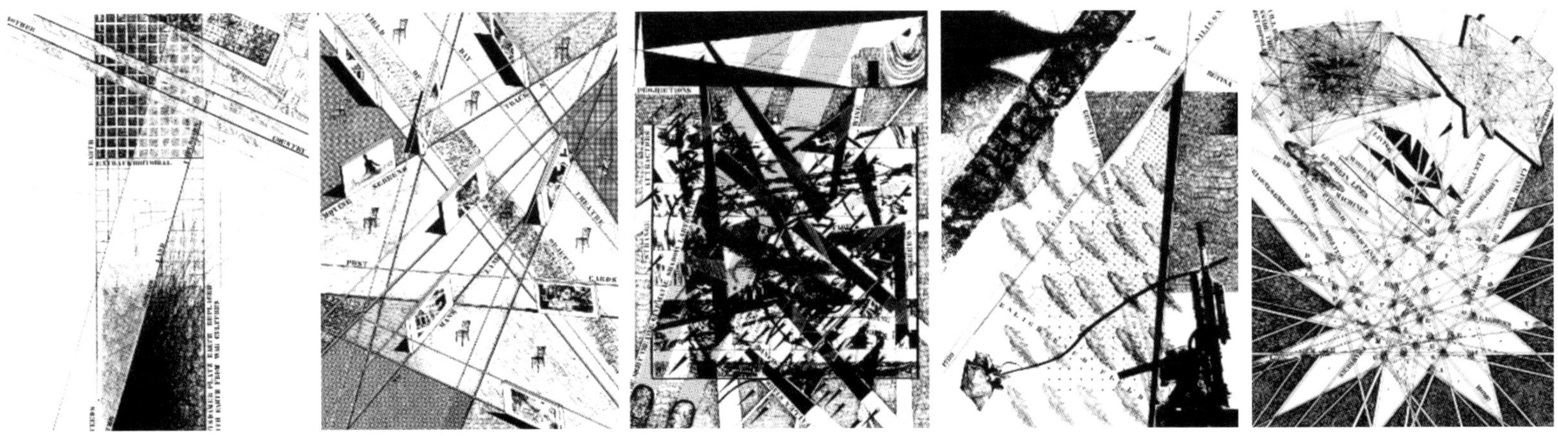
© Richard Weller

7. 德国波茨坦广场的5个层次

7. 5 layers of the Potsdamer Platz in Berlin, Germany

⑤ 埃德蒙德·胡塞尔认为任何知觉都是一种侧显，空间质料决定了从自我出发的意向会指向哪个对象及对象的内容；侧显中的统一性才使得高阶的对象、判断和知识成为可能。

⑥ 从现象学来说，主体认知借由“指月之指”对“目的地”进行占据并形成思考。马克·特雷布以此论述罗伯特·欧文的作品。

⑤ Edmund Husserl argued that any form of consciousness is abschattung; spatial materials determine the objects and the implications that the self-oriented intention projects; it is the unity of different visible sides that makes the advanced cognition of objects, judgments, and knowledge possible.

⑥ From the perspective of Phenomenology, the metaphor of the Finger Pointing to the Moon is referred to the occupation of the destination by subject's cognition, and the thoughts then inspired as well. Marc Treib used this to review the work of Robert Irwin.

时，主体意识的获取都是以侧显⑤的方式进行的，即通过角度摄取对若干部分侧面与信息产生理解，通过整合瞬时的碎片形成综合的认知形象与多元交叠的意义，而非在一次意识投射行为中把握事物整体。抽象的文化与社会结构性构成运动的物质化，在时空视角下，主体实施着对空间的记忆、想象与意义捕捉，促生在时空作用下情感与思维的相互影响[30]。

4.2 句法

针对本土化与全球化之间的明显张力，联系场所与地域性的设计方式虽会有助于加强场所意义，但也可能带来场地发展中幽闭的惯性和重复。针对景观表意文本，需要进行合理的句法建构，使用叙事缝合、混合叙事等方式，关注在审美表意过程中的“碰撞”“互动”与“缝合”，呈现出“超文本”和“超链接”的特征。通过对空间中异质结构的叠印关系进行强化，强调连续的震荡和反馈动作，深刻地揭示了易被忽视的类比关联。两个看似具有不同属性的要素既相对独立又形成碰撞，使混合表意强调了自身存在的可能、价值和意义，表现“指月之指”⑥的“感知跨越空间”能力。在人的身体运动中，非线性时空利用虚实空间结构与物境和影像中的节点，实现回忆增值。场地和运动之间的张力将故事与地点联系起来，通过在景观实践中使用叠印、错格、分隔、切换、消减、省略等方法将不同的时间折叠在一起[31]（图8）。

詹姆斯·科纳结合亨特有关场地、场所精神、场所营造等方面的文章中所提的相关观点，强调了“层化”与“想象”的关键技术，提出种群、混合体和克隆这三类空间结构。[32]种群是景观新陈代谢中的基础骨架与脉络，以及内部关系的结构；混合体则是利用缝合和嫁接的

form of integration, rendering, folding, juxtaposition, etc., the subject's consciousness is reflected through abschattung⑤—the understanding of the visible sides and the information of several space parts is shaped through fragment capture, and an overall cognitive image and overlapping meanings are formed through the integration of instantaneous fragments, rather than grasping the whole space with a single projection of consciousness. The abstract significance in culture and social structure constitutes the materialization of movement. From the spatio-temporal perspective, the subject projects his / her memory, imagination, and meaning capture of the space, which generates the spatio-temporal interplay between the emotion and thought[30].

4.2 The Syntax

In view of the obvious tension between localization and globalization, although the design method that connects the site and the context helps amplify the meaning of the site, it may bring about the confined inertia and repetition along with the evolution of the site. The creating of the ideographic texts of the landscape requires reasonable syntactical construction which employs methods such as “narrative seaming” and “mixed narrative,” focuses on the “collision,” “interaction,” and “stitching” in the ideography of aesthetics, and characterizes “hypertext” and “hyperlink.” By strengthening the superposition of heterogeneous structures in the space, the continuous shocks and reactions are accentuated, profoundly recounting the analogy connections that are easily overlooked. Two elements that seem with different attributes are both independent and collisional to each other, where the intermingling ideograms emphasize the possibility, value, and meaning of its existence and represent the ability of perception beyond space—like the Finger Pointing to the Moon⑥. During human's body movement, the non-linear temporality and spatial presence combines the virtual and real spatial structure with the physical and image nodes to achieve value increment of memories. The tension between the site and the movement connects the narration with the place and overlaps different time attributes through superimposition, anacoluthon, separating, switch, subduction, and omiting in landscape practice[31] (Fig. 8).

Upon Hunter's concepts on the site, the site spirit, placing making, etc., James Corner underlined the key techniques of “stratification” and “imagination” and proposed three types of spatial structure: species, hybrid, and clone.[32] Species is the skeleton and vein in landscape metabolism and constitutes the interrelation structure; Hybrid refers to the integrated space shaped with seaming and grafting—for example, the urban planning of Paris by George-Eugene Haussmann

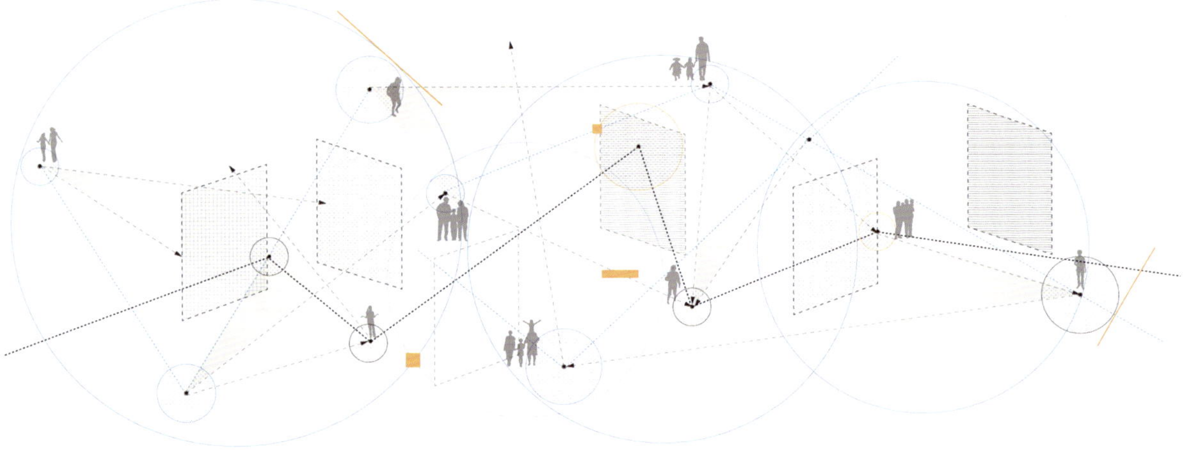

8 © 魏方，龚子舰

8. 意义空间中表意文本的侧显与完型

8. Abschattung and gestalt of ideographic texts in the meaning space

⑦ 更多关于法国喀桑采石场高速公路景观设计实践的讨论，请参见米歇尔·柯南所著的《伯纳德·拉索斯的喀桑采石场设计——论景观创建》一书。

⑦ For more criticism on the design of the moterway creation of the Quarries of Crazannes in France, please see Michel Conan's book *The Crazannes Quarries by Bernard Lassus—An Essay Analyzing the Creation of a Landscape*.

手段整合空间，例如，由乔治·豪斯曼提出的巴黎规划（图9）利用场地的未完成性和不确定性持续进化；克隆是以自治或通用的自我生长方式创造出极其多样、不可预料、充满互动的空间混合，用潜在的超文本创造不确定的事件与阅读。[32]

再如伯纳德·拉索斯提出的异质体[33]理念强调了异质要素的美学及历史价值，形成并置的层化设计方法，通过引入异质性布局形式，形成景观意义连续的串联体。景观空间片段被分解、切换、重组，类意识流般的文学叙述手法使景象与空间序列形成了特定的脉络组织。通过“情节”的分离、解构、重建，同时利用“最小公分母”统一差异性要素，可以建立表意过程中的关联性。拉索斯在法国喀桑采石场高速公路景观设计项目中未使用推平或炸毁的方式，而是使用了刮擦岩石面的方法，利用不同部分在色彩或形式上的统一要素作为最小公分母，建立视觉体验序列与连续的界面景观，并对被遮蔽的、历史沉积的文化差异痕迹进行发掘呈现。⑦

5 场域：空间中的统觉

约翰·杜威认为，“体验不仅是主体与世界相互作用的结果，而且是主体积极参与其中、发挥主观能动性的产物”[34][35]，当相互作用达

(Fig. 9) envisioned the continuous development of the site upon its incompleteness and uncertainty; Clone is to create a space mixture of an extreme diversity, unpredictability, and interactivity with autonomic or general self-growth methods, and to use the potential hypertext to inspire uncertain events and reading[32].

For another example, the concept of Heterodite[33] proposed by Bernard Lassus emphasizes the aesthetic and historical value of heterogeneous elements, forming a design method of juxtaposed stratification and creating a continuity of landscape meanings by introducing heterogeneous layout forms. Space sections are decomposed, switched, and reorganized in the landscape, and a quasi stream-of-consciousness literary narrative makes the scene and the space sequence form a specific contextual organization. Through the separation and decomposition of "plots," new connections are established, and by using the "least common denominator" to unify the elements of difference, the relatedness in the ideographic process occurs. In the moterway creation of the Quarries of Crazannes in France, Lassus, instead of using radical methods like flattening or blowing up, employed the design method that scrapes the rock surface and units different parts in color or form as the least common denominator, to organize the visual experience sequence and a continuous interface landscape and to celebrate the cultural uniqueness that was hidden within the historical traces.⑦

5 The Insight: Apperception in Social Field

John Dewey believes that "experience is not only the result of interaction of subject and world, but also the subject's reward when it transforms interaction into participation"[34][35]. The ultimate of

⑧ 统觉是指知觉内容和倾向蕴含着人们的已有经验、知识、兴趣和态度，因而不再限于对事物个别属性的感知。戈特弗里德·威廉·莱布尼茨的统觉是指人对其自身及其心灵状态的认识；通过统觉，人们理解、记忆和思考相互联合的观念，从而完成高级的思维活动。

⑧ Apperception means that people's consciousness and preference reflect their existing experience, knowledge, interests, and attitudes, which is not subject to the perception of an individual substance. In Gottfried Wilhelm Leibniz's philosophy, apperception is consciousness, or the reflective knowledge of this internal state; through apperception, human's thought, memory, and reflection are built upon interlinking concepts which are fundamental to higher thinking activities.

到极致，就会转化为参与和交流，最终成为知识的来源。“对象—视域”结构中的每一种体验是个人心智状态与筹划事件的互动结果——事件如同晶体一样，借由特定空间不断生成和发展。场景建立与重构中的自然与社会文化现象使自我与他人的结对和联想产生意义的递推与同感，从群体视角提升了公众意象力与社会效能，最终构成了统觉⑧，即个体对于他人身体和由之呈现出来的想象与意义合为一体。

5.1 事件空间

同感与统觉实现了个体与他人的通达和交互塑造，进而塑造群体化的生活世界。在当代，景观创作尝试为政治生活与知识生活寻求位置，它摒弃宏大叙事，强调了社群与地方性、场所与地域活动、社会运动、尊重他者等内容。当不同的文化形态与社会功用的空间形态被交叠并存时，触引经验、意义和价值的新形态出现，在有限的资源中显示出更高的活力，成为差异和他者的场所。

一方面，重拾的时间、土地的痕迹与文化现象[36]成为一种对空间压缩负面效应的抵抗，景观通过深层次的结构承载文化上的协和作用，为过去的存在提供了完成和永存的意义，以抵抗当代生活的快节奏[6]；另一方面，世界本身愈发杂交、多义和多元话语，种族、民族、文化、精神的主体日益多样化，促使景观不断在其中做出适应。多元化主体在空间中产生了复杂矛盾的感官认知与意义，以及多样的阅读与广泛的理解，并形成了情境意义的纠集[37]。这成为实体和场景融合的基本动力，感觉中的矛盾和超载也不断被重新纳入和整合。

在现代主义诞生初期，情境主义国际的理论思潮就探讨了景观创作中的日常生活性，居伊·德波创作的《巴黎心理地理学指南》利用心理感知层面的箭头将巴黎不同区域进行相互联系，形成了共时展现，并表达了个体化认知与心理距离作用下的重构的巴黎。[38]伯

9. 乔治·豪斯曼提出的巴黎规划（参见参考文献[32]）

9. The urban planning of Paris by George-Eugene Haussmann (Source: Ref. [32])

such an interaction will lead to a transform into participation and communication and ultimately become a source of knowledge. All the experience in the “object-view” structure is the result of the interaction between the individual's mental state and the designed event—events are the product that is continuously generated and developed in a given space. The nature and the socio-cultural phenomena in the construction and reconstruction of the scene make the subject be partnered with others and inspire recursion and empathy from meaningful implications, which enhances the public's imagination and social efficacy from a group perspective, and constitutes apperception⑧ in the end where the individual's imagination of the others' bodies and the associated meaning integrate as a whole.

5.1 The Event-Space

Empathy and appreciation attain the communication and interaction between individuals and shape the world of group life. Contemporary landscape creation attempts to reposition the political life and intellectual life by denying grand narratives while celebrating community and locality, place and regional activities, social movements, and respect for others. The overlapping and coexistence of spatial typologies of different cultural forms and social functions would activate new forms of experience, meaning, and value, presenting a higher vitality of the limited resources and becoming the site for differences and others.

On the one hand, the time to reclaim, as well as the trace and cultural phenomenon of the land[36] resist the negative impact of space compression. Landscape embraces a cultural harmony with its deep structure, and offers the existence of the past the meaning of completion and perpetuation that counteracts the fast pace of contemporary life[6]. On the other hand, the world itself is increasingly diverse in hybrid, polysemy, and discourses, where the subjects of race, ethnicity, culture, and spirit are also more and more diversified, making the landscape be in a continuous adaptation. Diversified subjects have brought complex and contradictory sensory cognitions and meanings in the space, as well as multiplicate reading and extensive understanding, gathering the meaning of a situation[37]. This becomes a driving force for the fusion of the entity and the scene, and the contradictions and overloads of one's feeling are constantly (re-)incorporated and (re-)integrated.

Among the early theories of Modernism, the Situationist International theory had emphasized the significance of daily life in landscape creation. Guy Debord's *Psychogeographic Guide of Paris* uses arrows indicating psychological perceptions to network different areas of Paris, which forms a synchronic

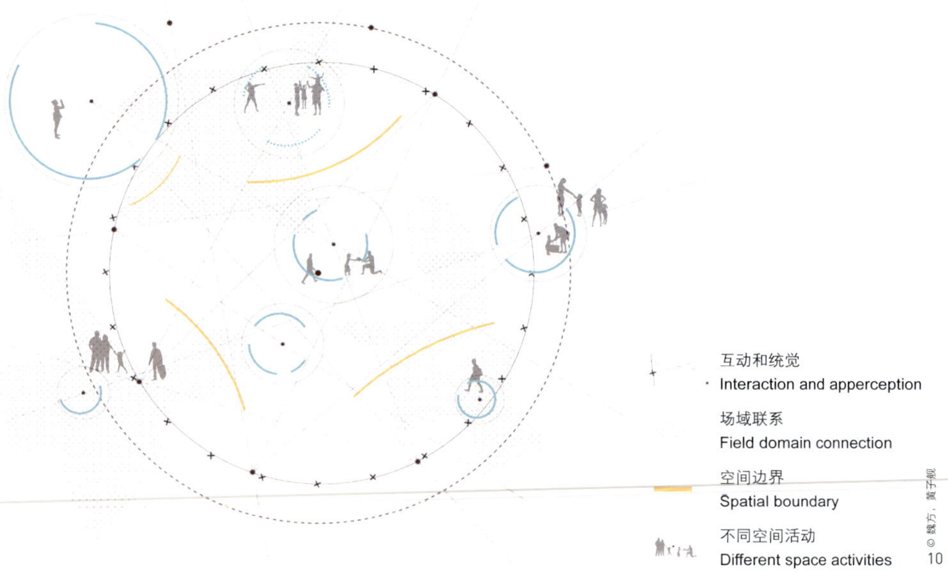

10. 场域空间中情境设定与社会效能提升下的统觉

10. Apperception constituted by scenarios of social field and the enhancement of social efficacy

纳德·屈米以“事件城市”作为主线设计的法国拉·维莱特公园，将事件作为构建场域与社会影响力的基本维度，进而将场地差异化的特征整合至人们对公园的感知之中。人在建筑空间中的各种主观体验活动和感受可以借由事件得以表达，脱离了传统“功能—形式”间的必然关系，以及综合、统一、精心管理的束缚，以结构系统差异层之间的冲突、碎片化、游戏性引发事件。设计以情景式的图层叠加的“程序”标记系统，激发了城市的社会活力，社会意义与形式创造经由事件得以显现。[39]

5.2 社会效能与意象力

主体基于个性化体验形成深刻的洞察，通过与场地对话，促使人们对自身的存在方式及意义进行思考。在特定情境设定、事件激发作用下的社会参与、互动、统觉的过程中，产生人与自然、人与社会、人与历史的关系，使主体从对形象的直观理解中获得概念构思、意象概括、譬喻性解释，形成基于个体经验的相对真理与认知原型，而具有发生学意义。景观通过参与社会运作甚至发挥政治职能，将自身构

display and represents the city reconstructed by individualized cognition and psychological distance.[38] Bernard Tschumi designed the Parc de la Villette, Paris with the narrative of “Event-Cities” which took events as the fundamental dimension to construct the social field and influence, and then integrated the attributes of differences of the site into people’s perception of the park. All kinds of subjective experience activities and feelings in architectural spaces can be expressed through events, which transcend the necessity of the traditional function-form relationship, and comprehensive, unified, and elaborate manipulates and controls, and trigger events upon the conflict, fragmentation, and gamification between different layers in the structural system. The design created a program system superimposed with scenario layers that activates the social vitality of the city and magnifies the social meaning and the formal creation with events.[39]

5.2 Social Efficacy and Social Image Ability

The subject’s profound insights are defined by his / her personal experience, and the dialogue with the site prompts people to think about the way and meaning of their own existence. In the social participation, interaction, and appreciation processes in specific scenarios and by event impulses, the relationships between man and nature, man and society, and man and history are built, so that the subject can obtain concepts, imagery, and metaphorical explanation from the intuitive understanding of images and form a relative truth and cognitive prototype based on individual experience of

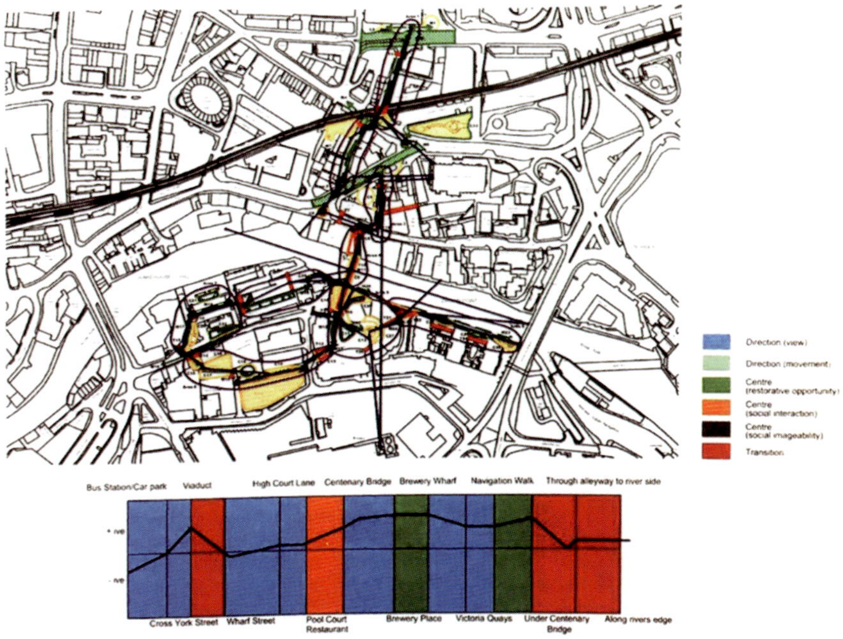

11

11. 基于CDTA要素的体验景观地图（参见参考文献[23]）

11. The map of people's experience of landscape with the CDTA System (Source: Ref. [23])

建为文化载体并影响现有文化，以在重塑世界中发挥作用（图10）。

为了调查社会公众的活动兴趣，劳伦斯·哈普林创作了“RSVP循环体系”（即资源—谱记—评价—绩效循环），并强调“谱记”的作用，同时参与式工作坊被首次运用在美国沃斯堡商业区项目的总体规划中。[40]这一体系梳理了设计者所应处理的各种差异性的物质要素与主体要素、公众期待的结果、决策分析、结果与绩效，鼓励人们参与环境创造过程。在此过程中，哈普林保持着一种对设计创造的本源与目的的极大兴趣，将创造“以人为本”的人性空间作为主要设计目标。为了说明体验景观中社会互动性的重要作用，凯文·斯韦茨还提出了CDTA[23]体系的社交互动与视野运动，认为整个城市可以形成可塑性的体验，一段穿越压力与真空的旅程。CDTA可运用于不同尺度，并具有不同的社会广度与丰富程度，利用“中心—方向—转折—面域”的原型组织方式，将人的体验折叠进入空间中，形成各种公共与社交活动（图11）。在景观组织中，基于视觉上的多样性和复杂性形成社会意

genetic significance. By participating in social operations or even political functions, landscape constructs itself as a cultural carrier that influences the existing culture, in order to play a role in the reshaping of the world (Fig. 10).

In order to investigate the public's interest in activities, Lawrence Halprin devised the RSVP Cycles (Resources-Scores-Valuation-Performance Cycles) and emphasized the role of “scores.” Participatory workshops were used for the first time in the Master Planning of the Fort Worth Downtown, the United States.[40] The RSVP Cycles sorts out all kinds of constituents that designers should deal with, including material and subject elements, the expected results by the public, the decision-making analysis, and the final results and actual performance. It encourages people to participate in the process of environmental creation, in which Harprin showed his enthusiasm for the essence and the purpose of design creation—in this project, Harprin took the creation of human-oriented space as the primary design goal. In order to illustrate the importance of social interaction in the experiencing landscape, Kevin Thwaites proposed the social interaction and vision movement of the CDTA (center, direction, transition, and area)[23] System. He believes that the one can form an experience of plasticity in the whole city and a journey through pressure and vacuum. CDTA can be applied at various scales for a wide-ranging social fields and objectives. It uses the prototypical organization of center-direction-transition-area to fold the one's experience into the space and to stimulate diverse public and social activities (Fig. 11). In the organization of landscape creation, the social imagery is formed

象力，并构成社会意义；通过不同体验方式、路径及汇合点，提供社会交往平台和用于休憩及精神恢复的城市空间。

可将差异要素进行折叠的景观空间原型的产生也与社会效能的提升目标相关，与艾力克斯·沃尔对城市表皮的阐述相似，这一空间组织方式将其自身作为动态的、对城市变化有响应的、能及时反映社会事件的空间载体。[41]格雷戈·林恩认为，空间折叠关注连续性与平滑性，力求将各种异质元素、复杂性、矛盾性在连续而又非均质的系统中被整合为统一体，并保持各自的特性[42]。德勒兹将"平滑性"描述为"连续的多样性"和"形式连续的展开"。保罗·维希留的"倾斜平面"理念强调了在流动中独立单元的消失，以及多维层次的空间互通。不明确性使人处于对内外认知的模糊状态，显示出空间定义的暧昧，形成无边界的景观。[43]日本横滨国际码头项目设计正是通过内部与外部空间的折叠，以表达时间的复杂性，并容纳全方位的社会想象。结合主体的互动体验，地平面本身成为拓扑的事件结构，溶解与重构了所谓的标准，以及新旧关系和图底关系，制造了差异的连续性，使人的活动与环境产生一种新的、深刻的相互作用。

6 结语

景观中的空间不只是容纳事物的容器，更是一种可以将差异性与多元要素相互连接起来的能力或力量。不同的表意方式将特定的情境或事物归诸于独特的特征与整体认知，形成不同的身体—时间—空间互动过程。身体体验与时空想象的原型关系决定了体验中的变化与相应的感知结果，决定了人与场所的沟通深度。当代学者不断研究空间中的情景创造，并将主客体交互深度的研究与探讨作为一种设计意识的觉醒，显示了身体—时间—空间中的多重视野和复合观察，以及对

upon visual diversity and complexity, and constitutes social meaning; through different experience methods, paths, and intersection, it creates urban spaces for social communication, recreation, and spiritual recovery.

The generation of spatial prototypes of the landscape that fold the elements of difference also serves for the goal of social efficiency improvement. Similar to Alex Wall's interpretation of urban surfaces, this spatial organization takes itself as a physical entity that is dynamic, responds to urban changes, and promptly reflects social events.[41] Greg Lynn holds that space folding emphasizes continuity and smoothness, and differences, complexity, and contradictions might be aligned into a continuous and heterogeneous system that also allows for pliancy[42]. Deleuze described smoothness as "continuous variation of matter" and "continuous discontinuity." The concept of "oblique circulation" proposed by Paul Virilio emphasizes the absence of independent units in the circulation and the interconnection between multi-dimensional spaces. The uncertainty makes people's perception of the inside and the outside ambiguous, which vaguely defines the space and forms a borderless landscape.[43] The design of the Yokohama International Port Terminal in Japan precisely used the folding of introvert and extrovert spaces to express the temporal complexity and to accommodate the full range of social imagination. Combining with the subject's interactive experience, the horizon itself becomes a topological event structure, dissolving and reconstructing the so-called standards and the relationships between new and old, and figure and ground, creating a continuity of differences and spurring a new, profound interaction between human activities and the environment.

6 Conclusion

The space in the landscape not only accommodates matters and things, but also becomes an ability or power to connect differences and various elements. Different ideographic methods attribute specific scenes or things to uniqueness and holistic cognition, forming diverse interactive processes between body, time, and space. The prototypical relationship between physical experience and space-time imagery determines the changes of one's experience and the corresponding perceptions, thus determining the depth of the communication between people and places. Contemporary scholars' continuous study and discussion on the depth of the interaction between the subject and the object for the creation of scenes, as a kind of awakening of design consciousness, shows the multiple visions and composite observations in the interactions between body, time,

不同层次的景观空间原型的关注。

基于物质、意义、场域的景观空间原型，展现了在实际空间中的异质要素与不同的感知组成部分如何在不同层面被不断展开与再组织。通过有意识的空间组织方法，可以提升主体感知的丰富性与社会互动效能，同时避免由感知过程中繁杂片段的不断链接造成的同质表意链断裂、时空链接过程中景观意义的过度扩散，以及空间细碎化导致的功用失效。不同空间维度中的关键性组织原型及其相应的身体参与过程构建可以进一步保持景观意义传达的有效性，使景观总体的续存力与活力可以在一种动态平衡中不断发展。**LAF**

and space, suggesting an emphasis on landscape prototypes at different scales and levels.

The space prototype of the landscape defined by the material, meaning, and field shows how heterogeneous elements and different constituents of perception in actual space continuously expand and constitute at different levels. Through a conscious organization of space, the subject's perception richness and the efficiency of social interaction could be enhanced, while avoiding the fracture of the homogenous ideographic chain caused by the hybrid of the links between the complex fragments in the subject's perception process, the excessive diffusion of the landscape meaning in the process of spatio-temporal linking, and the function failure caused by the space fragmentation. The key organizational prototypes in different space dimensions and the construction of the corresponding body movement process can further maintain the efficiency in conveying the meaning of the landscape, so that the overall sustainability and vitality of the landscape continue in a dynamic balance. **LAF**

REFERENCES

[1] Guo, G. (1985). What is die Lebensphilosophie?. International Philosophy Today, (4), 79.

[2] Ji, X. (2010). To Discuss the Breakthrough in Body-Mind Dualism by Body Phenomenology of Merleau-Ponty. Southeast Academic Research, (2), 154-162. doi:10.13658/j.cnki.sar.2010.02.011

[3] Wei, S. (2012). Body Turning and the Transformation of Aesthetics: The Theoretical Research of Shusterman's Somaesthetics (Doctoral dissertation). Shaanxi Normal University, Xi'an.

[4] Zhou, M. (2012). Research of Categorical Subjectivity under the View of Embodied Philosophy. Journal of Henan Normal University (Philosophy and Social Sciences Edition), 39(5), 19-22. doi:10.16366/j.cnki.1000-2359.2012.05.021

[5] Shusterman, R. (2002). Somaesthetics: A Disciplinary Proposal. In X. Zhou, & J. Gao (Eds.), Pragmatist aesthetics (pp. 360-366). Beijing: The Commercial Press.

[6] Balfour, A. (1999). Octagon: The Persistence of the Ideal. In J. Corner (Ed.), Recovering Landscape: Essays in Contemporary Landscape Architecture (pp. 89-90). New York: Princeton Architectural Press.

[7] Wang, L. (2013). The Carnival Sight in Network Field and its Social-Anxiety Mirror—Using Labeled "Discourse Symbol" as an Observation Window. New Horizons from Tianfu, (3), 96-102.

[8] Eisenman, P. D. (1970). Notes on conceptual architecture: Towards a definition. Design Quarterly, (78/79), 1-5.

[9] Feng, X. (2009). Genealogy and Somaesthetics: Nietzsche, Foucault and Deleuze. Theoretical Studies in Literature and Art, (2), 97-102.

[10] Hunt, J. D. (2016). Site, Sight, Insight: Essays on Landscape Architecture. Pennsylvania: University of Pennsylvania Press.

[11] Crary, J. (1992). Techniques of the Observer: On Vision and Modernity in the Nineteenth Century. Cambridge: MIT Press.

[12] Ye, C., Chai, Y., & Zhang, X. (2011). "Space Production" Theory, Research Progress and Enlightenment for Chinese Urban Studies. Economic Geography, 31(3), 409-413. doi:10.15957/j.cnki.jjdl.2011.03.010

[13] Zhang, Z., & Liu, J. (2019). The Source and Inspiration of Edward Soja's Thirdspace. Modern Communication (Journal of Communication University of China), (12), 14-20.

[14] Tilley, C., & Bennett, W. (2008). Body and Image: Explorations in Landscape Phenomenology 2. Walnut Creek: Left Coast Press.

[15] Herrington, S. (2016). Landscape Theory in Design. London: Taylor and Francis Group.

[16] Crawford, O. G. S. (1912). The Distribution of Early Bronze Age Settlements in Britain. The Geographical Journal, 40(2), 184-197.

[17] Hoskins, W. G. (2013). The Making of the English Landscape. London: Little Toller Books.

[18] Fox, C. (1924). The Archaeology of the Cambridge Region: A Topographical Study of the Bronze, Early Iron, Roman, and Anglo-Saxon Ages. The Geographical Journal, 63(4), 348-350. doi:10.1017/CBO9780511697739

[19] Aldred, O. (2014). An Archaeology of Movement: A Methodological Study (Doctoral dissertation). University of Iceland, Reykjavík.

[20] Stoss Landscape Urbanism. (2013). Herinneringspark, Belgium. Landscape Architecture Frontiers, 1(1), 122-128.

[21] Latz, P. (2017). Rust Red: The Landscape Park Duisburg-Nord. Munich: Hirmer Publishers.

[22] Thwaites, K., & Simkins, I. (2006). Experiential Landscape: An Approach to People, Place and Space. London: Taylor and Francis Group.

[23] Treib, M., & Ding, L. (2008). Modern Landscape Architecture: A Critical Review. Beijing: China Architecture and Building Press.

[24] Zhou, S. (2008). The Polysemy of Inverted Discipline, Image Media and Spatial Perception. Time + Architecture, (3), 24-31.

[25] Johnson, N. B. (2003). Mountain, Temple, and the Design of Movement: Thirteenth-century Japanese Zen Buddhist Landscapes. In M. Conan (Ed.), Landscape Design and the Experience of Motion. Washington, D. C.: Dumbarton Oaks Research Library and Collection.

[26] Deming, M. E. (2015). Values in Landscape Architecture and Environmental Design: Finding Center in Theory and Practice. Baton Rouge: LSU Press.

[27] Spirn, A. W. (1998). The Language of Landscape. New Haven: Yale University Press.

[28] Waldheim, C., Museum, I. S. G., & Hansen, A. (Eds.). (2014). Composite Landscapes: Photomontage and Landscape Architecture. Berlin: Hatje Cantz Verlag GmbH & Company KG.

[29] Weller, R., & Hunt, J. D. (2005). Room 4.1.3: Innovations in Landscape Architecture. Pennsylvania: University of Pennsylvania Press.

[30] Tuan, Y. F. (1977). Space and Place: The Perspective of Experience. Minneapolis: University of Minnesota Press.

[31] Zhou, S. (2007). Buildings and Images: The Image Logic of Remote Presence. Nanjing: Southeast University Press.

[32] Girot, C., & Imhof, D. (2016). The Thick and the Thin of It. In J. Corner (Ed.), Thinking the Contemporary Landscape (p. 119). New York: Princeton Architectural Press.

[33] Lassus, B. (1998). The Landscape Approach. Pennsylvania: University of Pennsylvania Press.

[34] Leddy, T. (2006, September 29). Dewey's Aesthetics. Retrieved from https://plato.stanford.edu/entries/dewey-aesthetics/

[35] Dewey, J. (2005). Art as Experience. New York: Tarcher Perigee.

[36] Marot, S. (1999). The Reclaiming of Sites. In J. Corner (Ed.), Recovering Landscape: Essays in Contemporary Landscape Architecture (pp. 45-58). New York: Princeton Architectural Press.

[37] Holl, S. (2012). Steven Holl: Vol. 1. 1975-1998. Tokyo: A. D. A. Edita Tokyo.

[38] Mcdonough, T. (Ed). (2004). Guy Debord and the Situationist International: Texts and Documents. Cambridge: MIT Press.

[39] Tschumi, B. (2014). Tschumi Parc de la Villette. London: Artifice Books.

[40] Olin, L. D. (2012). An American Original: On the Landscape Architecture Career of Lawrence Halprin. Studies in the History of Gardens and Designed Landscapes, 32(3), 139-163. doi:10.1080/14601176.2012.687904

[41] Wall, A. (1999). Programming the Urban Surface. In J. Corner (Ed.), Recovering Landscape: Essays in Contemporary Landscape Architecture (pp. 233-249). New York: Princeton Architectural Press.

[42] Lynn, G. (Ed.). (1993). Folding in Architecture (Vol. 102). Berkshire: Academy Editions Limited.

[43] Redhead, S. (2004). Paul Virilio: Theorist for an Accelerated Culture. Toronto: University of Toronto Press.

本文引用格式 / PLEASE CITE THIS ARTICLE AS

Aziz, N. A. A. E. (2020). Space Syntax as a Tool to Measure Safety in Small Urban Parks—A Case Study of Rod El Farag Park in Cairo, Egypt. Landscape Architecture Frontiers, 8(4), 42-59. https://doi.org/10.15302/J-LAF-1-020034

https://doi.org/10.15302/J-LAF-1-020034 收稿时间 RECEIVED DATE / 2020-07-25 中图分类号 / TU984 文献标识码 / A

运用空间句法衡量小型城市公园的安全性——以埃及开罗市罗德–法拉格公园为例

SPACE SYNTAX AS A TOOL TO MEASURE SAFETY IN SMALL URBAN PARKS —A CASE STUDY OF ROD EL FARAG PARK IN CAIRO, EGYPT

诺哈·艾哈迈德·阿卜杜勒·阿齐兹
开罗大学城市与区域规划学院城市设计系博士、副教授

Noha Ahmed Abd El AZIZ*
PhD and Associate Professor at Urban Design Department, Faculty of Urban and Regional Planning, Cairo University

*Corresponding Author
Address: 1 Gamaa Street, Giza 12613, Egypt
Email: noos2000@yahoo.com

摘要

数十年来，厘清犯罪行为及其发生场所之间的关系一直是设计和社会领域的研究重点。尽管空间句法理论为研究环境的布局特征及其对人们活动与犯罪方式的潜在影响提供了有力支持，其在景观设计中的运用却仍然较少。本研究借助空间句法理论，使用depthmapX软件分析了埃及开罗市一座公园的空间布局并预测了其安全水平，以期填补这一空白。研究通过现场观察和采访公园工作人员收集了该公园2019年的犯罪记录，并运用ArcGIS 10.3软件对其进行分析。结果表明，空间深度、整合度、连接度和犯罪模式分布之间存在较强的相关性。公园的可见性分析图则显示了夏季和冬季植被（常绿乔木 / 落叶乔木）对视觉连接度和犯罪类型的不同影响。研究指出，将空间句法理论应用于景观设计仍面临挑战，但该方法在预测城市公园犯罪情况方面具有较大潜力。此类研究结果可为改进公园的概念设计提供参考，以创造更安全的公园环境。

关键词

CPTED；空间句法；开罗公园；安全公园；depthmapX软件；环境设计

ABSTRACT

Decoding the relationship between crime and place has been the focus of researchers in both design and social fields for a few decades. Space syntax theory offers the possibility of examining the configuration characteristics of the environment and their potential influences on people's activities and crime patterns; however, its implementation in landscape architecture has been limited. This study responds to such a gap by exploring the effectiveness of applying space syntax theory to predict safety levels in a park in Cairo, Egypt. depthmapX was used to analyze the spatial configuration of the park. Crime records from 2019 were collected through site observation and staff interviews, and analyzed using ArcGIS 10.3 software. Results indicated a strong correlation between space depth / integration / connectivity and crime pattern distribution. The park visibility graphs indicated the different impacts of vegetation (evergreen tree / deciduous trees) in summer and winter on visual connectivity and crime types. The research concluded that applying space syntax theory to landscape architecture is challenging; nevertheless, it represents a promising approach to predict committing crimes in urban parks, and the findings can be adopted to enhance park conceptual designs to achieve higher safety level.

KEYWORDS

CPTED; Space Syntax; Cairo's Parks; Safe Parks; depthmapX; Environmental Design

编辑 王胤瑜 田乐 **翻译** 王胤瑜
EDITED BY WANG Yinyu Tina TIAN **TRANSLATED BY** WANG Yinyu

1 引言

在过去数十年间，全球的城市化进程十分迅速，包括埃及开罗在内的许多大都市区都面临着如何提供更好、更安全的城市开放空间（如公园）的挑战。城市公共开放空间可供人们休闲娱乐、亲近自然，有利于促进居民的身心健康[1][2]，对生活品质具有深远的影响。有研究指出，安全性是影响公园使用情况的主要因素之一，对使用者行为和态度起决定性作用，令人缺乏安全感的城市空间使用率较低[3]。那

么，如何设计安全的公园？首先需要承认的是，实现这一目标并非易事，因为“安全感”是一种复杂的感受，受到环境诱因，以及建筑、社会和生态维度等多种因素影响[4]。

城市环境中的安全性可以借助环境设计手段来提升，在这个过程中，设计师需要了解物质环境与复杂的个人需求和行为之间的相互联系，从而通过设计来预防潜在的犯罪行为[5]。早在1830～1880年间，欧洲的“制图学派”已开始尝试研究犯罪与物质环境及其他社会因素之间的关系[6]。20世纪20～40年代，“芝加哥犯罪学派”提出的“社会解组论”，以及克利福德·R·肖和亨利·D·麦凯伊的研究关注于解释为何某些社区的犯罪率要高于其他社区[5][7]。

20世纪60年代，简·雅各布斯在《美国大城市的死与生》一书中强调，规划良好的城市社区有助于保障公共安全[8]。美国佛罗里达州立大学雷伊·杰弗里的著作《通过环境设计预防犯罪》所提出的同名理论（CPTED）阐述了如何通过建筑和景观设计预防犯罪，亦颇具影响力[5]。奥斯卡·纽曼在《防御空间：通过城市设计预防犯罪》一书中进一步指出，地产所属权明确、管控得力且容易使犯罪者暴露或有所忌惮的地区的犯罪率较低[5][9]。20世纪70年代末至80年代初，英国家庭研究办公室提出了“情境犯罪预防”理论，认为犯罪机会的增加导致了更多的犯罪[10]。另有许多其他研究为CPTED理论的进一步完善做出了贡献。例如，保罗与帕特丽夏·布伦蒂汉姆研究

1 Introduction

Over the past decades, the world has experienced an extraordinary increase in urbanization where many metropolitan cities, such as Cairo City, Egypt, are challenged to offer better, safer urban public open spaces like parks, which are well-acknowledged for their profound impact on the quality of the citizens' life by providing places to relax, play, interact, and connect with nature, and to enhance the physical and psychological health of communities[1][2]. When analyzing the factors shaping the use of parks, studies concluded that safety is a prominent factor, controlling and maneuvering the users' behaviors and attitudes. Lacking a sense of safety in urban spaces results in underuse, consequently hindering their benefits to the community[3]. So how to design safe parks? Achieving the sense of safety is not easy, as it is a very complicated feeling and combines a wide range of factors, including environmental cues, architectural, social, and ecological dimensions[4].

Environmental design is one of the approaches tackling safety in the urban context. It offers a platform to understand the interconnected relationship between physical environments and complex individual needs and behaviors. Such an approach advocates that crime can be reduced by designs that deter potential offenders from committing the crime[5]. The first attempts to examine the relationship between crime and the physical environment and other social factors started during 1830 ~ 1880 under the name of the "Cartographic School" in Europe[6]. From 1920s till 1940s, immerged the Social Disorganization Theory, a theory issued by the "Chicago School of Criminology," and the work of Clifford R. Shaw and Henry D. McKay sought to understand why crime and delinquency rates were higher in some neighborhoods than others[5][7].

In the 1960s, in her book *The Death and Life of Great American Cities*, Jane Jacobs declared the impact of well-planned urban neighborhoods in endorsing public safety[8]. Another influential figure is Ray Jeffery of Florida State University, who introduced the concept of "Crime Prevention through Environmental Design" (CPTED) in his book with the same title, and identified how architectural and landscape design could discourage possible offenders from committing crimes[5]. Completing the rally, Oscar Newman's book *Defensible Space: Crime Prevention through Urban Design* claimed that properties with high degrees of ownership and control and making criminals exposed and vulnerable could discourage crime[5][9]. From the late 1970s to early 1980s, the Situational Crime Prevention (SCP) theory was developed at the British Home Research Office; it suggested that more crime opportunities lead

了佛罗里达州的盗窃案及其与城市设计的关系[11]；詹姆斯・威尔逊和乔治・科林提出了“破窗理论”，认为修复和改善残旧的城市空间以营造此处有人使用或占有的感觉是遏制犯罪率上升的必要举措[5][11]。非营利组织对此也有所贡献，例如，加拿大“安全设计委员会”提出了传统的环境犯罪预防方法，即在提高安全性的同时通过建筑和景观设计减少公众对犯罪的恐惧[5]。近期的一些研究已开始将这一领域与地理空间技术相结合，例如美国德克萨斯州立大学运用该技术识别和预测犯罪；另一些研究则运用空间句法理论分析空间布局对邻里社区或城市中犯罪的影响，但基于该理论研究公园或小型空间中犯罪情况的案例相对不足。因此，本文试图通过将CPTED概念与空间句法理论相结合来填补这一空白，以评估景观设计对小型城市公园犯罪发生情况和犯罪类型的影响。

2 犯罪场所理论和CPTED原则

许多理论都聚焦于分析城市犯罪多发于某些特定地点的原因，它们大致源于三种基本理论：一是“理性选择理论”，该理论认为实施犯罪的决定取决于个人需要和情境因素（如监视情况和被抓住的可能性）；二是“行为地理学理论”，该理论关注犯罪场所的“可达性”，认为犯罪者更倾向于在其工作地、居住地等日常活动区域附近作案[12]；三是“日常活动理论”，主要关注三个因素的相互作用：能够接近有吸引力的目标、缺乏有效监视，以及有犯罪动机者[13]。环境设计能够对日常活动理论中的两个因素产生影响，即犯罪目标和犯罪者的暴露程度。

保罗・科岑斯与特伦西・拉夫将犯罪发生场所归纳为5种类型：产生犯罪型、吸引犯罪型、转化犯罪型、恶化犯罪型和临时起意型。产生犯罪型场所可吸引大量人群，其中便包括犯罪动机尚不确定但可能实施犯罪的人；吸引犯罪型场所是指能激起人的犯罪欲望的场所；

to more crimes[10]. Many others contributed to the development of CPTED. For example, Paul and Patricia Brantingham examined burglaries in Florida, USA and their relation to urban design[11]. James Wilson and George Kelling developed the “Broken Windows Theory,” and claimed that in order to prevent escalating crimes it is a must to repair and improve dilapidated urban sites to build a sense of control and ownership[5][11]. Non-profitable organizations also joined the ride. For example, Safe Design Council in Canada has developed traditional environmental crime prevention approaches to reduce the public fear of crime by using architectural and landscape design[5]. More recent studies introduced geo-spatial technologies; for example, at Texas State University, USA they were applied to identify and predict crime. Other studies included using space syntax theory in studying the impact of the spatial configuration on crime in neighborhoods or cities. Nevertheless, applying space syntax theory in detecting crime in parks or small spaces is rare. Therefore, this paper seeks to fill this gap by integrating CPTED concepts with space syntax theory to evaluate landscape design impact on crime appearance and typology in small urban parks.

2 Crime Place Theories and CPTED Principles

Numerous theories seek to explain why urban crime occurs in certain places; basically they can be grounded into three primary theories. The first one is Rational Choice Theory, which claims that the decision to commit a crime depends on personal needs and situational factors such as surveillance and the possibility to be caught. The second theory is Behavioral Geography Theory that considers places closer to the offender’s work or residency are at higher risk than areas not within the offender’s daily route, in other words, referring to accessibility[12]. The last theory is the Routine Activity Theory, which looks at the interaction of three factors: the availability of an attractive target, the absence of guardians, and the presence of motivated offenders[13]. The environmental design has proven the ability to intervene two of them: the physical target and the offenders’ exposure.

Regarding the urban crime location, Paul Cozens and Terence Love summarized the places where crimes occur into 5 types: crime generators, crime attractors, crime detractors, crime facilitators, and crime precipitators. Crime generators are places that attract a mass of people, some with undetermined motivations to offend that can change to criminal acts. Crime attractors are places that are appealing to perform offending actions. Crime detractors are places that have few people, thus

转化犯罪型场所则指那些少有人来往、可能供潜在犯罪者实施犯罪的场所；恶化犯罪型场所是指那些可供犯罪者藏匿枪支、同党、酒精和毒品的场所，可帮助他们实施犯罪；临时起意型场所的物质环境会促使本无犯罪意图者犯罪，如在没有公共厕所的环境下随地小便的行为[11]。

本研究关注的CPTED方法旨在通过扩大监视者视野、建立明确的场所边界，以及创建和维护城市空间的正面形象来减少犯罪机会。在按照CPTED建议设计的场所中，犯罪者会更容易暴露并更有被捕的危机感[11]。除了设计建议外，CPTED还为保障设计效果提供了相应的管理策略建议，例如通过对城市环境的妥善维护与恰当使用，充分营造“为人所有、为人所用”的氛围，从而减少犯罪的发生。CPTED提出了7个设计原则，即空间领地性、监视、形象和周边环境、地理环境、出入口控制、合法活动引导，以及目标强化[11]，非营利组织“公共空间工程”在此基础上又增加了可理解度和物理通透性——可理解度是指环境空间结构的清晰度和易识别度，物理通透性则是指在某一环境中人们可自由选择如何活动的程度。根据CPTED的建议，充足的照明、可见的入口、适度疏朗的绿植、栅栏和积极的空间使用均有助于提高公共空间的安全性[3][9][12]。

3 空间句法理论与犯罪预防

3.1 空间句法

空间句法（space syntax）是一种城市分析模型，可对城市环境的品质进行定量描述，包含一系列用于量化和分析建筑及城市空间布局的指标[9]。空间句法理论由英国伦敦大学学院巴特莱建筑学院的比尔·希里尔和尤利安·汉森于20世纪80年代首次提出[13]。希里尔在《空间即机器：建筑的布局理论》一书中将空间句法定义为从空间和形态学布局视角解释人类行为及社会活动的一种客观方式[14][15]，认为对空间布局进行分析与理解极为必要，因为空间的系统结构会影响使用者在其中的活动和回避情况，进而决定其对空间的使用及社会关系的形成[2][15]。空间句法理论还认为空间的拓扑属性比地理特征更为重要，因为人们更倾向于遵循基于图论的拓扑学规律来使用空间[16]。空间句法还提供

to encourage use by potential offenders. Crime facilitators are places that contain things that assist offenders such as firearms, gangs, alcohol, and drugs. Finally, Crime precipitators are places where its physical combinations push non-offenders to commit crimes; for example, public urination due to the lack of public toilets[11].

This research concentrates on CPTED, an approach that seeks to optimize prospects for surveillance, clearly define boundaries, and create and maintain a positive image of the urban area, all to reduce opportunities for offending. Within CPTED recommendations, offenders would be more visible and would feel more at risk of being apprehended[11]. Besides offering design interventions, CPTED provides management strategies to support its cause, such as amplifying the sense of ownership and social control by well-maintained and appropriately used urban environment to hinder offenders. CPTED proposes 7 concepts for design: territoriality, surveillance, image and milieu, geographical juxtaposition, access control, legitimate activity support, and target hardening[11]. Project for Public Spaces added legibility and physical permeability. The former refers to the clarity of the environment and the degree to which a space is understandable, while the latter means to what extent an environment allows people to alternate choices of movement in it. Sufficient lighting, visible entrances, less dense foliage, fences, and active space use are recommended by CPTED to increase the safety of the public spaces[3][9][12].

3 Space Syntax Theory and Crime Prevention

3.1 Space Syntax

Space syntax is a kind of analytical urban model, and a quantitative method aiming to capture the quality of urban environments with a set of measures for space configuration and for quantifying and analyzing the properties of architectural and urban spaces[9]. It was first developed in the 1980s at the Bartlett Unit for Architectural Studies, University College London by Bill Hillier and Julienne Hanson[13]. In Hillier's book *Space is the Machine: A Configurational Theory of Architecture*, space syntax is defined as an objective way to interpret human behaviors and social activities from a spatial and morphological configuration point of view[14][15]. The theory postulates that the system structure of space in which various activities happen can affect users' movement and avoidance, shape their uses, and produce social relations; therefore, the spatial configuration must be analyzed and understood[2][15]. Space syntax privileges the topological properties of a space over its geography, as people are likely to move or behave based on topology under

了一系列工具来分析空间的语言学特征，如整合性、布局、使用者选择、可见性及视域等。

3.2 空间布局对犯罪的影响

“空间布局”（spatial configuration）是指两种元素之间受同时存在的其他至少一种元素，甚或全部其他元素影响的相互关系[14]，即某一时间点上空间之间存在的一系列关联，而这些关联不一定是肉眼可见的或物理层面上的。空间布局会影响人们的认知，随着时间的变化且在特定条件下，认知要素反过来也会影响空间布局。此外，空间布局能够改变日常活动理论中的环境吸引力（即目标）及犯罪机会（即缺乏有效监视），并影响CPTED中空间领地性、监视、出入口控制和目标强化等相关设计（图1），因此空间布局在犯罪预防领域得到了广泛重视。

已有大量研究探讨了犯罪的发生与空间布局之间的关系，但主要关注于居民区或城市尺度[9]。对犯罪环境的研究有助于理解犯罪事件，并深入了解与特定犯罪类型（如入室盗窃、街头抢劫、毒品交易和偷窃）高度相关的空间布局特征[4]。例如，有研究指出，非法活动与其发生地点的行人流量、可达性和渗透性具有内在联系[17]。关于空间布局如何影响犯罪和社区安全主要存在两种观点：其一受简·雅各布斯影响并由“新城市主义派”引导，提倡开放、可渗透的混合功能空间；另一种观点则以奥斯卡·纽曼的理论为代表，强调对公共领域加强控制。空间句法分析研究印证了这两种观点[17]：一项在伦敦进行的研究发现，巡警巡视较少的地点与毒品犯罪事件存在相关性，这与新城市

Graph Theory[16]. It delivers tools to analyze the linguistic characteristics of space, such as integration, configuration, user choice, visibility, and isovists.

3.2 Impacts of Space Configuration on Crime

The term spatial configuration refers to “a relation affected by the simultaneous co-presence of at least a third element and possibly all other elements in a complex”[14]. Thus, spatial configuration is a set of relations between spaces that exist at a particular time, which may enable or limit the possibility for visual and physical linkages. Spatial configuration is responsible for shaping cognition, while over a time and certain circumstances, cognitive constructs shape spatial configuration. Moreover, spatial configuration is able to alter the attractiveness of the environment (target) and the opportunity (the absence of a capable guardian) as mentioned in the Routine Activity Theory. In addition, it can control territoriality, surveillance, access control, and target hardening in the CPTED approach (Fig. 1), thus to be widely used in the domain of crime prevention.

A considerable body of research devoted efforts to investigate the relationship between the occurrence of criminal events and spatial configuration, mainly in residential areas or at a city scale[9]. Studying crime settings can help understand crime events and gain more knowledge about configurations that are highly connected with particular types of crime such as burglary, street robbery, drug dealing, and theft[4]. Studies have shown that illegal activity is intrinsically linked to pedestrian flows, accessibility, and permeability of the place where crime occurs[17]. Generally, there are two competing schools of thought on how spatial configuration may influence crime and community safety. The first, driven by “new urbanism school”

1. 空间句法理论与CPTED原则及日常活动理论的关系（改绘自参考文献[11][12]）

1. The contribution of space syntax theory to the CPTED principles and Routine Activity Theory (Adaptation sources: Refs.[11][12])

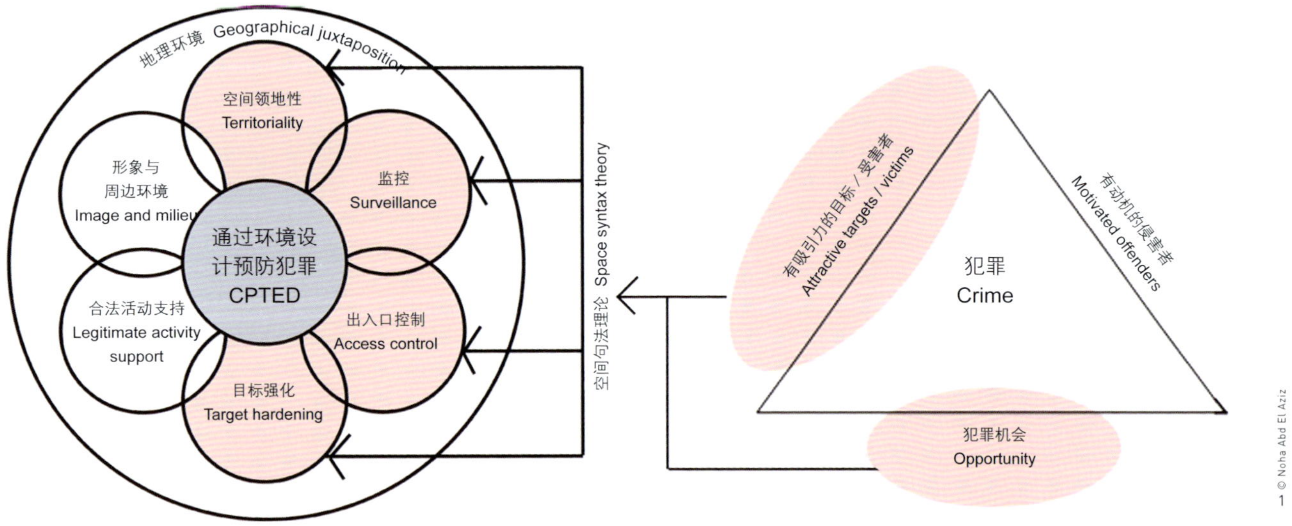

主义学派的观点相一致[17]；另一方面，雷伊·杰弗里认为建立具有明确边界、出入口控制有序且景观维护良好的城市空间有助于预防犯罪[5]，而另一项针对加拿大某居民区的研究亦发现支路与主干街道的可达性与犯罪率呈正相关[18]，二者均印证了第二种观点。

可见性是增强空间安全性及人类安全感的重要因素，其同样受空间布局影响。可见性、自然监视和共现程度的不同也会对犯罪产生不同的影响[17]。较高的视线通透性可以使人们清晰地看到周围的其他人并发现潜在的威胁来源，从而感到更加安全。茂密的植被、栅栏、墙体、尖锐的拐角、仓储构筑，以及建筑物的遮挡均会影响视线通透性[19]。一些研究表明，公园内低矮且茂密的植被会遮挡视线、为犯罪者提供藏身之所，从而降低人们的安全感[20]。然而，也有一些研究发现空间中的植被可以吸引更多的使用者，从而降低犯罪率；同时，没有植被的街道和无地面铺装的区域通常被视为“无人地带”，由于缺少社交活动，犯罪者在这些空间中更不易被发现。相反，维护良好的植被往往意味着该区域为人所有或处于管护之下，因而有助于减少犯罪[21]。尽管不同的植被类型与犯罪发生之间的关联可能存在差异，但整体而言，低矮且茂密的植被与犯罪发生之间的正相关性更为显著；相反，场所的空间开阔度与犯罪发生之间存在负相关性[21]。

4 案例研究：罗德－法拉格公园

本研究选取埃及开罗市的罗德—法拉格公园（以下简称REF公园）来探索运用空间句法理论预测城市公园中犯罪行为的可能性。该公园位于一处高密度非正式聚居区，周边居民大多是低收入者。公园面积为3.82hm^2，于1997年建成，场地原为当地的一座蔬菜市场。REF公

and influenced by Jane Jacobs, calls for open and permeable mixed-use environments, whereas the opposition emphasizes the importance of control over people’s territory like Oscar Newman’s theory. Space syntax analysis has shown that both the theoretical standpoints have their strengths and weaknesses[17]. An example supporting the new urbanism school is a study based in London, which showed that locations less likely to be surveyed by police patrol were associated with drug crime[17]. In contrast, Ray Jeffery claimed that crime could be prevented by creating urban spaces with well-defined boundaries, well-controlled access points, and well-maintained landscapes[5], and another study in a residential area in Canada found that an increasing accessibility to secondary and arterial streets is associated with an increase in crime[18], both supporting the second vision.

Visibility is an essential factor in enhancing space security and the sense of safety, which is also affected by spatial configuration. Different degrees of visibility, natural surveillance, and co-presence also impact crimes[17]. Higher visual permeability can make people feel safer as they can see other people around with clear sightlines, which allows for identifying sources of threat. Visual permeability can be negativity affected by the presence of shrubbery vegetation, fences, walls, sharp corners, storage sheds, and buildings[19]. Several studies confirmed that low, dense vegetation in parks obstructs views and offers criminals a place to hide, thus reducing the sense of safety[20]. Yet, some other studies have found that vegetation is associated with decreased crime rates due to higher attractiveness to people. Meanwhile, streets and unpaved areas with no vegetation are often seen as “no man’s lands,” which would discourage social interaction, making it easier for criminals to go unnoticed. In contrast, well-maintained vegetation might reduce crime since it can be seen as a “territorial marker” or a “cue to care”[21]. Generally, this discrepancy can be explained by differences in the types of vegetation analyzed, as the positive correlation with crime appearance were found more in low, dense vegetation; however, the contradicting results might be concluded to more open areas[21].

4 Case Study: Rod El Farag Park

This research selected Rod El Farag Park in Cairo City, Egypt to assess the possibility of using space syntax theory in predicting crime patterns in urban parks. The park is located in a high-density informal district, and residents here are mostly low-income citizens. The 38,200-square meter park was built up in 1997 after the regional vegetable market was relocated outside

2-1

1 文化中心 Cultural center
2 消防站 Fire station
3 中央办公室 Central office
4 医院 Hospital
5 儿童图书馆 Children's library
6 学校 Schools
7 青年中心 Youth center
8入口与售票处 Entrance and ticket outlet
9 洗手间 Toilets
10 公园管理处 Administration
11 广场 Plaza
12 木制凉亭 Wooden pergolas
13 电力设备箱 Electrical box

© Noha Abd El Aziz

2-2

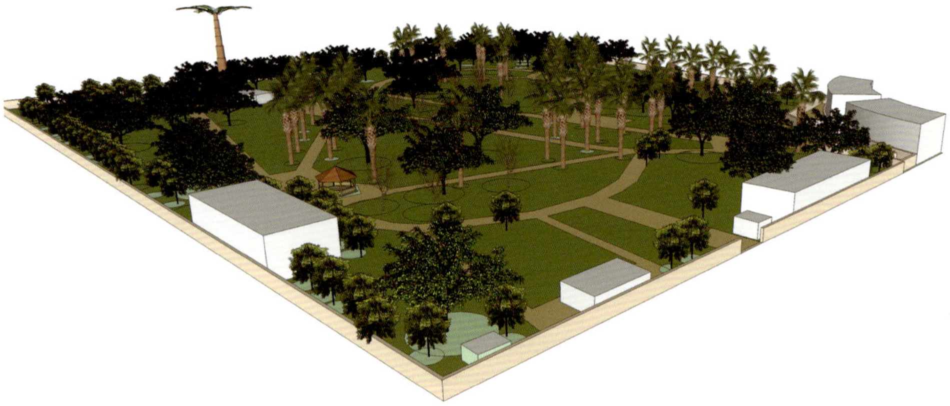

© Noha Abd El Aziz

2-3

2. REF公园区位、周边土地利用情况及整体透视图（底图来源：Google Earth）

2. The location, surrounding land use, and overall perspective of Rod El Farag Park (Base map source: Google Earth)

园隶属于一个服务综合体，内有大片草坪和带有木制凉亭的广场（图2）。尽管公园交通便利，门票价格合理，但由于存在安全隐患及犯罪率较高而难以吸引当地居民前来，公园内多处区域现已无人使用，反而成了犯罪分子的聚集区——正如约翰尼斯·努特森所说，许多吸毒者和贩毒者都认为公园是吸毒或毒品交易的理想场所[22]。公园只有一个通往城市主干道的入口，而通往罗德—法拉格文化中心的大门则常年关闭。

4.1 研究方法

研究首先进行了两组采访：一组针对公园管理人员，目的是获取已记录在案的公园非法活动相关资料；另一组针对公园保安团队，通过他们的日常观察与记忆了解那些未被正式记录的公园犯罪情况。研

the city. The park is a part of a service complex, with large lawn areas and plazas with wooden pergolas (Fig. 2). Although the park is highly accessible and with a reasonable entry charge, it fails to attract most locals due to its bad reputation in poor safety and offending acts. Many criminal incidents were recorded here, driving out users from utilizing some zones in the park, which echoes Johannes Knutsson's opinion that drug users and drug dealers find parks to be appealing locations to get high or to trade[22]. The park has one entry from the main street, and a gate (always closed) connects it to Rod El Farag Cultural Center.

4.1 Research Methods

In the first section of this research, two sets of interviews were conducted: one with the park's management staff to collect data of illegal activities that were officially recorded, and the

究跨度为2019年全年，其中部分犯罪事件已由警方处理，另一些则由当地保安人员处理解决或由公园游客制止。研究者根据这些信息判别已记录及未记录犯罪发生的地点与类型，并绘制了公园内犯罪事件的分布图。REF公园内发生的犯罪分为4种类型：自我危害行为、危害他人行为、严重危害他人行为，以及危害公园行为（如破坏公物）。研究在ArcGIS 10.3软件中根据犯罪发生情况对公园各区域进行编码，0表示无犯罪，1表示有犯罪发生；并分别在2019年夏季（7月）和冬季（12月）一天中的不同时段对公园场地进行观察，以了解使用者活动及分布情况。

第二部分是使用depthmapX软件分析公园的空间布局参数，涉及的工具主要包括：

1）深度分析图：用于表示从某一空间到达另一空间必须经过的拓扑节点数量；数值越小代表空间深度越浅，数值越大代表空间分离度越高[14]。

2）全局整合度（句法意义上空间的可达程度）分析图：用于表征空间可达性或数学意义上的邻近中心度，即反映了空间网络中某一特定路段为行人所踏足的可能性[23]，可据此预测行人的移动趋势或网络中潜在的目的地。

3）连接度分析图：用于衡量直接与原点空间相连的空间数。连接度是指与给定线段直接相连的线段数量。

4）可理解度分析图：反映环境中寻路的难易程度，即观察者在整个空间系统中从任一位置到达另一位置的容易程度[14]。

5）可见性分析图：用于表示公园向使用者或路过者所提供的自然监视的质量[2]。

分析得出的具体空间布局数值范围均以从深蓝色到红色的色阶表示。蓝色表示低值，红色表示高值。

植被对空间可见性、连接度和可达性的影响较为复杂。与充斥着大量建筑物、视线极易受阻的建成环境相比，透过乔木和灌木枝叶进行观察可以增强视觉连接度、连续性，并提供更开阔的视线。经过实地考察，研究将建筑物、凉亭及售货亭作为可见性分析图中的阻碍

other with the park security team to acquire information about the non-documented incidents depending on their observations and memories. The collected crime data records were for the year 2019. Some violations were intervened by police forces; the others were solved by the local security personnel or the response of other visitors. The occurring places and types of both the recorded and non-documented crime events were then identified, and used to create a crime mapping to highlight the crime distributions. Crimes in the park were categorized into 4 types: crimes against oneself, crimes against others, dangerous crimes against others, and crimes against the park (e.g. vandalism). Criminal data were coded, 0 for none, and 1 for appearance, then mapped in ArcGIS 10.3. Besides, site observations were carried out in July (summer) and December (winter) at different hours of the day to record the activities and users' distribution.

The second section was analyzing the parameters of the spatial configuration of the park using depthmapX, and the following tools were adopted:

1) Depth graph shows the number of topological nodes that must be crossed to go from one space to another. In a depth graph, low values mean shallowness of space, while high values mean segregation[14].

2) Integration graph showing global integration values (degrees of syntactic accessibility) measures accessibility or mathematical closeness centrality, showing how likely a particular path segments is to be the destination for those using the network based on the position of the path segment in the network[23]. It can be used to predict users' movements or their potential destinations.

3) Connectivity graph measures the number of spaces immediately connecting a space of origin.

4) Intelligibility shows how the environment is easily navigable, which means how easy an observer can be acquainted with his / her position in any location he / she may potentially occupy within the whole spatial system[14].

5) Visibility map presents the quality of natural surveillance by either park users or commuters passing by the park[2].

In these graphs, the analysis value ranges are represented by a gradient of colors ranging from dark blue to red: dark blue indicates lowest values and red indicates highest.

The impact of vegetation on visibility, connectivity, and accessibility is complex. Looking through branches of trees and shrubs enhances the visual connection and continuity, and offers more open sightlines when compared with doing so in urban built environments, where buildings block users' sightlines. Site visits helped with selecting objects that may block sightlines

表1：公园中树木分类
Table 1: Tree classification in the Rog El Farag Park

树木名称 Species	种类 Type	树冠大小 Size of canopy	树冠不透明度 Opacity of canopy
阔荚合欢 *Albizia lebbeck*	落叶树 Deciduous tree	大 Large	低 Low
印楝 *Azadirachta indica*	落叶树 Deciduous tree	大 Large	低 Low
腊肠树 *Cassia fistula*	常绿树 Evergreen tree	大 Large	高 High
节果决明 *Cassia nodosa*	落叶树 Deciduous tree	大 Large	低 Low
地中海柏木 *Cupressus sempervirens*	常绿树 Evergreen tree	大 Large	高 High
凤凰木 *Delonix regia*	落叶树 Deciduous tree	大 Large	低 Low
垂叶榕 *Ficus benjamina*	常绿树 Evergreen tree	大 Large	高 High
绿黄葛树 *Ficus virens*	落叶树 Deciduous tree	大 Large	低 Low
榕树 *Ficus microcarpa*	常绿树 Evergreen tree	中 Medium	高 High
非洲楝 *Khaya senegalensis*	常绿树 Evergreen tree	大 Large	高 High
山榄科植物 *Mimusops laurifolia*	常绿树 Evergreen tree	大 Large	高 High
乌墨 *Syzygium cumini*	常绿树 Evergreen tree	中 Medium	高 High

因素，但不包括座椅等不会遮挡视线的户外家具。根据实地观察结果将公园内的植被分为两类，一类是树冠茂密但树干分叉较低的中型及大型乔木（视线通透性低，即树冠不透明度高），它们被视为可见性分析中的阻碍因素；另一类包括棕榈树（树干极高）、树冠较小且树干较高的其他乔木（树冠视觉通透性高），以及低矮灌木（高度低于50cm）和地被植物，本研究不将它们看作视线阻碍因素。由于公园中绝大部分为成熟植被，一年中公园的植被密度变化较大，这会影响空间的可见性和使用情况，于是研究分别计算了夏季与冬季公园空间的视觉连接度及相应的犯罪事件分布情况。夏季情景将常绿和落叶乔木都考虑在内，冬季情景则不考虑落叶乔木（表1）。笔者收集了这些树木在夏季和冬季的照片（图3），以确定每种树木树冠的不透明度和树干高度。

4.2 研究方法的局限性

运用空间句法对景观进行研究也存在许多困难，因为景观中的空间并不像建成环境中的空间那样，以墙体或建筑物作为明确的边界

3 © Noha Abd El Aziz

3. 以凤凰木为例示意同一种乔木夏季与冬季的树冠视觉通透性差异

3. An example of *Delonix regia* showing the difference of a tree's canopy opacity in the summer and the winter

to be added to the visibility graph, such as buildings, pergolas, kiosks, and obstructing vegetation. Seats and other site furniture were excluded as they rarely block people's sight. Based on site visits, vegetation in the site was categorized into two groups. One group is medium and large trees with dense canopies and relatively short trunks (providing low visual permeability, i.e. high opacity), which were added to the visibility map. The other group included palm trees (very high trunks), trees with small crowns and high trunks (providing low opacity), short shrubs (less than 50 cm), and ground covers, which were excluded as they do not affect sightlines. Considering that most vegetation in the park is mature and the dynamic vegetation density throughout the year would impact the visibility and the use of space, scenarios of both the summer and the winter were implemented to acquire the fluctuation in visual connectivity with the crime pattern. The summer scenario took both evergreen and deciduous trees into consideration, while the winter one excluded deciduous trees as they do not represent visual obstacles (Table 1). Pictures of the park trees in the summer and the winter were collected to determine the opacity of their canopies and trunk heights (Fig. 3).

4.2 Limitations

Using space syntax in landscape studies arises many predicaments, such as defining clear boundaries of spaces since they are not well defined by walls or buildings as in urban context (Fig. 4). In their research, Zhai Yujia and Perver Baran[2]

4. REF公园中的空间边界类型

4. The boundary types of the spaces in Rod El Farag Park

（图4）。翟宇佳和珀维尔·巴兰指出，空间的边界是由空间功能和设计意图决定的，进而提出了一个问题：在空间句法分析中是否应对道路和活动区域运用同样的处理方式？[2]因此，本研究在定义公园空间布局时将小径和广场同等对待，但不包括原本未被设计为活动区域的草坪（尽管实际上已有人在这些草坪上活动）。其他难点包括：研究只能依靠保安团队的回忆来获知未记录在案的犯罪行为的发生地点和时间，而这些数据的准确性无法保证；作为2D软件，depthmapX不支持输入乔木的树冠通透度、高度、覆盖率和生长速率等数据，也无法模拟地形特征，因此本研究的空间句法分析没有考虑颜色和纹理/材质等环境外观特征，以及活动对人群的吸引效果。

5 研究结果

5.1 公园犯罪地图

对犯罪数据（表2）的分析结果表明，吸毒和酗酒等自我危害行为在REF公园中最为常见，可以通过留下的垃圾（针头及酒瓶等）对其进行追踪；其次是危害公园行为，包括乱抛垃圾、随地小便、涂鸦，以及破坏公物行为（包括爬树、折断树枝、在树上乱涂乱画、喷涂座椅和凉亭，以及破坏木凳和垃圾桶）。其后是青少年的不雅行为、争吵及寻衅滋事行为。在公园发生的严重危害他人行为中，盗窃的比例最高，其次是持刀斗殴，绑架儿童事件也偶有发生。犯罪行为主要发

proposed that boundaries between spaces are defined by spatial functions and design intentions, and they raised the question that whether to consider activity areas and pathways equally in the system. Thus, this study regarded paths and plazas equally in defining the park's spatial configuration, excluding lawn areas that are not intended for use though some people do use. In addition, the research had to acquire locations and occurrence time of those unrecorded crimes depending on the memory of the security team, which was therefore not accurate. depthmapX is a 2D software that cannot deal with data regarding tree opacity, height, spread, or growth rate. Moreover, terrains were not included in the model. Finally, space syntax in this research ignored the superficial appearance of the environment, including surface colors and textures, and discarded the effect of activities in attracting pedestrian flows.

5 Results

5.1 The Crime Mapping of the Park

After analyzing the crime data (Table 2), results showed that crimes against oneself, like drug and alcohol abuse, were the most common crimes in the park. They can be tracked by the waste left behind (e.g. needles and bottles). In the second place came crimes against the park represented by littering, public urinating, graffiti, and vandalism including breaking tree branches, carving in trees, spraying seats and pergolas, and dismantling wooden benches and trash bins. Teenagers' inappropriate behaviors, quarrels, and harassment followed in the third place. As for dangerous offenses against others, theft was in the lead, then armed fights, and few cases of kid's

表2：公园中犯罪类型分析

Table 2: Crime typology analysis in the Rog El Farag Park

犯罪种类 Crime types	犯罪行为 Crime activities	占总犯罪数百分比 Percentage (%)
自我危害行为 Crimes against oneself	毒品交易 吸毒 酗酒 Drug trading Drug abuse Alcohol abuse	46
危害他人行为 Crimes against others	不雅行为 争吵 寻衅滋事 Inappropriate behaviors Quarrels Harassments	20
严重危害他人行为 Dangerous crimes against others	偷盗／扒窃 持械斗殴 绑架儿童 Thefts / pocket-picking Armed fights Child kidnapping	7
危害公园行为 Crimes against the park	乱丢垃圾 随地小便 涂鸦 破坏公物 Littering Public urinating Graffiti Vandalism	27

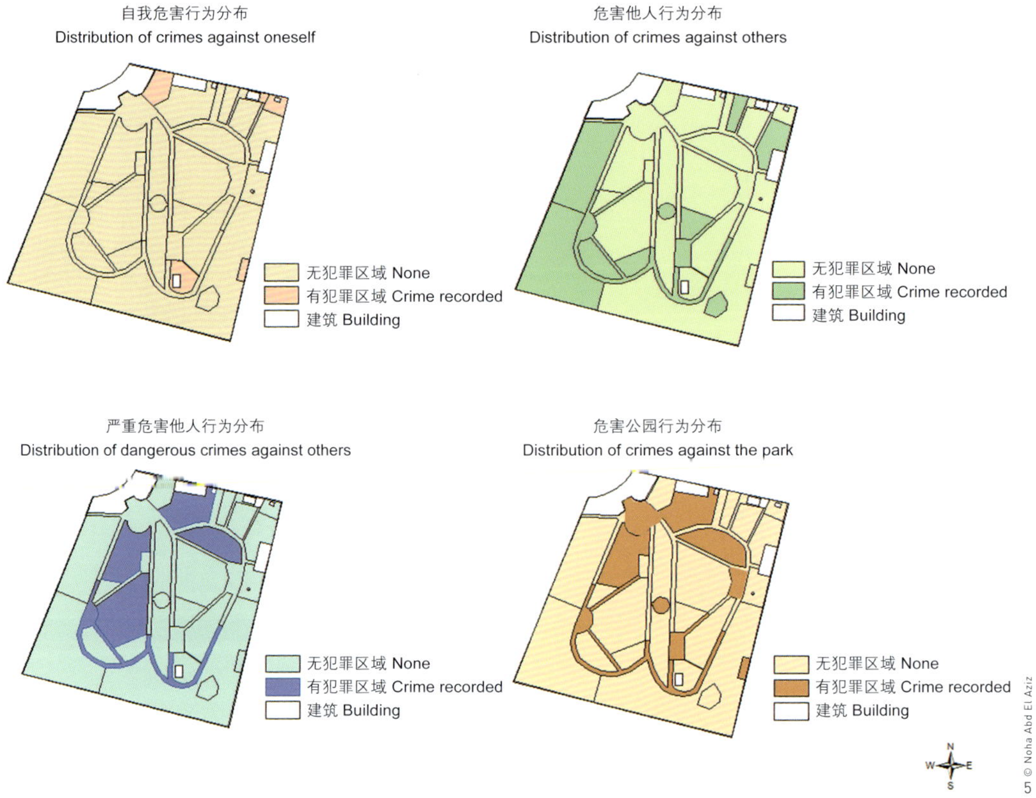

5

5. 不同类型犯罪事件在REF公园中的分布情况

5. The distribution of different crime types in the Rod El Farag Park

生在公园外围和西侧，而公园中心区域较为安全，几乎没有犯罪发生（图5）。

5.2 公园空间布局分析

空间深度分析的结果（图6–1）表明，公园北部的洗手间周边和南部区域的空间深度值最大，即洗手间周边区域和南部区域在空间上是高度隔离的；北部广场和公园中部两条主要道路的空间深度值最小；公园的其余区域深度值为中等。连接度分析结果（图6–2）表明，公园中部的两条道路和东北部的广场连接度最高，公园入口、中央广场和南部连接度最差。整合度分析结果（图6–3）则表明，将北部广场和公园南部区域相连的道路空间整合度最高，东侧和南侧道路的整合度最差。

kidnapping attempts. Crimes were mainly found at the park periphery and the west section, whereas the central area of the park was considered safe and free from criminal activities (Fig. 5).

5.2 Spatial Configurations Analysis of the Park

The result of the space depth analysis (Fig. 6-1) shows that the area around the toilet in the north and the southern section of the park had the highest depth values, indicating that these two areas were the most spatially isolated, while the plaza in the north section and the two main paths in the center of the park had the least depth values. The rest of the park is intermediate in space depth. As for the connectivity analysis (Fig. 6-2), the two paths in the center of the park and the north plaza were the most connected areas; the entrance, the plaza in the center, and the southern section were the most disconnected areas. In regards to integration analysis shown in Figure 6-3, it was found that the most spatially integrated path is the one connecting the north plaza with the southern section. In contrast, paths in eastern and southern parts of the park had the least integration with the other paths and spaces.

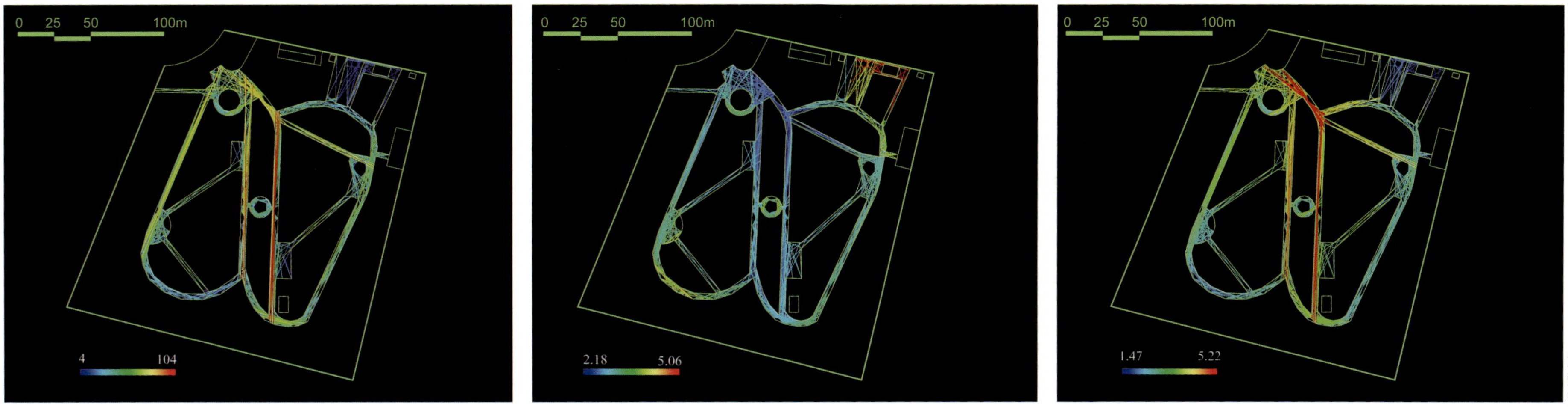

平均深度分析结果
Mean depth graph

连接度分析结果
Connectivity graph

整合度分析结果
Integration graph

© Noha Abd El Aziz 6

6. REF公园空间布局分析结果

6. The spatial configuration analysis of the Rod El Farag Park

图7显示了整合度值分布的偏差情况，其表明公园内约一半地点的空间整合度值适中且较为接近，而另一半地点的空间整合度值则呈显著的两极分化。此外，研究也分析了空间连接度与整合度之间的关系，即空间的可理解度（图8）：整合度和连接度之间的相关系数为0.70，表明整合度高的空间或路径连接度也较高，而整合度与平均空间深度，以及平均空间深度与连接度之间则呈负相关（相关系数分别为–0.94和–0.69）。各项空间布局分析结果见表3。

5.3 可见性图分析

在可见性研究中对道路和草坪区域进行了无差别处理。值得注意的是，由于存在树木、建筑物及覆盖着金属薄板的栅栏等遮挡物，无法透过公园外围看到其内部（图9）。

结果表明，整个公园的可见性在夏季和冬季均呈辐射状分布，即中心区域可见性最高，外围可见性最低。由于公园内建筑物和凉亭极少，因此对可见性的影响范围较小。落叶乔木（图中黑色圆点）对可见性的负面影响在夏季较为显著，致使高可见性区域明显缩小（图10–1）；在冬季，树冠的通透度较高，因此公园东部和西部区域的可见性有所提升（图10–2）。

Figure 7 displays the integration value deviation, showing that half of the park integration values are close while the other half is either highly integrated or disconnected. Additionally, the intelligibility of the park was measured by investigating the relation between the connectivity of space and its integration (Fig. 8). In terms of the degree of intelligibility, the correlation coefficient between integration and connectivity was 0.70, indicating that spaces / paths with high integration are also highly connected and intelligible. However, integration and mean depth saw a negative correlation (correlation coefficient was -0.94), so did mean depth and connectivity (correlation coefficient was -0.69). The spatial configuration analyses are summarized in Table 3.

5.3 Visibility Graph Analysis

In the visibility analysis, paths and lawn areas were treated the same. It is important to note that the park cannot be seen from the surroundings due to trees, buildings, or metal sheets covering the park fence (Fig. 9).

A radial visibility distribution pattern was found in both the summer and the winter. The park center was the most visible zone, while the park periphery was the least visible section. Since there are few buildings and pergolas at the site, their impact on visibility was localized. The negative effect of the deciduous trees (black dots on the graph) can be noticed in the summer scenario (Fig. 10-1), as they shrunk highly visible areas. In the winter scenario, the eastern and western sections were more visible due to sightline penetrating the translucent tree canopies (Fig. 10-2).

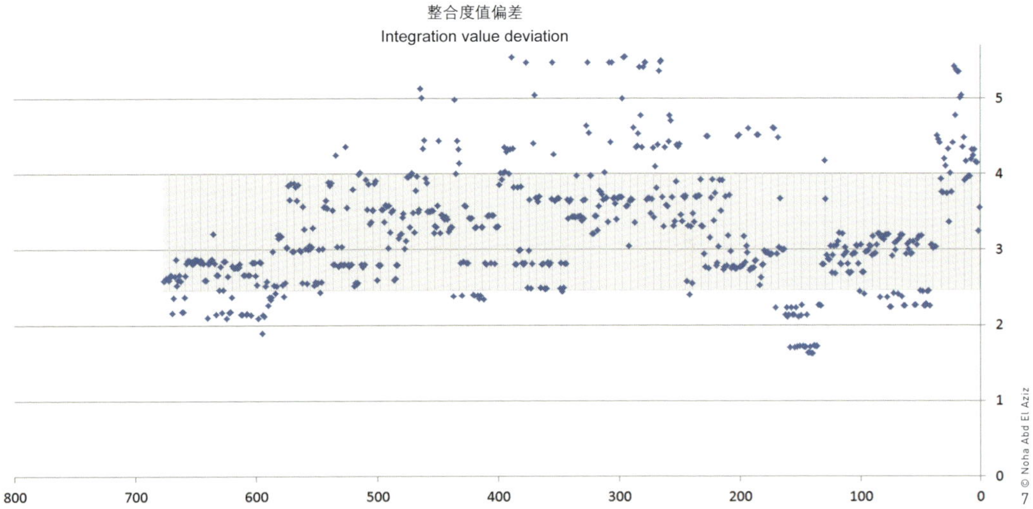

表3：公园空间布局分析结果
Table 3: Results of the spatial configuration analysis of the park

	整合度 Integration	平均深度 Mean depth	连接度 Connectivity
平均值 Average	3.1	3.1	47.8
最小值 Minimum	1.4	2.1	4.0
最大值 Maximum	5.2	5.2	105.0
标准差 Standard deviation	0.8	0.5	20.8

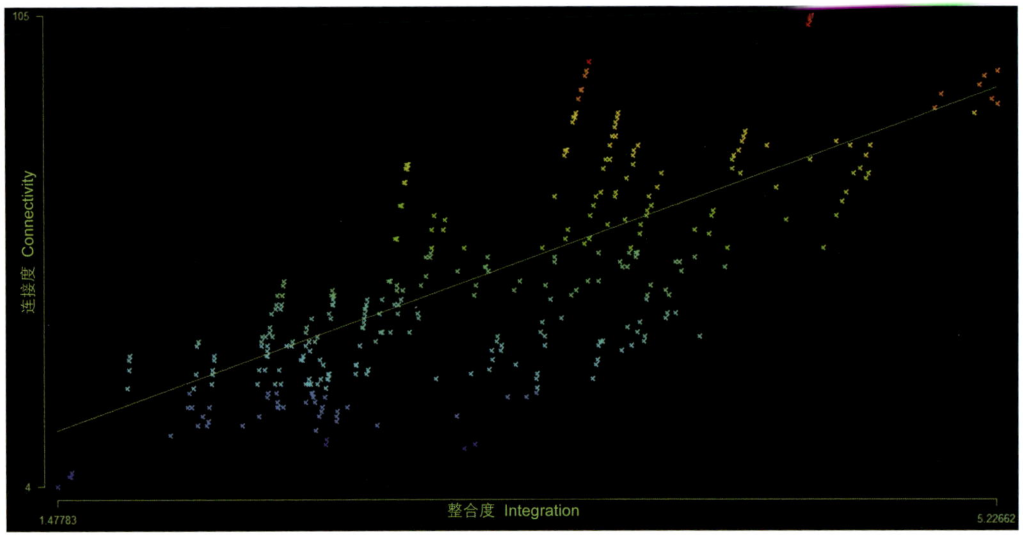

7. 空间整合度值偏差分布图
8. 空间整合度-连接度散点图，从中可看出公园空间布局的可理解度较好。

7. Integration value deviation analysis
8. The scatter graph of integration and connectivity implying that the park has a good intelligibility of spatial configuration

6 结论

6.1 空间布局对犯罪类型及其分布的影响

研究发现，公园中犯罪类型与特定的空间布局相关。例如，空间深度小、整合度及连接度高的区域犯罪记录最少，且犯罪类型以乱抛垃圾为主；在空间深度、整合度与连接度均中等的区域发生的犯罪活动主要为言语骚扰、破坏公物、不雅行为和乱抛垃圾；空间深度大、整合度与连接度极低的区域最容易发生严重犯罪活动，如酗酒、吸

6 Conclusions

6.1 The Impact of Spatial Configuration on Crime Types and Distribution

The research found that certain spatial configuration characteristics had relations with crime types. For example, the areas with low depth, high integration, and high connectivity recorded the least crimes, and crimes in these areas were basically littering. Spaces with medium depth, medium integration, and medium connection recorded criminal activities such as verbal harassment, vandalism, inappropriate behaviors, and littering. Serious criminal activities such as alcohol / drug abuse, public urination, and physical harassment took place mostly in spaces with high depth, minimal integration, and minimum connectivity. Most crimes against oneself did not occur in the paths or plazas

© Noha Abd El Aziz 9

9. 来自REF公园外部被阻挡的视野

10. 夏季和冬季情境下的可见性分析图

9. The blocked views from outside of the Rod El Farag Park

10. Visibility analyses in summer and winter scenarios

毒、随地小便和肢体骚扰。大多数自我危害行为发生在空间整合度低的区域，而非道路或广场上。

此外，公园入口处更易发生绑架和持刀斗殴等犯罪活动，因为犯罪者逃脱的可能性相对较大。此外，现场观察结果表明，游客更喜欢坐在公园的入口和出口附近，这里的扒窃犯罪也更为多发。从表4所示的各类型犯罪发生场所的空间整合度数值范围可知，除入口区域和具有自然监视的公园管理处周边区域以外，无犯罪区域的整合度相对较高（可达5.2）。

but in the areas with low integration values.

Additionally, the entrance of the park attracted crimes like kidnapping and fights with pocket knives, as this area maximizes the probability of escaping. Moreover, site observation found that the park visitors prefer to sit near the park access, where pocket-picking crimes were mostly occurred. Table 4 shows the range of integration values for each crime type. The integration values of non-crime zones were relatively higher (up to 5.2), except for the entrance and the area near the administration that provided natural surveillance.

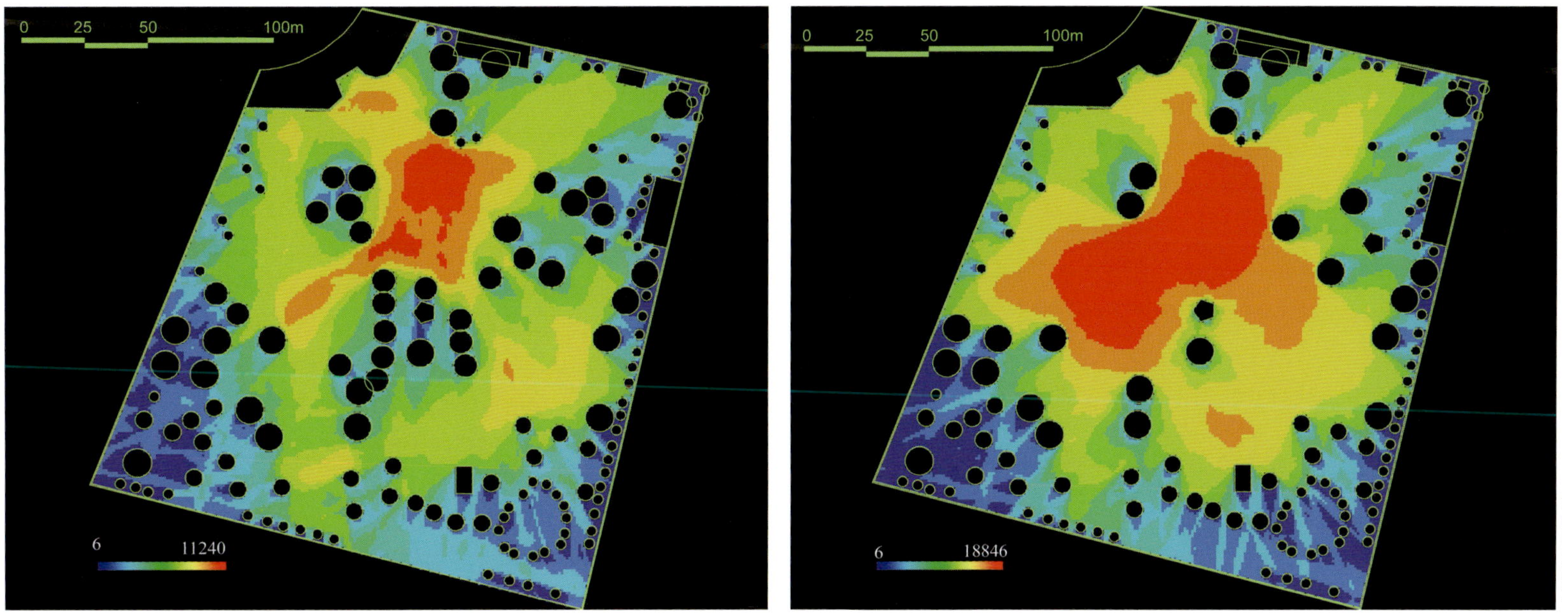

© Noha Abd El Aziz 10

表4：各类型犯罪发生区域的空间整合度值
Table 4: Integration value for each crime type

犯罪类型区域 Crime type areas	整合度值 Integration value
自我危害行为区域 The area of crimes against oneself	1.4 ~ 2.0
危害他人行为区域 The area of crimes against others	2.0 ~ 3.9
严重危害他人行为区域 The area of dangerous crimes against others	2.0 ~ 3.2
危害公园行为区域 The area of crimes against the park	2.0 ~ 4.6
无犯罪区域 No-crime area	2.0 ~ 5.2

表5：冬季情境下各类型犯罪发生区域的可见性值
Table 5: Visibility value of the areas of each crime type in the winter scenario

犯罪类型区域 Crime type areas	可视性值 Visibility value
自我危害行为区域 The area of crimes against oneself	1,000 ~ 9,500
危害他人行为区域 The area of crimes against others	800 ~ 14,000
严重危害他人行为区域 The area of dangerous crimes against others	2,500 ~ 17,000
危害公园行为区域 The area of crimes against the park	2,500 ~ 14,000
无犯罪区域 No-crime area	15,000 ~ 18,000

6.2 场地可见性对犯罪类型和分布的影响

将公园的可见性分析图与犯罪类型及其分布图进行比较可知，空间可见性越高，发生非法行为的可能性就越小（如公园中心区域）：围栏附近可见性较差的区域会发生酗酒、吸毒等事件；危害他人行为（尤其是不雅行为）多发生于公园西南部和东北部的低可见性区域；可见性中等或较高但人群密集的空间容易发生严重危害他人行为，如盗窃、扒窃和绑架儿童，因为这些地点邻近出入口，更便于犯罪者逃脱；危害公园行为则多发生在可见性中等及较低的区域，个别发生在高可见性区域。表5总结了不同犯罪类型发生区域所对应的可见度取值范围（平均值为10 600）之间的关系，图11展示了公园内不同位置的植被对视线的影响。

综上，公园南部区域的低空间整合度助长了犯罪活动的发生。此外，遮阴植被虽然提升了公园的舒适度和视觉吸引力，但也带来了空间安全隐患，尤其是在公园外围地区。公园保安队伍的监视活动主要集中于入口区域，无法覆盖整个公园。作为自然监视的来源，公园入口和公园管理处的位置对犯罪行为的分布有明显影响，而人群分布则与特定类型的犯罪有关。

6.2 The Impact of Site Visibility on Crime Types and Distribution

When comparing the park's visibility graph with crime types and distribution, it was found that the more visible the area was, the fewer illegal actions occurred, e.g. the park center. The less visible area near the fence recorded alcohol / drug abuse incidents. Crimes against others, especially inappropriate behaviors, appeared in the low visible zones in the southwest and northeast sections. High and medium visible spaces occupied by crowds were prone to dangerous crimes against others, like thefts / pocket-pickings, and child kidnapping due to their proximity to the escape point (entrance). As for vandalism against the park, it occurred in medium to low visible areas and a few spots with high visibility. Table 5 summaries the visibility value ranges of areas for different crime types (average visibility value is 10,600). Figure 11 illustrates the impact of vegetation on sightlines in different locations in the park.

It can be concluded that the poor integration of the southern sections encouraged the crimes. Furthermore, the lack of a balance between shading trees for thermal comfort / visual appeal and high visibility compromised safety levels, particularly at the park periphery. The surveillance of the security team was concentrated at the entrance gate, and cannot cover the whole park visually. The locations of the entrance and the administration affected the crime distribution by offering natural surveillance, while crowd distribution had an impact on the appearance of some crime types.

11. 3D模拟图展示了公园内不同位置的植被对可见性的影响

11. 3D models illustrating the impact of vegetation on visibility at different locations in the park

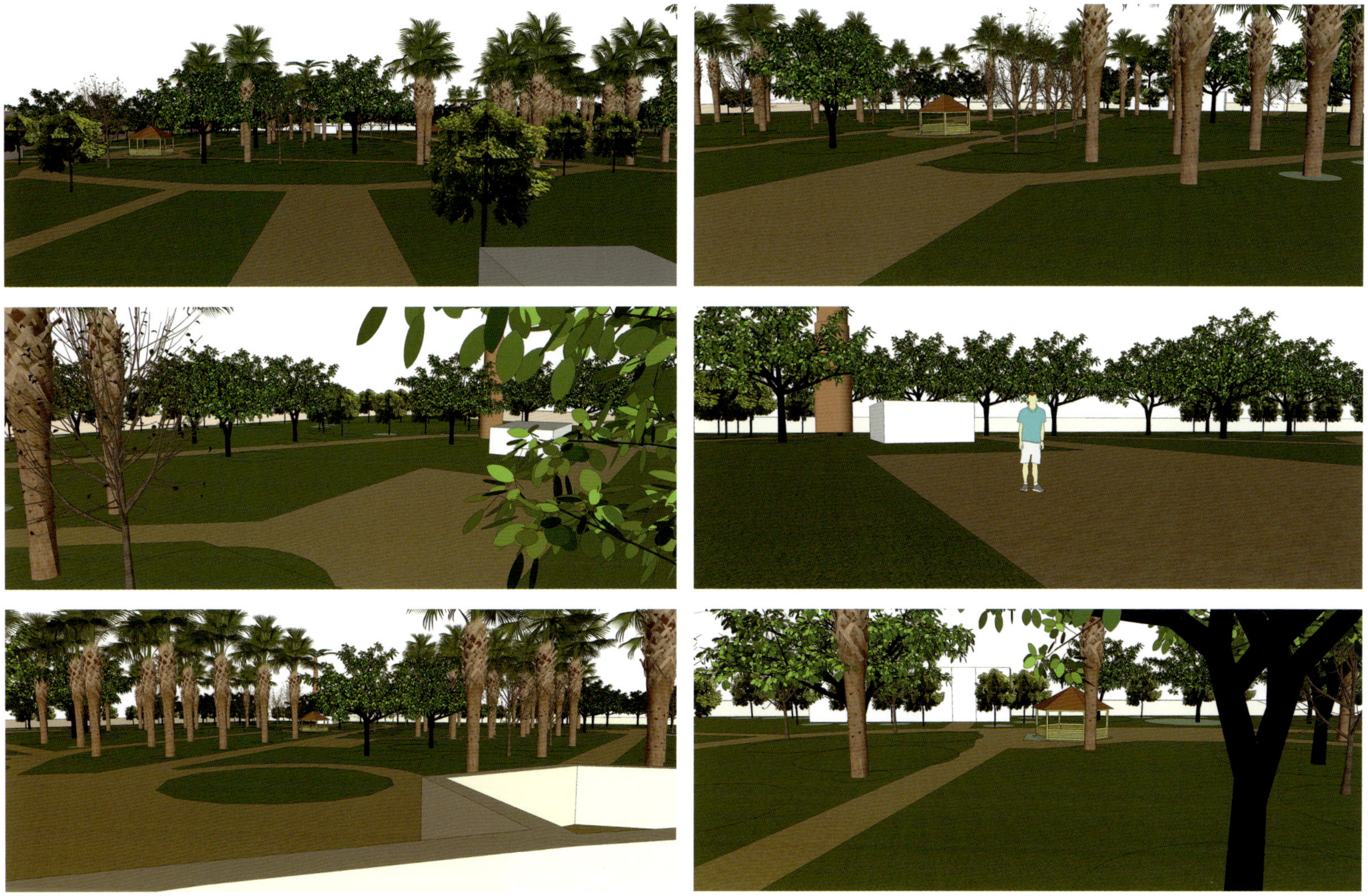

7 讨论

空间句法理论被用于研究城市环境空间布局与人类活动模式／行为之间的关系已有20余年的历史。本研究选择了位于埃及开罗市非正式聚居区且犯罪频发的REF公园为研究对象，探究了公园空间布局与在此发生的犯罪类型及空间分布的影响。结果表明，空间连接度、整合度、深度均与犯罪行为存在相关性。具有较大空间深度、与周边连接度较低的地点易发生吸毒、不雅行为和寻衅滋事等犯罪活动；连接度较高的道路及区域能吸引更多人群，有助于减少大多数的犯罪行为，

7 Discussion

In the past 20 years, space syntax theory has been adopted to examine the relationship between the spatial configuration of urban contexts and human activity patterns / behaviors. In this study, Rod El Farag Park situated in an informal district in Cairo City, Egypt, with a noticeable criminal records, was selected to investigate the effect of its spatial configuration on crime distribution and types. The results indicated a correlation between measurements as space connectivity / integration / depth and crime commitment. Deep, isolated spaces offered opportunities for drug use, inappropriate behaviors, and harassment. As for well-connected paths or areas that welcomed more people and hindered most crimes nevertheless offered

却是盗窃和持械斗殴的易发场所。危害公园行为（如破坏公物）常见于除中心区域以外的任何区域，与空间整合度的关联性不明显。研究对空间深度的分析结果印证了比尔·希利尔和奥兹莱姆·萨巴兹的观点，即可达性差的街道（空间深度值较大）每单位长度发生的抢劫事件更多[24]；但也有一些研究得出了相反的结论，如伊琳娜·马蒂诺塞汀在美国纽黑文市和立陶宛考纳斯市进行的研究表明，公共区域中抢劫案的发生率更高[25]；托比·戴维斯和肖恩·约翰逊在加拿大进行的另一项研究也发现，潜在使用者更多的街道周边更易发生入室盗窃[18]。

本研究还指出公园树木现状分布和类型对视线存在的负面影响，这些树木有可能成为犯罪者的藏身之处；公园四周种植的常绿乔木带使公园丧失了来自周边街道的自然监视；落叶乔木使得公园冬季的视线通透性较高，而在夏季，常绿和落叶乔木庞大、茂密的树冠则大大降低了许多区域的可见性。自我危害行为和（严重）危害他人行为的发生地点都具有一定的隐蔽性，而危害公园行为则多发于开阔场所，这与另一项研究的发现——可达性或可见性较高的场所犯罪率整体较低[9]——基本一致。席恩·E·迈克尔、R·布鲁斯·胡尔与戴安·L·扎姆[26]在对当地警察的陈述资料进行研究后，发现犯罪分子经常在植被茂密区域藏匿或处置赃物。但本研究并不建议公园对乔灌木进行清除（因为这类植被能为公园营造空间私密性和神秘感），而是倡导公园的种植设计应在考虑植物的观赏性与遮阴功能的同时，也能够保障周围环境的可见性。需要指出的是，本研究存在许多局限性，其中之一是未考虑空间使用对犯罪的影响，因为入口和管理区域在一定程度上提供了自然监视，从而预防了大多数犯罪行为的发生。

尽管空间句法已被广泛运用于邻里及城市尺度的研究，其在开放空间和公园等场地尺度研究中的应用仍然非常有限。本研究证明了运用空间句法理论预测埃及城市公园内犯罪发生区域的可行性，鼓励在公园设计阶段即引入安全性模拟分析，从而最大限度地提高公园安全性。未来还需进一步探究本研究方法在其他地域背景下的适用性，运用3D软件对空间布局进行更准确的模拟；在研究对象方面，应对活动及设施类型更多样、更具吸引力的公园予以更多关注。**LAF**

the opportunity for thefts and armed fights. Crimes against the park (e.g. vandalism) did not associate with a specific integration level as it occurred all over the park except for the center. The finding about space depth supported the finding of Bill Hillier and Ozlem Sahbaz that less accessible segments (with more space depth) were associated with more robberies per unit of street length[24]. But some other studies held the opposite opinions: Irina Matijosaitiene's study in New Haven, USA, and Kaunas, Lithuania[25] declared that more robberies happened in common use areas. Another study in Canada by Toby Davies and Shane Johnson concluded a higher risk of burglary for streets with more potential usage[18].

The results of this study also reveal the negative impact of the existing tree distribution and types on the sightlines, as they create blind spots for crime to hide. The evergreen buffer placed around the periphery deprived the park of natural surveillance from the streets around it. The use of deciduous trees enhanced the park's visual connectivity in winter, while in summer, large, dense canopies of evergreen and deciduous trees obstructed the visibility to many zones. Crimes against oneself and (dangerous) crimes against others sought hiding places, while crimes against the park did not need such secrecy. This conclusion supports a study showing that places with higher accessibility / visibility tend to have lower crime rates[9]. Sean E. Michael, R. Bruce Hull, and Diane L. Zahm[26] discussed in their research on statements by local police that dense vegetation was used by criminals to hide or dispose unwanted goods. Nevertheless, this does not mean removing shrubs or trees, as parks need intimate private places and some mystery. Vegetation should be designed in such a way to ensure the visibility of the surroundings while performing its ornamental and shading functions. Meanwhile, this study has many limitations, one of which is failing to consider the impact of space uses on crimes, as the entrance, the administration, and the office provided some natural surveillance hindering most of the crimes.

Although space syntax has been widely used in research at the neighborhood or city scale, its site-scale implementation, such as open spaces and parks, is still very limited. This study proves that space syntax theory is able to predict the crime zones in urban parks in the Egyptian context. The results open the door to including safety simulations in the design stage of parks to improve the safety level as much as possible. More studies should be conducted to evaluate the method's applicability in other regional contexts, preferably through utilizing 3D software for more accurate representation of the spatial configuration, and with parks accommodating various activities and attraction points. **LAF**

REFERENCES

[1] UN Habitat. (2017). Global Public Space Programme Annual Report 2017. Retrieved from https://unhabitat.org/global-public-space-programme-annual-report-2017

[2] Zhai, Y., & Baran, P. (2013). Application of space syntax theory in study of urban parks and walking. Proceedings of the ninth international space syntax symposium (p. 32). Seoul: Sejong University.

[3] Project for Public Spaces. (2008, December 31). What role can design play in creating safer parks?. Retrieved from https://www.pps.org/article/what-role-can-design-play-in-creating-safer-parks

[4] Çamur, K., Roshani, M., & Pirouzi, S. (2017). Using Space Syntax to Assess Safety in Public Areas—Case Study of Tarbiat Pedestrian Area, Tabriz-Iran. IOP Conference Series Materials Science and Engineering, 245(8), 082022. https://doi.org/10.1088/1757-899X/245/8/082002

[5] Sundberg, K. W. (2013). Preventing crime through informed urban design. Security Solutions Magazine, (87), 30-35.

[6] Courtright, K., & Mutchnick, R. (2002). Cartographic School of Criminology. In D. Levinson (Ed.), Encyclopedia of Crime and Punishment. Thousand Oaks: SAGE Publications, Inc.

[7] Hardyns, W., & Pauwels, L. J. R. (2017). The Chicago School and Criminology. In R. A. Tripplett (Ed.), The Handbook of the History and Philosophy of Criminology (pp. 123-139). Hoboken: Wiley-Blackwell. https://doi.org/10.1002/9781119011385.ch7

[8] Jacobs, J. (1961). The Death and Life of Great American Cities. New York: Vintage Books.

[9] Pourmohammadi, M. R., & Ghorbanian, M. (2013). Crime prevention in urban design: Towards space syntax approach as a quantitative analytic modeling of qualitative. Armanshahr Architecture and Urban Development, 6(10), 157-166.

[10] Clarke, R. V. (1983). Situational Crime Prevention: Its Theoretical Basis and Practical Scope. In M. Tonry (Ed.). Crime and Justice: An Annual Review of Research, (4), 225-256. https://doi.org/10.1086/449090

[11] Cozens, P., & Love, T. (2015). A Review and Current Status of Crime Prevention through Environmental Design (CPTED). Journal of Planning Literature, 30(4), 393-412. https://doi.org/10.1177/0885412215595440

[12] Nubani, L. N. (2006). Targets for crime: Measuring the spatial and visual attributes of crime locations using space syntax (Doctoral thesis). University of Michigan, Michigan.

[13] Hillier, B., & Hanson, J. (1984). The Social Logic of Space. Cambridge: Cambridge University Press.

[14] Hillier, B. (1996). Space is the Machine: A Configurationally Theory of Architecture. Cambridge: Cambridge University Press.

[15] Abd El Raheem, A. A. (2019). Spatial Conditions for Sustainable Communities: The Case of Informal Settlements in GCR (Master's thesis). Al Azhar University, Cairo.

[16] Ostwald, M. J. (2011). The mathematics of spatial configuration: Revisiting, revising and critiquing justified plan graph theory. Nexus Network Journal, 13(2), 445-470. doi:10.1007/s00004-011-0075-3.

[17] Bolton, T., Froy, F., Khan, S., & Francis, N. (2018). Crime Policy and Place Layout. Retrieved from http://spacesyntax.com/wp-content/uploads/2018/03/3.-Crime-policy-and-place-layout_2018.pdf

[18] Sahajramani, D., Purkayastha, S., Ranjit, R., & Vyas, A. (2018, October). Determination of correlation between street accessibility and crimes using space syntax network graph analysis. Paper presented at the 39th Asian Conference on Remote Sensing, Kuala Lumpur, Malaysia.

[19] Iqbal, A. (2015). Assessment of Crime and Safety Issues in Parks (Licentiate thesis). Royal Institute of Technology, Stockholm.

[20] Lis, A., Pardela, L., & Iwankowski, P. (2019). Impact of vegetation on perceived safety and preference in city parks. Sustainability, 11(22), 1-20. https://doi.org/10.3390/su11226324

[21] Troy, A., Grove, M., & O'Neil-Dunne, J. (2012). The relationship between tree canopy and crime rates across an urban-rural gradient in the greater Baltimore region. Landscape and Urban Planning, 106(106), 262-270. doi:10.1016/j.landurbplan.2012.03.010

[22] Knutsson, J. (1997). Restoring public order in a city park. Stockholm: National Council for Crime Prevention Sweden.

[23] Summers, L., & Johnson, S. D. (2017). Does the configuration of the street network influence where outdoor serious violence takes place? Using space syntax to test crime pattern theory. Journal of Quantitative Criminology, (33), 397-420. https://doi.org/10.1007/s10940-016-9306-9

[24] Hillier, B., & Sahbaz, O. (2005). High Resolution Analysis of Crime Patterns in Urban Street Networks: An Initial Statistical Sketch from an Ongoing Study of a London Borough. In A. V. Nes (Ed.), Proceedings of the 5th International Space Syntax Symposium (pp. 451-478). Delft: Delft University of Technology.

[25] Matijosaitiene, I. (2016). Combination of CPTED and space syntax for the analysis of crime. Safer Communities, 15(1), 49-62. doi:10.1108/SC-05-2015-0013

[26] Michael, S., Hull, R., & Zahm, D. (2001). Environmental factors influencing auto burglary—A case study. Environment and Behavior, 33(3), 368-388. doi:10.1177/00139160121973034

本文引用格式 / PLEASE CITE THIS ARTICLE AS

Wang, G., & Genovese, P. V. (2020). Categorization of the Spatial Elements between Courtyards in Historical Villages and Interpretation of Their Morphological Characteristics—A Case Study on Guanlu Village in Huangshan City, Anhui Province. Landscape Architecture Frontiers, 8(4), 60-75. https://doi.org/10.15302/J-LAF-1-020033

https://doi.org/10.15302/J-LAF-1-020033 收稿时间 RECEIVED DATE / 2020-05-10 中图分类号 / TU981, TU24 文献标识码 / A

古村落宅间元素的分类及其平面特征解读——以安徽省黄山市关麓村为例

CATEGORIZATION OF THE SPATIAL ELEMENTS BETWEEN COURTYARDS IN HISTORICAL VILLAGES AND INTERPRETATION OF THEIR MORPHOLOGICAL CHARACTERISTICS —A CASE STUDY ON GUANLU VILLAGE IN HUANGSHAN CITY, ANHUI PROVINCE

王国伟
天津大学建筑学院博士候选人

罗杰威*
天津大学建筑学院教授、博士生导师

*通讯作者
地址：天津市南开区卫津路92号天津大学建筑学院
邮编：300072
邮箱：pavic@163.com

WANG Guowei
PhD Candidate of School of Architecture, Tianjin University

Paolo Vincenzo GENOVESE
Professor and Doctoral Supervisor of School of Architecture, Tianjin University

摘要

宅间元素是古村落景观的重要组成部分。在乡村景观同质化的当下，现有地方元素的研究倾向于传统符号或建筑细部等，而较少关注构成古村落宅间平面形态的核心元素。本文以安徽省黄山市关麓村为例，梳理了28种古村落宅间元素的分类，绘制了相应的元素图式，并从面积、圆形度、矩形度、紧凑度和宽长比5个方面量化分析了元素的平面特征。本研究不仅有益于细化古村落平面形态的理论研究，还有助于促进地方元素的挖掘及应用。这一基于元素分类、图式及其平面特征量化分析的方法模型为以延续地域特征为目的的村落景观平面设计提供了客观依据，同时丰富了村落景观设计语汇，避免设计元素模块化和千村一面等现象。

关键词

古村落；宅间元素；设计元素；景观；平面特征；设计语汇；关麓村

ABSTRACT

Spatial elements between courtyards are an important component of the landscape of historical villages. With an increasingly homogenous rural landscape in China, most existing studies focus on traditional symbols and architectural details, while little research is conducted to explore the core elements that shape the spaces between village courtyards. Taking Guanlu Village in Huangshan City, Anhui Province as an example, the research team identified 28 sorts of spatial elements, developed the corresponding diagrams, and quantified their morphological characteristics in area, circularity, rectangularity, compactness, and width-length ratio. This research not only contributes to the theoretical development on the morphology of ancient villages, but also helps promote the exploration and application of local elements. This village landscape design model constituted with element categorization, diagram drawing, and morphological quantitative analysis would provide scientific evidences that help inform the practices to revitalize village localities, showing its practical significance of enriching the design vocabulary of village landscapes and avoiding the prevailing, generic usage of modular designs with urban landscape elements.

KEYWORDS

Historical Village; Spatial Element between Courtyards; Design Elements; Landscape; Morphological Characteristics; Design Vocabulary; Guanlu Village

编辑 田晓劼 田乐 **翻译** 田乐 田晓劼 肖杰
EDITED BY TIAN Xiaojie Tina TIAN **TRANSLATED BY** Tina TIAN TIAN Xiaojie XIAO Jie

1 研究背景

随着城镇化的不断推进，城乡二元体制下的中国乡村和城市之间的差距日益扩大，并引发了一系列社会矛盾[1]。村落城镇化的模式主要有“拆村并点”[2]和“村落拟城化”[3]。部分破坏性建设致使村落的景观多样性和传统生产生活方式等发生剧烈变化[4]，村落和谐的人居环境及地域景观特色面临被破坏和异化的窘境[5]。其中，过度使用城市设计元素以及设计语汇的模块化是村落景观设计中存在的主要问题，趋同的城市设计元素（如广场、草坪、树池）不可避免地导致地域特征弱化和千村一面的现象[6]，使乡村景观缺乏场所精神和乡土气息[7]。村落地域特征的弱化引发了相关专家学者的广泛讨论，他们呼吁村落建设应注重地方村落景观特质的延续，不应盲目效仿城市景观[8][9]。村落景观应使当地居民拥有地方文化认同感[10]，但目前很多乡村的规划和设计并没有实现这一目标。

村落景观本身具有地域性、文化性、多样性、复合性、延续性和稳定性等特征[11]，相关空间元素具有特定的形状、功能和含义，是村落设计语汇的重要组成，但却没有得到足够的重视，也缺乏相应的研究。2011年，联合国教科文组织大会通过了《关于城市历史景观的建议书》，其中提到挖掘和沿用地方元素对村落景观可持续发展的重要性[12]。然而，目前对村落地方元素的挖掘主要集中在古村落建筑细部、建筑材料等宅院部分的研究[13]，以及古村落耕读文化、宗教文化、名人轶事等文化层面的研究[14]。为了提升乡村居民的文化认同感，本文认为，在村落景观设计过程中可以将具有村落地域特征的元素作为景观设计语汇。

村落所处的自然环境、村民的生产生活方式，以及当地的文化习俗等共同塑造了其景观特色，其中，古村落宅间元素便是村民日常生活与村落环境长期相互适应发展的结果[15]。村落宅间元素是针对村落景观平面形态构成的细化研究提出的概念，这些元素是中国乡村在长期的农耕社会发展中积累的优秀人居文化遗存，是践行可持续性村落景观设计的重要资源。本文认为，延续村落地域特征、营造和谐人居环

1 Background

The urban-rural dualism long-time existing in China's rapid urbanization process results in development disparities and social conflicts between the urban and rural areas[1]. Urbanization in rural China is mostly realized by merging a number of small villages into a larger one[2] or adopting urban / town development patterns[3]. In some cases, the aggressive construction has dramatically changed the local landscape diversity and the traditional production patterns and lifestyles[4], eliminating or dissimilating the harmony of human settlements and regional landscape features[5]. Particularly, the prevailing use of urban elements and vocabulary (e.g. squares, lawns, tree pools) has caused stereotyped rural designs that neglect the place spirit and country indentities[6][7]. Scholars and experts' criticisms on the disappearing localities in China's urbanization call for a halt to the generic rural development and an emphasis on protecting and celebrating the uniqueness of vernacular landscapes[8][9] which ensure people having a sense of local cultural identity[10]. However, such concepts have still not been practiced in the current planning and design of rural construction.

Village landscapes are, and should be regional, cultural, diverse, compound, sustaining, and persisting[11], and the associated spatial elements have particular shapes, functions or services, and cultural implications, which, however, have not been studied as key components of the village design vocabulary. In 2011, the UNESCO approved the Recommendation on the Historic Urban Landscape, which highlights the importance of exploring and integrating local spatial elements into the sustainable development of village landscapes[12]. However, most existing studies on local elements focus on architectural details, building materials[13], and rural culture such as farming-reading traditions, religions, and ancient anecdotes[14]. To strengthen locals' cultural identity, indigenous elements can be used in village landscape design to enrich the design vocabulary.

Village landscape is defined by the natural environment and people's production patterns and lifestyles, as well as cultural traditions. Being part of the village landscape, the spatial elements between the courtyards of a historical village are shaped by the generations' interaction between the locals' daily activities and the nature[15]. The research on the existing spatial elements between village courtyards is considered a subfield of the study on the morphological and typological constitution of village landscapes. It examines such elements as cultural legacies of rural settlements of China's agricultural society, and provides a source for enhancing the rural sustainability through landscape

境需要保护、传承和善用这些村落宅间元素，通过创造性转化来实现这些元素的活态再生[16]。

在将这些村落宅间元素作为景观设计语汇之前，设计师面临的一个问题是，这些元素的平面特征大多并非几何形。那么，这些地方性的、在人与环境的长期相互适应中发展而来的元素平面特征是什么？如何用其指导设计？惯常的图式方法是设计过程中的常见工具，也是设计表达和交流的语言[17]，其优点是可以概括和总结村落宅间元素非几何形态的综合特征[18]，但不能准确、严谨地表述元素具体的平面特征，如面积、圆形度、矩形度、紧凑度和宽长比等。然而，对非几何形的村落宅间元素平面特征的准确描述至关重要，因为这决定了研究成果能否准确地用于指导设计实践，以有效地延续地域特征。因此，本研究提出了图式与图形特征量化分析相结合的研究方法，基于实例分析对村落宅间元素进行了分类，并借由量化工具对这些元素的平面特征进行了解读。

2 概念界定与文献综述

2.1 古村落宅间元素释义

古村落宅间元素是指村落宅院之间平面形态的各个构成部分，包含了实体聚落边界范围内非建筑部分的诸要素，研究对象是属于公共活动区范畴的平坦、晒场、巷道等空间，以及棚架、圈舍、添灯等构筑物。

2.2 图式释义

图式的形式可以为概念模型或抽象简图，也可以理解为一种设计工具或示意符号[19]。影响宅间元素形式的因素包括比例、结构及其他不可见的参数，这些因素具有模糊性，但这种模糊性不是随意的、无边际的，而是有着严格的范畴。较文字而言，图式可以更为准确地捕捉这种模糊性，可以对平面特征进行更为直观的概括和提炼。

2.3 文献综述

在元素形态特征研究方面，设计学领域现有研究以文本描述和图式为主。例如，以图式语言对古村落公共开放空间类别和形态特征进行梳理[20]；通过图式语言对徽州传统村落宗族图谱中的宅院图进行研究[21]；以图式与文本分析相结合的方法对古村落中的集中型、组团型、带状、放射型、象征型、灵活型等平面形态进行定性分析[22]等。

村落平面形态量化研究大多集中在整体空间形态方面，缺少对单个元素形态的量化分析。例如，基于三种数学原型——“群”“序”“拓扑”——对太湖流域古镇进行的空间结构解析[23]；运用空间句法对古村落空间形态进行的定量分析[24]；运用计算机编程

design means. The authors believe that, to preserve localities of historical villages and to rebuild harmonious human-land relationships, landscape designers are encouraged to preserve, adopt, and regenerate such elements in village landscape design for rural revitalization[16].

Before extracting the existing spatial elements between village courtyards as design vocabulary, landscape design needs to understand that most of these elements in historical villages are often in irregular shapes. What are the morphological characteristics of such elements? How can they inform the design practice? Diagram is a conventional design tool that expresses and communicates design ideas[17]. It can map and extract the overall typological characteristics of the non-geometric spatial elements[18], but fails to accurately describe detailed morphologies, such as area, circularity, rectangularity, compactness, and width-length ratio. However, such an accuracy is necessary, because it determines the application of the research findings in guiding design practices to honor the localities. Illustrating with a case study, this paper proposes to combine diagrams with a quantitative method of graphic characteristics, in order to describe and interpret the morphology of the spatial elements between village courtyards.

2 Concept Definitions and Literature Review

2.1 The Spatial Elements between Village Courtyards

The spatial elements between village courtyards refer to the morphological components defined by the non-architectural elements within a village settlement, such as the flat ground in front of gate, sunning ground, alleys, and structures (e.g., canopy frames, colony houses, and ever-burning lamps).

2.2 Diagrams

Diagrams can be conceptual models or sketches; they are also a design tool and a graphic symbol[19]. The forms of the spatial elements are defined by proportion, structure, and other invisible factors, which are of ambiguity, but not randomly. Compared with texts, diagrams can more accurately describe and represent such an ambiguity through a direct extraction of the morphological characteristics.

2.3 Literature Review

Texts and diagrams are mostly employed in morphological studies. Diagrams' effectiveness has been proven in categorizing the public space in historical villages and sorting out their morphological characteristics[20]; in studying the courtyard maps of the genealogies of Huizhou historical villages[21]; and

1. 关麓村航拍平面图

1. The aerial image of Guanlu Village

软件绘制建筑节点网络图，对聚落平面形态的方向性秩序特征进行科学而精准的量化描述[25]；运用数理分析方法，从住居面积、住居间距离、住居中心性和方向性等方面对传统村落空间形态的结构和秩序进行分析[26]；通过多智能体技术平台对村落形式结构自组织动态演变进行模拟等[27]。

另外，既有村落整体形态方面的研究多以建筑及其围合的巷道为对象讨论村落平面形态特征[28]，较少涉及古村落平面形态构成元素的详细类别。从语言学的角度来看，对单体元素（语汇）进行分析是研究村落整体形态（语法）的必要步骤。本文的创新性在于从语言学视角探讨了村落平面形态的构成内容及图式分类，并援引信息工程学图形特征量化分析方法计算了古村落宅间元素的平面特征数值。

3 研究方法

3.1 案例选取

关麓村位于安徽省黄山市黟县，是“中国历史文化名村”[29]及“中国传统村落”[30]（图1）。村内目前有150余位常住居民，他们传承了当地的生产及生活方式。鉴于村落的整体空间结构和宅间元素得到了较好的保护，故本文选取关麓村作为研究案例。

3.2 宅间元素分类

研究团队主要采用实地走访及文献检索的方法确认关麓村宅间元素的分类，这一过程分为三个步骤：1）通过走访当地年长村民（包括前任村长、书记和当地学校的退休教师），初步收集宅间元素的名称

in supporting qualitative analysis of the centralized, clustering, belt-like, radial, symbolic, and flexible morphologies in historical villages[22], etc.

Most quantitative research on the morphologies of villages studies the overall spatial forms, rather than individual spatial elements. For instance, three mathematical prototypes, i.e. group, order, topology, were employed to interpret spatial structures of historical towns in Taihu Lake Basin[23]; the space syntax methodology was applied in quantitative analyses of the spatial forms of historical villages[24]; computing-mapped architectural node network was used for accurate quantitative description of the directional order of settlement morphologies[25]; mathematical analysis methods were introduced to analyze the area, spacing distance, centrality, and directionality of settlements in traditional villages[26]; and multi-agent technology platform was developed to simulate the spontaneous dynamism of village structures[27].

The existing studies on the overall forms of villages mainly focus on the morphologies of architectures and alleys[28], paying insufficient attention to detailed spatial element categorization. In a linguistic analogy, understanding grammars (the overall form of villages) necessitates the study on vocabulary (individual spatial elements). This paper innovatively explores the components and diagram categories of village morphologies from the linguistic perspective and quantifies the morphological characteristics of the spatial elements between village courtyards with the graphic method adopted from Information Engineering.

3 Research Methods

3.1 Case Selection

The Guanlu Village of Yi County in Huangshan City, Anhui Province was selected as one of China's Historic and Cultural Villages[29] and of Traditional Chinese Villages[30] (Fig. 1). Now there are more than 150 villagers who keep the traditional production patterns and lifestyles. The overall form and structure of the village is well preserved, including the spatial elements between village courtyards, making it an ideal place for case study.

3.2 Categorization of the Spatial Elements between Village Courtyards

In this research, the spatial elements between village courtyards were categorized according to the collected data from interviews, field visits, and literature review with three steps: 1) primarily recording and categorizing the spatial elements by interviewing the elder (including the former village head, former

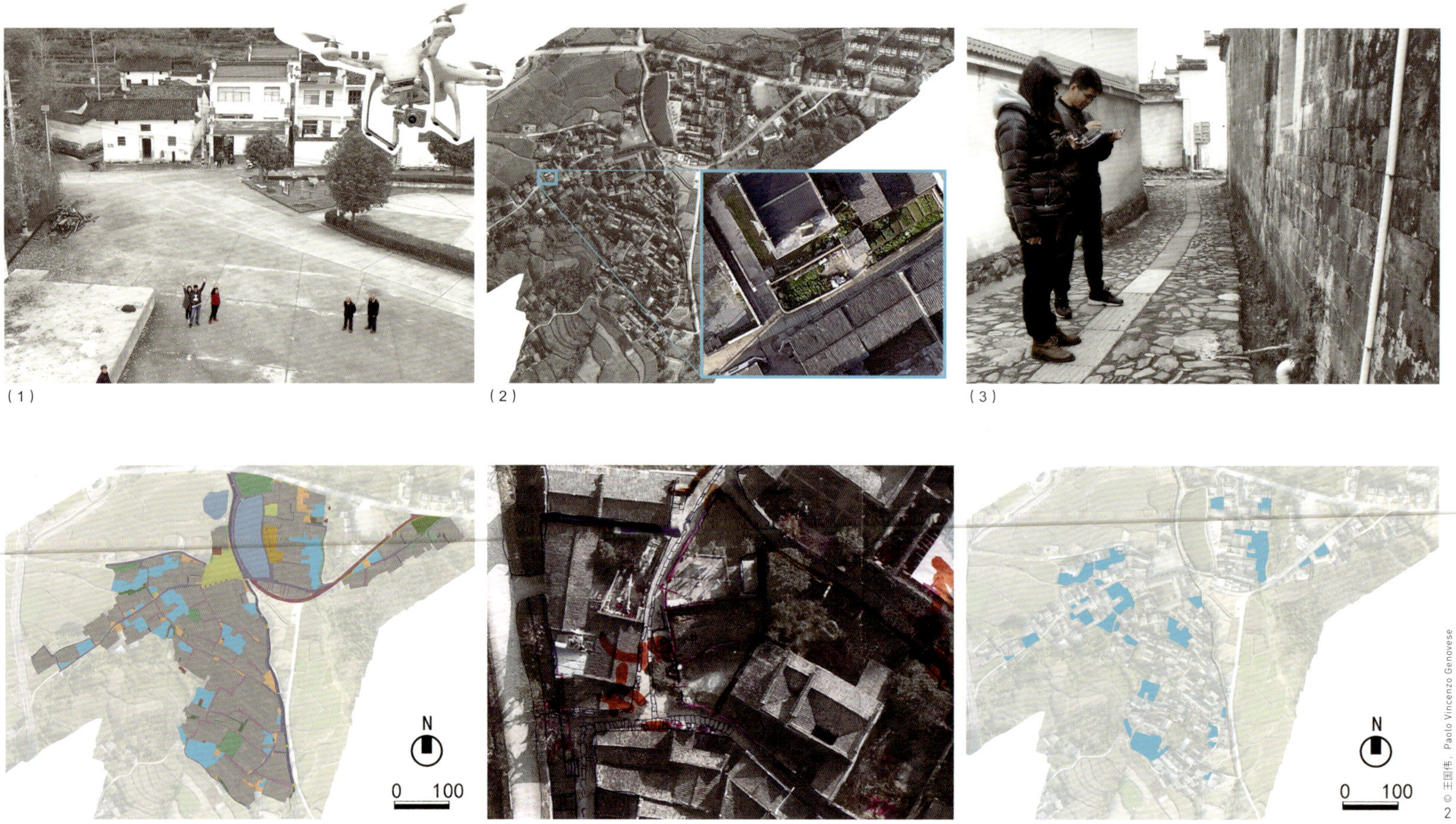

(1) (2) (3) (4) (5) (6)

2. 绘制宅间元素图式的6个步骤

2. Six steps of diagram drawing of the spatial elements between village courtyards

及含义，并对这些元素进行分类整理；2）与这些村民在村落中进行实地考察，并在地图上标记宅间元素的位置，查漏补缺；3）通过文献检索（包括县志、村落志，以及相关文件及出版物等）进一步收集、补充与该地区村落相关的宅间元素分类。

3.3 绘制宅间元素图式

古村落空间类型元素的边界确定工作十分复杂，针对这一问题，研究团队采用“六步骤”来绘制宅间元素图式（图2）：

1）研究团队借鉴王云才团队以Google Earth和AutoCAD为平台通过分析遥感影像获取图式的思路[31]，采用无人机结合Agisoft PhotoScan和AutoCAD的方法绘制采样精度为5cm的村落航拍平面图；设定无人机以

secretary of village committee, and local retired teachers); 2) conducting field investigations with the interviewed villagers to map the spatial elements and add the missing ones; and 3) further supplementing the spatial element categorization based on literature review, including county annals, village annals, and related documents and publications.

3.3 Diagram Drawing of the Spatial Elements between Village Courtyards

Diagram drawing of the spatial elements between village courtyards was very challenging, because the boundaries of such elements are difficult to measure or describe precisely. This research came up with a 6-step mapping method (Fig. 2) as a solution:

1) Inspired by Wang Yuncai et al.[31] who conducted diagram drawing with remote sensing image analysis by Google Earth and AutoCAD, the research team produced the village plan

100m左右的恒定高度飞行——过高难以保证拍摄照片的精度，过低则会造成透视角过大，不利于照片的后期合成；随后设定扫描轨迹和拍摄照片数量，保证每两张照片有2/3以上的重叠区域，对村落平面进行扫描。

2）将扫描照片导入Agisoft PhotoScan，合成高精度村落平面图。

3）以1:200的比例分区块在A2图纸上打印彩色村落平面图，确保所有宅间元素在地图上清晰可见，共打印了6张A2图纸；随后组织团队成员通过实地调研，在图纸上标记出各分区内不同元素之间的边界。

4）将标记的元素边界转换为AutoCAD文件。

5）如遇信息缺失或模糊的情况，则需返回场地重新描绘边界并补充信息。

6）最后将宅间元素图式按照元素分类分图层导出。

3.4 宅间元素平面特征量化分析

宅间元素图式可以使人们直观了解元素的综合形态特征，而平面特征量化分析则可以明确每个元素平面特征的数值范围，以对其特征有更为清晰具体的描述。宅间元素平面特征量化分析参考信息工程学图形特征计算方法，注重分析元素图式的轮廓特征，包括面积、圆形度、矩形度、紧凑度、宽长比5个方面[32][33]。其中，图式的面积描述了元素的大小，其数值可直接通过AutoCAD获取。

圆形度是用来表示元素图式圆形程度的指标，其常用计算公式如下：

$$C=\frac{P^2}{S_0}$$

式中，C为圆形度，P^2为该元素周长的平方，S_0为该元素的面积；C的最小值为4π，元素形状越狭长，C值越大。

矩形度体现元素图式对其外接矩形的充满程度，其计算公式如下：

$$R=\frac{S_0}{S_{\mathrm{MER}}}$$

式中，R为矩形度，S_0为该元素的面积，S_{MER}为该元素的最小外接矩形面积。R的最大值为1，当元素为圆形时，R为π/4；元素越狭长、弯曲，R值越小。

(accuracy of 5 cm) based on the photos taken by a UAV with Agisoft PhotoScan and AutoCAD. The UAV was set at a constant flight altitude of about 100 m, for accuracy and post-production considerations. Then, the flight path and the amount of photos to be taken were determined, ensuring that the overlapping area between two continuous photos is not less than 2/3 of the photograph.

2) All the UAV photos were uploaded into Agisoft PhotoScan to produce a high-resolution plan of the village.

3) The plan was color printed on 6 pieces of A2 sheets at the scale of 1:200, ensuring all spatial elements can be clearly identified. Then the research team marked the element boundaries on the map in field investigations.

4) All the marked boundary data were used to generate AutoCAD drawings.

5) The boundary data and other information were completed by re-mapping if blurred or missing.

6) Diagrams of the spatial elements between village courtyards were generated by categories.

3.4 Quantitative Analysis of the Morphologies of the Spatial Elements between Village Courtyards

Diagrams are used to visualize the overall forms and typologies of the spatial elements, and the graphic method sourced from Information Engineering can analyze and quantify the morphological characteristics of each element, including area, circularity, rectangularity, compactness, and width-length ratio[32][33]. Particularly, the area indicates the size of the element, data of which can be obtained from AutoCAD directly.

Circularity measures the roundness of an element. The commonly used calculation formula is as follows:

$$C=\frac{P^2}{S_0}$$

where, C is the circularity, P^2 is the square of the element's perimeter, and S_0 is its area. The minimum value of C is 4π; as the value grows, it indicates an increasingly elongated polygon.

Rectangularity measures the proximity of an element to its enclosing rectangular. The calculation formula is as follows:

$$R=\frac{S_0}{S_{\mathrm{MER}}}$$

where, R is the rectangularity, S_0 is the area of the element, and S_{MER} is the area of the minimal enclosing rectangle. The maximum value of R is 1, and for circles, R is π/4. The more elongated and curved the element is, the smaller the value will be.

表1：关麓村宅间元素列表
Table 1: The categories of the spatial elements between courtyards in Guanlu Village

类型 Categories	宅间元素名称 Items of the spatial elements between countyards
节点 Node elements	平坦、垱、埠头、塘、晒场、宅间农田、花池、竹林、草坪（新建）、广场（新建） Flat ground in front of the gate, earth dike, pier, pond, sunning ground, farmland among courtyards, planting bed, bamboo forest, lawn (newly built), and square (newly built)
线域 Linear elements	滴水沟、塝、路、巷道、坝、排水渠、溪、茅草墙、石墙 Ditch, side slope, path, alley, dam, drainage channel, creek, twitch-grass wall, and stone wall
构筑物 Structure elements	门当、添灯（已毁）、桥、井、石阶、石凳、圈舍、棚架、树池（新建） Stone drum, ever-burning lamp (ruined), bridge, well, stone step, stone seat, colony house, canopy frame, and tree pool (newly built)

紧凑度是指图式边界的光滑度，常用计算公式如下：

$$F=\frac{4\pi S_0}{P^2}$$

式中，F为紧凑度，S_0为该元素的面积，P^2为该元素周长的平方。当元素为圆形时，F为1；当元素为其他形状时，$F<1$；元素边界越弯曲、越复杂，F值越小。

宽长比是指图式最小外接矩形的宽长比，这一特征用于指征元素形态的狭长程度（或接近方形或圆形的程度），其计算公式如下：

$$r=\frac{W_{\mathrm{MER}}}{L_{\mathrm{MER}}}$$

式中，r为宽长比，W_{MER}为图式最小外接矩形的宽，L_{MER}为图式最小外接矩形的长。当元素为圆形和正方形时，r为最大值1；元素越狭长，r值越小。

4 研究结果

4.1 宅间元素分类及其图式

关麓村宅间元素共计28种，包括24种现存本土元素、1种已被破坏的本土元素、3种在村落旅游开发过程中新建的元素（表1）。为了清晰表述不同的元素类型，本研究将28种古村落宅间元素归纳为三类：

Compactness measures the smoothness of an element's boundary. It is often calculated as follows:

$$F=\frac{4\pi S_0}{P^2}$$

where, F is the compactness, S_0 is the area of the element, P^2 is the square of the perimeter. When the element is in a circular shape, F is 1; when in other shapes, $F<1$. The more complicated or curved boundary of the element is, the smaller the value will be.

Width-length ratio refers to the ratio of the width and the length of an element's minimal enclosing rectangle. It indicates the elongated degree (or the square or circular degree) of an element and is calculated as follows:

$$r=\frac{W_{\mathrm{MER}}}{L_{\mathrm{MER}}}$$

where, r is the width-length ratio, W_{MER} and L_{MER} are the width and length of the minimal enclosing rectangle, respectively; r reaches its maximal value, i.e.1, when the element is in a square or circular shape; an increasingly elongated element will have a smaller r value.

4 Research Findings

4.1 Categorization and Diagrams of the Spatial Elements between Village Courtyards

This research identified 28 sorts of the spatial elements between courtyards in Guanlu Village, including 24 existing indigenous spatial elements, 1 ruined indigenous element, and 3 new elements introduced during the tourism development (Table 1). These spatial elements were roughly in 3 categories, namely node

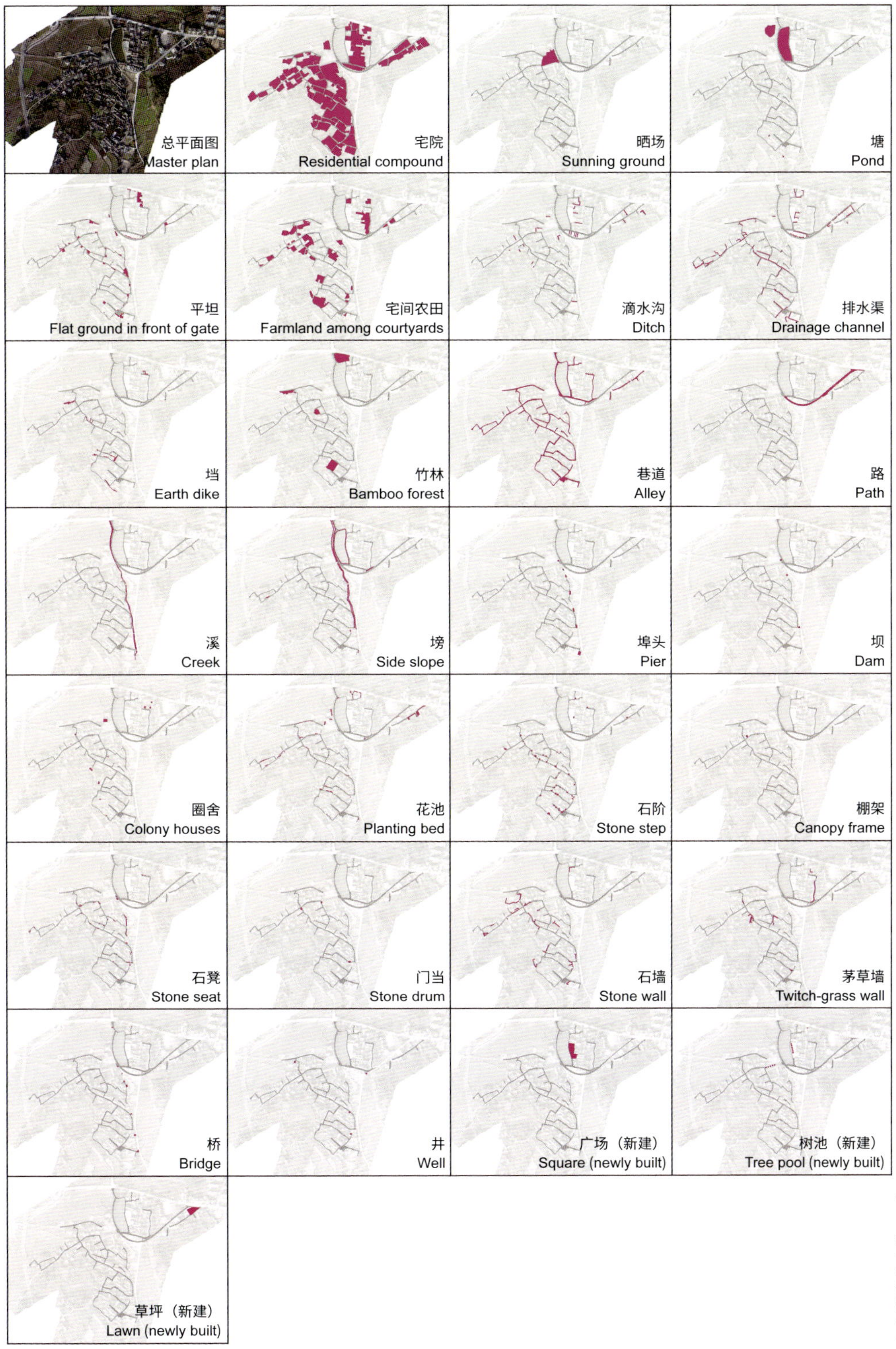

3

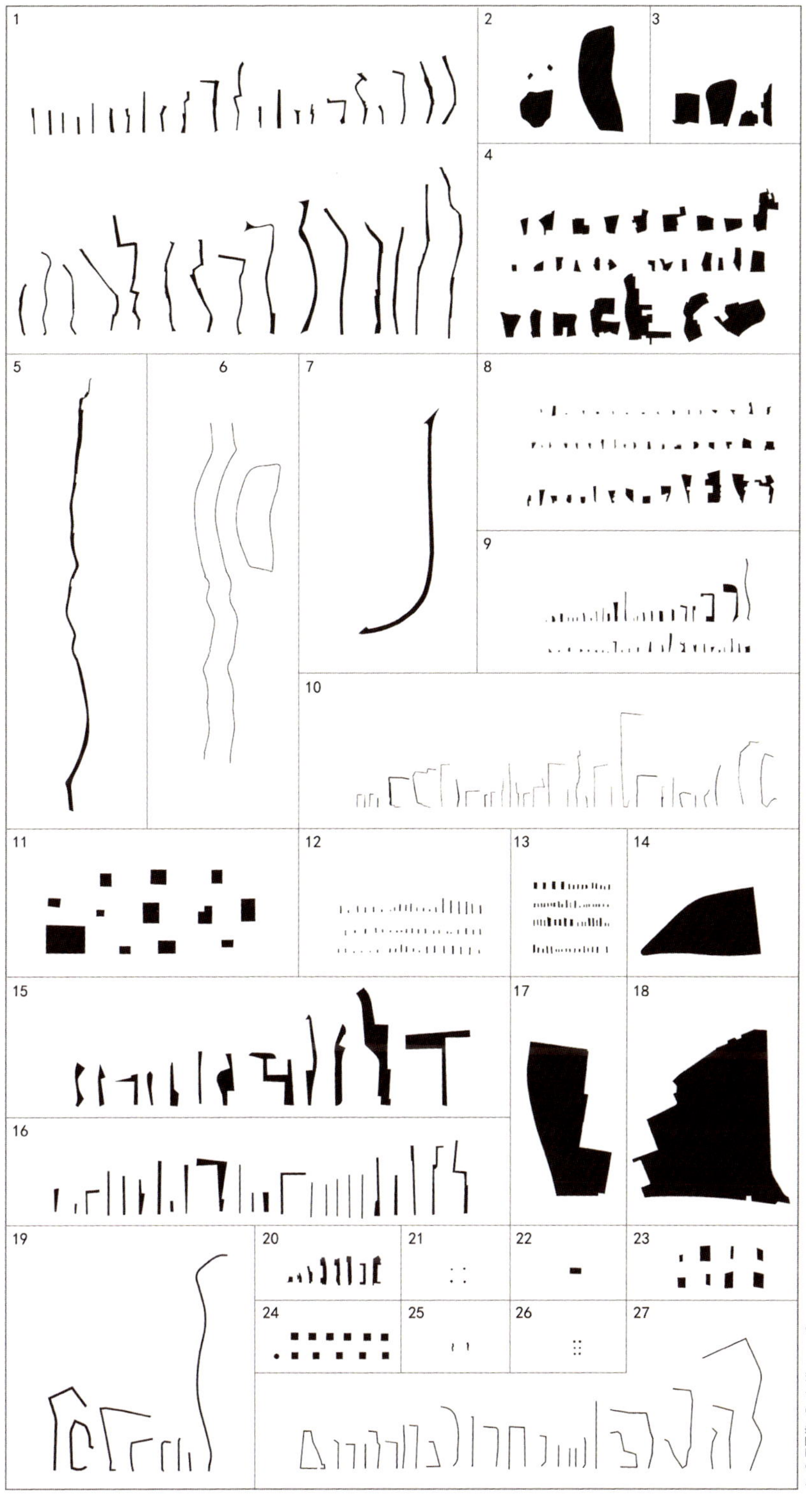

4

图例 Legend

1 巷道 Alley
2 塘 Pond
3 竹林 Bamboo forest
4 宅间农田 Farmland among courtyards
5 溪 Creek
6 塝 Side slope
7 路 Path
8 平坦 Flat ground in front of gate
9 花池 Planting bed
10 排水渠 Drainage channel
11 圈舍 Colony houses
12 石凳 Stone seat
13 石阶 Stone step
14 草坪 Lawn
15 垱 Earth dike
16 滴水沟 Ditch
17 广场 Square
18 晒场 Sunning ground
19 茅草墙 Twitch-grass wall
20 埠头 Pier
21 井 Well
22 棚架 Canopy frame
23 桥 Bridge
24 树池 Tree pool
25 坝 Dam
26 门当 Stone drum
27 石墙 Stone wall

3. 关麓村宅间元素分布
4. 关麓村宅间元素图式列表

3. The distribution of the spatial elements between courtyards in Guanlu Village
4. The diagrams of the spatial elements between courtyards in Guanlu Village

节点、线域和构筑物。其中，节点和线域可用于界定空间，构筑物可涵盖空间中的设施和物品。

由于添灯这种元素在村落发展中已逐渐消失，所以关麓村仅包含27种宅间元素图式（图3）。研究团队进一步将属于同一类别的元素图式放在一起，以更清晰地展示不同元素的图形特征（图4）。

4.2 宅间元素图形特征取值

通过上述公式，研究团队共计算了27种宅间元素共计500个图形在面积、圆形度、矩形度、紧凑度和宽长比方面的具体取值、极值、均值和标准差（数值的离散程度）。图5是各个元素图式特征在上述5个方面的极值和数值范围，图6则体现了均值和标准差。

以石墙（元素27）和滴水沟（元素16）为例，在面积方面，滴水沟的均值（8.96:4.30）和标准差（7.03:2.84）是石墙的两倍多；但在圆形度方面，石墙要比滴水沟的均值大得多（299.96:101.56），即石墙要比滴水沟更细长，石墙在圆形度方面的标准差也比滴水沟更高（190.55:51.52）；在矩形度方面，滴水沟的均值是石墙的两倍多（0.73:0.30），但两者具体值的标准差非常接近（0.30:0.36）；在紧凑度方面，无论是均值（0.18:0.06）还是标准差（0.13:0.03），滴水沟都数倍于石墙；在宽长比方面，两者较为相近，石墙略高于滴水沟（0.24:0.16），两者具有相同的标准差（0.18:0.18）。

5 讨论

通过图4可知，古村落宅间元素与新建设计元素存在明显区别。虽然平坦、塝、埠头、垱、滴水沟等元素反映了徽州古村落平面形态地域特征，但这些元素却很少出现在当地村落景观设计中。设计师经常使用城市平面元素，忽略了对本土元素的挖掘和传承。例如，关麓村针对部分区域进行的旅游景观提升项目中充斥着广场、草坪、树池等

elements, linear elements, and structure elements. The former two define the boundary of a place, and the latter one covers the facilities and objects in the place.

As the ruined ever-burning lamps are disappearing in the village, the research team further studied the other 27 sorts of elements (Fig. 3) by categories to clearly display the graphic characteristics of different elements (Fig. 4).

4.2 Values of the Graphic Values of the Spatial Elements between Village Courtyards

The research calculated the values, extreme values, mean values, and standard deviations (the discreteness of the values) of the 27 sorts of elements (500 graphs in total) in the area, circularity, rectangularity, compactness, and width-length ratio. Figure 5 shows the extreme values and value range of the 5 graphic characteristics of each element, and Figure 6 indicates the corresponding mean values and standard deviations.

Stone wall (Element 27) and ditch (Element 16) are illustrated here for a further explanation. In terms of the area, ditches have a twice-higher value than stone walls in both the mean value (8.96:4.30) and standard deviation (7.03:2.84). The mean value of circularity of stone walls is much higher than that of ditches (299.96:101.56), suggesting that the stone walls in the village are more in elongated shapes than the ditches. The circularity standard deviation of the stone walls are higher than those of the ditches (190.55:51.52). The rectangularity of ditches is more than twice that of stone walls (0.73:0.30), but their standard deviations are very close (0.30:0.36). In terms of the compactness, the mean value (0.18:0.06) and standard deviation (0.13:0.03) of ditches are much higher than those of stone walls. The width-length ratio of stone walls is slightly higher than that of ditches (0.24:0.16), with the standard deviations (0.18:0.18) being the same.

5 Discussions

Figure 4 displays the significant differences between the existing spatial elements between village courtyards and the newly built elements. The indigenous spatial elements such as flat grounds in front of gate, side slopes, piers, earth dikes, and ditches all reflect the regional qualities of Huizhou villages, but are rarely found in the local landscape design, which are dominated by the generic use of urban landscape elements, ignoring the exploration and revitalization of local elements. For instance, squares, lawns, and tree pools were prevailingly used in the tourism development (e.g. the Guanlu Village regeneration project) to reshape the village's image. For a

5. 宅间元素平面特征极值和数值范围

5. The extremums and value ranges of the morphological characteristics of the spatial elements between village courtyards

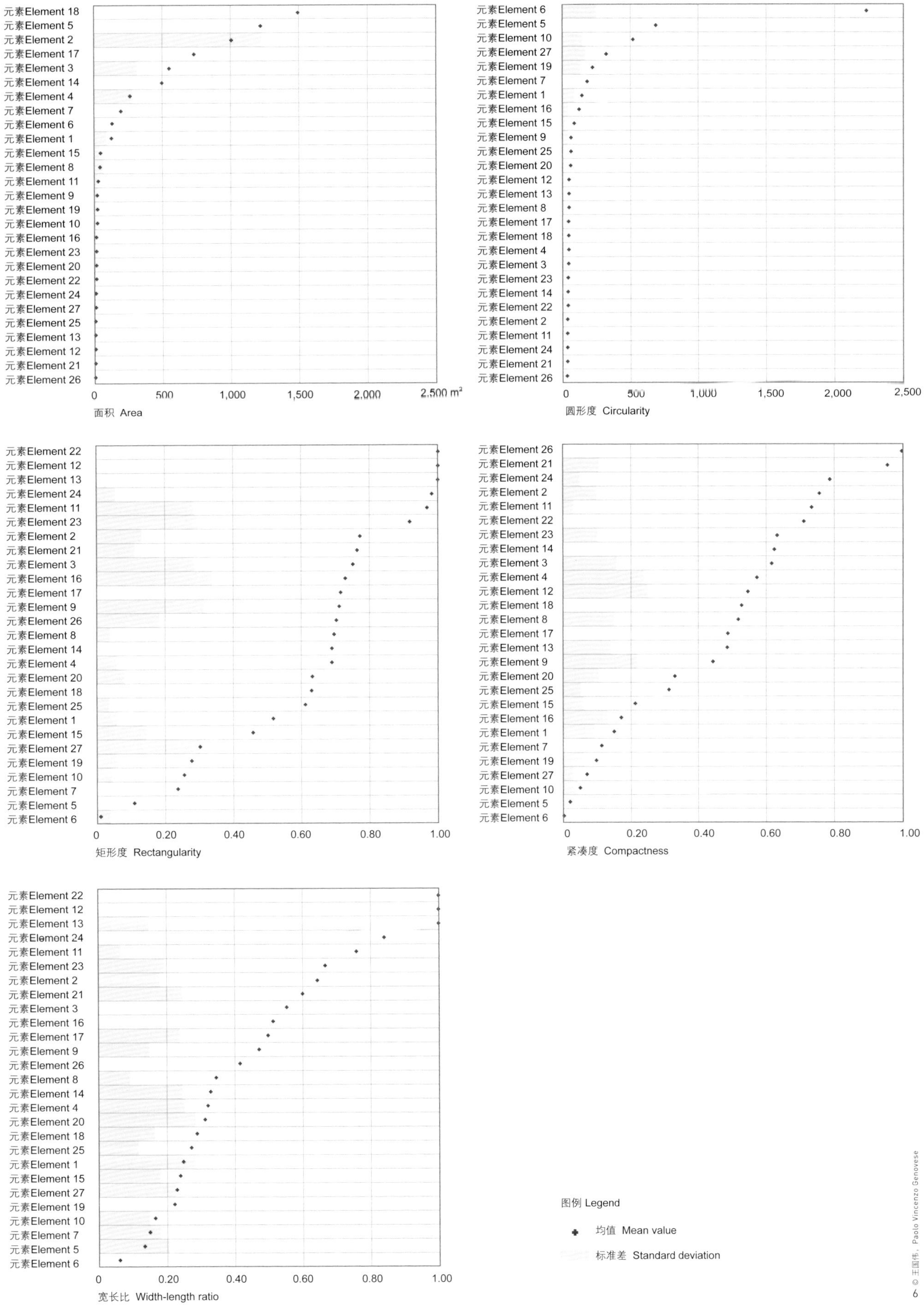

© 王国伟，Paolo Vincenzo Genovese
6

6. 宅间元素平面特征的均值和标准差

6. The mean values and standard deviations of the morphological characteristics of the spatial elements between village courtyards

表2：黄山市古村落（关麓村）与新建村落的宅间元素对比
Table 2: The comparison between historical village (Guanlu Village) and a newly built village in the same city in the spatial elements between village courtyards

	古村落（关麓村） Historical village (Guanlu Village)	新建村落 Newly built village
宅间元素 Spatial elements between village courtyards	平坦、垱、埠头、塘、晒场、宅间农田、花池、竹林、草坪（新建）、广场（新建）、滴水沟、塝、路、巷道、坝、排水渠、溪、茅草墙、石墙、门当、添灯（已毁）、桥、井、石阶、石凳、圈舍、棚架、树池（新建） Flat ground in front of the gate, earth dike, pier, pond, sunning ground, farmland among courtyards, planting bed, bamboo forest, lawn (newly built), square (newly built), ditch, side slope, path, alley, dam, drainage channel, creek, twitch-grass wall, stone wall, stone drum, ever-burning lamp (ruined), bridge, well, stone step, stone seat, colony house, canopy frame, and tree pool (newly built)	广场、儿童活动场、草坪、亭、岗亭、廊架、雕塑、车行道、人行道、挡土墙、羽毛球场、停车场、坡道、庭院墙、景墙、长凳、宅间绿化、树池 Square, playground, lawn, pavilion, watch house, corridor, sculpture, roadway, sidewalk, revetment, badminton court, parking lot, ramp, courtyard wall, landscaped wall, bench, greening among courtyards, and tree pool

元素。本文随机选择了与关麓村同属黄山市的一个新建村落，将其宅间元素与关麓村进行比较，结果显示差异元素的比例高达近87%（表2）。需要说明的是，研究团队仅对构成宅间平面形态的核心元素进行了对比分析，尽可能排除建筑细部构成元素（如灯柱、音箱、花钵等）对研究结果可能造成的影响。

元素平面特征的量化分析可以进一步明晰同类型元素的形式特征。例如，“石墙”“滴水沟”“排水渠”“巷道”均属于线域元素，研究团队提取了这4种元素的图形特征数据，将面积、圆形度、矩形度、紧凑度、宽长比这5个平面特征影响因素作为象限坐标，分别生成雷达图（图7），呈现了同类型元素平面特征的不同之处。

此外，当前村落景观设计多依赖主观经验指导设计，设计师的个人能力与专业素养在很大程度上影响着设计品质，这导致量大面广的村落景观设计品质良莠不齐。研究团队提出的这一基于元素分类、图式及其平面特征量化分析的方法模型从以下三个方面为以延续地域特征为目的的村落景观平面设计提供了客观依据：1）古村落宅间元素分类明确了元素在地方村落景观平面设计中的适用范围；2）宅间元素图式概括了元素的综合平面特征；3）宅间元素平面特征量化分析清晰地界定了元素平面的图形特征。

元素分类和图式的价值是辅助设计师进行初步设计，而量化分析的意义则是校验设计元素是否契合面积、圆形度、矩形度、紧凑度、

comparative study, this paper randomly selected a newly built village in the same city with the Guanlu Village, and examined the spatial elements between courtyards of the both villages. The analysis demonstrated the significant difference of such spatial elements (nearly 87%) between the villages in two contrastive typologies (Table 2). Specifically, the research team only analyzed the core spatial elements between village courtyards; architectural decorations such as lamp poles, sound boxes, and flower pots were excluded to avoid research bias.

Quantitative analysis of the morphological characteristics can highlight the differences among similar elements. For instance, stone wall, ditch, drainage channel, and alley are all linear elements. The research team visualized the area, circularity, rectangularity, compactness, and width-length ratio of the 4 elements in radar maps to clearly illustrate their morphological differences (Fig. 7).

Besides, current practice of village landscape design is still guided by individual experience, and the design quality is largely subject to the designer's personal ability and capacity, resulting in disparities in design quality across the vast rural China. This village landscape design model constituted with element categorization, diagram drawing, and morphological quantitative analysis would provide scientific evidences that help inform the practices to revitalize village localities: 1) the categorization of the spatial elements between courtyards offers guidelines for the elements' regeneration; 2) the diagrams extract the overall characteristics of the elements; and 3) the quantitative analysis defines the values of the morphologies of the elements.

Element categorization and diagrams are used to help form preliminary design plans, and quantitative analysis

宽长比等元素的平面特征取值范围，在计算机辅助设计中，有助于实现设计方案的快速调整与迭代。以元素“石墙”为例，设计师首先初步设计元素形态，随后计算其平面特征的取值并与当地的真实元素进行对比，也可将设计元素的个体雷达图置入地方元素类型雷达图中，从而观察具体取值偏差并进行调整。平面特征量化分析提供了一个符合地域特征的设计区间，在区间内的设计既具有严谨性又不失灵活性（图8）。研究团队提出的这一村落景观设计方法模型，尽管可在计算

is used to verify whether the designed element' fit in its morphological value ranges in area, circularity, rectangularity, compactness, and width-length ratio. The computer-aided design process allows for prompt adjustments and iteration. Take the stone wall as an example: After the design of a conceptual or preliminary scheme, the values of the designed elements will be calculated and compared with those of the authentic elements; the designer can also compare their radar maps to identify deviations. The quantitative analysis helps define the “intervals” for element design and ensures the rationality and flexibility of the design (Fig. 8)—In this research, the computer-aided design process still greatly requires human intelligence and manual labor; In the future, software engineers are expected

7. 线性元素图式取值对比

7. Comparison of morphological characteristics of the linear elements

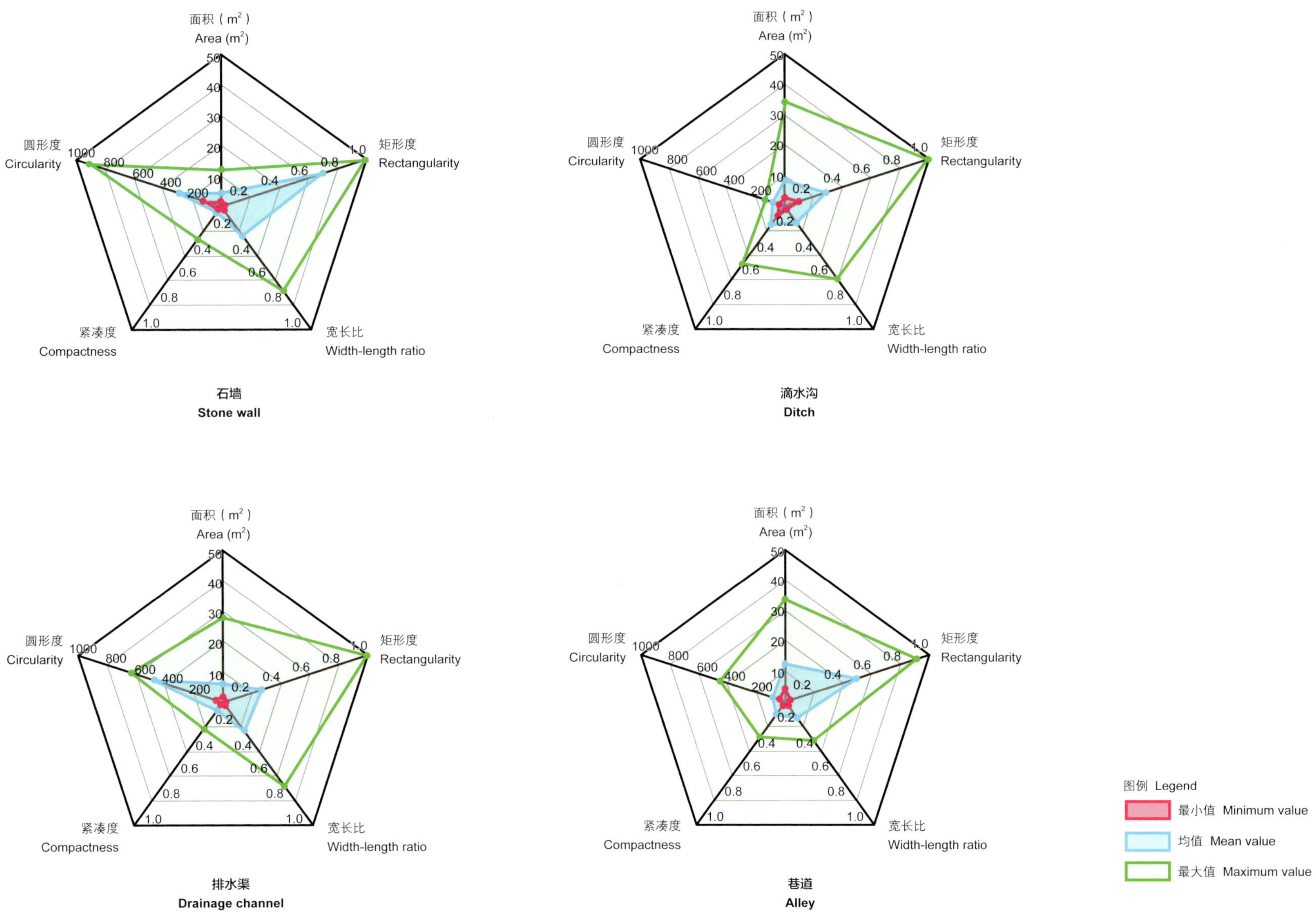

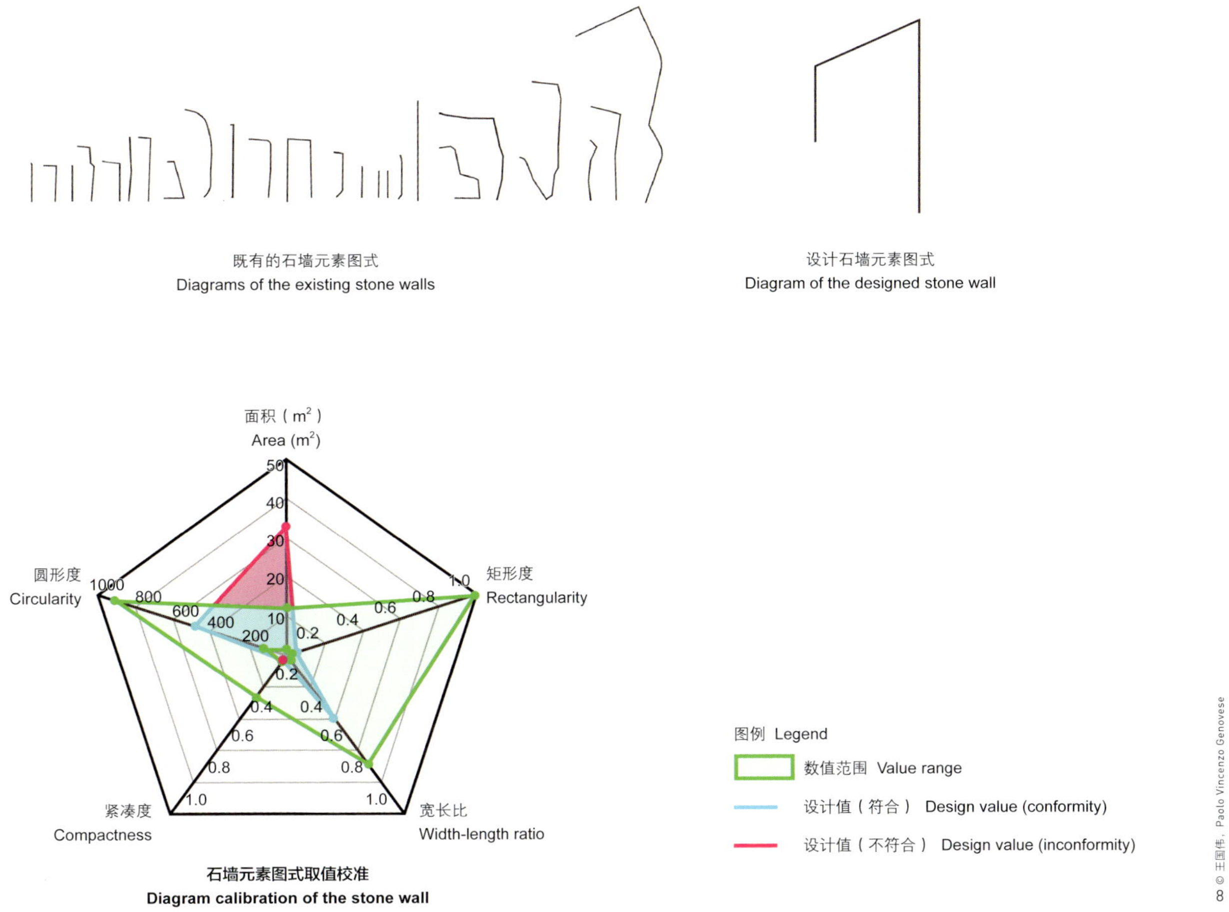

8. “石墙”元素图示校准

8. Diagram calibration of the design of stone wall

机平台上进行辅助设计，但全程均离不开人工参与。如果软件工程师可以据此开发出一款根据设计元素平面特征进行动态数值校验并生成建议元素形状的工具，必将大大提高设计师的工作效率。

6 结语

首先，本文以黄山市关麓村为例梳理了当地28种古村落宅间元素分类及相应的元素图式，并量化分析了其平面特征。元素分类为设计师提供了更丰富的设计语汇，从而避免一味使用城市景观元素。虽然每个村落的形态特征不同，但在特定地区内，村落的宅间元素特征存在共性规律，元素图式及其量化分析则有助于设计师更好地辨识这些

to develop tools that support dynamic numerical verification on elements' changing morphological characteristics and offer design recommendations, which will greatly improve the design efficiency.

6 Conclusions

First, this paper identifies 28 sorts of the spatial elements between courtyards in Guanlu Village of Huangshan City and the corresponding diagrams, and quantifies their morphological characteristics. Element categorization provides designers with an enriched vocabulary, thus avoiding the mindless use of urban landscape elements. Although the morphological characteristics of different villages might vary, the spatial elements in a region see a consistent style, which can be used as references for village landscape design with aids of diagraming and quantitative analysis. As a methodological exploration, this paper also underlines the fact that the acquisition of the

特征，为元素在村落景观设计中的应用提供参考。地方元素特征取值区间的确定需要以大量案例数据的收集和统计为基础，本文仅作为一种方法论上的探索。宅间元素的形态特征亦不能用于直接解决村落的综合性生态、社会及文化问题。

其次，对元素平面特征的研究除了图形特征量化分析之外，还包括图像特征量化分析。本文聚焦于图形特征量化分析，通过数值区分不同元素图式的形状特征取值范围、辨别不同元素图式特征的差异，同时也允许不同元素间存在取值相似或相同的情况。图像特征研究方法包括元素的方向梯度直方图法、傅里叶功率谱法等[32]。未来，研究可关注如何将元素的图形和图像特征研究与计算机深度学习相结合，以实现村落宅间元素的自动识别。

最后，古村落宅间元素之于村落景观如同词汇之于语言——语言的完整性不仅包括词汇，还应包含语法结构、修辞与隐喻等[34]。研究团队认为，古村落宅间元素的分类及其平面特征的研究只是基础，未来需要进一步深入研究元素之间的空间关系，以建立村落景观语言体系，进一步探讨古村落平面形态的演变规律，从而促进村落平面形态演变模型的细化与完善，使其更具科学性和完整性。**LAF**

value ranges of local elements requires a large amount of data collection and statistics work, and the morphological characteristics of spatial elements cannot be used to deal with synthetic ecological, social, or cultural issues directly.

Second, in addition to the quantitative analysis of graphic characteristics, the study of element's morphology also includes the quantitative analysis of image characteristics. This paper focuses on the former, aiming to distinguish the value ranges of the graphs of different elements, where different elements may have similar or same morphological value ranges. Quantitative analysis of image characteristics includes gradient histogram and Fourier power spectrum[32]. In the future, the auto-identification of village spatial elements can be realized by combining deep learning technology with quantitative analyses of both graphic and image characteristics.

Last, the spatial elements between courtyards of historical villages to the village landscape is what the vocabulary is to the language—Languages are constituted not only by vocabulary, but also grammars, rhetoric skills, and metaphors[34]. The research team believes that the study on the categorization and the analysis of morphological characteristics needs more efforts in studying the spatial relations among the elements to form and complete the "lingual system" of village landscapes, exploring the evolution pattern of the morphology of ancient villages, refining the simulation of villages' morphological evolution, and contributing to the scientific and systematic development of associated research. **LAF**

致谢

本文为第一作者在天津大学建筑学院攻读博士期间的研究成果。作者感谢天津大学唐晨教授提出的宝贵建议，安徽农业大学张云彬教授、王迪、王明瑞提供的设备支持及帮助，以及《景观设计学》期刊编辑部及匿名审稿专家对本文提出的中肯意见。

ACKNOWLEDGMENTS

This study is part of the first author's doctoral dissertation in the School of Architecture at Tianjin University. The authors would like to thank Professor Tang Chen for her valuable advice, Professor Zhang Yunbin, Wang Di, and Wang Mingrui from Anhui Agricultural University for their device support and help, the efforts of the editorial team of *Landscape Architecture Frontiers* journal, and anonymous peer reviewers' comments on this paper.

REFERENCES

[1] Sun, Y., & Ma, H. (2017). Overview on the Research of Urban Fringe Villages in China. City Planning Review, 41(1), 95-103. doi:10.11819/cpr20170114a

[2] Qiu, B. (2010). Scientific Planning for a New Urbanization Strategy. Planners, 26(7), 7-12.

[3] Zhang, J. (2006). Study on the Phenomenon of the Village Imitating the City in the Process of Urbanization. Tongji University Journal Social Science Section, 17(4), 36-40. doi:10.3969/j.issn.1009-3060.2006.04.006

[4] Li, J. (2013). Great Changes in the Rural Landscape. Landscape Architecture, (4), 149-150. doi:10.3969/j.issn.1673-1530.2013.04.019

[5] Chen, Z. (2016). Flexible Urbanization: A Hypothesis Based on Pluriactivity and Mobility of Rural Employment. City Planning Review, 40(9), 59-66. doi:10.11819/cpr20160908a

[6] Wang, G., & Genovese, P. V. (2020). Classification and Discussion of Planar Elements for the Space between Residential Compounds in the Landscape Environment Study of Ancient Villages. Landscape Design, (2), 22-29. doi:10.12145/202002022

[7] Li, J. (2016). A Study on the Approaches of Rural Revival and Rural Landscape Protection in China. Chinese Landscape Architecture, (9), 16-19.

[8] Liu, B., & Chen, W. (2000). The Exploration of Chinese Rural Landscape and Garden. Urban Planning Forum, (6), 66-68. doi:10.3969/j.issn.1000-3363.2000.06.015

[9] Li, J., Zhang, Y., Liu, K., & Hu, B. (2007). Thoughts on Rural Landscape Planning in China. Journal of Beijing University of Agriculture, 22(3), 52-56. doi:10.3969/j.issn.1002-3186.2007.03.015

[10] Oktay, D. (2002). The Quest for Urban Identity in the Changing Context of the City. Cities, 19(4), 261-271. doi:10.1016/S0264-2751(02)00023-9

[11] Liu, Z., & Jin, Q. (1999). Study on the Types of Rural Cultural Landscape and its Evolution. Journal of Nanjing Normal University (Natural Science), 22(4), 120-123. doi:10.3969/j.issn.1001-4616.1999.04.030

[12] UNESCO World Heritage Convention. (2019, March). The UNESCO Recommendation on the Historic Urban Landscape. Retrieved from https://whc.unesco.org/en/hul

[13] Shan, D. (2010). Chinese Vernacular Dwellings. Beijing: China Intercontinental Press.

[14] Huang, Q., Zhu, X., & Chen, C. (2016). Research on the Landscape Genetic Code and Derivation Model of Traditional Settlement—Taking Nanxi River Famous Scenic Site as an Example. Chinese Landscape Architecture, 32(10), 89-93.

[15] Mahmoud, R. A. (2016). Old Gourna: The Complexity of Vernacular Architecture / Urbanism and Cultural Heritage. Procedia: Social and Behavioral Sciences, (225), 200-215. doi:10.1016/j.sbspro.2016.06.020

[16] Yang, G. (2019). Spatial Interpretation of Rural Human Settlements Culture and Its Revitalization. Journal of Human Settlements in West China, 34(6), 102-108. doi:10.13791/j.cnki.hsfwest.20190614

[17] Meng, X. (2016). Pattern Language Expression of Landscape Based on the Graphics. Chinese Landscape Architecture, 32(2), 18-24. doi:10.3969/j.issn.1000-6664.2016.02.004

[18] Wang, Y. (2017). The Logical Thinking and Framework of Landscape Space Pattern Language. Landscape Architecture, (4), 89-98. doi:10.14085/j.fjyl.2017.04.0089.10

[19] Hu, Y., & Ding, W. (2010). Interpretation of Peter Eisenman's Schematic Theory—Basic Connotation of Architectural Schematic Concept. The Architect, (4), 21-29.

[20] Wang, Y., & Liu, B. (2003). Chinese Rural Landscape and Rural Landscape Planning in China. Chinese Landscape Architecture, 19(1), 55-58. doi:10.3969/j.issn.1000-6664.2003.01.015

[21] Pei, Y., Leng, J., & Gong, K. (2019). The Research of Classification and Quantification Based on Village Residential Drawing: A Case Study of Huizhou Traditional Village Group. The Architect, (1), 106-111.

[22] Ye, Z. (2001). The Exploration of the Structure of Traditional Settlement Environmental Space. Architectural Journal, (12), 21-24. doi:10.3969/j.issn.0529-1399.2001.12.008

[23] Duan, J., Ji, S., & Wang. H. (2002). Urban Spatial Analysis: Spatial Structure and Form of Ancient Towns in Taihu Basin. Beijing: China Architecture and Building Press.

[24] Chen, D. (2017). Research on the Spatial Form of Ancient Village Based on Spatial Syntax: A Case Study of Zhukou Village in Qimen County. Urban Studies, 24(8), 29-34.

[25] Pu, X., Wang, Z., Gao, L., & Huang, Q. (2013). Study on the Ordinal Value of Directionality of the House Plane Figure in Rural Settlement. Architectural Journal, (5), 111-115. doi:10.3969/j.issn.0529-1399.2013.05.019

[26] Wang, Y. (2016). The Spatial Concepts in the Traditional Settlement Structure (Second Edition). Beijing: China Architecture and Building Press.

[27] Du, R., & Dong, W. (Ed). (2015). Research on the Evolution of Urban Space Based on Urban Modeling and Simulation. Nanjing: Southeast University Press.

[28] Ding, W., & Li, Q. (2013). Study on the Morphological Identities and Its Elements of Southern Jiangsu Village. Architectural Journal, (12), 64-68. doi:10.3969/j.issn.0529-1399.2013.12.013

[29] Ministry of Housing and Urban-Rural Construction of the People's Republic of China, & National Cultural Heritage Administration. (2003, October 8). First batch of famous historical and cultural towns (villages) in China. Retrieved from http://www.mohurd.gov.cn/wjfb/200611/t20061101_157345.html

[30] Ministry of Housing and Urban-Rural Construction of the People's Republic of China, Ministry of Culture and Tourism of the People's Republic of China, National Cultural Heritage Administration, & Ministry of Finance of the People's Republic of China. (2012, August 22). Notice on the Evaluation and identification index system of traditional villages (Trial). Retrieved from http://www.mohurd.gov.cn/wjfb/201208/t20120831_211267.html

[31] Wang, Y., Zhang, Y., & Han, L. (2014). The Pattern Language and Its Application in Meso- and Micro scale Eco-interface. Chinese Landscape Architecture, 30(9), 46-50.

[32] Xie, F. (2016). Digital Image Processing and Application (2nd ed.). Beijing: Publishing House of Electronics Industry.

[33] Sun, J. (2005). Image analysis. Beijing: Science Press.

[34] Spirn, A. W. (2016). The Language of Landscape. Landscape Architecture Frontiers, 4(6), 20-27.

本文引用格式 / PLEASE CITE THIS ARTICLE AS

Yin, Y., Shao, Y., Xue, Z., Thwaites, K., & Zhang, K. (2020). An Explorative Study on the Identification and Evaluation of Restorative Streetscape Elements. Landscape Architecture Frontiers, 8(4), 76-89. https://doi.org/10.15302/J-LAF-0-020005

https://doi.org/10.15302/J-LAF-0-020005 收稿时间 RECEIVED DATE / 2020-04-08 中图分类号 / TU984 文献标识码 / A

疗愈性街景元素识别与评价研究

AN EXPLORATIVE STUDY ON THE IDENTIFICATION AND EVALUATION OF RESTORATIVE STREETSCAPE ELEMENTS

殷雨婷
英国谢菲尔德大学景观建筑系博士候选人、社会空间城市主义研究中心成员

邵钰涵*
同济大学建筑与城市规划学院景观学系、上海市城市更新及其空间优化技术重点实验室助理教授，英国谢菲尔德大学社会空间城市主义研究中心成员

薛贞颖
同济大学建筑与城市规划学院景观学系硕士研究生

凯文 · 斯韦茨
英国谢菲尔德大学景观建筑系高级讲师、社会空间城市主义研究中心联合创始人

张克新
山东省烟台市城市规划编研中心高级工程师

YIN Yuting
PhD Candidate at Department of Landscape Architecture and Member of Socio-spatial Urbanism Unit (SsUU), The University of Sheffield

SHAO Yuhan
Assistant Professor at Department of Landscape Studies, College of Architecture and Urban Planning and Shanghai Key Laboratory of Urban Renewal and Spatial Optimization Technology, Tongji University; Member of Socio-spatial Urbanism Unit (SsUU), The University of Sheffield

XUE Zhenying
Master Student at Department of Landscape Studies, College of Architecture and Urban Planning, Tongji University

Kevin THWAITES
Senior Lecturer at Department of Landscape Architecture and Founder and Co-Leader of Socio-spatial Urbanism Unit (SsUU), The University of Sheffield

ZHANG Kexin
Senior Engineer at Development and Research Center on Urban Planning in Yantai, Shandong Province

*通讯作者
地址：上海市杨浦区四平路1239号同济大学建筑与城市规划学院
邮编：200092
邮箱：shaoyuhan@tongji.edu.cn

摘要

街道作为一种重要的城市公共空间，疗愈潜能是其社会价值的体现之一。本研究从注意力恢复理论出发，以其提出的疗愈性环境的4个特征因子——“远离性”“延展性”“迷人性”“兼容性”为依据，阐明了街道空间具有疗愈性对于高密度城市环境中居民的重要意义。研究通过将传统的疗愈性量表问卷与移动式眼动仪相结合，了解使用者在城市街道环境中能够获得的疗愈性体验，并识别出与疗愈性相关的街景元素，用以探究不同元素对人们疗愈性体验的影响程度。研究结果表明，“绿植”“人”“汽车”等是显著影响街道使用者疗愈体验的街景元素。此外，不同街景元素对疗愈环境4个特征因子的影响程度也不尽相同，如：对于远离性、延展性和迷人性三个维度来说，“绿植”的影响最为重要；而对于兼容性维度来说，“人”是核心影响因素。研究结果可为归纳提升街道疗愈性的设计导则提供参考，并帮助专业人员依据不同类型街道的疗愈性侧重点制定具有针对性的设计改善思路。

关键词

疗愈性；街景元素；感知评价量表；移动式眼动仪；注意力恢复理论

ABSTRACT

The street is a type of important urban public space with multiple social values, one of which is the restorative potential. Based on the "being-away," "extent," "fascination," and "compatibility" constructs of restorative environments proposed by the Attention Recovery Theory, this study elaborated the significance of restorativeness provided by street environments to people living in high-density cities. It used the traditional restorativeness scale with mobile eye trackers to explore the restorative experience provided by an urban street, and identified the specific streetscape elements related to restorativeness and the degree of their influences. The results show that "greenery," "people," and "cars" perform significant influences, and different streetscape elements have different degrees of influences on the 4 constructs of the restorative environment. For example, for the"being-away," "extent," and "fascination" constructs, the influence of "greenery" is the most important, while "people" plays the core role in "compatibility." The findings can help professionals develop targeted design strategies to improve diverse street environments for a better restorativeness.

KEYWORDS

Restorativeness; Streetscape Elements; Perception Evaluation Scale; Mobile Eye Tracker; Attention Recovery Theory

基金项目
国家自然科学基金青年科学基金项目“城市自然景观视觉舒适度感应机理研究”（编号：51808393）
国家自然科学基金面上项目“城市景观视觉空间网络感应机理与评价”（编号：51678417）

RESEARCH FUNDS
Urban Natural Landscape Visual Comfort Mechanism Research, Youth Program of National Nature Science Foundation of China (No. 51808393)
Urban Landscape Visual Spaces Network Perception and Reaction Assessment, General Program of National Nature Science Foundation of China (No. 51678417)

编辑 王胤瑜 田乐 **翻译** 张健 王胤瑜 王颖 田乐
EDITED BY WANG Yinyu Tina TIAN **TRANSLATED BY** Angus ZHANG WANG Yinyu WANG Ying Tina TIAN

1 引言

通常而言，自然环境能够带来疗愈体验，但高密度城市的空间及资源供给极大限制了城市居民与自然环境的接触。对于高密度城市空间营造而言，在日常场景中满足居民的疗愈性体验需求比为其提供前往郊野的机会更为重要。街道是人们在“外界”生活的主要空间载体[1]~[3]，利用街道环境为人们提供短暂而多次的疗愈体验显然更加实际。因此，街道环境中任何可能通过设计手段赋予或增强的疗愈潜能，对塑造有利于健康的城市环境都有着巨大的价值。上海是中国典型的高密度城市，人口规模庞大，城市资源紧张。依托城市支路形成的丰富多样的街道空间[4][5]具备为居民提供便捷、连续的疗愈体验的潜力。研究选取上海市杨浦区支路国康路作为研究对象，通过问卷调查和眼动追踪相结合的方法，探究了影响行人在街道环境中获得疗愈性体验的街景元素，以寻求通过设计手段提升街道环境疗愈性的方法。

2 城市街景疗愈性

2.1 相关理论发展

疗愈环境理论起源于环境心理学，侧重于探究能够帮助人们恢复在日常生活工作中消耗的心理、生理和社会资源的特定环境体验及特征[6]~[8]。早期的疗愈环境理论研究普遍认为，即使仅与自然环境进行极短的接触或仅向窗外眺望自然景色，也能够帮助人们提升注意力[9]~[11]，改善情绪和精神状态[12]~[14]，从而显著提升认知能力、改善行为表现[15]~[20]。为将人们在环境中获得的疗愈性体验应用于以疗愈为导向的环境设计，诸多学者曾尝试建立标准化的疗愈性评价方法[11][21][22]。这些研究大多以疗愈环境的心理学构成为基础构建多维度心理学量表，通过问卷获得使用者对环境疗愈性的评价。蕾切尔与斯蒂芬·卡普兰提出的聚焦于注意力衰竭的“注意力恢复理论”（ART）[15][17]和罗杰·S·乌尔里希[16]~[18]提出的聚焦于生理和情绪的负面变化的“压力舒缓理论”是两大主流疗愈环境理论（图1）。其中，ART所总结的疗愈环境的4个特征因子——远离性、延展性、迷人性和兼容性，成为了构建疗愈性评价量表的主要理论支撑[15]，相关量表包括疗愈感知量表[22]和疗愈

1 Introduction

Natural environment can bring restorative experience, which is, however, usually limited to the residents in high-density cities. In this sense, it is more important for space making to help people get “healed” in urban spaces within dense built environments rather than in suburbs. Streets, as primary places for daily outdoor activities[1]~[3], may offer temporary yet repeatable restorative experiences through design interventions, which contribute largely to shaping a healthy urban environment. As a typical high-density city in China, Shanghai sees such potential in its urban street system of diverse spatial experiences[4][5] that may create convenient and continuous restorative benefits for people. Focusing on the Guokang Road in Yangpu District of Shanghai, this study used questionnaire survey with eye tracking technology to identify streetscape elements that influence the restorative experience of pedestrians, so as to provide evidence for streetscape design for restorativeness improvement.

2 Restorativeness of Urban Streetscapes

2.1 Theoretical Development

Originating from Environmental Psychology, theories of restorative environments mainly focus on probing into specific environmental experiences and features that help with the recovery of humans’ psychological, physiological, and social resources from daily exhaustion[6]~[8]. Early research commonly found that even spending a little time in the nature or just looking at natural scenes through a window can help recover humans’ attention[9]~[11] and improve emotional and mental state[12]~[14], significantly enhancing cognitive competence and ameliorating behaviors[15]~[20]. In order to leverage such benefits to guide the environmental design for restorativeness improvement, scholars have established standardized methods to evaluate restorativeness[11][21][22]. Most of these studies employed multi-dimensional psychological scales based on psychological constructs of restorative environments to evaluate people’s recovery through questionnaire surveys. There have been two mainstream theories of restorative environments: Attention Restoration Theory (ART)[15][17] proposed by Rachel and Stephen Kaplan and focusing on attention fatigue, and the Stress Reduction Framework proposed by Roger S. Ulrich[16]~[18] and focusing on physiology and emotion decline (Fig. 1). Particularly, the former summarizes 4 constructs of restorative environments, namely being-away, extent, fascination, and compatibility, which have become the theoretical foundation for restorativeness evaluation scales[15], including the Perceived Restorativeness

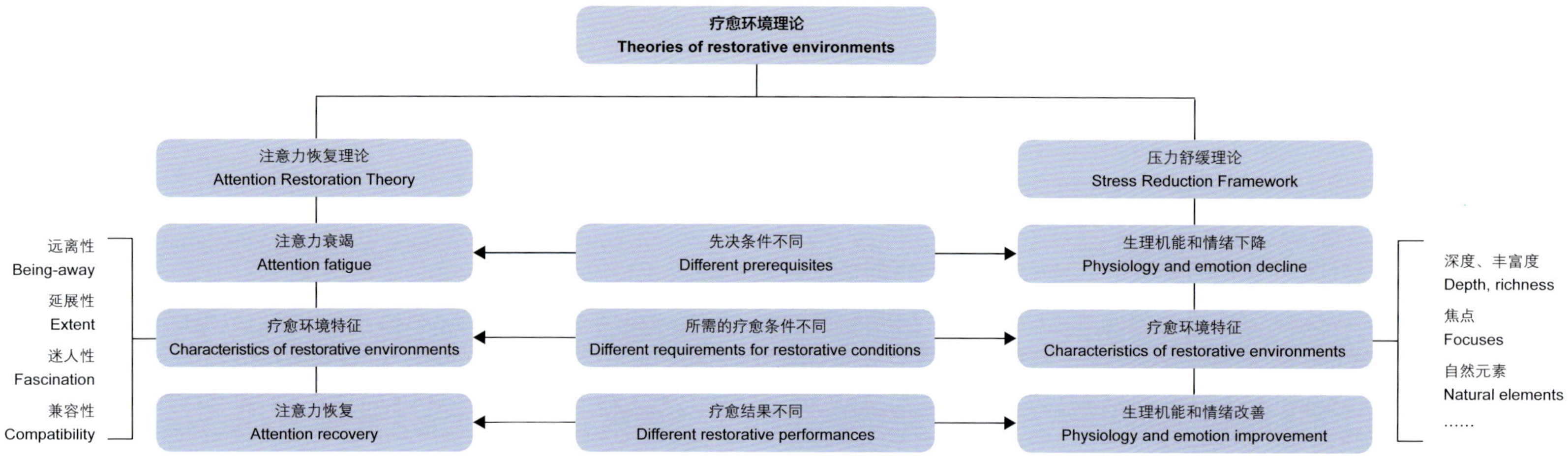

1

因子量表（RCS）[11]等。值得注意的是，此类量表多以数字量化评价被试者的心理状态[23]，单纯使用这些量表无法识别出与疗愈性相关的具体环境特征。

近年来，在城市化的影响下，越来越多的研究开始探索建成环境中自然元素的疗愈潜能[24]~[27]。已有研究表明，疗愈性环境不必同时具备ART的4个特征因子[28]；经过精心设计的具有这些特征因子的街道[29]、广场[30]等城市空间同样能够提供疗愈性体验[31][32]。相较于公园、广场等公共场所，尽管人们在街道上停留的时间通常较短，但使用街道的频率却明显更高。国外针对街景开展的疗愈性研究发现，街道两侧的建筑越高，且街道熵值（街道环境中各元素的混乱度）越大，人们获得疗愈性体验的可能性越小[33]。此外，行道树及种植池数量的增加也能显著提高街道的疗愈潜能[29]。然而，由于街道环境的复杂性，这类评价研究多针对建筑物、行道树等特定街景元素或沿街界面延伸性、复杂性和天际线变化等特定街道环境特征展开，未能对街景元素进行系统的考量。

2.2 疗愈性评价方法回顾

早期的景观视觉评价大多以图片、视频、三维立体模型或虚拟现实场景等作为视觉媒介[34]，要求参与者以偏好排序[35]、打分[36]等形式进行评估。但无论是图像还是模型，都可能因为缺乏真实感[37]而影响评价

Scale[22] and the Restorative Component Rating Scale (RCS)[11]. However, these tools can be hardly used to identify specific environmental features related to restorativeness as they quantify merely the restorativeness perception of the participants[23].

The process of urbanization has encouraged more and more studies in recent years to explore the restorative potential of natural elements in built environments[24]~[27]. Some suggest that a restorative environment does not always satisfy all the 4 constructs of ART[28]. Moreover, urban spaces such as streets[29] and squares[30] that are designed of these constructs can provide restorative experience[31][32]. As frequently used places in people's everyday life, streets are designed for passing through—in comparison to other types of urban spaces (e.g. parks and squares) to stay in. Studies on restorative streetscapes proved that people's restorative experience correlates negatively with the height of buildings in the streets and the street's entropy value (describing the disorder of a street environment)[33], while positively with the quantity of street trees and planting beds[29]. However, street environment is complex. Existing research mainly focuses on individual streetscape elements (buildings, street trees, etc.) or street characteristics (extensibility, complexity, and skyline changeability of the street interface, etc.), and efforts that systematically examines all the streetscape elements are absent.

2.2 A Review on Methods of Restorativeness Evaluation

Most early research performed visual evaluation of landscapes via images, videos, 3D models, or VR scenes[34],

1. 两种主流的疗愈环境理论

1. Two mainstream theories of restorative environment

结果的准确性。近年来飞速发展的眼动追踪技术能够通过捕捉人眼球的注视点和运动轨迹，有效地建立视觉感知与环境中特定媒介之间的联系[38]-[40]，为突破这一局限性提供了技术基础。学界已有充足证据表明，人们对环境的视觉偏好与环境疗愈性密切相关[11][31][41]，注视时长与视觉偏好的正相关性[42]-[44]则引导学者们进一步探索眼动仪在ART相关研究中的应用。他们尝试运用眼动追踪技术捕捉疗愈性环境中人们注视点的运动轨迹，以注视频次表征视觉偏好，由此发掘与疗愈性相关的环境元素[11][31][41]-[44]。例如，丽塔·博托等人发现疗愈性不同的环境会引发不同的眼球运动模式[41]；此后又有研究在探寻小型城市公共空间中与疗愈性相关的景观元素时，进一步证实了眼动仪所记录的高频注视点与对应元素的疗愈性之间的关系[45]。

3 研究方法

为了在真实环境中系统地理解疗愈感知和街景元素之间的关系，本研究尝试在已有方法的基础上，将基于疗愈性评价量表的定性方法与基于眼动追踪技术的定量方法结合使用。已有研究认为，当使用疗愈性评价量表来调查人们的疗愈感知时，人们大脑对量表问题的思考将会带动眼球运动[46]-[48]，而该过程中眼动仪捕捉到的注视点即可表征街道环境中与疗愈性有关的街景元素。

3.1 主观疗愈性感知评价——问卷调查法

本研究选取卡琳·劳曼等人[11]制定的RCS作为主观疗愈性感知的评价工具。验证性因子分析结果表明，相较于其他基于ART的疗愈性量表，RCS的因子结构与ART提出的疗愈环境特征因子更为贴合，且描述ART4个特征因子的措辞方式一致，更加有利于人们理解量表含义，作出准确评价。

问卷第一部分在原RCS基础上略作修改，保留了其中15项适用于街道环境评价的问题，分别评价ART提出的4个疗愈环境特征因子（表1），被试者用0~6分来描述每个问题与自身实际感知的相符程度，完

where the evaluations were based on participants' preference ranking[35] and scoring[36]. However, the lack of authenticity of such visual media might lead to a low accuracy of evaluation[37]. In recent years, this problem has been addressed by the advance of eye tracking technology which helps discover the relations between visual perception and specific environmental agencies by capturing the fixation points and movement tracks of eyes[38]-[40]. It has widely evidenced that human's visual preference is closely related to the restorativeness of environment[11][31][41], and the fixation duration positively correlates to visual preference[42]-[44] that inspires scholars to further use eye trackers in ART-based research. By capturing the movement track of fixation point and taking the fixation frequency to indicate the viewer's visual preference, the environmental elements related to restorativeness can be identified[11][31][41]-[44]. For example, Rita Berto et al. found that environments with varied level of restorativeness may result in different eye movements[41]. Other researchers confirmed the correlations between high-frequency fixation points recorded by eye trackers and the restorativeness of corresponding landscape elements[45] in small urban spaces.

3 Study Methods

This study explores the relations between restorativeness perception and streetscape elements in the real world by adopting both qualitative and quantitative methods—utilizing a restorativeness evaluation scale supported by eye tracking technology. This is based on the prerequisite that when people are working on questions of a scale, their thinking would stimulate the eye movements[46]-[48] and the fixation points captured by the eye tracker can be considered the restorative streetscape elements in the environment.

3.1 Self-Reporting Evaluation on Restorativeness Perception with Questionnaire

This study employed the RCS developed by Karin Laumann et al.[11] to evaluate the restorativeness perception, because confirmatory factor analysis has proved that the factor structure of RCS better echoes the 4 constructs in ART. Besides, RCS adopts a consistent wording in describing the 4 constructs, which helps participants better understand the meaning of scale questions for a higher accuracy of evaluation.

The questionnaire used in this study consisted of 2 parts: the first part adapted 15 questions of the original RCS that are

表1：本研究中使用的疗愈因子量表
Table 1: The restorative component scale used in this study

疗愈环境特征因子 Constructs of a restorative environment	疗愈性因子评价问题 Evaluation questions to each restorative construct	
远离性（B） Being-away (B)	B1	这里让我能够暂时忘记工作和日常的生活中的烦恼。 When I am here I feel free from work and daily routine.
	B2	这里让我能够暂时忘记他人的要求和期望带来的压力。 When I am here I feel free from other people's demand and expectations.
	B3	这里让我能够暂时忘记所承担的责任与义务。 When I am here I do not need to think of my responsibilities and obligations.
延展性（E） Extent (E)	E1	这里的所有东西都是互相联系的。 The elements here go together.
	E2	这里的所有东西都很好地融入环境之中。 The existing elements belong to here.
	E3	周围的环境整体上是连贯的。 The surroundings are coherent.
迷人性（F） Fascination (F)	F1	这里有很多我想要探索的东西。 There is plenty to discover here.
	F2	这里有很多令我感到好奇的东西。 This setting has many things that I wonder about.
	F3	这里有很多吸引我的东西。 There are many objects here that attract my attention.
	F4	这里有许多事物使我流连忘返。 There is plenty that I want to linger on here.
	F5	我感到深深地沉浸在周围的环境中。 I am absorbed in these surroundings.
兼容性（C） Compatibility (C)	C1	这里让我有机会去做我喜欢做的事情。 The environment gives me the opportunity to do what I like.
	C2	我能够解决在这里出现的问题。 I can handle the kinds of problems that arise here.
	C3	我能够很快地适应周围的环境。 I rapidly adapt to this setting.
	C4	我想做的事情能够在这一环境中得到实现。 There is an accordance between what I like to do and this environment.

注
量表内容改编自参考文献[11]。

NOTE
The scale is adapted from Ref. [11].

全不符为0分，完全符合为6分；第二部分采集了参与者的性别、年龄及专业背景等个人信息。

3.2 客观疗愈性街景元素识别——眼动追踪技术

研究采用由同济大学人因智能与环境行为实验中心提供的Tobii Pro Glass 2移动式眼动仪捕捉被试者的眼球运动轨迹，所采集的数据包括动

applicable to streetscape evaluation, corresponding to the 4 constructs in ART (Table 1). Participants were required to score the consistency degree of the description in each question to their own perception with 0 ~ 6 points: 0 means not consistent at all and 6 points means totally consistent; and the second part collected participants' personal information, including gender, age, and occupation / profession.

3.2 Identification of Restorative Streetscape Elements with Eye Tracking Technology

The study employed the Tobii Pro Glass 2 mobile eye tracker provided by the Experimental Center of Ergonomical Intelligence

2. 视频图像经过语义分割后进行注视点匹配
3. 研究方法框架

2. Semantic segmentation and fixation point match of the video images
3. The study method framework

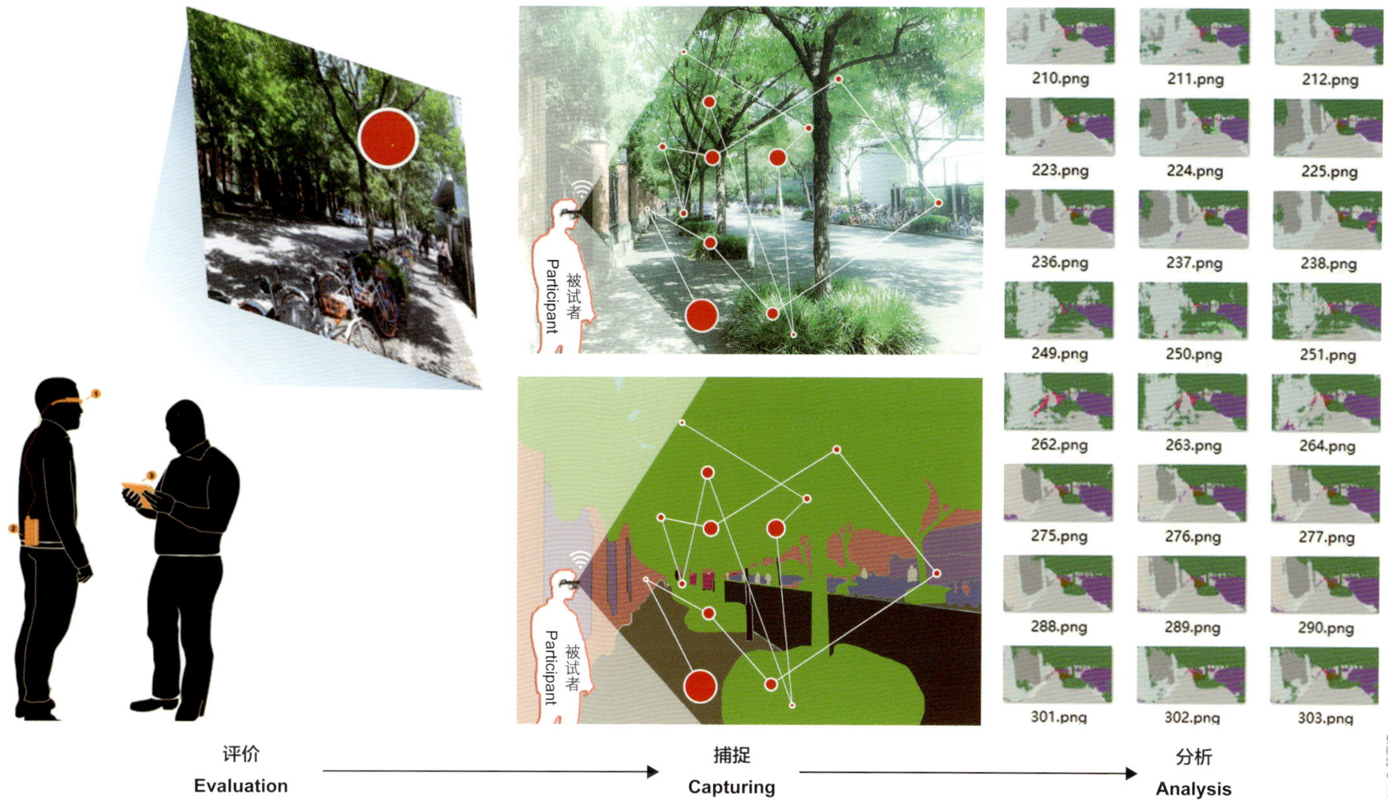

2

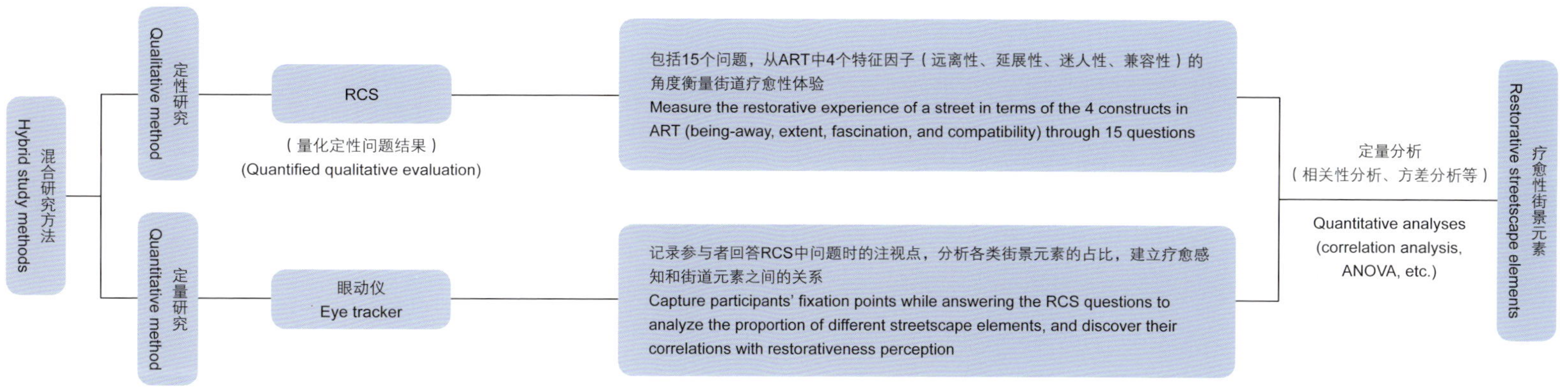

3

态视频及带有坐标和时间信息的注视点。研究采用基于机器学习的图像语义分割技术，将视频输出为图像后进行画面分割，再与注视点的坐标进行匹配，找到每一帧画面中参与者注视的环境元素（图2）；随后将上述匹配结果与RCS中疗愈性问题的评价结果进行比对分析，了解在参与者回答有关街道疗愈性问题的过程中各类街景元素被注视的累积频次，其中的高频注视点即可表征研究环境中与疗愈性密切相关的街景元素[11][31][41]-[44]（图3）。

and Environmental Behavior of Tongji University to collect data of eye movement tracks, including videos and fixation points with location and time information. The collected videos were first framed into images for semantic segmentation by machine learning. Then the results were matched with the coordinates of the fixation points to locate the environmental elements that the participant looked at (Fig. 2). These elements were further compared with the evaluation results of the RCS to calculate the cumulative fixation frequency of each type of element. The elements of higher fixation frequency were considered the restorative components within the investigated environment[11][31][41]-[44] (Fig. 3).

© 殷雨婷
4

3.3 确定研究地点

由于目前在真实场景中综合运用问卷调查和眼动追踪技术的研究较少，结合单次问卷调查所需时长（3~5分钟），研究宜选择长度为300~1 000m，具有明确的起、终点，两侧沿街界面功能类型明确、元素组成较为简单的街道环境进行实验。国康路两侧主要为教育科研机构与行政办公场所，是一条以通勤功能为主的城市支路（图4），长约720m，全程步行约需8分钟；沿街界面主要由植被和围栏构成，中段毗邻少量店铺（与路面之间有绿篱分隔），界面构成较为均质。根据沿路公交站点的分布位置，结合街道两侧的建筑功能及前期的场地调研分析，最终选择人群出现较为频繁的区域作为实验路段。该路段涵盖

3.3 Research Site Selection

Due to a lack of reference adopting similar methods, this study proposed its own metrics in research site selection—a street of 300 ~ 1,000 meters (considering that the participants should finish the questionnaire in 3 ~ 5 minutes), with clear starting and end points, and the types and elements of frontage can be easily identified. The Guokang Road was selected: as a commuting urban street along which there are a number of educational, research, and administrative workplaces (Fig. 4), it stretches for 720 meters, taking 8 minutes to walk through, and the streetscape is largely defined by greenery and fences, with a few shops in its middle section (separated from the the lanes by hedges). Further, based on the locations of bus stops and the frontage types along the street, as well as a preliminary site investigation, a 380-meter-long section where the working people visit most frequently was chosen for this experiment. This section covers all typical frontage types of the street, and allows participants to finish the questionnaire while walking through it within 5 minutes (Fig. 5).

3.4 Participant Selection

Participants recruited on-site on Guokang Road for this experiment were workers aged between 25 and 55, who are

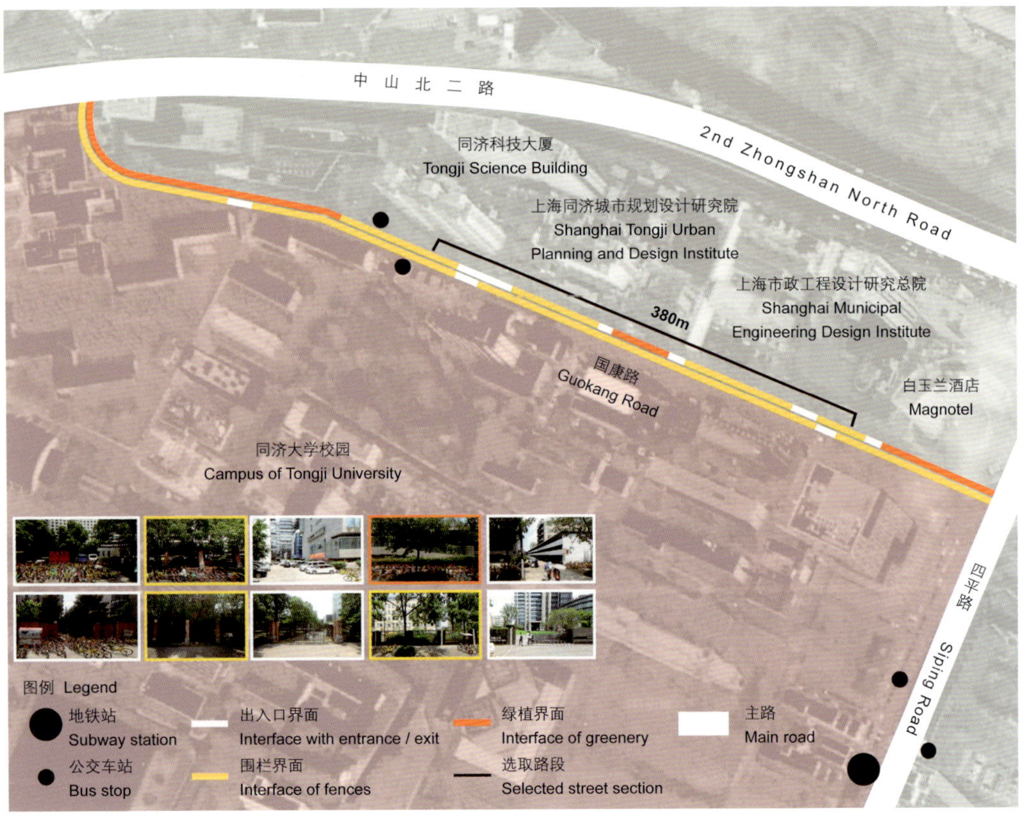

© 殷雨婷
5

4. 国康路实景
5. 研究地点（地图来源：百度地图、百度街景）

4. The real environment of Guokang Road
5. The research site (Map sources: Baidu Map, Baidu Streetscape)

表2：参与者组间差异分析显著性值（n=25）
Table 2: Significance values by ANOVA analyses on the participants (n = 25)

	B1	B2	B3	E1	E2	E3	F1	F2	F3	F4	F5	C1	C2	C3	C4
性别 Gender	0.730	0.884	0.388	0.693	0.513	0.513	0.329	0.950	0.807	0.980	0.489	0.053	0.515	0.880	0.150
年龄 Age	0.497	0.399	0.010	0.268	0.417	0.208	0.896	0.262	0.519	0.259	0.142	0.297	0.350	0.113	0.303
专业背景 Occupational / professional information	0.398	0.987	0.26	0.746	0.284	0.133	0.322	0.653	0.953	0.062	0.263	0.964	0.753	0.693	0.757

整条路段中所有界面种类，具有代表性；长度约380m，步行通过时长与答题时长基本吻合（图5）。

3.4 选择参与者

参与者由研究人员在国康路现场招募，主要为承受较大生活压力、易产生心理疲劳等问题的工作人群（25~55周岁）[50]。因已有研究发现，在保证安全的前提下，人们在独处时获得疗愈体验的可能性更高[51]，本次试验仅选择独自出行者参与。最终共31人参与实验，男性15人，女性16人，其中具有专业背景的（指工作或学习背景与规划、景观和建筑有关）19人。最终筛选出有效样本①29份。

3.5 实验过程

实验于2019年5月6~10日（均为工作日）午休时间（11:00~14:00）展开，实验日天气均温度适宜、无雨且空气质量良好。参与者在佩戴移动式眼动仪后需首先进行校准与行走适应，以保证在正式实验中所收集数据的准确性。校准成功并适应后，被试者以自然状态向前方行走，研究人员随行其后进行RCS的提问，以免进入被试者视线范围。眼动仪从量表提问开始时进行视频录制，结束时终止。

4 数据分析

实验获得的29份RCS问卷数据均通过了内部一致性信度检验[52]。对问卷数据进行组间（性别、年龄及是否具有相关专业背景）差异分析，发现29名被试者在疗愈性体验上不存在感知能力差异，说明数据有效可靠（表2）。眼动仪对29名被试者的眼动捕捉率为2%~90%②，平均值为53%（标准差为28.5%）。结合前人研究经验[53]，将捕捉率低于20%的样本剔除，最终保留有效样本25个。

prone to mental fatigue and pressure[50]. Considering that in a safe environment, people might perceive higher restorativeness when they are alone[51], only single passers-by were selected. In the end, totally 15 males and 16 females participated in the experiment; 19 of them are occupationally / professionally associated with planning, landscape design or architecture. 29 valid samples① were finally collected.

3.5 Experiment Process

The experiment was carried out during lunch hours (11:00 ~ 14:00) from May 6 to 10 (all were working days) in 2019, the weather was sunny with moderate temperature and good air quality. Participants were asked to test and calibrate the eye tracker before the experiment. During the formal measurement, the participants were required to walk casually through the street, accompanied with a researcher asking them the RCS survey questions while walking behind them to avoid visual distractions. The eye tracker started recording videos as the survey began, and ended when it was finished.

4 Data Analyses

The data of the 29 completed RCS questionnaires were verified in internal consistency[52]. The ANOVA analyses (in terms of gender, age, and occupational / professional information) revealed that no difference was found in the competence of restorativeness perception among the participants, proving that the data were valid and reliable (Table 2). The capture ratio for eye movement of the 29 participants ranged from 2% to 90%②, with an average of 53% (SD = 28.5%), and those under 20% were eliminated, referencing previous research[53]. Finally, 25 valid samples were retained.

① 本研究中，“有效样本”指完成了所有量表评价项目且提供了被试者完整背景信息的样本。
② 由于仪器受室外光线及无线信号影响较大，即使经过仪器校准和行走适应，不同被试者的眼动捕捉率仍然可能存在较大差异。

① "Valid samples" in this study are those with completed evaluation results and participants' individual information.
② Despite device calibration and adjustment, the capture ratio for different participants may still vary because the eye trackers are also subject to outdoor light and wireless signals.

表3：实验路段街景疗愈性RCS评价结果（n=25）
Table 3: The evaluation results of RCS on the streetscape restorativeness of the selected section (n = 25)

	远离性（B） Being-away (B)			延展性（E） Extent (E)			迷人性（F） Fascination (F)					兼容性（C） Compatibility (C)			
	B1	B2	B3	E1	E2	E3	F1	F2	F3	F4	F5	C1	C2	C3	C4
子特征因子平均得分 Mean score of each sub-construct	3.24	3.32	2.60	4.48	4.16	3.44	2.60	2.72	3.04	2.84	3.16	3.48	4.12	4.84	3.80
特征因子平均得分 Mean score of each construct	3.05			4.03			2.87					4.06			

6. 各街景元素对应的注视累积频次占比

6. The percentage of the cumulative fixation frequency for each streetscape element

4.1 选取路段街景的疗愈性

问卷结果（表3）显示，被试者对选取路段现状街道环境的疗愈性评价适中（总平均分3.50分），4个特征因子中远离性（3.05分）和迷人性（2.87分）得分低于延展性（4.03分）和兼容性（4.06分）得分。选取路段是一条主要服务于周边工作人群的通勤道路，与工作紧密相关是导致环境远离性得分较低的主要原因，这一点在B3项的评价结果（2.60分）上体现得尤其明显。迷人性因子的5个评价小项均得分偏低，特别是对街道环境的好奇心（F1项，2.60分）和探索欲（F2项，2.72分）的评价。这是由于国康路两侧界面形式较为单一，缺少沿街店铺、特色景观等可供注视、停留或进行其他活动的界面，故而对行人的吸引力有限。

4.1 Restorativeness of the Streetscape of the Selected Section

The questionnaire results (Table 3) showed that the participants' evaluation on the restorativeness of the street section was moderate (with an overall average of 3.50 points). Among the 4 constructs, "being-away" (3.05 points) and "fascination" (2.87 points) scored lower than "extent" (4.03 points) and "compatibility" (4.06 points). The low score in "being-away" may result from that the street is surrounded by workplaces and the walking might evoke the participants' commuting and working experience, especially affected their scoring in the sub-construct associated with "responsibility and obiligation" (B3, 2.60 points). In addition, the scores of all the 5 sub-constructs in "fascination" were low—particularly in "curiosity to the street environment" (F1, 2.60 points) and "desire to explore the environment" (F2, 2.72 points)—because the monotonous streetscape of the selected section less encouraged the participants to look at or stay in.

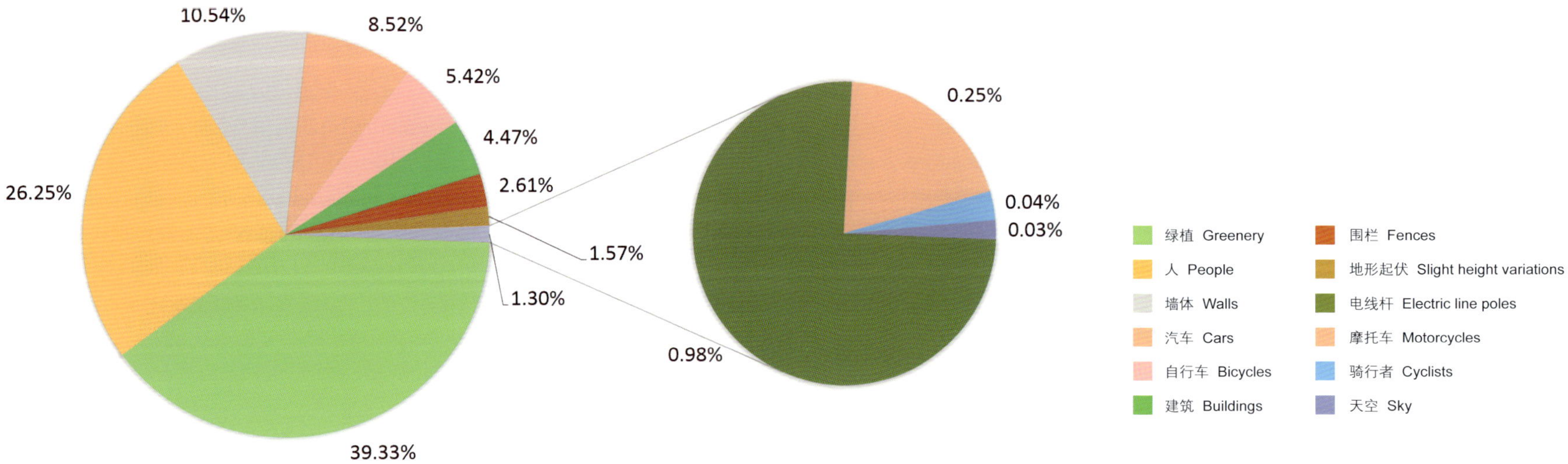

7. 各特征因子评价过程中各类街景元素的注视频次占比

7. The percentage of fixation frequency for each streetscape element during the evaluation of each construct

③ 根据语义分割技术所依据的训练模型分类标准，此处的“人”专指街道空间中未使用交通工具，或站立或行走或坐的人，故而与“骑行者”为两类不同的街景元素。

③ According to the classification standard of the training model used in semantic segmentation, "people" here refers to people standing, walking, or sitting. "People" and "cyclists" thus are two different types of streetscape elements.

4.2 疗愈性街景元素的识别

根据眼动仪所记录的注视点坐标信息将其在视频帧画面中定位，经语义分割并剔除占画面面积比例过大的“道路”与“人行道”元素后，得到12类与疗愈体验相关的街景元素（图6）。结果显示，被试者在进行疗愈性评价时，注视“绿植”的百分比最高（39.33%），其次为“人”[③]（26.25%）、“墙体”（10.54%）、“汽车”（8.52%）、“自行车”（5.42%）、“建筑”（4.47%）、“围栏”（2.61%）及“地形起伏”（1.57%）等，说明实验路段内“绿植”“人”“墙体”是对疗愈性体验影响最大的三类街景元素。

4.3 街景元素对疗愈环境特征因子的影响机制

研究人员按照被试者回答量表中4个特征因子相关问题的起止时间将视频切割为4段，对每一时间段中各类街景元素的注视频次进行统计，以进一步探索影响每个特征因子的街景元素及具体的影响机制。结果显示，各类街景元素对各因子的影响程度存在差异（图7）。其中，在评价远离性、延展性和迷人性的过程中，“绿植”的注视

4.2 Identification of Restorative Streetscape Elements

With coordinates recorded by the eye tracker, the fixation points were positioned in each video frame, and 12 types of streetscape elements related to people's restorative experience were identified through semantic segmentation and by screening out "road" and "sidewalks"—they took a larger proportion in the whole image that might impact the results (Fig. 6). The results showed that the top 3 elements that participants looked at were "greenery" (39.33%), "people"[③] (26.25%), and "walls" (10.54%), followed by "cars" (8.52%), "bicycles" (5.42%), "buildings" (4.47%), "fences" (2.61%), and "slight height variations" (1.57%).

4.3 Influencing Mechanism of Streetscape Elements on Restorative Constructs

The researchers divided each video into 4 segments by the participants' evaluation to each construct, and audited the percentage of fixation frequency for each streetscape element in each segment, in order to identify the influencing elements to each construct and the corresponding mechanism. The results showed a significant variety in the influence degree (Fig. 7):

频次占比依次为33.19%、42.61%和43.03%，在所有元素中最高，是影响这三个因子的最主要的街景元素；但对于兼容性，“人”（占比31.57%）的影响则比“绿植”（占比27.18%）更大，这主要是由于兼容性衡量的是街道环境对人们需求的满足程度，进行必要的社交活动是人的一种内在需求，而社会交往则是街道空间承载的主要功能之一[54]。“墙体”“建筑”“围栏”元素在远离性评价中的注视频次占比明显高于其他三个因子，这是由于选取路段两侧多为透绿性较高的栅栏围墙，且其中一侧为校园内的红砖建筑，外观优美且具有年代感；校园作为与人们的特殊记忆或情感密切相关的一类场所[55]，也能够激发已步入社会的工作人群的回忆和遐想。此外，“汽车”“自行车”两类元素在延展性评价中的注视频次占比之和较其它三个因子显著增加。结合延展性因子中包含的连贯性和范围两个子因子[56]可以推测，“汽车”“自行车”为暂时存在的通过性元素，会影响街道环境内部元素之间的协调性，从而影响人们的疗愈性感知[57]。

4.4 疗愈性街景元素影响的正负性

利用SPSS 26.0软件对疗愈性感知评价结果与对应的注视点元素百分比进行皮尔逊相关性分析，以正、负相关性表征各街景元素对环境疗愈性感知的促进或遏制影响，发现“地形起伏”及“绿植”能够促进被试者获得疗愈性体验；“自行车”“围栏”“建筑”“墙体”“骑行者”“汽车”元素会不同程度地阻碍被试者获得疗愈性体验（表4）。对比图6的结果可知，在注视频次占比较高的几类元素中，“人”与任何疗愈性因子的正、负相关性皆不显著。部分已有的实证研究表明，对于环境中“人”这一元素的疗愈性与被评价的环境是否安全有关，在保证安全的前提下，被试者在人少的环境中能够获得更好的疗愈体验[51][58][59]；同时，也有研究认为被试者本身的性格会影响他们对环境中“人”这一要素及疗愈性体验的感知[59]。此外，相关性分析中出现的“骑行者”（对B2有促进作用，对E3有阻碍作用）却并非本次实验中注视频次较高的街景元素。

“greenery” was the most frequently recorded fixation element during the evaluation of “being-away” (33.19%), “extent” (42.61%), and “fascination” (43.03%), showing the highest effect on restorativeness. For the construct of “compatibility,” “people” (31.57%) was more important than “greenery” (27.18%), because “compatibility” measures the satisfaction degree of a street environment to people’s needs, and streets are main places accommodating citizens’ social interactions[54]. “Walls,” “buildings,” and “fences” were the most influencing elements to the constructs “being-away,” because the greenery can be seen through the fencing-walls along the selected section; besides, a group of red-brick college buildings on the one side are distinctively attractive, which can arouse the working group’s memories and affections to their school life[55]. The sum percentage of fixation frequency of “cars” and “bicycles” increased significantly during the evaluation of “extent” compared with the other 3 constructs. This is because according to the connectedness and scope defined as 2 sub-items of “extent”[56], “cars” and “bicycles” are “passing-through” elements that temporarily occur in a streetscape and may decrease the participants’ restorativeness perception of the streetscape[57].

4.4 The Positive and Negative Effects of Restorative Streetscape Elements

Assisted with SPSS 26.0, the Pearson correlation analysis between the evaluation results and the proportion of fixation frequency of each element revealed the positive or negative effects on restorativeness perception. Results showed that “slight height variations” and “greenery” would help augment participants’ restorative experience, while “bicycles,” “fences,” “buildings,” “walls,” “cyclists,” and “cars” would decline such an experience to varying extents (Table 4). Compared with the other elements with high fixation frequency shown in Figure 6, the element of “people” presented neither evident positive nor negative correlation with any construct, which might be explained by different evidences by existing empirical studies: some argue that the restorativeness perception on “people” depends mainly on whether the investigated environment is safe—being in a safe environment, the participant can get better restorative experience when the place is less crowded[51][58][59]; others hold that the characters of participants determine their perception of “people,” which would influence their restorative experience in the environment[59]. For another interesting finding, “cyclists,” though positively correlating to “pressure from others’ demands and expectations” (B2) and negatively to “continuous environment” (E3), did not get a high fixation frequency in this experiment.

表4：与实验路段街道环境疗愈性显著相关的街景元素（n=25）
Table 4: The streetscape elements with significant correlation to the restorativeness of the selected section (n = 25)

	地形起伏 Slight height variations	绿植 Greenery	自行车 Bicycles	围栏 Fences	建筑 Buildings	墙体 Walls	骑行者 Cyclists	汽车 Cars
促进的疗愈性因子（正相关） Promoted sub-constructs (positive correlated)	B1 (0.013)	B1 (0.043)	—	—	—	—	B2 (0.032)	—
阻碍的疗愈性因子（负相关） Inhibited sub-constructs (negatively correlated)	—	—	E1 (0.003), E2 (0.000)	E1 (0.004), E2 (0.011)	F1 (0.018), F2 (0.016), F4 (0.020), E3 (0.038)	C2 (0.038), C3 (0.011)	E3 (0.017)	F1 (0.040)

注
p=0.05；括号内数字为相关性分析显著性值。

NOTE
p = 0.05; the given figures in the brackets are the significance values of sub-constructs.

5 结论与讨论

街道环境的疗愈潜力近年来已逐渐受到业界学者的关注[29][33]，但对疗愈性元素的系统性研究一直较为缺乏。考虑到当前高密度城市发展语境中人们对于日常疗愈环境的迫切需求，本研究探索了城市街道这一日常空间的疗愈性，并通过定性与定量结合的方式建立了抽象的疗愈性感知与具象的街道元素之间的联系，为以提升街景疗愈性为目的的设计提供了思路。

研究结果发现，“绿植”是人们在进行疗愈性评价时关注最多的街景元素，表明“绿植”对于街道环境的疗愈性具有重要贡献，这一点与已有研究[8]-[11]所证明的绿色自然元素的显著疗愈功能相一致。进一步的分析表明，不同街景元素对ART中4个特征因子影响的重要程度及机制不尽相同。例如，“绿植”对远离性、迷人性和延展性三个因子的核心影响、“人”对兼容性的重要影响，以及“汽车”的影响在延展性因子评价中的增强等都揭示了规划设计能够介入的环节和手段，也为制定针对性的疗愈性街景设计提供了实证依据。

然而，因目前聚焦于街道环境的研究较少，且“问卷调查+眼动追踪”的方法仅能识别出街道的内容元素，无法识别其特征属性（如

5 Conclusion and Discussion

In recent years, the restorative potential of street environment has attracted increasing attention of the academia[29][33], but systematic research on the restorative elements is absent. In response to the urgent needs of daily restorative environment against the current backdrop of high-density urban development, this study attempted to examine the restorativeness of urban streets as an everyday place for citizens, and explored the relations between the intangible restorativeness perception and the tangible streetscape elements by combining qualitative and quantitative methods, so as to inspire design practices to improve the restorativeness of streetscapes.

The study found that “greenery” was the focal streetscape element when participants were evaluating the restorativeness, indicating that “greenery” played an important role in providing restorative experience within streetscapes, corroborating the significant restorativeness of green natural elements proved in previous studies[8]-[11]. Further analyses in this study manifested that the importance and influential mechanism of different streetscape elements on the 4 ART constructs varied, including the significant influence of “greenery” on “being-away,” “fascination,” and “extent,” the influence of “people” on “compatibility,” and the increasing influence of “cars” on “extent” and “compatibility.” All these findings may support landscape planning and design practices with an empirical basis for targeted restorativeness in specific cases.

However, except for “greenery,” “people,” and “cars,” there has been no existing research paying attention to the other 9 elements or drawing similar conclusions to this study. This may be due to the lack of existing research on the street environment,

复杂度、开阔度等[33][61][62]），导致除“绿植”“人”“汽车”外，未能在已有研究中发现有关其他9类街景元素的类似结论。因此，应在未来的研究中进一步探索建立既包含内容元素又涵盖特征属性的街景疗愈性评估框架。未来研究亦可采用除RCS以外的基于其他理论基础的量表，以丰富街景疗愈性的内涵。同时，鉴于“问卷调查+眼动追踪”的混合研究方法能在主观感知和客观环境之间构建联系，也可灵活运用于其他环境心理学研究。

另一方面，本研究在方法和技术上仍存在不足之处，有待在后续研究中改进。研究选取路段为通勤类街道，两侧界面的功能、形式均质单一，元素构成较为简单；由于被试者的疗愈感知会随着街道功能（如商业街、景观街等）和特征的变化而变化，因此研究使用的疗愈性量表中4个特征因子影响疗愈性体验的重要程度也会相应发生变化；未来还需针对其他不同类型的街道展开相关研究，以针对性地总结出提升各类街道疗愈潜能的方法。此外，研究发现街景元素在视频图像中的占比与其注视频次占比之间具有显著相关性（p=0.05），表明某一元素的注视频次占比较高可能是由于其在视野中占比较大。在以后的研究中应继续改进实验方法，尽量消除这一影响，进一步提高高频注视点与疗愈性街景元素之间关系识别的准确性。

综上，本研究强调在城市生活的日常环境中获得疗愈体验的重要性，并探究了街道环境具备的疗愈性。通过发掘不同街景元素对疗愈体验的促进或遏制作用，建立街景元素与疗愈性之间确切的对应关系，可有效服务于差异化街道的疗愈性提升改善实践，帮助专业人员依据不同类型街道的疗愈性侧重点制定相应的设计改善思路。研究结果表明，街道环境本身具有较多待挖掘的社会价值，城市环境中也存在许多能够媲美自然环境的疗愈性场所，值得进一步探索。**LAF**

and the failure of the "questionnaire-and-eye-tracking survey" method in describing the qualitative attributes of streetscapes (e.g. complexity, openness[33][61][62]). Therefore, it is necessary to establish a restorativeness evaluation framework which examines both physical and qualitative attributes of streetscape elements. In addition to RCS, future analysis may also adopt more scales from other related theories to expand the research domain of streetscape restorativeness. Linking self-reporting perception and technical identification of physical environment, this method can also be applied to other environmental psychology studies.

The research methods and technologies employed in this study need to be improved in the future: the investigated street mainly serves commuters and the streetscape is homogeneous in frontage type and form; as the participants' perceptions might vary with street characteristics and types (e.g. commercial streets, landscape streets), the influence distributions among the 4 constructs of the adapted RCS may change accordingly. Therefore, the conclusion in this study is not yet widely applicable, and more diverse restorativeness improvement strategies to varied street environment are required. The study did not eliminate the contribution of the proportion of each element in a participant's vision to the percentage of their fixation frequency (p = 0.05), thus causing errors in identifying the restorative streetscape elements. It should be avoided in future research through improved experimental methods for more accurate identification of the correlations of restorative streetscape elements with high-frequency fixation points.

In conclusion, this study reinforces the significance of daily urban environment in providing restorative experience for citizens by focusing on street environment. Manifesting the positive and negative effect of different street elements on the restorative experience, the findings of this study would offer guidance for the design practice that improves restorativeness performance of different street environments. This study also evidences the social potential a street environment should perform but now has less been explored or recognized, as well as that many other urban places can also offer restorative experience for people as what natural environment does. **LAF**

注释

本文部分内容基于第一作者殷雨婷在谢菲尔德大学的博士论文研究课题“探索城市街道疗愈性设计途径——以上海市为例”写作。

NOTE

This paper is partly based on Yin Yuting, the first author's doctoral dissertation "Towards Delivering Restorative Street Design Principles in Shanghai, China" at The University of Sheffield.

REFERENCES

[1] Gehl, J. (2010). Cities for People. Washington D.C.: Island Press.

[2] Ewing, R., & Clemente, O. (2013). Measuring Urban Design: Metrics for Livable Places. Washington D.C.: Island Press.

[3] Jacobs, A. B. (1993). Great Streets (1st ed.). Boston: MIT Press.

[4] Cai, J. (2005). Study on the Importance of Access Roads. City Planning Review, 29(3), 84-88.

[5] Yang, T, & Zhou, W. (2009). Local Street Systems: The Key to a Healthy Urban Road Hierarchy. Planners, 25(6), 11-15.

[6] Ulrich, R. S. (1979). Visual Landscapes and Psychological Well-Being. Landscape Research, 4(1), 17-23. https://doi.org/10.1080/01426397908705892

[7] Ulrich, R. S. (1984). View through a Window May Influence Recovery from Surgery. Science, (224), 420-421.

[8] Hartig, T., Mang, M., & Evans, G. W. (1991). Restorative Effects of Natural Environment Experiences. Environment and Behavior, 23(1), 3-26.

[9] Hartig, T., Evans, G. W., Jamner, L. D., Davis, D. S., & Gärling, T. (2003). Tracking Restoration in Natural and Urban Field Settings. Journal of Environmental Psychology, 23(2), 109-123. doi:10.1016/S0272-4944(02)00109-3

[10] Van den Berg, A. E., Koole, S. L., & Van der Wulp, N. Y. (2003). Environmental Preference and Restoration: (How) Are They Related?. Journal of Environmental Psychology, 23(2), 135-146.

[11] Laumann, K., Gärling, T., & Stormark, K. M. (2001). Rating Scale Measures of Restorative Components of Environments. Journal of Environmental Psychology, (21), 31-44. doi:10.1006/jevp.2000.0179

[12] Ekkekakis, P., Hall, E. E., VanLanduyt, L. M., & Petruzzello, S. J. (2000). Walking in (Affective) Circles: Can Short Walks Enhance Affect?. Journal of Behavioral Medicine, 23(3), 245-275.

[13] Van den Berg, A. E., Hartig, T., & Staats, H. (2007). Preference for Nature in Urbanized Societies: Stress, Restoration, and the Pursuit of Sustainability. Journal of Social Issues, 63(1), 79-96.

[14] Korpela, K. M., Ylén, M., Tyrväinen, L., & Silvennoinen, H. (2008). Determinants of Restorative Experiences in Everyday Favorite Places. Health and place, 14(4), 636-652.

[15] Kaplan, S., & Talbot, J. F. (1983). Psychological Benefits of a Wilderness Experience. In I. Altman & J. F. Wohlwill (Eds.), Behaviour and the Natural Environment. New York: Plenum.

[16] Ulrich, R. S. (1983). Aesthetic and Affective Response to Natural Environments. In I. Altman & J. F. Wohlwill (Eds.), Human Behaviour and Environment: Vol. 6. Advances in Theory and Research (pp. 85-125). New York: Plenum Press.

[17] Kaplan, S. (1995). The Restorative Benefits of Nature: Toward an Integrative Framework. Journal of Environmental Psychology, (15), 169-182.

[18] Ulrich, R. S., Simons, R. F., Losito, B. D., Fiorito, E., Miles, M. A., & Zelson, M. (1991). Stress Recovery during Exposure to Natural and Urban Environments. Journal of Environmental Psychology, 11(3), 201-230.

[19] Kaplan, R. (1993). The Role of Nature in the Context of the Workplace. Landscape and Urban Planning, 26(1-4), 193-201.

[20] Kaplan, R. (2001). The Nature of the View from Home: Psychological Benefits. Environment and Behavior, 33(4), 507-542.

[21] Han, K. -T. (2003). A Reliable and Valid Self-Rating Measure of the Restorative Quality of Natural Environments. Landscape and Urban Planning, (64), 209-232. doi:10.1016/S0169-2046(02)00241-4

[22] Hartig, T., Korpela, K., Evans, G., & Gärling, T. (1997). A Measure of Restorative Quality in Environments. Scandinavian Housing and Planning Research, 14(4), 175-194. https://doi.org/10.1080/02815739708730435

[23] Wakita, T., Ueshima, N., & Noguchi, H. (2012). Psychological Distance between Categories in the Likert Scale: Comparing Different Numbers of Options. Educational and Psychological Measurement, 72(4), 533-546.

[24] Korpela, K., & Hartig, T. (1996). Restorative Qualities of Favourite Places. Journal of Environmental Psychology, (16), 221-233.

[25] Nordh, H., Hartig, T., Hagerhall, C. M., & Fry, G. (2009). Components of Small Urban Parks that Predict the Possibility for Restoration. Urban forestry & urban greening, 8(4), 225-235.

[26] Nordh, H., & Østby, K. (2013). Pocket Parks for People—A Study of Park Design and Use. Urban Forestry and Urban Greening, 12(1), 12-17.

[27] Karmanov, D., & Hamel, R. (2008). Assessing the Restorative Potential of Contemporary Urban Environments: Beyond the Nature versus Urban Dichotomy. Landscape and Urban Planning, 86(2), 115-125.

[28] Kaplan, R., Kaplan, S., & Ryan, R. (1998). With People in Mind: Design and Management of Everyday Nature. Washington D.C.: Island Press.

[29] Lindal, P. J., Hartig, T. (2005). Effects of Urban Street Vegetation on Judgments of Restoration Likelihood. Urban Forestry and Urban Greening, 14(2), 200-209.

[30] Kaplan, S., Bardwell, L. V., & Slakter, D. B. (1993). The Museum as a Restorative Environment. Environment and Behavior, 25(6), 725-742.

[31] Ivarsson, C. T., & Hagerhall, C. M. (2008). The Perceived Restorativeness of Garden—Assessing the restorativeness of a Mixed Built and Natural Scene Type. Urban Forestry and Urban Greening, 7(2), 107-118.

[32] Karmanov, D., & Hamel, R. (2008). Assessing the Restorative Potential of Contemporary Urban Environments: Beyond the Nature versus Urban Dichotomy. Landscape and Urban Planning, 86(2), 115-125.

[33] Lindal, P. J., & Hartig, T. (2013). Architectural Variation, Building Height, and the Restorative Quality of Urban Residential Streetscapes. Journal of Environmental Psychology, (33), 26-36.

[34] Xu, L., Meng, R., Huang, S., & Chen, Z. (2019). Healing Oriented Street Design: Experimental Explorations via Virtual Reality. Urban Planning International, (1), 38-45.

[35] Brush, R. O. (1981). Landform and Scenic Preference: A Research Note. Landscape Planning, 8(3), 301-306.

[36] Arthur, L. M. (1977). Predicting Scenic Beauty of Forest Environments: Some Empirical Tests. Forest Science, 23(2), 151-160.

[37] Xu, L., Meng, R., & Chen, Z. (2017). Fascinating Streets: The Impact of Building Facades and Green View. Landscape Architecture, (10), 27-33.

[38] Meissner, M., & Oll, J. (2019). The Promise of Eye-Tracking Methodology in Organizational Research: A Taxonomy, Review, and Future Avenues. Organizational Research Methods, 22(2), 590-617.

[39] Buswell, G. T. (1935). How People Look at Pictures: A Study of the Psychology and Perception in Art. Oxford: The University of Chicago Press.

[40] Deubel, H., & Schneider, W. X. (1996). Saccade Target Selection and Object Recognition: Evidence for a Common Attentional Mechanism. Vision Research, 36(12), 1827-1837.

[41] Berto, R., Massaccesi, S., & Pasini, M. (2008). Do Eye Movements Measured across High and Low Fascination Photographs Differ? Addressing Kaplan's Fascination Hypothesis. Journal of Environmental Psychology, 28(2), 185-191.

[42] Noland, R. B., Weiner M. D., Gao, D., Cook, M. P., & Nelessen, A. (2016). Eye-Tracking Technology, Visual Preference Surveys, and Urban Design: Preliminary Evidence of an Effective Methodology. Journal of Urbanism: International Research on Placemaking and Urban Sustainability, 10(1), 98-110.

[43] Birmingham, E., Bischof, W. F., & Kingstone, A. (2009). Saliency does not Account for Fixations to Eyes within Social Scenes. Vision Research, (49), 2992-3000.

[44] Glaholt, M. G., Wu, M., & Reingold. E. M. (2009). Predicting Preference from Fixations. PsychNology Journal, (7), 141-158.

[45] Nordh, H., Hagerhall, C. M., & Holmqvist, K. (2013). Tracking Restorative Components: Patterns in Eye Movements as a Consequence of a Restorative Rating Task. Landscape Research, 38(1), 101-116.

[46] Grant, E. R., & Spivey, M, J. (2003). Eye Movements and Problem-Solving Guiding Attention Guides Thought. Psychological Science, 14(5), 462-466.

[47] Just, M. A., & Carpenter, P. A. (1985). Cognitive Coordinate Systems: Accounts of Mental Rotation and Individual Differences in Spatial Ability. Psychological Review, 92(2), 137-172.

[48] Ehrlichman, H., & Weinberger, A. (1978). Lateral Eye Movements and Hemispheric Asymmetry: A Critical Review. Psychological Bulletin, 85(5), 1080-1101.

[49] Bartels, M. (2019). Eye-Tracking Technology. American Society of Safety Engineers, 64(1), 17.

[50] Zhaopin.com., & Institute of Psychology, Chinese Academy of Sciences. (2012). An Investigation Report about Working Group's Psychological Health. Openings, (18), 78-79.

[51] Staats, H., & Hartig, T. (2004). Alone or with a Friend: A Social Context for Psychological Restoration and Environmental Preferences. Journal of Environmental Psychology, 24(2), 199-211.

[52] Hinton, P. R. (2014). Statistics Explained (3rd ed.). New York: Routledge.

[53] Vries, S. (2017). Using a Wearable Eye-Tracking Device on Bicyclists to Explore the Possibility of Measuring Motorcyclist Eye Movements (Master's thesis). University of Twente, Enschede.

[54] Carstensen, L. L. (1993). Motivation for Social Contact across the Life Span: A Theory of Socioemotional Selectivity. Nebraska Symposium on Motivation, (40), 209-254.

[55] Brunelli, M. (2019). "Non-Places" of School Memory. First Reflections on the Forgotten Places of Education as Generators of Collective School Memory: Between Oral History, Public history and Digital History. History of Education and Children's Literature, 14(1), 49-72

[56] Kaplan, R., & Kaplan, S. (1989). The experience of nature: A psychological perspective. Cambridge: Cambridge University Press.

[57] Norberg-Schulz, C. (1990). Existence, Space, and Architecture (P. Yin Tran.). Beijing: China Architecture and Building Press.

[58] Collado, S., Staats, H., & Sorrel, M. A. (2016). A Relational Model of Perceived Restorativeness: Intertwined Effects of Obligations, Familiarity, Security and Parental Supervision. Journal of Environmental Psychology, (48), 24-32.

[59] Korpela, K., & Staats, H. (2014). The Restorative Qualities of being Alone with Nature. In Coplan, J. & Bowker, C. (Eds.), The Handbook of Solitude: Psychological Perspectives on Social Isolation, Social Withdrawal, and Being Alone. Oxford: Wiley-Blackwell.

[60] Wang, H. (2015). The Research about the Differences of Friendship Perception and Friend Preference among Students with Different Personality Type—Taking an Example of Students Learning in HUST (Master's thesis). Huazhong University of Science and Technology, Wuhan. Retrieved from CNKI database.

[61] Galindo, M. P., & Hidalgo, M. C. (2005). Aesthetic Preferences and the Attribution of Meaning: Environmental Categorisation Processes in the Evaluation of Urban Scenes. International Journal of Psychology, (40), 19-27.

[62] Fredrickson, B. L., & Levenson R. W. (1998). Positive Emotions Speed Recovery from the Cardiovascular Sequelae of Negative Emotions. Cognition and Emotion, (12), 191-220.

本文引用格式 / PLEASE CITE THIS ARTICLE AS

Li, J., Dong, H., & Jiang, J. (2020). Prototyping in the Design of Built Landscapes. Landscape Architecture Frontiers, 8(4), 90-103. https://doi.org/10.15302/J-LAF-1-030018

https://doi.org/10.15302/J-LAF-1-030018　收稿时间 RECEIVED DATE / 2020-05-30　中图分类号 / TU986　文献标识码 / B

原型思维在广义建成景观中的设计应用

PROTOTYPING IN THE DESIGN OF BUILT LANDSCAPES

摘要

"原型"起源于"本质主义"——认为万物均拥有其客观存在的本质，人们可以对典型现象进行抽象、描述并揭示该事物的本质。在建筑学发展过程中，由于本质主义无法描述形态变体的差异性，因而产生了类型学的概念。类型学强调对建筑形式进行变化和组合，形成与历史、文化或环境具有内在联系的新的空间形式。而在景观领域，面对复杂多变的设计对象，自类型学衍化而来的原型概念由于包含时间维度而被更广泛应用。可以说，原型思维是一种空间秩序的描述及测试，从提取特征、确定形式、测试模拟，到最终引入实体空间，形成了"抽象－衍化－测试－结果"的设计方法。在景观都市主义语境下，设计者首先必须了解场地的特定文脉，了解过去和未来及使用人群的设计语言，而后进行原型推演，并将时间性纳入考虑。本文主要探讨了原型概念的演化过程，并进一步讨论原型思维在广义建成景观设计过程的三个阶段——研究设计对象、推敲设计策略及测试最优策略——中起到的作用。

关键词

原型思维；建成景观；切片；情境分析；模拟

ABSTRACT

The concept of "prototype" originated from "essentialism"—the theory holds that everything is found in its own pure realm that can be typically abstracted, described, and represented. In the development of Architecture, essentialism fails to describe the differences between formal variations, and then Typology was born which manifests the new spatial forms that are embedded within the historical, cultural, and environmental contexts through the changes and combinations of architecture. Prototype, stemming from Typology, highlights the qualities of the time dimension and has been broadly used in the field of landscape architecture to address the objects that are often complex and chaotic. Prototyping is to profile and test the spatial order and characterized by a process of "extraction–deduction–test–outcome": through the scenario analysis upon understanding and perception of the site, the design extracts the elements, deduces the forms, tests the simulations, iterates the strategies, and finally realizes the outcome physically. In the discourse of Landscape Urbanism, designers must understand the specific material language of the site, the design language of the site's history (past and future), and the design language of the human activities proposed, while considering the changes over time. This article primarily reviews the evolution of the concept of prototype, and discusses its role in benefiting the design of built landscapes, ranging from the design investigation to the conceiving and testing of design strategies.

KEYWORDS

Prototyping; Built Landscape; Site Section; Scenario Analysis; Simulation

李静芸
J'Studio景观研究工作室研究员，哈佛大学设计研究生院景观设计学硕士研究生

LI Jingyun
Researcher at J' Studio Research LAB; Master Student in Landscape Architecture at Harvard Graduate School of Design

董华冠*
J'Studio景观研究工作室联合创始人，北京林业大学园林专业农学学士

DONG Huaguan
Co-founder of J' Studio Research LAB; Bachelor of Agriculture in Landscape Architecture, Beijing Forestry University

姜佳怡
J'Studio景观研究工作室研究员，千叶大学风景园林学博士研究生

JIANG Jiayi
Researcher at J' Studio Research LAB; PhD Candidate of Landscape Architecture, Chiba University

*通讯作者
地址：北京市海淀区清华东路35号北京林业大学北林印刷厂5号楼
邮编：100083
邮箱：donghuaguan@163.com

编辑、翻译　田乐
EDITED AND TRANSLATED BY　Tina TIAN

1 引言

"原型"（prototype）概念最初起源于社会哲学，而后在建筑学、城市规划、景观设计学等领域的语境中逐渐发展演变，经历了从"本质形式"（form）到"类型"（type）再到"原型"的认知过程。

早在希腊古典时期，柏拉图提出了基于形而上学的形式理论，认为任何的实体都有具有其永恒不变的本质形式[1]。在古典哲学比喻《洞穴之喻》中，柏拉图认为形式是构成可感知世界的基础[2]。文艺复兴时期，建筑师菲拉雷特提出建筑的本质表现为一个坡屋顶及其4根支撑立柱；而后，建筑理论家马克—安托万·洛吉耶在《建筑随笔》中呼吁建筑应当摒弃装饰，返璞归真[3]。

18世纪末，第一次工业革命推动了生产力的发展，促使建筑师提出更高效的设计方法。法国新古典主义建筑师让—尼古拉—路易·迪朗成为现代主义以来基于类型学（Typology）进行设计的开创者。他在《古代与现代各类建筑汇编》一书中倡导使用类型学将古典主义建筑语言进行分类，利用轴线和网格来布局模块单元演化建筑形式，从而使类型学成为一种简单的模式化生产工具，并满足新时代对建筑标准的需求[4]。直至勒·柯布西耶提出"多米诺"体系，引入空间、结构、功能等要素，才终于使类型学走出了形而上的秩序性探讨[5]。自此，类型学成为一种设计方法：通过基于建筑单体的变化和组合，形成与历史、文化或环境相融合的建筑空间形式。

推动类型学研究在城市规划中进一步发展的重要人物是阿尔多·罗西，他在《城市建筑》一书中提出："城市自身就是一个建筑体"[6]。罗西认为城市是各种类型的构筑物的集合，具有普遍性和集体特征，并批评当时的功能主义在研究城市空间时忽略了它在时间影响下的品质与特性变化[7]。此时，人们已开始将时间概念引入设计过程。与相对静态的类型学方法相比，"原型"设计方法将时间维度纳入讨论，即包含了原始模型或参照对象在不同时间维度下的各个状态[4]。景观语境中更多运用的是"原型思维"（prototyping）概念，即在理解和认知场地的基础上进行情境分析，提出策略，并修正策略。由于广义下的建成景观是人类主观能动性改造自然的产物，具有动态性和复杂性[8]，原

1 Introduction

Initiatively proposed in Social Philosophy, the concept of "prototype" has gradually adopted and developed in the fields of Architecture, Urban Planning, Landscape Architecture, etc., having been cognized through an evolution from "form" and "type."

As early as in the Ancient Age of Greek, Plato put forward his metaphysical view, the Theory of Forms, which believed that the things being defined are to be found in an eternal, unchanging, and ontologically pure realm[1]. Plato's *Allegory of the Cave* notes that knowledge is gained primarily by coming to know the Form[2]. In the age of Renaissance, architect Filarete exemplified the essence of architecture as four columns and a pitched roof on top of it; In his *Essai sur l'Architecture* (*An Essay on Architecture*), architectural theorist Marc-Antoine Laugier believed that architectural conceptions should be "unnecessarily decorative in nature"[3].

At the end of the 18th century, the first industrial revolution propelled the advances in productivity which spurred architects to conceive new design methods for higher efficiency. Among modern designers, French neoclassical architect Jean-Nicolas-Louis Durand is considered the pioneer who practiced the ideas of Typology. In the book *Recueil et Parallèle des Édifices de Tout Genre*, he advocated classifying the language of classical architecture with typological concepts, using axes and grids to handle the composition, where "a simple enough method of coping with the programs and the new building requirements demanded by a new society" was offered[4]. It was not until the ideas of the Dom-ino System proposed by Le Corbusier that exceeds the "objective view of the autonomous rules of architecture"[5] by introducing the concepts of space, structure, function, etc. Typology has been employed as a design method: through the changes and combinations of building units, an architectural spatial form that is intrinsically embedded within the historical, cultural, and environmental contexts is shaped.

Aldo Rossi is key to push forward typological research in the field of urban planning. In his book *The Architecture of the City*, Rossi regarded the city itself as an artifact[6]. He also emphasized that the city is as a totality where "all urban artifacts and the city are a collective," and criticized that the naïve functionalism ignores the quality and uniqueness developed in time[7]. In this process, the concept of time has begun to be introduced into the design process. Compared with the design methods in Typology that examine "frozen mechanisms," those in Prototype amplify the varying status of the dimension of time what a form or an object has[4]. In landscape architecture, prototyping is used to generate

型思维成为了景观设计师“否定过去和展望未来的方式”[4]。原型的作用也已超出对空间的主观改编：设计者首先必须了解场地的特定文脉，了解过去和未来及使用人群的设计语言，而后进行原型推演[9]。总之，景观设计语境下的原型思维可以帮助设计者做出更合理且具有适应性的决策。

2 空间设计原型起源：对自然的模仿和再造

目前大多数关于空间设计原型的研究主要集中在建筑和城市空间，然而，最初的空间设计原型很可能源于自然景观。罗西提出，建筑和城市类型学首先建立在自然“初型”（archetype）的基础上[9]。在《城市建筑》中，他认为城市“是由建筑和一切人类改造自然形成的产物构成的”[6]。建筑师约瑟佩·米利齐亚指出，“尽管现实中的建筑缺乏自然的模型，但在人类建造他的第一所房屋时，它已经具备了另一种源自自然劳动的属性”[10]。

古罗马建筑师维特鲁威在《建筑十书》中想象了史前人类受到自然启发而主动搭建庇护所的过程[11]。他指出这些房子正是对自然的模仿：有些是用树枝扎成棚架，有些是在山上挖洞，有些则模仿燕子的巢穴和栖息地，将树枝的房屋交织在一起并用泥土或粘土覆盖。通过观察和改善彼此的庇护所，他们很快开始建造更好的屋子。因此，那些天生喜欢模仿的人，为自己的发明感到自豪，也通过先前的方法获得了日常经验，从而在建造的品质方面相互竞争”[11]。维特鲁威的描述中暗含的信息是：建筑起源于自然，即从混沌和不断变化[9]的自然语言中找到规律，提取为人类所用的部分，来满足人类生存的需要。随着时间推移，一种共享的空间设计原型语言慢慢地扎根于人类的精神世界中。安东尼·维德勒在《类型思想》一文中引用了法国建筑师里巴

scenario analyses upon the understanding and perception of the site, and to propose strategies that can be altered accordingly. Broadly defined, the built landscape is the product of human transformation on the nature which contains the “dynamic multiplicity of urban process”[8]. For landscape designers, prototype “becomes a way of denying the past, as well as a way of looking at the future”[4]. The role of the prototype has also gone beyond the subjective adaptation of the space: designers must first “understand the specific material language of the site, the design language of the site’s history (past and future), and the design language of the human activities proposed”[9]. In short, prototyping, in landscape design, can help designers make more reasonable and adaptive decisions.

2 The Initial Prototype of Spatial Design: The Imitation and Reconstruction of Nature

At present, most of the research on the prototypes of spatial design mainly focuses on architecture and urban spaces. However, the initial prototype of spatial design likely stemmed from natural landscapes. Rossi suggested that “building and urban typology rests on a foundation of natural archetypes”[9]. In *The Architecture of the City*, Rossi argued that the city “is constituted of its architecture and of all those works that constitute the true means of transforming nature”[6]. Architect Giuseppe Milizia defined that “although architecture in reality lacks a model in nature, it has another model derived from man’s natural labor in constructing his first house”[10].

In *De Architectura*, the ancient Roman architect Marcus Vitruvius Pollio imagined that prehistoric humans built shelters which were learnt from the nature[3]. He described that “some by making arbors with the boughs of trees, some by excavating caves in the mountains, and others in imitation of the nests and habitations of swallows, by making dwellings of twigs interwoven and covered with mud or clay. From observation of and improvement on each other’s expedients for sheltering themselves, they soon began to provide a better species of huts. It was thus that men, who are by nature of an imitative and docile turn of mind, and proud of their own inventions, gaining daily experience also by what had been previously executed, vied with each other in their progress towards perfection in building”[11]. This implies that architecture originates from the nature by extracting the laws of nature—the impressive landscape of chaos, and a state of constant change[9]—to meet the needs for human survival. As time goes by, a shared prototype language of spatial design has taken root in the spiritual world of human beings. In The Idea of Type, Anthony Vidler adopted the definitions of

特·狄·夏姆斯特在概述类型历史时对“类型”和“初型”的定义：“类型”反映了人类为了满足自身使用或愉悦需求而进行的改造自然的首次尝试；而画家从自然中有理有据地选择出那些既能激发又能指引其想象力的可感知对象，则称之为“初型”。[12][13]

据此，本文认为，空间设计原型的提出并非完全是人类对自然要素的直接提取，而是源于人类的主观能动性，是利用自然规律并反作用于自然的改造行为。这些空间设计原型的提出最初聚焦于生产功能，在漫长的演化中逐步衍生为一系列空间美学体验；而且建筑和城市的原型也建立于自然原型之上。也就是说，在封闭建筑内或开放空间中，我们的空间体验不存在本质的区别。

人类最早期形成景观空间原型之一是空地。居住在森林中的史前人类在清理森林的过程中产生了空间体验的对比：森林是郁闭的、昏暗的、神秘的，而采伐后的空地则是开阔、明亮的、焦灼的[9]。这种对于空间体验的对比作为一种经验扎根于人类的意识中；直到现在，设计师在建筑或景观中编排连续空间序列时，还是会通过控制明暗、开闭等手法来影响观者的空间认知和情绪。

在西方海洋文明语境中，典型的景观空间原型包括生产性的果园，以及贸易和交往所需要的公共空间，如剧场、台地等[9]。相比之下，“圃”和“囿”是中国最早的景观空间原型——前者指栽种蔬菜的地方，即菜圃；后者最初指稻田，后指饲养禽兽的地方——圃、囿的甲骨文文字就表示出古人成行成畦栽植稻米果蔬的形象（图1），是最早对建成景观的一种原型呈现。

3 原型思维在设计过程中的作用

运用类型学方法的设计过程可以说是将空间对象的要素（即该空间对象的形式结构的基础元素）引入场地，使之在适应性处理后达到精确状态的一种方式[4]。能够体现该过程的一个典型案例是意大利乌尔

1

1. “圃”和“囿”是中国最早的景观空间原型

1. In China, "Pu" (圃) and "You" (囿) are the earliest landscape prototypes.

“type” and “archetype” proposed by French architect Rebart de Chamoust in his overview on Typology history: The word type reflects “the first attempts of man to master nature, render it propitious to his needs, suitable to his uses, and favorable to his pleasures; The perceptible objects that the Artist chooses with justness and reasoning from nature in order to light and fix at the same time the fires of his imagination, I call archetypes.”[12][13]

On these grounds, this article holds that human’s extraction of the prototype of the spatial design is not merely a simple selection of natural elements, but a utilization to meet human needs that transforms the nature by imitating the nature. Initially developed for productive uses, such prototypes have manifested a series of spatial aesthetic experience and evolved into the prototypes for architecture and the city. In other words, essentially there is no difference between people’s experience in enclosed buildings and open spaces.

One of the earliest landscape prototypes is the clearing, which dramatically shaped the spatial experience of prehistoric human beings: the forest is gloomy, shady, and inviting, and the clearing is alternatively brilliant, exposed, and scorching[9]. Such a contrast is rooted in human consciousness as an experience. Up to now, the choreography of brightness and darkness as well as opening and enclosure in continuous spatial sequences is still used in architectural and landscape design.

In the Western marine civilization, typical landscape prototypes include production places (e.g., orchards), and trading or commercial public spaces (e.g., theaters, terraces)[9]. In China, “Pu” (圃) and “You” (囿) are the earliest landscape prototypes. The former refers to vegetable gardens and the latter initially refers to rice paddy fields and then animal farms—the oracle inscriptions of Pu and You express the image of the ancients planting rice, fruits, and vegetables in rows and plots (Fig. 1), profiling the earliest prototypes of built landscapes.

3 Prototyping in Design Process

The design process employing typological methods is a way of bringing the elements of a typology (the formal structure of a given spatial object), through adaptive interventions, “into the precise state that characterizes the single work”[4]. A typical example of such a process is the Collegio del Colle project in Italy (Fig. 2), where the architect Giancarlo De Carlo attempted to integrate the shape of the structure with the contours of the hill: a series of “boxes” (the building) was perfectly configurated in accordance to the terrain, as the orchestration of spatial experience. Like the Dom-ino System which became a design paradigm of modernist architecture, Carlo, rather than simply

2

2. 意大利乌尔比诺学生公寓平面图及实景照片

2. The plan and photo of Collegio del Colle project in Italy

比诺学生公寓（图2）。建筑师吉卡洛·德·卡洛尝试将建筑的形状与山丘的形态相互渗透："方盒子"被巧妙地排布在山体之上，适应等高线和微地形变化，使建筑与场地形成了一组空间合奏。正如"多米诺"体系所奠定的现代主义建筑设计范式，卡洛并不是将建筑单体进行单纯的组合，而是通过类型学的设计方法来创造空间变化[5]。

在狭义景观的范畴，传统设计过程往往通过类型的组合或变体来适应场地，并构成新的空间。这是一种感性的、微观的设计技巧。如今，景观的概念已不再仅限于狭义的公园等绿地，而是广义下人类活动改造自然的产物，即建成景观。詹姆斯·科纳在《流动的土地》一文中指出，景观都市主义认为景观首先是动态的过程，受到城市化进程、资本积累、放松管制、全球化、环境保护的影响而不断变化[8]。在面对具有复杂时间性和动态性的设计对象时，需要运用源自类型学的、具有时间维度的原型概念：原型不是静止或永恒的；原型可以被认为是设计随着场地条件的变化而发生转变时记录下的瞬时影像。因而，原型思维也是一种动态设计方法：在理解和认知场地的基础上进行情境分析、提取场地特征、确定设计形式、测试模拟、修正策略，

combining individual structures together, exercised typological design methods to create changes of space[5].

In the narrow sense of the landscape, traditional design processes often adapt to the site through typological combination or variation to constitute new spaces, representing a sensitive micro-scale technique. Today, landscape no longer simply refers to green spaces such as parks; it has been broadly defined as the products of human's transformation of the nature, i.e. built landscapes. James Corner pointed out in the article Terra Fluxus that landscape urbanism processes over time, and the processes of urbanization are shaped by urban relationships such as capital accumulation, deregulation, globalization, and environmental protection[8]. In landscape design, the understanding of complicated objects in time and dynamism necessitates using the concept of prototype that contains typological ideas to examine how things work in space and time. Rather than being unchanging or eternal, prototype can be considered a series of instantaneous images of the design changes when the changes of the site occur. Therefore, prototyping is also a dynamic design method which is characterized by a process of "extraction-deduction-test-outcome": through the scenario analysis upon understanding and perception of the site, the design extracts the elements, deduces the forms, tests the simulations, iterates the strategies, and finally realizes the outcome physically. At the same time, in the discourse of modern landscape, designers need to observe the world from a more rational and macro perspective, with the advancement of

3 斯蒂芬·M·韦勒对全球24个大都市区的建成景观原型进行了提炼（来源：参考文献[14]）

3. Stephen M. Wheeler studied 24 metropolitan regions across the world to extract the prototypes of built landscapes (Source: Ref. [14])

再最终引入实体空间，构成了“抽象—衍化—测试—结果”的设计过程。同时，在现代广义的景观范畴下，设计师需要以更为理性、宏观的角度去观察世界，理解景观与人类文化、社会、经济、政治等因素之间的联系[8]。本文将通过场地切片、情境分析和模拟三个途径来讨论现代广义景观设计下的原型思维应用。

3.1 场地切片——利用原型思维研究设计对象

场地切片是一种从研究场地中提取、简化或抽象推演空间原型，以对建成景观进行研究归纳的手段。在研究建成景观（包括一切受到人类干预的自然景观）时，尤其是在面对后现代复杂的“拼贴城市”的过程中，选择有代表性的地块进行场地切片研究，将有助于指导更合理的空间设计。

在此方面的代表性研究是斯蒂芬·M·韦勒的《大都市地区的建筑景观：国际类型学》[14]。韦勒利用卫星地图研究了建筑—景观—街道格局，依此提炼出全球24个大都市区的建成景观原型（图3）。这些建成景观的场地切片通常为1km^{2}以上，场地使用者具有固定的使用习惯——原型的形态反过来也影响了居民行为和空间使用模式。韦勒同

“more socially just, politically emancipatory, and ecologically sane mix(es) of the spatio-temporal production process”[8]. This article demonstrates the application of prototyping in landscape design in the forms of site section, scenario analysis, and simulation.

3.1 Site Section—Prototyping as Site Investigation

The site section is an approach to extract, simplify, or abstractly deduce spatial prototypes from the given sites for the investigation and induction of built landscapes. When studying built landscapes (including all natural landscapes under human interventions), particularly the post-modern complex “collage cities,” selecting representative site sections would help generate more reasonable design schemes.

Typically, in the Built Landscapes of Metropolitan Regions: An International Typology[14], Stephen M. Wheeler used satellite maps to study the architecture-landscape-street pattern of 24 metropolitan regions across the world to extract the prototypes of built landscapes (Fig. 3). Most of the site sections covered an area of 1 km^2 or larger and the sites had been shaped by the observed usage patterns—which had been shaped by the typology of the prototypes in turn. Wheeler also analyzed the formation and historical backgrounds of each prototype. This typology of built landscape forms can help decision-makers and

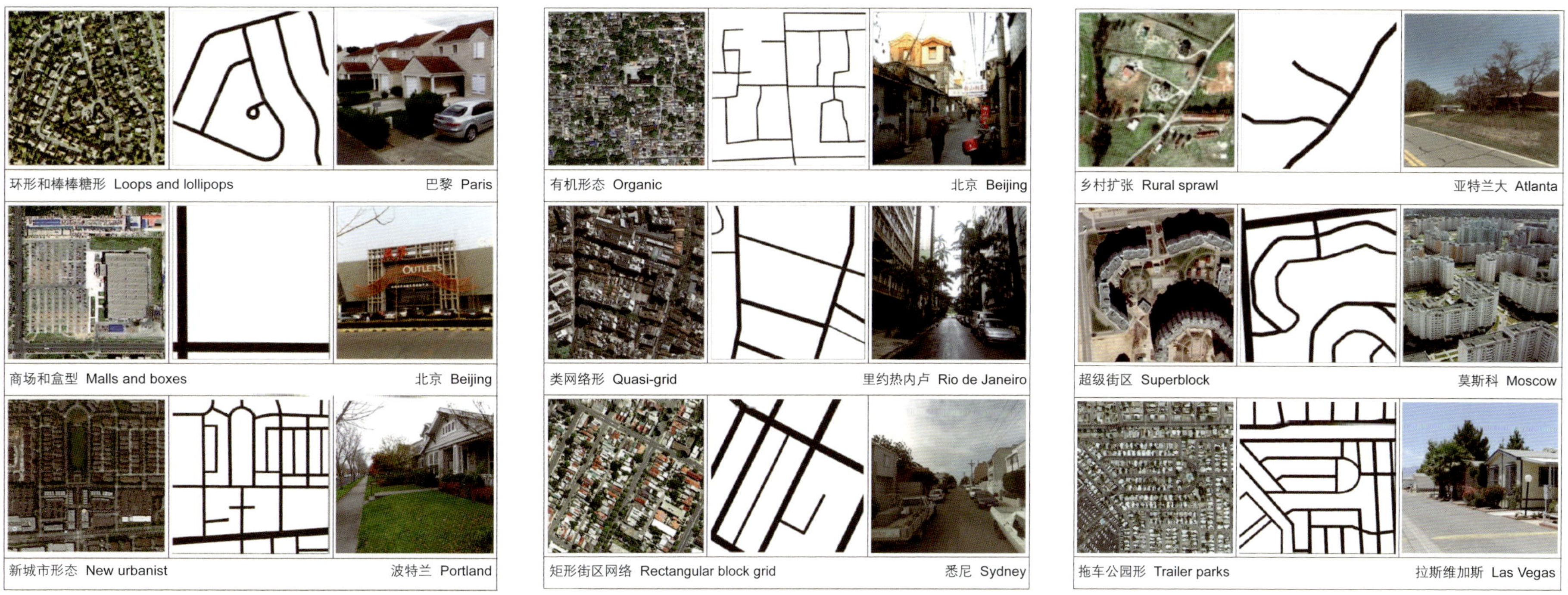

3

时分析了不同原型的形成原因和历史背景。这种建成空间类型学能够帮助决策者和公众理解复杂的城市街区或更大规模的土地利用，并指导设计师解读某种建成空间类型背后的政治、经济和文化因素，从而促进在宜居性和可持续性方面的反思与创新。在此基础上，韦勒归纳了全球大都市区的27种建成景观基本类型，并指出目前由传统邻里构成的有机城市类型仅占全球多数大都市地区的一小部分，剩下的绝大部分为郊区和郊区形式的其他区域[14]。

从城市建成景观的角度而言，城市蔓延是发达国家和发展中国家的城市所共同面临的当代问题。在中国，该问题主要表现为因农业用地空置及城市建设用地扩张而导致的城市无序发展。本文以城镇化问题尤为突出的云南省宜良县为例，在空间划分层面采用类型学研究方法，将宜良县按照人口密度分为城市、郊区、乡村三个圈层，并最大程度地利用城郊的可种植界面，分别对三个圈层提出连续性生产景观设计原型，旨在在缓解城市环境问题的同时引导城市合理增长。在城市圈和郊区圈区域，根据人口密度，将现有的城市聚落组团进行切片研究和分类，得到9种空间切片（超高层住宅、超级街区、板楼、旧城、商业空间、开放空间、工业区、山地，以及郊区），并在每种空间切片的基础上探讨增加生产性景观界面的可能性。针对具有改造潜力的城市界面（如公共建筑的屋顶、高层或老城住房的双坡屋顶），提出了一系列弹性的改造策略与设计原型（图4，5）。

3.2 情境分析——利用原型思维推敲设计策略

如上文所述，原型思维和原型设计方法使得设计师可以适应微妙的场地要素变化和时间变化的要求，甚至对可能出现的条件变化做出假想和预判。这可称为情境分析，即通过设立不同情景，预测对象可能出现的情况或产生的后果。

在全球气候变化的影响下，斯堪的纳维亚半岛的西部沿海地区普遍存在冻土融化问题。尤其在挪威，封冻的土地在春季提早消融，阻碍了当地的萨米人和鹿群的回迁路线。[15]相关研究资料显示，冻土融化

the public understand the land use of complex urban blocks or in larger-scale cases, and help designers interpret the political, economic, and cultural threads of a certain type of built spaces, to promote the reflection and innovation in livability and sustainability. Through such case studies, Wheeler found that 27 basic types of built landscape made up metropolitan regions worldwide; neighborhood-scale urban types of tightly knit organic patterns now "make up a small fraction of most metropolitan areas, while suburbs and suburban forms comprise the vast majority of the land area"[14].

In terms of urban built landscapes, urban sprawl is a contemporary problem faced by cities in both developed and developing countries. In China, there is a contrast between the vacancy of agricultural land and the expansion of urban construction land, leading to disordered urban development. In the case study on the urbanization in Yiliang County of Yunnan Province, the authors adopt typological research methods to restructure the spaces of the county into three types—urban, suburban, and rural—according to the population density. The proposal maximally leverages the plantable land in the suburban areas with the designed prototypes that support continuous productive urban landscapes to each type of space. This can not only alleviate urban environmental problems but also bring the possibility to spur a smart urban growth. In the urban and suburban areas, the proposal extracts 9 types of site sections of the existing urban clusters with consideration of population density: incremental, superblock, apartment block, organic, commercial, open space, industrial, mountainous, and suburban. Flexible transformation strategies and design prototypes for each site section that would increase productive landscape interfaces (such as the roofs of public buildings, and the pitched roofs of high-rises or the housing buildings in the old town) are then developed (Fig. 4, 5).

3.2 Scenario Analysis—Prototyping for Design Strategies

As mentioned above, prototyping and prototype design methods enable designers to be sensitive to the subtle alterations of the elements within the site, as well as time changes, and to prepare responding strategies upon the predictions of possible changes. This is the approach of scenario analysis, which allows designers to simulate various possibilities and the corresponding consequences.

Under the impact of global climate change, the problem of permafrost thawing is increasingly observed in the western coastal areas of Scandinavia, especially for the Saami people in Norway where snows melt earlier in the springtime and reindeer heading becomes more difficult as the ice is weak,

4. 连续性生产景观：城乡结构及空间原型
5. 连续性生产景观：城市界面改造设计原型

4. Continuous productive urban landscapes: the urban-rural structure and spatial prototypes
5. Continuous productive urban landscapes: design prototypes of urban interface regeneration

什么是连续性生产城市景观设计?
What is Continuous Productive Urban Landscape (CPUL)?

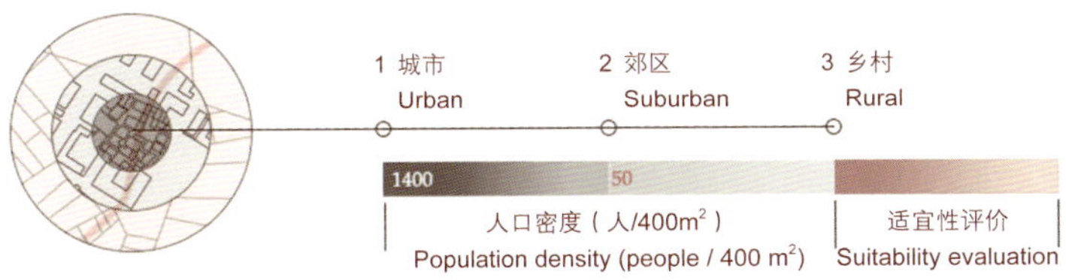

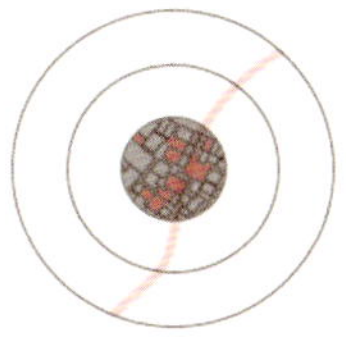

1 城市圈 Urban cycle

城市圈层中的连续性生产景观界面的人口密度较高，可利用屋顶、墙体、绿地等界面来生产食物
Characterized by high population density, CPULs in urban cycle use various interfaces like rooftop, wall, and green space to produce food

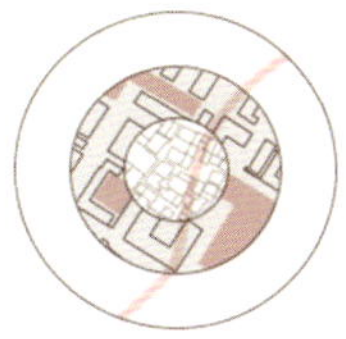

2 郊区圈 Suburban cycle

由于郊区圈层的人口密度低，其连续性生产景观会利用工厂附属绿地等闲置土地建设低维护的农业园区
Given a low population density, CPULs in suburban cycle use spare land like green space of factories to construct agriculture park of low-maintenance

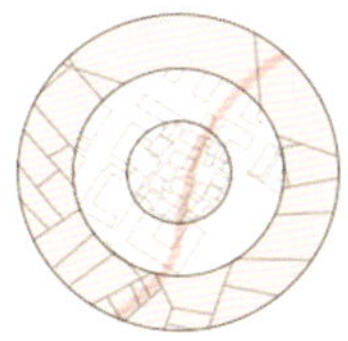

3 乡村圈 Rural cycle

在乡村圈层中，通过加权计算（对当前场地类型、可达性和水安全性进行评价和打分）来确定连续性生产景观土地的选址
In this cycle, CPULs land is selected by weighted calculation: current field type, accessibility, and water security are evaluated and scored

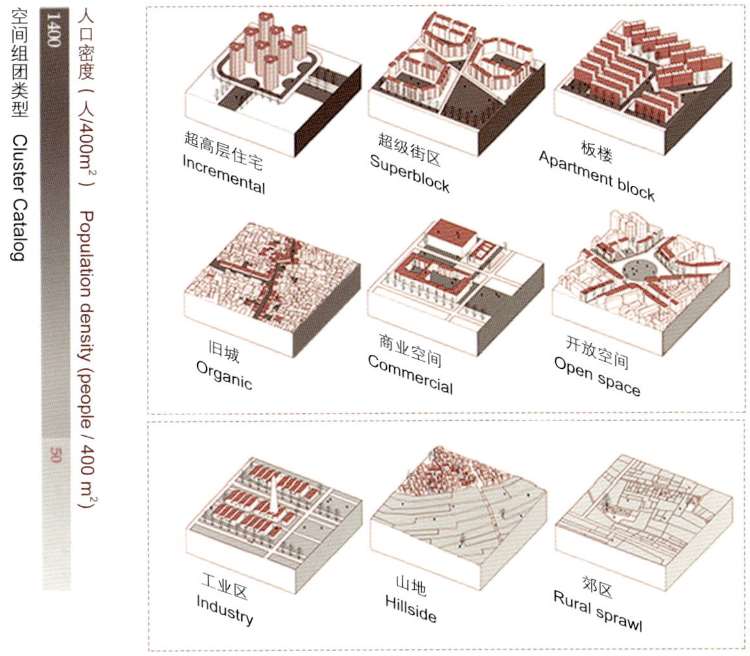

4

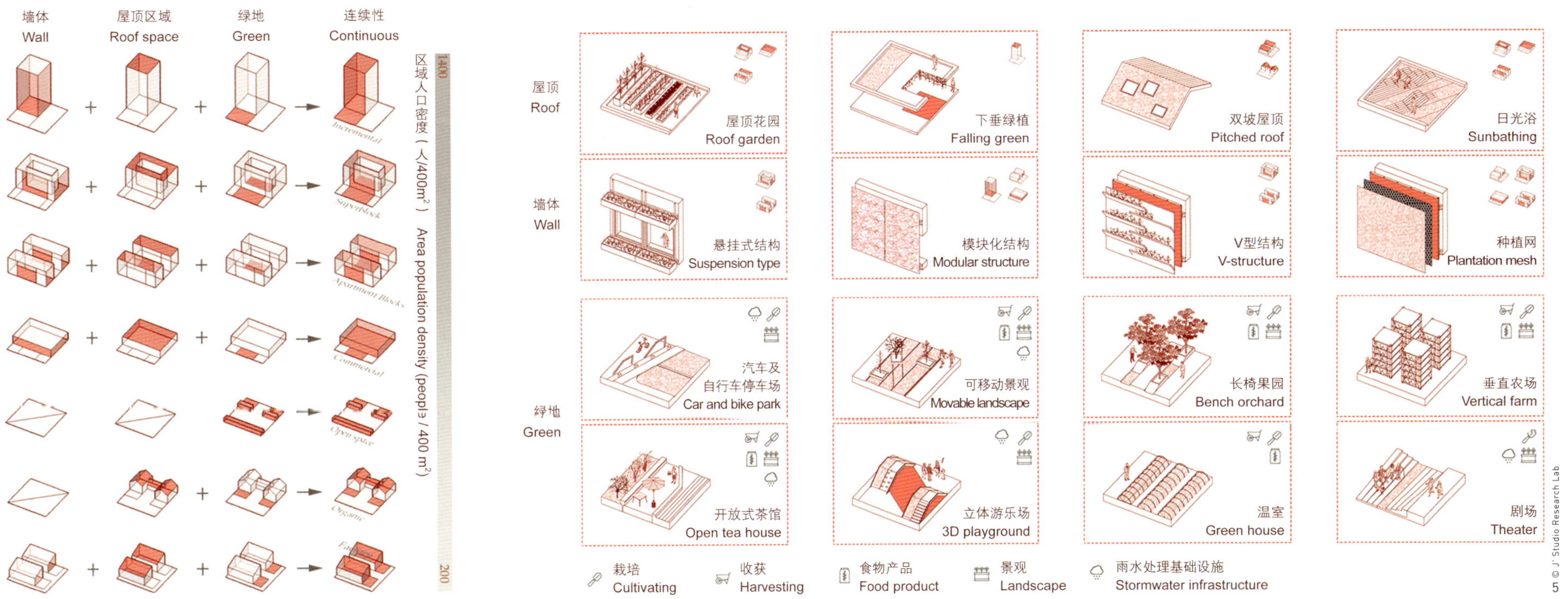

5

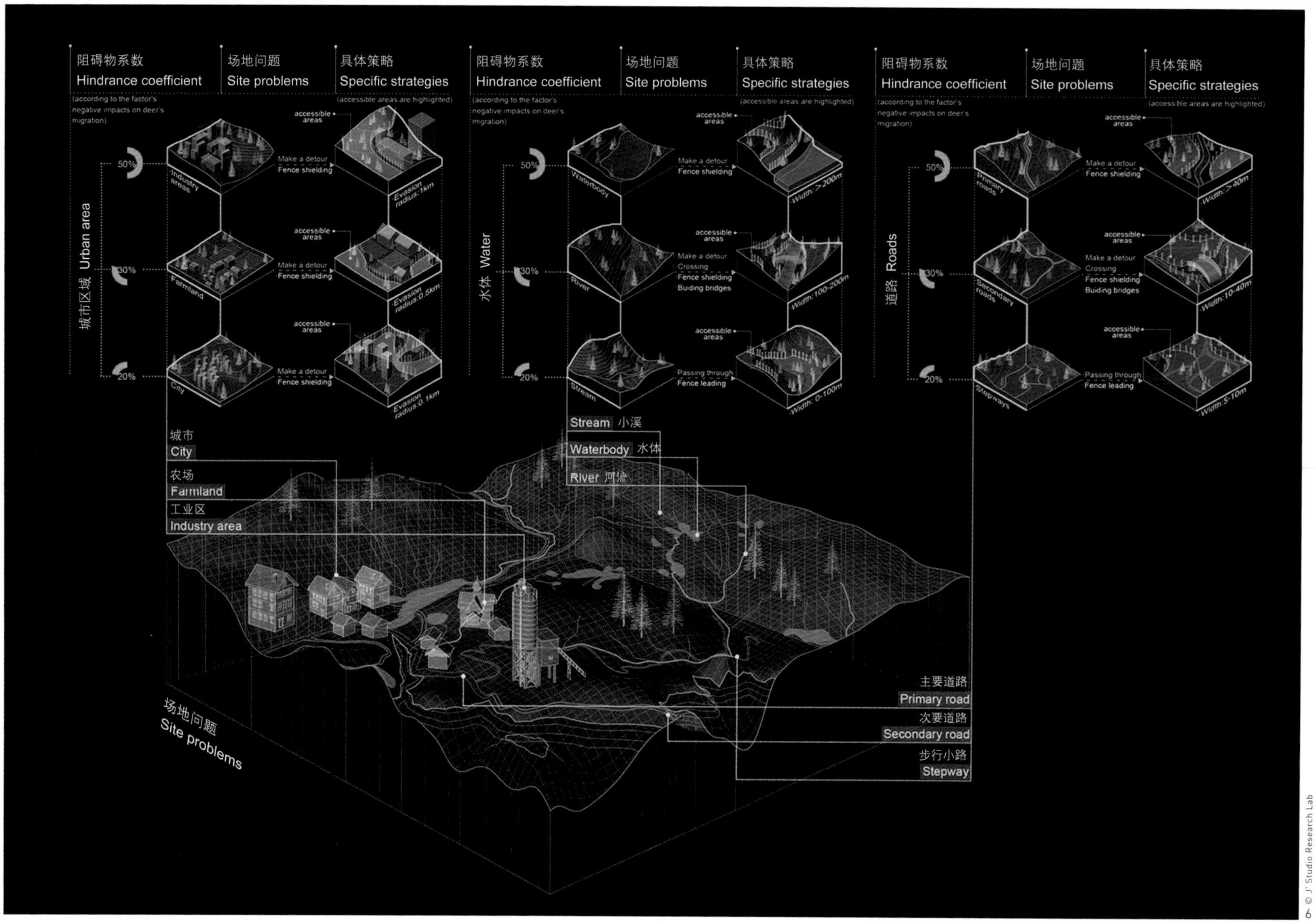

6 © J' Studio Research Lab

6. 应对气候变暖的驯鹿迁徙廊道设计

6. Reindeer migration corridor design in response to climate change

最严重的区域集中在密林区，高大林木在雪地上投射阴影，吸收大量的热量。科学家利用卫星图比较了被鹿群啃食和未啃食的地块，发现被啃食的苔原或灌木丛能够反射更多的太阳光，其效果足以减慢冻土的融化[16]。因此，笔者通过运用情境分析方法设计了一条迁徙路线，在保障驯鹿的可通过性与安全性（主要包括对驯鹿迁徙途中可能遇到的阻碍物进行归类分级，并提出不同的穿行策略）的同时，通过引导鹿群啃食植被来缓解冻土融化问题（图6）。

making the herders have to navigate the migration differently.[15] Relevant research reveals that the most heavily thawed frozen soil is largely distributed in dense forests, where the shadow of tall trees on the snow absorbs more heat. By using satellite images to compare with the grazed and un-grazed snow-covered sites, scientists found that grazed tundra or bushes can have a higher solar reflectance that is enough to offset the heat absorbed, which can greatly help slow the melting of frozen soils[16]. Through scenario analysis, the authors planned a new migration route that can ensure the passing and safety of the reindeers—primarily by classifying the possible obstacles on the route and arranging alternative route if necessary, and alleviating the permafrost thawing by leading the reindeers to the targeted vegetation areas (Fig. 6).

① 关于该课程的更新信息，请访问建筑联盟学院网站。

① For more information about this program, please visit the website of the Architectural Association School of Architecture.

3.3 模拟——利用原型思维测试最优设计策略

在建成景观中，设计师面对的环境是不断变化的。如今，计算机技术的发展使得设计师可以对场地环境的各个要素（风、光照、水文、沉积物等）进行模拟，最大程度接近场地的真实条件变化。其中，模拟推导设计原型的设计方法论在全球前沿院校的景观课程中受到了广泛关注。

英国建筑联盟学院开展的景观都市主义研究生项目强调将自然过程和城市发展整合为可持续的人工生态方式，对景观过程进行大量的模拟研究，并以此指导设计。①以2015年的"重塑海岸"项目为例，设计者从尼罗河三角洲沿海地区达米埃塔海岬鱼塘里使用的装置中获取了设计原型：使用泥沙围栏和泥沙幕布进行不同方向的空间围合，可以减慢泥沙的运动，改变沉积物的偏转和积累方向。同时，养鱼作业中形成的构筑物本身就有利于泥沙的沉积，这反过来又能有利于当地居民扩大生产。[17]

计算机技术支持设计者在迭代模拟运行时实时做出决策。当沉积物到达与潟湖边缘土地相接的高度时，设计者根据他们规划的引导角度设置了更多的泥沙截取装置，这些岛屿起到了控制和形成额外潟湖的作用。这一过程的不断重复不仅形成了一系列堆叠的潟湖，也为当地沿海居民提供了新的生存环境（图7）。

此外，以模拟验证原型设计过程的还有由克里斯托弗·吉鲁特教授指导的苏黎世联邦理工学院的景观设计课程——机器人自动化建造的景观。该课程将计算机模拟设计方法论与机械臂实验相结合，要求学生随着时间的推移开发创新的河道地形原型，以确保河流在这种动态景观中的长期平衡。[18][19]

J' Studio景观研究工作室同样将模拟作为测试设计原型，从而指导设计的重要手段。模拟方法包括计算机模拟和物理实验模拟；模拟对象涵盖水文、城市扩张、流体、泥沙、群聚、风环境、太阳辐射等。例如，位于佛得角共和国福戈岛的"岩浆引流——火山灾害下的农业景观"项目通过使用流体模拟，指导策略生成、原型选择，以及最终

3.3 Simulation—Prototyping for Optimizing Design Strategy

The environment of the built landscape is constantly changing. Nowadays, the advance of computer technology allows designers to simulate various site elements (wind, light, hydrology, sediment, etc.), as close as possible to the authenticity. The methodology that deduces design prototypes through simulation has been widely employed in landscape courses of leading colleges in the world.

The AA Landscape Urbanism (AALU) is a research graduate program in the Architectural Association School of Architecture. This program offers a way in which it allows the integration of natural processes and urban development into a sustainable artificial ecology and contextualizes the practice through stimulations of landscape processes.① Taking the Littoral Negotiations project in 2015 as an example, the AALU designers extracted a design prototype from a fishery device in the Damietta Spit, a coastal area of the Nile Delta. Techniques such as silt fences and silt curtains are used to slow sediment movement and for deflection and accumulation. The fish farmers themselves have an incentive to deploy this technique given that it has the capacity to accumulate land, which in turn allows them to expand their production.[17]

Computer technology supported the designers making real-time decisions during the iterative simulations. When the spit reached the point at which it touched the land forming a lagoon, the designers inserted more islands as sediment interception devices arranged in a designed angle, which serve to control and provoke the formation of an additional lagoon, offering implications upon the lives of the people who live in the Damietta Spit (Fig. 7).

Another program that verifies the prototyping design process through simulations is the Robotic Landscapes at ETH Zürich, led by Professor Christophe Girot. This program introduces an experimental robotic arm into the computer simulation, and requires students to develop innovative river typology that changes over time, to ensure the long-term dynamism of the river landscape.[18][19]

J' Studio Research Lab also uses simulation as a primary means to test prototypes to optimize the design. The simulations employed include computational simulation and physical simulation, and the application ranges from hydrology, urban expansion, flux, sediment, clusters to the wind,and solar radiation. For example, in the project "Lava Diversion—Structure Strategy for Volcanic Hazards and Barren Land" in Fogo, Cape Verde, flux simulation was used for developing design strategies, selecting prototypes,

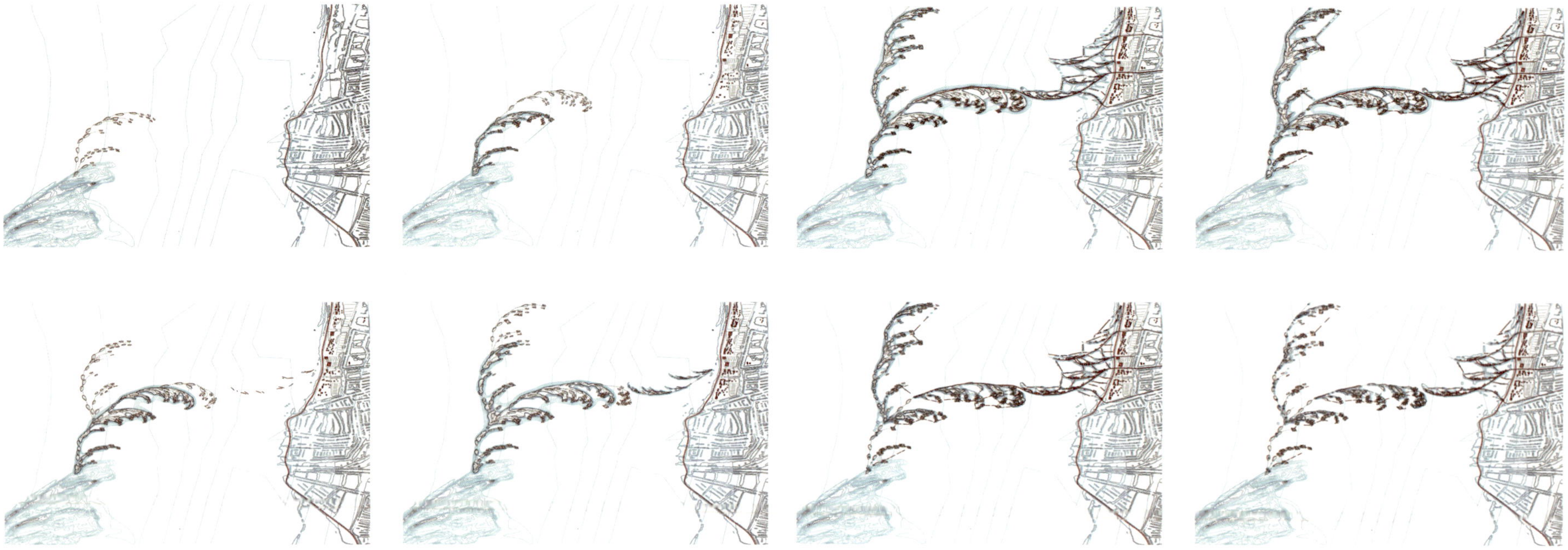

7 © _. Mouritz

设计的形成（图8，9）。该项目旨在利用引流装置将火山灾害转化为机遇：火山喷发是一种自然灾害，但是它同时也是一种潜在资源——火山灰是良好的农业肥料。设计者通过调查场地的地质条件、村落分布、岩浆的喷发及流动情况等，在结合流体模拟的基础上提出了引流装置的设计原型，以在火山喷发时将岩浆引流至人烟稀少、土壤贫瘠的地方。同时，项目利用火山喷发后的风化物质改善当地土壤肥力，促进岛屿农业和旅游业的发展，以及岛民生活条件的改善。

4 讨论与结论

在人类主观能动性改造自然的过程中，空间设计原型作为一种经验始终贯穿于人的意识中，其在设计领域中发挥的作用也不断演变——原型思维既是一种研究方法，也是一种设计和验证的手段。

自20世纪80年代末以来，景观都市主义理论在查尔斯·瓦尔德海姆、理查德·韦勒、科纳、莫森·莫斯塔法维等人的推动下逐渐完善，建成景观的历史背景、复杂性及时间性都被纳入设计师的考虑范

and forming the final schemes (Fig. 8, 9). The project aims to turn volcanic disasters into opportunities with designed drainage devices. A volcanic eruption is a natural disaster but it can also bring a potential resource: the volcanic ash is good fertilizer for plants. By investigating the geological conditions of the site, the distribution of villages, and the eruption and the flow of lava, the designers proposed design prototypes of the drainage devices through the flux simulation—Lava can be diverted to the sparsely populated and barren areas when the volcanic eruption occurs. At the same time, the project uses the volcanic ash to improve the fertility of the island, promoting the agriculture and tourism development of the island and improving the living standards of the locals.

4 Discussion and Conclusion

The process of transforming the nature manifests human's use of prototypes of spatial design as a conscious experience, and the role of these prototypes in the field of design is continuously evolving: Prototyping is not only a research method but also a means of design and a way of testing design ideas.

Since the end of the 1980s, the theory of Landscape Urbanism has seen an improvement with the efforts by scholars—including Charles Waldheim, Richard Weller, Corner, and Mohsen Mostafavi—and the historical background, the complexity, and the dimension of time of the built landscape

7. 鱼塘与潟湖的地形演化
8. 岩浆引流设计策略：通过物理实验进行火山喷发模拟

7. Topographical intersection evolution of the fishery area and the lagoon
8. Lava diversion strategy: simulation of eruption with physical experiments

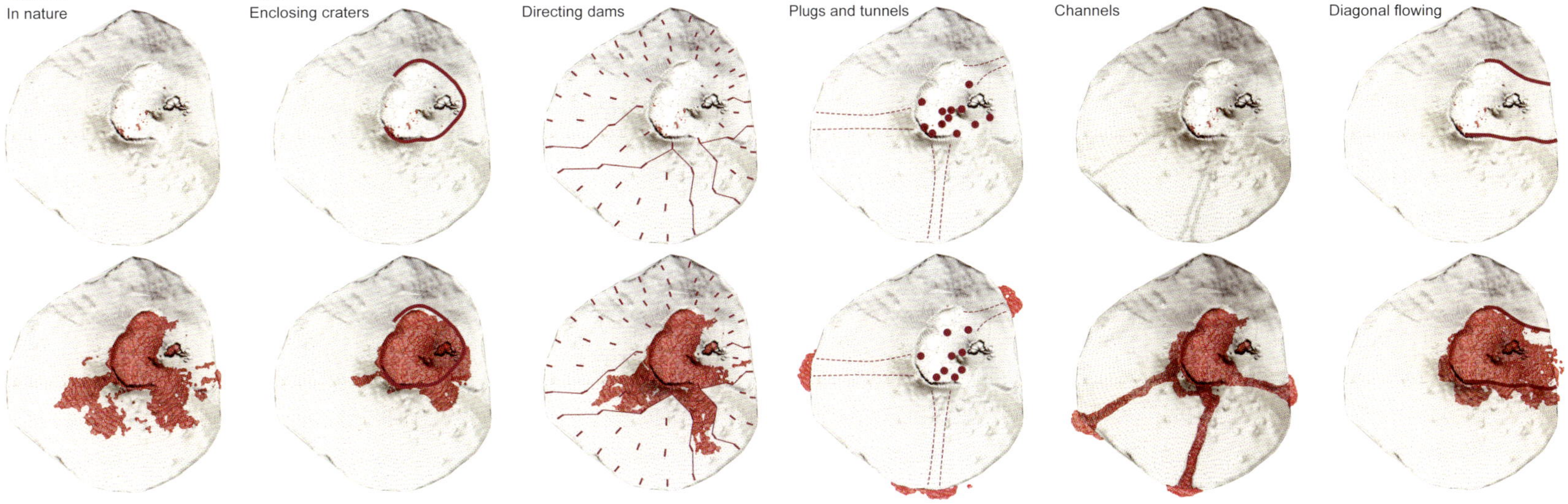

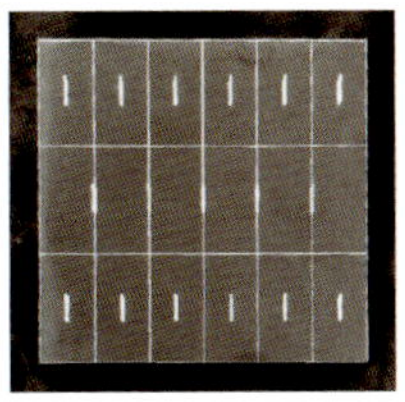

在18cm × 18cm的丙烯酸板上划分出3排6列网格，将凹槽切穿，并将代表“导流坝”的短板插入凹槽中

With 3 × 6 reference lines in 18 cm × 18 cm acrylic plate, the groove is cut through and the short-plate dams are inserted into the groove

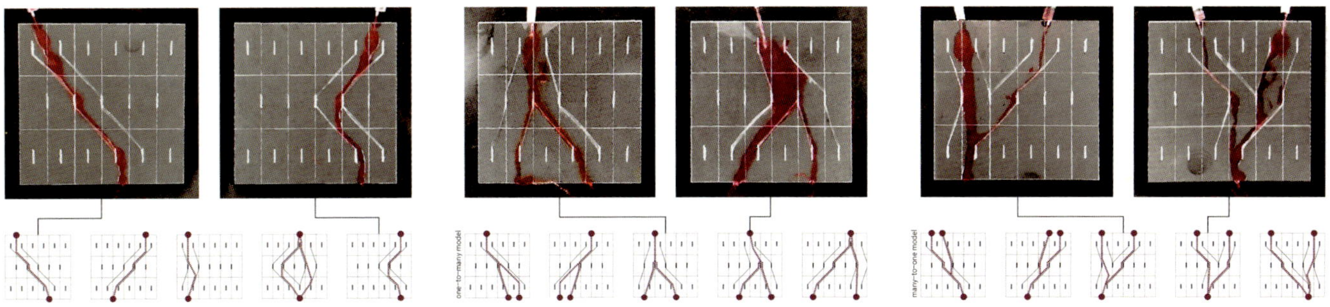

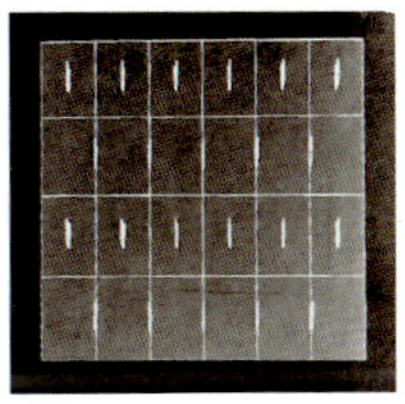

在18cm × 18cm的丙烯酸板上划分出4排6列网格，将凹槽切穿，并将代表“导流坝”的短板插入凹槽中

With 4 × 6 reference lines in 18 cm × 18 cm acrylic plate, the groove is cut through and the short-plate dams are inserted into the groove

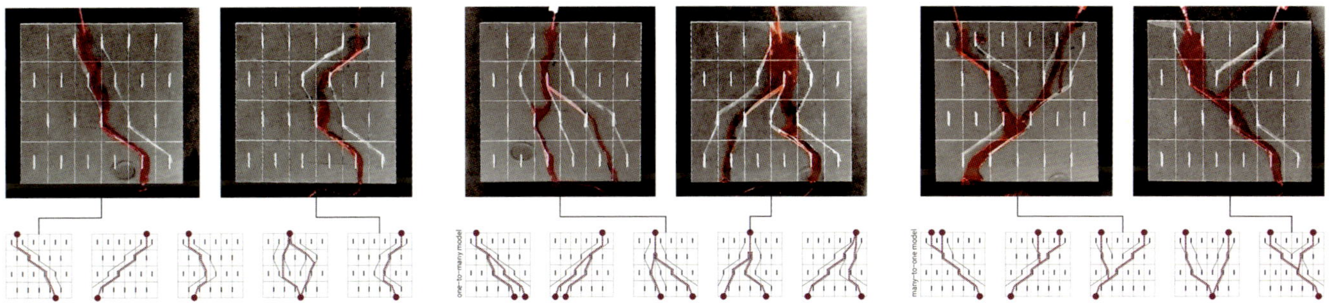

在18cm × 18cm的丙烯酸板上划分出6排6列网格，将凹槽切穿，并将代表“导流坝”的短板插入凹槽中

With 6 × 6 reference lines in 18 cm × 18 cm acrylic plate, the groove is cut through and the short-plate dams are inserted into the groove

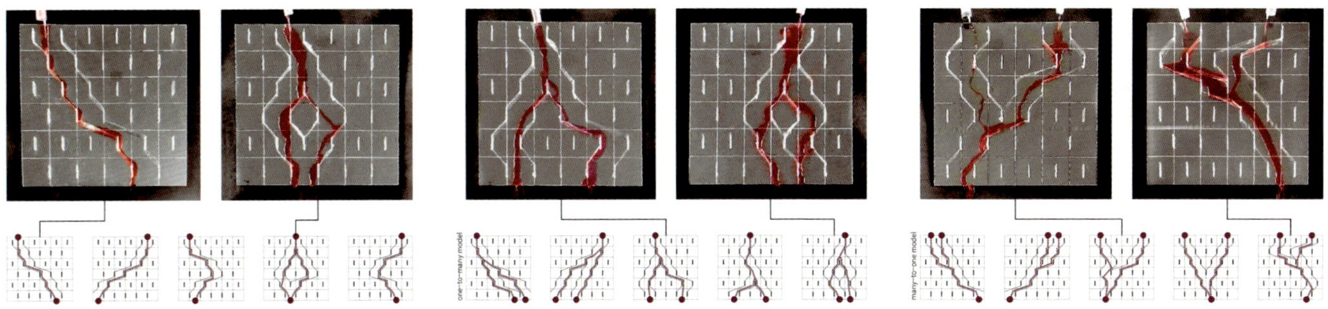

8 © J' Studio Research Lab

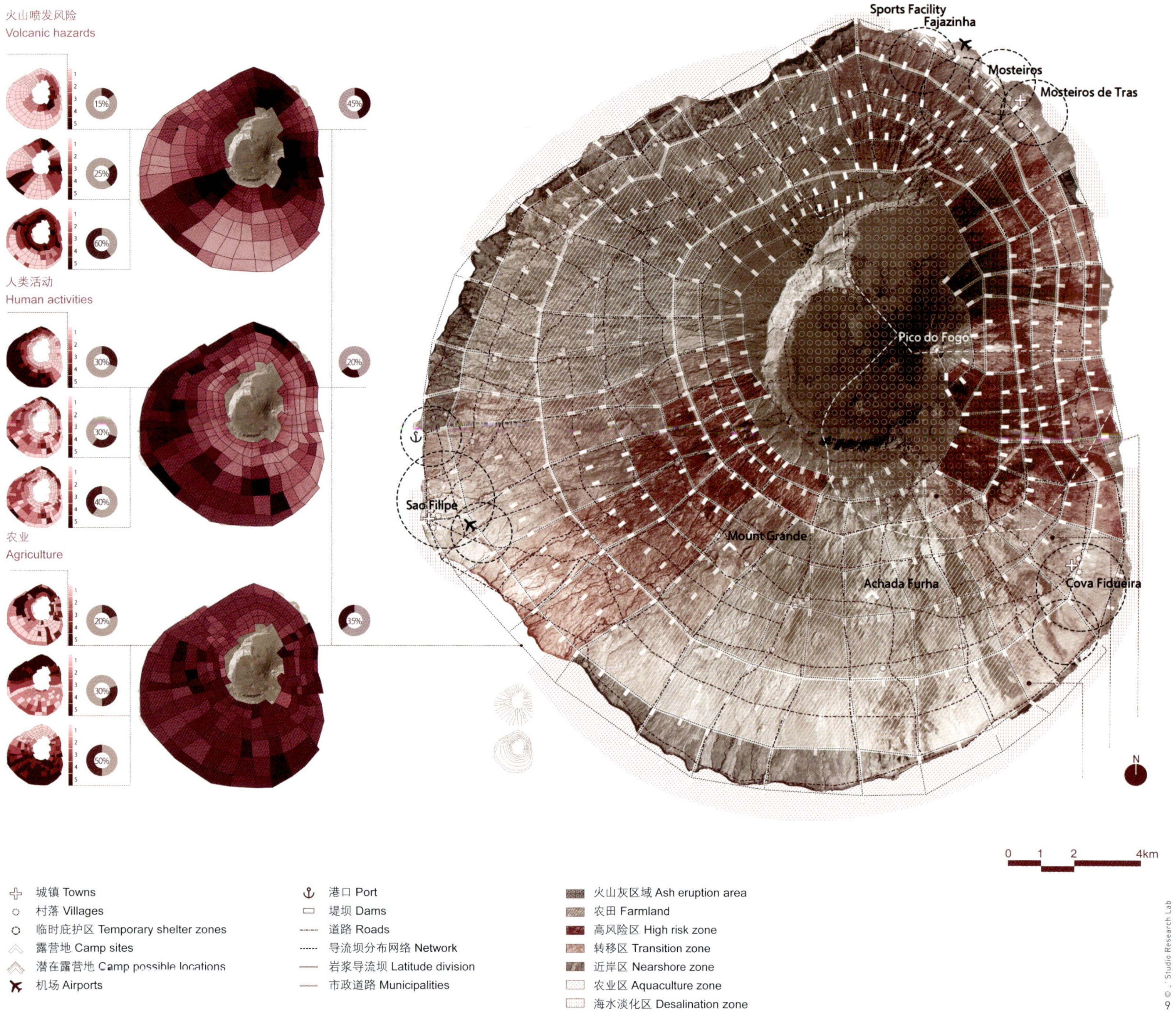

9. 岩浆引流设计策略：设计方案评估

9. Lava diversion strategy: evaluation of plan

畴。设计师可以利用场地切片的方法，从研究场地中提取、简化或抽象推演空间原型，对建成景观的历史背景进行研究归纳；通过情境分析，设计师可以对可能出现的条件变化做出假想和预判，从而提出应对情境的设计原型；在时间景观的语境下，使用计算机技术对场地所

are all underscored in the design process. Designers can use the approaches of site section to extract, simplify, or abstractly deduce the prototypes of spatial design, as a way of investigating the historical background of the given site; Through scenario analysis, designers can make predictions on possible changes of site situations to conceive the design prototype accordingly; Highlighting that landscapes process over time, computer

处环境要素进行模拟，使设计师能够根据实时变化及时调整原型的组合或变体。

与此同时，原型思维也存在一定的局限性。例如，虽然原型思维在抽象—衍化—测试—结果的过程中作为一种预判设计方法是可行的，但在现实条件中，这种强调过程的设计方法忽略了设计受到的政治和社会层面的制约[20]。再比如，由于景观设计师面临的设计对象（如城市、自然）都属于混沌系统，具有不确定性和不可预知性[21]，任何初始条件的细微差异都有可能导致原型设计从理论到应用过程中出现偏差[22]。

但是，总的来说，得益于在生成设计策略与推敲设计方案时的优势，越来越多的景观实践和研究将原型思维纳入其方法论中。这不仅是由于现代景观的动态性和复杂性，更突显了跨学科合作的必要性。事实上，原型思维不仅是设计师理解场地、深入设计和验证结果的工具，更可作为一种简单有效的沟通方法，帮助公众、政府部门、开发商等不同群体理解设计师所做的干预。相信在未来，原型思维会帮助景观设计师制定出更具有实践意义和创新性的解决方案。**LAF**

technology supports designers to simulate the alternations of environmental elements of the site, during which real-time adjustments and iterations on the prototypes, be it combinations or variants, can be made.

Meanwhile, the limitations of prototyping cannot be denied. For example, although prototyping is applicable in the process of extraction-deduction-test-outcome, as a prediction means, in reality "the idea of process is limiting today because it works against the agency of design as a political and social project"[20]. For another example, in landscape design, the objects are often chaotic systems, such as cities and the nature, which are characterized by uncertainty and unpredictability[21], and any subtle or sensitive dependence on initial conditions would lead to a disparity in the formation process of a prototype or in its application in design practice[22].

However, in general, prototyping has benefited the development of design strategies and design schemes, and more and more landscape practices and studies demonstrate the working integration of prototyping with methodology. This not only results from the dynamics and complexity of the modern landscape but also comes to prominence of interdisciplinary collaboration. In fact, besides being a tool for designers to comprehend the site, improve proposals, and test outcomes, prototyping can also help with designers' communication with the public, the government, developers, etc., who can better understand the design interventions simply and effectively. In the future, prototyping will witness a broader application in landscape design practice as impulses to innovative solutions. **LAF**

REFERENCES

[1] Dancy, R. M. (2004). The Genesis of the Theory of Forms: Aristotle's Account. Plato's Introduction of Forms (pp. 11-19). Cambridge: Cambridge University Press.

[2] Watt, S. (1997). Introduction: The Theory of Forms (Books 5–7). Plato: Republic (pp.14-16). London: Wordsworth Editions.

[3] Ozkan, S. (2001). Development of Thinking and Theory in Architecture. Center for the Study of the Built Environment. Retrieved from https://www.csbe.org/development-of

[4] Moneo, R. (1978). On Typology. Oppositions, (13), 22-45.

[5] Anderson, S. (1984). Architectural research programmes in the work of Le Corbusier. Design Studies, 5(3), 151-158. doi:10.1016/0142-694x(84)90007-3

[6] Rossi, A., & Eisenman, P. (1982). The Architecture of the City (pp. 27-35, 111). Cambridge: MIT Press.

[7] Canniffe, E. (2012). Aldo Rossi: The Architecture of the City (1966). Retrieved from http://architectureandurbanism.blogspot.com/2012/06/aldo-rossi-architecture-of-city-1966.html

[8] Corner, J. (2006). Terra Fluxus. In C. Waldheim (Ed.), The Landscape Urbanism Reader (pp. 21-33). New York: Princeton Architectural Press.

[9] Condon, P. (1994). A Built Landscape Typology: The Language of the Land We Live in. In K. A. Franck, & L. H. Schneekloth (Eds.), Ordering Space: Types in Architecture and Design (pp. 79-94). New York: Van Nostrand Reinhold.

[10] Milizia, F. (2018). Principi di architettura civile Vol. 3 [Principles of civil architecture Vol. 3]. London: Forgotten Books.

[11] Pollio, V. (2012). The Architecture of Marcus Vitruvius Pollio: In Ten Books (Book II, Chapter I). London: Forgotten Books.

[12] Vidler, A. (1977). The idea of type: The transformation of the academic ideal, 1750-1830. Oppositions, (8), 95-111.

[13] De Chamoust, R. (1783). L'Ordre Francois Trouve dans la Nature [The Order Francois Found in the Nature]. Paris: Nyon.

[14] Wheeler, S. M. (2015). Built landscapes of metropolitan regions: An international typology. Journal of the American Planning Association, 81(3), 167-190. doi:10.1080/01944363.2015.1081567

[15] Arctic Climate Impact Assessment. (2005). Arctic Climate Impact Assessment, ACIA Overview Report (p. 1020). Cambridge: Cambridge University Press. Retrieved from https://www.amap.no/documents/doc/arctic-arctic-climate-impact-assessment/796

[16] Beer, C., Zimov, N., Olofsson, J., Porada, P., & Zimov, S. (2020). Protection of Permafrost Soils from Thawing by Increasing Herbivore Density. Scientific Reports, (10), 4170. https://doi.org/10.1038/s41598-020-60938-y

[17] Mouritz, L., Chang, T., & Hu, X. (2015). Littoral Negotiations. London: Architectural Association Landscape Urbanism.

[18] Fahmi, F. (2020, February 05). Design Studio HS2019: Robotic Landscapes III. Retrieved from https://girot.arch.ethz.ch/courses/design-studios/design-studio-hs2019-robotic-landscapes-iii-2

[19] Girot, C., & Hurkxkens, I. (2018). Robotic Landscapes—Nature, Computation, and the Design Space of Autonomous Terrain Modeling. Landscape Architecture Frontiers, 6(2), 64-75.

[20] Berrizbeitia, A. (2016). On the Limits of Process: The Case for Precision in Landscape (pp. 110-117). In D. Daou, & P. Pérez-Ramos (Eds.), New Geographies 08: Island. Cambridge: Harvard University Press.

[21] Alexander, C. (1967). A city is not a tree. Ekistics, 23(139), 334-348.

[22] Worster, D. (1990). The ecology of order and chaos. Environmental History Review, 14(1/2), 1-18.

本文引用格式 / PLEASE CITE THIS ARTICLE AS

Zhang, J., Yu, Z., & Zhao, B. (2020). Impact Mechanism of Urban Green Spaces in Promoting Public Health: Theoretical Framework and Inspiration for Practical Experiences. Landscape Architecture Frontiers, 8(4), 104-113. https://doi.org/10.15302/J-LAF-1-030019

https://doi.org/10.15302/J-LAF-1-030019 收稿时间 RECEIVED DATE / 2020-03-31 中图分类号 / TU984 文献标识码 / A

城市绿地促进人群健康的作用途径：理论框架与实践启示

IMPACT MECHANISM OF URBAN GREEN SPACES IN PROMOTING PUBLIC HEALTH: THEORETICAL FRAMEWORK AND INSPIRATION FOR PRACTICAL EXPERIENCES

摘要

城市绿地不仅可以提供广泛的生态系统服务，也能提升人群健康。当前，已有大量研究论述了城市绿地与人群健康的关系并取得了诸多进展，但尚缺少对两者复杂潜在作用途径的探讨。本文首先论述了城市绿地对人群健康的积极与消极影响，其次从鼓励体力活动、缓解精神压力、提高社会凝聚力和提供生态系统调节 / 支持服务4个方面构建了城市绿地促进人群健康的作用途径理论框架。在此框架研究基础上初步提出了健康导向下的城市绿地系统规划应对策略，具体包括：1）提升城市绿地的可获得性；2）提高城市绿地的可达性；3）增强城市绿地的可视性；4）优化城市绿地的空间要素组成；5）构建网络状城市绿地空间格局；6）降低城市绿地对人群健康的消极影响。研究成果可为人群健康和城市可持续发展提供有效的理论基础和经验启示，让有限的城市绿地发挥更大的健康效益。

关键词

人群健康；城市绿地；基于自然的解决方案；生态系统服务；城市绿地系统规划

ABSTRACT

Urban green spaces can not only offer a wide range of ecosystem services, but also promote public health. Most of existing studies have effectually explored the correlation between urban green spaces and public health, but failed to dig the complex impact mechanism behind. This article firstly goes into the positive and negative impacts of urban green spaces on public health, and proposes a theoretical framework of the impact mechanism from perspectives of physical activity encouragement, stress management, social cohesion enhancement, and regulating / supporting services provision by ecosystems. On this basis, 6 health-oriented urban green space system planning strategies are proposed, including promoting the availability, improving the accessibility, enhancing the visibility, optimizing the spatial composition, constructing a network pattern of urban green spaces, and reducing the negative impacts of urban green spaces on public health. The research results can provide theoretical grounding and reference for public health promotion and sustainable urban development to exert more health benefits with limited urban green spaces.

KEYWORDS

Public Health; Urban Green Spaces; Nature-Based Solutions; Ecosystem Services; Urban Green Space System Planning

张金光
南京林业大学风景园林学院与哥本哈根大学地球科学与自然资源管理系联合培养博士研究生

ZHANG Jinguang
Joint PhD Student of College of Landscape Architecture, Nanjing Forestry University and Department of Geosciences and Natural Resource Management, Faculty of Science, University of Copenhagen

余兆武
哥本哈根大学地球科学与自然资源管理系助理教授、博士生导师

YU Zhaowu*
Assistant Professor and PhD Supervisor, Department of Geosciences and Natural Resource Management, Faculty of Science, University of Copenhagen

赵兵
南京林业大学风景园林学院教授、博士生导师

ZHAO Bing
Professor and PhD Supervisor, College of Landscape Architecture, Nanjing Forestry University

*Corresponding Author
Address: Department of Geosciences and Natural Resource Management, Faculty of Science, University of Copenhagen, 1958, Copenhagen, Denmark
Email: zhyu@ign.ku.dk

编辑 冉玲于 **翻译** 王颖 冉玲于 张金光
EDITED BY RAN Lingyu **TRANSLATED BY** WANG Ying RAN Lingyu ZHANG Jinguang

1 引言

随着城市化的不断发展，人口从乡村流向城市，城市已成为人类最主要的栖息地。然而，快速的城市化进程也带来了严峻的环境和人群健康问题。快速的生活节奏、日益加大的社会竞争压力、多坐少动等缺乏体力活动的生活方式，以及城市高密度发展所导致的绿色空间的不断减少，成为引发各类精神疾病和慢性疾病的重要因素[1]~[3]。“基于自然的解决方案”（NBS）正是科学家为应对复杂的城市生态环境问题和人群健康问题所提出的一项重要行动策略，旨在高效利用自然资源，以有效且强适应的方式来应对一系列环境挑战，同时带来经济、社会和环境效益[4]。作为一种创新的可持续设计理念，NBS强调从设计实践层面实现理论价值，以达到城市韧性提升、人与自然和谐共处和资源可持续利用的目的[5]。城市绿地作为城市中重要的自然资源，是NBS的重要组成部分。城市绿地不仅为城市提供了广泛的生态系统服务[6]，也是居民亲近和感受自然的重要场所，能够缓解居民的生活和工作压力、改善人群健康[7]~[9]。玛娅·武伊契等人[10]通过跨学科方法研究了城市自然环境与人群心理健康的关系，发现NBS能有效帮助改善实验参与者的压力过大、抑郁和焦虑等状况；马蒂尔达·范·登·波什等人[11]则引入“NBS框架”综述了城市自然环境对人群健康的各类积极效益。然而，当前的NBS研究多集中于探讨生态环境问题的缓解，仅有少量研究将其与人类健康和福祉相互关联。因此，如何将城市绿地与人群健康研究和NBS理论研究相结合仍有待深入探索。此外，现有研究虽然在城市绿地与健康效益关系的探索上取得了诸多进展，但是，关于系统构建城市绿地与人群健康之间复杂潜在作用途径的相关研究仍显欠缺[12]~[14]，这直接阻碍了城市绿地系统在规划设计层面的策略实施[15]。

鉴于此，本文通过论述城市绿地对人群健康的积极与消极影响，构建了城市绿地促进人群健康的作用途径理论框架，最后从实践视角提出了相应的城市绿地系统规划应对策略和启示，以期推动实现自然解决方案的价值。

2 城市绿地对人群健康的影响

《世界卫生组织组织法》将“健康”定义为“不仅为疾病或羸弱之消除，而系体格、精神与社会之完全健康状态”[16]。据此可将“健

1 Introduction

The rapid urbanization has caused people to migrate from rural to urban areas, where have become the primary habitat for human beings. In the meantime, the living environments and health status of people are heavily challenged. For instance, mental disorders and chronic diseases are prone to happen either due to fast pace of living, increasing competitive pressure, sedentary lifestyles without physical activity, or the shrinking of green spaces[1]~[3]. Under such circumstances, “Nature-Based Solutions” (NBS), aiming at using natural resources to effectively and adaptively address a range of environmental challenges while bringing economic, social, and environmental benefits, have become a key course of action[4]. With its innovative response, NBS emphasizes the theoretical value via design practices to achieve urban resilience, harmonious human-nature relationship, and sustainable resource utilization[5]. In this regard, urban green spaces could act as a crucial NBS because it provides not only extensive ecosystem services[6], but also opportunities for people to get close to and enjoy the nature with benefits such as stress relief and health improvement[7]~[9]. Specifically, Maja Vujcic et al.[10] found that NBS can effectively relieve participants’ feelings of stress, depression, and anxiety in an interdisciplinary research on the linkage between urban natural environments and human psychological health. Matilda van den Bosch et al.[11] further introduced an NBS framework to summarize positive effects of urban natural environments on public health. However, such studies on how urban green spaces may impact public health and human well-being are insufficient as most of the current NBS-related research focus mainly on mitigating ecological and environmental problems. Moreover, although considerable studies have explored the links between urban green spaces and public health, there is still a gap in identifying and structuring their complex mechanism of action[12]~[14], which directly impedes the implementation of relevant strategies in urban green space system planning and design[15].

In response, this study explores the positive and negative impacts of urban green spaces on public health, constructs a theoretical framework for the mechanism of urban green spaces in promoting public health, and finally proposes potential strategies and inspirations for health-oriented urban green space system planning to realize the value of NBS.

2 Impacts of Urban Green Spaces on Public Health

The Constitution of the World Health Organization defines that health is a state of complete physical, mental, and social

康”分为生理健康、心理健康和社会健康。目前已有大量文献通过实验研究、典型案例研究或追踪调查等方法探索了城市绿地与人群健康的关系。

在生理健康层面，城市绿地能够降低人群罹患慢性疾病和临床疾病的风险，进而降低人群死亡率。如米雷娅·加斯康等学者综述了12篇研究绿地与死亡率相关性的文献，发现在绿化覆盖率较高的居住区，居民的死亡率相对较低——其中患心血管疾病人群的死亡风险显著降低[17]。现有研究也表明绿地与心脏病、呼吸系统疾病、肝癌、慢性乙肝等临床疾病的发病率有很大关系[11]。此外，城市绿地能够降低人群罹患代谢性疾病的风险，如肥胖症、糖尿病等[18]。

在心理健康层面，居住区周边的绿地面积（或可达性）与居民的心理健康程度有着密切联系。现有文献讨论了城市绿地对特定精神疾病的缓解效应，主要包括焦虑症[19]、多动症[20]、精神分裂症和抑郁症等[21]。同时，大量文献通过实验设计和自我报告等方法表明绿地体验（活动）能够提升情绪积极性。这些研究主要围绕由罗杰·乌尔里希提出的压力缓解理论[22]和史蒂芬·卡普兰提出的注意力恢复理论展开[23]，包括对人群与城市绿地接触情况进行的单次或连续多次的跟踪调研。如相关研究证实了城市绿地不仅能够提升人群的积极情绪和幸福感指数[24]，而且对记忆力和注意力[25]，儿童的认知功能[26]、学习行为[27]，以及想象力和创造力等方面都有着积极影响[28]。

在社会健康层面，城市绿地提供了社区居民社交活动的空间，能够促进社会互动，进而增强居民归属感、支持感和参与感[29]，促使居民感悟生活意义[30]，增加场所依恋性[31]，进而增强社会凝聚力和社会资本，促进人群的社会健康。

然而，相关研究表明城市绿地偶尔也会对人群健康产生负面影响，主要包括三个方面：1）城市绿地中某些植物的花粉传播会导致过敏性疾病[32]；2）城市绿地（尤其是水体周边）中的蚊子会加速疟疾等传染性疾病的传播[33]；3）因城市绿地的维护工作而造成的伤害[34]。

3 城市绿地促进人群健康的作用途径

3.1 城市绿地暴露度与人群健康

绿地能够充分地“暴露”（exposure）于城市居民之中，是其实现各类健康效益的基本前提和必要途径。“暴露”是一个较为宽泛的学术用语，指的是基于一定的绿地特征（如面积、类型、设施品质）的城市绿地暴露度[35]，可以通过多种指标进行评估，如城市绿地的可获得性、可达性和可视性[36]。可获得性是一种数量指标，通常表示为一定范围内的绿地总量（主要指绿地总面积或面积占比）或一定范围内的平均归一化植被指数（NDVI）[37]。可达性是一种距离／时间指标，通常指到达公园绿地的距离或所耗用的旅行时间，往往通过ArcGIS来估测居

well-being and not merely the absence of disease or infirmity[16], according to which it may cover physical health, mental health, and social health. A large collection of papers have studied the link between urban green spaces and public health via experimental research, case study, and longitudinal research.

Regarding the physical health, urban green spaces are proved effective in reducing people's risks of suffering from chronic and clinical diseases, thus lowering the mortality rate. For example, Mireia Gascon et al. systematically reviewed 12 papers and found that the mortality rate is relatively lower in residential areas with higher greenery coverage—especially for mortality caused by cardiovascular diseases[17]. Studies have also indicated a close relation between urban green spaces and the incidence of clinical diseases such as heart disease, respiratory diseases, liver cancer, and chronic hepatitis B[11]. Furthermore, urban green spaces can help decrease the morbidity of metabolic diseases, such as obesity and diabetes[18].

The area (or accessibility) of surrounding green spaces is closely associated to residents' mental health. Recent reviews have pointed out that some mental illnesses, such as anxiety disorder[19], attention deficit hyperactivity disorder (ADHD)[20], schizophrenia, and depression[21], can be ameliorated with urban green spaces. Additionally, a large amount of research with experimental data and self-reports showed that experience and physical activities in green spaces may catalyze positive moods. These studies were normally conducted on the basis of two main theories, i.e. the Stress Reduction Theory proposed by Roger Ulrich[22] and the Attention Restoration Theory by Stephen Kaplan[23], and developed by the investigations of single as well as cumulative occasions of nature contact. Relevant research confirmed that urban green spaces improve not only the positive moods and happiness of the public[24], but also children's memory and attention[25], cognitive functioning[26], learning behavior[27], imagination, and creativity[28].

On the level of social health, urban green spaces provide opportunities for residents to interact, which enhances their sense of coherence, support, and participation[29] with a better understanding of the worthwhile or good life[30]. In the meantime, place attachment[31] would also come into being with increased social cohesion and social capital, and finally the social health.

However, studies have shown that urban green spaces may also have negative impacts on public health: 1) pollen allergy caused by pollen emission[32]; 2) the spread of infectious diseases (such as malaria) accelerated by mosquitoes flying in urban green spaces (especially around water bodies)[33]; and 3) injuries caused by urban green spaces management activities[34].

住地和公园绿地之间的欧氏距离或网络距离[38]，或通过网络地图的API接口获取出行时间值。可视性指的是居民通勤出行时或者其住宅附近绿地的可视情况，通常借助调研问卷的自我报告形式或Google地球街景模式等方式获取[36]。

不同的“暴露”指标的选取，一定程度上依赖于城市绿地对人群健康的作用途径[7]。例如，可获得性适用于描述城市绿地所能提供的生态系统服务的能力，尤其是生态系统的调节服务所带来的健康效益；可达性指标更多被用于评估与人类活动相关的健康效益——如促进体力活动；可视性指标则更适用于城市绿地对心理健康的影响作用，常被应用于以注意力恢复理论和压力缓解理论为基础的科学问题上（图1）。

3.2 作用途径的理论框架建构

城市绿地促进人群健康的作用途径理论框架主要包含鼓励体力活动、缓解精神压力、提高社会凝聚力和提供生态系统调节 / 支持服务4个方面（图2）。

3.2.1 鼓励体力活动

居住在（或易于到达）有一定活动设施的城市绿地附近，有利于人群的生理和心理健康，其中最重要的作用途径就是鼓励居民开展散步、慢跑等体力活动[39]。在城市居民三大活动领域（工作、交通和休闲）中，城市绿地主要通过交通（步行或骑自行车）和休闲（运动或游憩）促进体力活动。例如，伊娃·海宁等人指出在前往目的地途

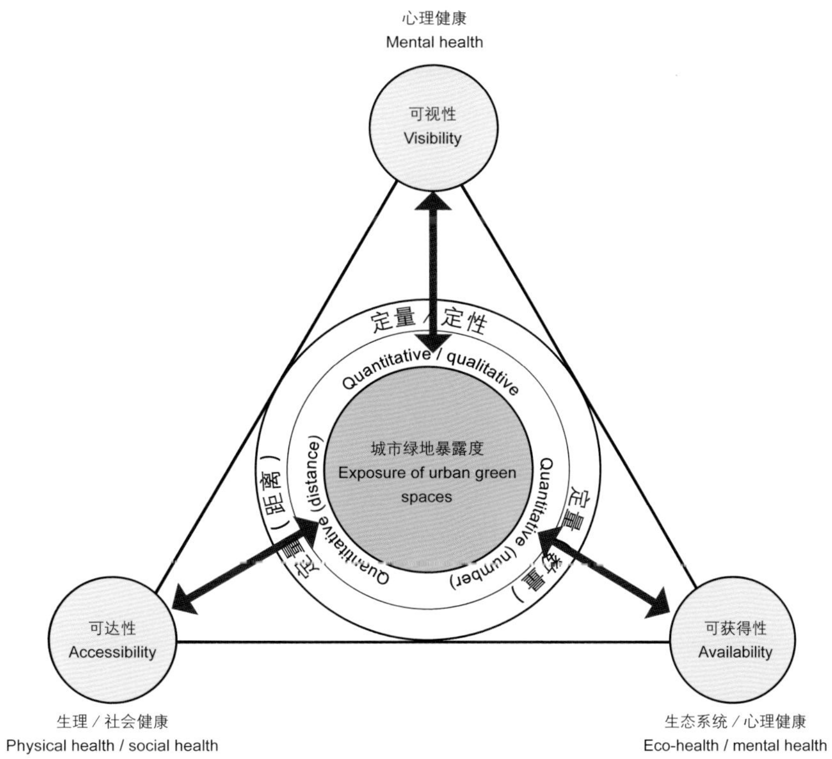

© 张金光，余兆武，赵兵

1

1. 城市绿地暴露度与人群健康的关系

1. The relationship between exposure of urban green spaces and public health

3 Impact Mechanism of Urban Green Spaces in Promoting Public Health

3.1 Exposure of Urban Green Spaces and Public Health

In realizing the health promotion benefits, urban green spaces should be able to have full “exposure” to residents. “Exposure,” as a broad term, here means the exposure degree of urban green spaces based on their natural features (size, type, and qualities such as configuration)[35], which is often assessed by various indicators including the availability, accessibility, and visibility[36]. Availability refers to the total area or proportion of the green spaces, or the average NDVI within a defined spatial distance[37]. Accessibility is the distance or time spent from residence to parks, which can be estimated by the Euclidean Distance or network distance by ArcGIS or travel times via API data from digital maps[38]. Visibility represents the green spaces that can be seen visually when residents commute or move around the residential communities, which are usually accessed from self-reports or Google Earth Street View[36].

The selection of different “exposure” indicators, to a certain extent, depends on the mechanism of urban green spaces impacting public health[7]. For example, when emphasizing the ecosystem services provided by urban green spaces, especially the health benefits as regulating services, the indicator of availability is preferable; accessibility is usually used to assess the health benefits associated with human activities, such as the promotion of physical activity; visibility is more applicable in evaluating the effect of urban green spaces on mental health—especially concerning questions based on Attention Restoration Theory and Stress Reduction Theory (Fig. 1).

3.2 Theoretical Framework Construction of the Impact Mechanism

In this study, the impact mechanism of urban green spaces in promoting the public health was summarized to 4 approaches: 1) physical activity encouragement; 2) stress management; 3) social cohesion enhancement; and 4) ecosystem regulating / supporting services provision (Fig. 2).

3.2.1 Physical Activity Encouragement

Easily accessible urban green spaces with certain recreational facilities is significant to human physical and mental health, as it could encourage residents to carry out physical activities such as walking and jogging[39]. For citizens, physical activities are usually realized via commuting (walking or cycling) and recreation (sports or touring). For example, Eva Heinen et al. pointed out that people prefer walking or cycling in paths with beautiful and greenery-covered scenes[40]. Studies also confirmed that physical activities in green spaces bring about more health benefits than activities

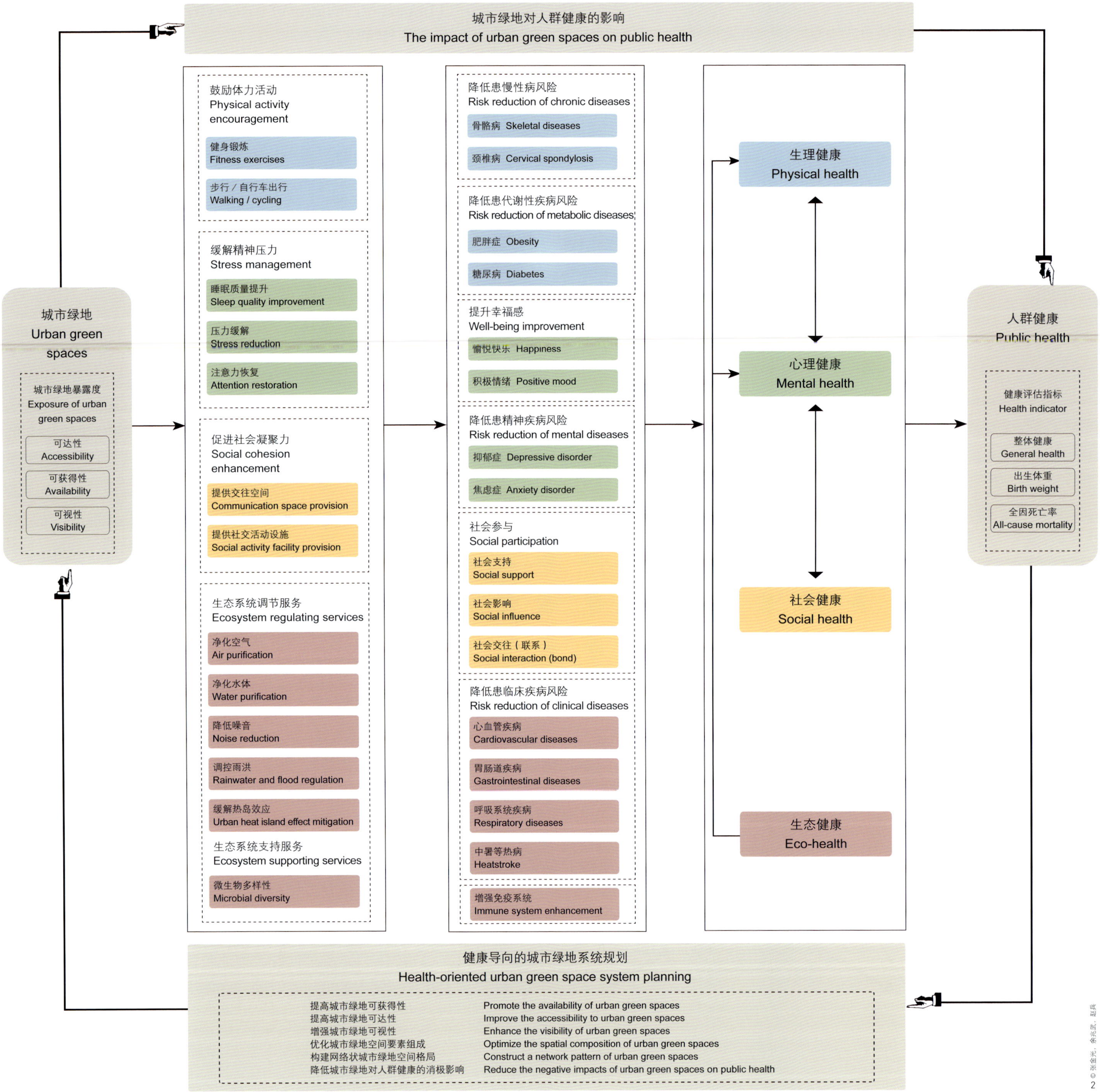
城市绿地对人群健康的影响
The impact of urban green spaces on public health
城市绿地
Urban green spaces
城市绿地暴露度
Exposure of urban green spaces
可达性
Accessibility
可获得性
Availability
可视性
Visibility
鼓励体力活动
Physical activity encouragement
健身锻炼
Fitness exercises
步行 / 自行车出行
Walking / cycling
缓解精神压力
Stress management
睡眠质量提升
Sleep quality improvement
压力缓解
Stress reduction
注意力恢复
Attention restoration
促进社会凝聚力
Social cohesion enhancement
提供交往空间
Communication space provision
提供社交活动设施
Social activity facility provision
生态系统调节服务
Ecosystem regulating services
净化空气
Air purification
净化水体
Water purification
降低噪音
Noise reduction
调控雨洪
Rainwater and flood regulation
缓解热岛效应
Urban heat island effect mitigation
生态系统支持服务
Ecosystem supporting services
微生物多样性
Microbial diversity
降低患慢性病风险
Risk reduction of chronic diseases
骨骼病 Skeletal diseases
颈椎病 Cervical spondylosis
降低患代谢性疾病风险
Risk reduction of metabolic diseases
肥胖症 Obesity
糖尿病 Diabetes
提升幸福感
Well-being improvement
愉悦快乐 Happiness
积极情绪 Positive mood
降低患精神疾病风险
Risk reduction of mental diseases
抑郁症 Depressive disorder
焦虑症 Anxiety disorder
社会参与
Social participation
社会支持
Social support
社会影响
Social influence
社会交往（联系）
Social interaction (bond)
降低患临床疾病风险
Risk reduction of clinical diseases
心血管疾病
Cardiovascular diseases
胃肠道疾病
Gastrointestinal diseases
呼吸系统疾病
Respiratory diseases
中暑等热病
Heatstroke
增强免疫系统
Immune system enhancement
生理健康
Physical health
心理健康
Mental health
社会健康
Social health
生态健康
Eco-health
人群健康
Public health
健康评估指标
Health indicator
整体健康
General health
出生体重
Birth weight
全因死亡率
All-cause mortality
健康导向的城市绿地系统规划
Health-oriented urban green space system planning
提高城市绿地可获得性
提高城市绿地可达性
增强城市绿地可视性
优化城市绿地空间要素组成
构建网络状城市绿地空间格局
降低城市绿地对人群健康的消极影响
Promote the availability of urban green spaces
Improve the accessibility to urban green spaces
Enhance the visibility of urban green spaces
Optimize the spatial composition of urban green spaces
Construct a network pattern of urban green spaces
Reduce the negative impacts of urban green spaces on public health

2 © 张金光，余兆武，赵兵

2. 城市绿地对人群健康作用途径的理论框架

2. The theoretical framework of urban green spaces' impact mechanism on public health

中，风景优美、绿地覆盖率较高的路径会促使人们选择步行或骑自行车出行[40]。多项研究证实，在绿地上开展的体力活动比在其他环境（如室内）中的活动更具健康效益[1]。体力活动能够降低罹患慢性疾病和代谢性疾病的风险，如预防和治疗业已成为"全球头号杀手"的心血管疾病[11]。

3.2.2 缓解精神压力

在城市绿地进行体验（活动）后，人群能更好地消除疲劳、缓解压力，产生更多的积极情绪。实证表明，居住在绿地周边的人群所承受的心理压力普遍较低，恢复能力更强，且更能集中注意力。大量研究通过参与者自我报告，统计绿地暴露度与各类健康指标之间的相关性，证实了绿地体验（活动）能够改善睡眠和减轻压力[41][42]——二者是人群罹患精神疾病（尤其是抑郁症）的主要因素[35][43]。格雷戈里·N·布拉特曼等人的研究表明，实验对象在进行绿地体验（活动）后，大脑内的前扣带回皮层、背外侧前额叶皮层和背内侧前额叶皮层的活跃度会增强，这将有效降低罹患精神疾病的风险[44]。

3.2.3 提高社会凝聚力

社会关系可以通过以下机制影响健康：社会参与、社会支持、社会影响，以及社会交往（联系）[31]。城市绿地（尤其是社区公园）能够提供居民社会交往所需的公共空间，促进人群或邻里之间频繁的社会接触和联系，提升群众参与感，进而为其带来自我认同感和幸福感[45]。例如，一项聚焦于伦敦东部区域的研究案例表明，城市绿色空间中的社交互动空间可以提高参与者与他人建立联系的机会，发展其社区意识，并从日常生活需求中重组人际关系[46]。芝加哥的研究人员发现，在树木和草地等植被覆盖率较高的公共空间中，邻里之间的非正式社交更加频繁[47]。

3.2.4 提供生态系统调节 / 支持服务

近年来，有学者提出了"生态系统健康"概念[48][49]，即城市绿地通过广泛的生态系统服务（尤其是调节服务和支持服务）促进人群的心理和生理健康。从这一层面而言，"生态系统健康"能够相应地促进人群健康。以调节服务为例，城市绿地能够通过净化空气和水体、降低噪音、调控雨洪、缓解热岛效应等方式降低人群感受到的环境压力，在一定程度上促进人群健康。比如，有研究表明，城市绿地通过

happened in other (such as indoor) environments[1]. Moreover, along with physical activities, risks of chronic and metabolic diseases, e.g., cardiovascular diseases known as the "No.1 killer worldwide," could be decreased[11].

3.2.2 Stress Management

For the public, more positive emotions with less fatigue and stress will generate after urban green spaces experience or outdoor physical activities. Empirical evidence showed that people living adjacent to green spaces are much more emotionally resilient with less mental stress and better attention focusing. With self-reports by participants and analytical analysis of the correlation between each indicator of exposure and health, a great deal of research proved that experience or activities in green spaces could help improve sleep quality and relieve stress[41][42], which are two main causes of mental illness, especially depression[35][43]. The study of Gregory N. Bratman et al. suggested that the activation of anterior cingulate cortex, dorsolateral prefrontal cortex, and dorsomedial prefrontal cortex increased after the interaction between human and nature, thereby enhancing people's resistance to mental illness[44].

3.2.3 Social Cohesion Enhancement

Public health can be affected by social relations through the avenues of social participation, support, influence, and interaction (bond)[31]. Urban green spaces (especially community parks) can provide public spaces for people to constantly interact with neighbors, during which process their sense of participation, self-identity, and happiness will be enhanced[45]. For example, a case study in East London showed that social interaction happened in urban green spaces catalyzed relationship building between participants and others, while encouraging their sense of community and desire of reorganizing relationships to meet daily needs[46]. Researchers in Chicago have found that public spaces with higher vegetation coverage, such as trees and grass, see more informal social interactions between neighbors[47].

3.2.4 Ecosystem Regulating / Supporting Services Provision

In recent years, many scholars have put forward the concept of "Eco-health"[48][49], and defined it as an exporter of extensive ecosystem services—especially regulating and supporting services—to promote the mental and physical health, i.e. public health. In terms of ecosystem regulating services, urban green spaces can play a key role in reducing people's pressure from the environment by air and water purification, noise reduction, rainwater and flood regulation, urban heat island effect mitigation, etc. to promote public health to some extent. For instance, studies have evinced that

净化水体、改善空气质量等调节服务可减少胃肠道疾病、呼吸道疾病等临床疾病的发生[49]。就支持服务而言，研究人员主要关注丰富的微生物组（微生物多样性）所带来的健康效益：城市绿地中丰富的微生物组能够增强使用者的免疫系统，进而减少过敏性城市疾病的发生[50]。

4 健康导向下的城市绿地系统规划设计启示

4.1 提升城市绿地的可获得性

城市绿地可获得性是健康导向下城市绿地系统规划的基础指标之一。规划设计师和决策者在城市规划初期，尤其是新城规划建设阶段，应设定合理的绿地评估指标，提升城市绿地的可获得性，满足人与自然的交互需求。中国现行的对城市绿地数量的评估指标主要包括“城市绿地率”“城市绿化覆盖率”和“人均公园绿地面积”，而此类指标主要应用于城市或街道尺度。未来应继续细化评估模式和尺度，以社区或居住小区为基本单元，精准识别因缺乏可获得的城市绿地而具有潜在健康问题的居住小区。另外，在建筑高度密集的城市建成区，由于很难大范围开展绿地建设，研究学者应深入探索城市绿地可获得性与人群健康之间的阈值关系。比如，杰洛·科佩尔等学者[51]探讨了绿地可获得性（住址周围250m缓冲区内的绿化覆盖率）与人群健康之间的关联，发现绿化覆盖率低于2.5%的住区对居民的（自评）健康有显著的负面影响。

4.2 提高城市绿地的可达性

良好的城市绿地可达性不仅可以提高居民到访频次，增加居民与自然接触的机会，还能促使居民开展各项体力活动，进而带来更多健康效益[52][53]。研究表明，客观情况下（即居民没有明确的绿地接触意图时），300 ~ 400m是绿地布置的距离阈值区间[54][55]，超过这一阈值区间，居民的到访意愿将会大幅下降。玛格丽塔·特里盖罗—马斯等人的研究表明，300m距离以内的自然环境与心理健康指标呈正相关[56]。雷吉纳·格拉祖列维等人[57]的研究表明，与城市绿地的距离每增加300m，正常血压值就会增加9%，中高血压值增加14%。因此，规划设计师和决策者应当增加居民与绿地的接触机会，确保居民在300 ~ 400m的出行距离内“见绿”。此外，随着城市的高度集约化发展，新建大

urban green spaces can reduce the risk of clinical diseases such as gastrointestinal and respiratory diseases through some of the above regulating services[49]. Regarding the ecosystem supporting services, researchers mainly focus on the health benefits brought by the rich microbiome (microbial diversity) in urban green spaces as it can strengthen the immune system of users and reduce allergic diseases[50].

4 Health-Oriented Urban Green Space System Planning

4.1 Promote the Availability of Urban Green Spaces

The indicator of availability is basic for health-oriented urban green space system planning. Urban planners and policy makers are responsible to set reasonable urban green space assessment indicators at the early stage of urban planning, especially regarding new urban areas, aiming at increasing the interaction between human and nature. Existing indicators, e.g. urban green rate, urban green coverage rate, and the per capita green area of the park, are primarily used to assess the quantity of urban green spaces at city or sub-district scales. Given this condition, future research should refine the mode and scale of urban green spaces assessment, better at the community level, to help accurately identify communities suffering from the potential health problems caused by limited urban green spaces. For built-up areas in a high-rise city with less availability to urban green spaces, studies should focus on examining the threshold relationship between urban green spaces and public health. For example, Gero Coppel et al.[51] found that spatial coverages of urban green spaces of less than 2.5% (within a 250-meter-long buffer around the residence) would negatively impact the self-reported health.

4.2 Improve the Accessibility to Urban Green Spaces

Reasonable accessibility to urban green spaces can encourage citizens to not only contact with the nature more frequently, but also participate in various physical activities that bring about more health benefits[52][53]. Research suggested that the use frequency of urban green spaces steeply declined once the distance exceeded the interval of 300 ~ 400 meters for citizens without definite trip plans[54][55]. Margarita Triguero-Mas et al. found a positive association between natural outdoor environments and mental health indicators within the distance of 300 meters[56]. Regina Grazuleviciene et al.[57] pointed out that the probability of normal blood pressure increased by 9%, and that of high-normal blood pressure by 14% for every 300 meters increase in the distance to urban green spaces. On these findings, urban planners and policy makers should take into consideration the distance threshold of 300 ~ 400 meters to urban green spaces for citizens. In addition,

型绿地难度加大，未来以社区公园和街旁游园为代表的小型绿地将成为提升绿地可达性、改善城市居民健康的关键因素[58]。

4.3 增强城市绿地的可视性

城市绿地的可视性是缓解人群精神压力的关键因素。因此，在城市绿地系统规划中应充分考虑绿地对周边环境的视觉呼应，明确绿色景观的视觉焦点与人群活动的主要观赏面。特别是在居住区、办公区及商业区等人群活动密集的空间中，户外环境设计应充分考虑与室内观赏面（如窗户）的融合与呼应，增加人们在室内活动时外界“绿色”的可视性。另外，城市绿地可以作为城市标志性景观（如观光塔等）的背景，其设计形态应与城市标志性景观的视觉焦点相融合，使人们在观赏标志性景观的同时能够最大程度地获得绿色视野[59]。最后，应加强人行道两侧的绿色环境营造，鼓励采用以攀缘型绿植为主的垂直绿化模式来装饰两侧围墙和建筑立面，提升“绿色”可视性。

4.4 优化城市绿地的空间要素组成

既有研究表明，城市绿地的空间特征会对人群健康产生一定影响。黄秋韵等人[60]通过虚拟现实技术探究了草地、林地及硬质铺装在缓解人群压力方面的作用，发现草地的积极效应最高。帕亚姆·塔布里赞等人[61]基于沉浸式虚拟环境评估不同绿地组成环境对人群的注意力恢复能力，发现混交林、疏林草地和落叶树种对人群注意力恢复能力的影响最大，而建筑物及硬质铺装则存在负面影响。邓莉等人[62]的研究表明，具有天然森林形态和水景特征的地貌景观可能是最佳的生理和心理恢复环境。因此，规划设计师应合理配置城市绿地内部的空间要素组成，协调“硬质”与“软质”空间的配比——既要建造满足人群体力活动、社交活动的“硬质”空间，也要兼顾“软质”空间在缓解精神压力方面的功效。

4.5 构建网络状城市绿地空间格局

规划设计师和决策者应考虑构建网络状的城市绿地空间格局和公园系统。一方面，“翡翠项链”式的网络状结构可达性高，有利于促进居民开展户外活动；且其以线性游憩型绿色开放空间（如绿道等）

by embracing the strategies of constructing small green spaces such as community parks and street gardens, both the accessibility to green spaces and public health will get promoted effectively in the trend of highly intensive urban development[58].

4.3 Enhance the Visibility of Urban Green Spaces

Viewing urban green spaces may significantly relieve stress. In view of this, the visual contact in urban green space system planning, including the visual focus of the landscape and the main viewing interface during daily activities of the public, should echo with the surroundings. For instance, outdoor spaces that support intensive activities, e.g. residential areas, offices, and commercial zones, should fully consider the integration and echo with the indoor viewing interface (such as windows) for more visible urban green spaces. Furthermore, urban green spaces may also act as the background of landmarks, e.g. the sightseeing tower, for which its designed form should match up with visual focuses of these landmarks to provide a wider green vision for visitors[59]. Finally, the visibility of urban green spaces could also be realized by increasing vertical greening (introducing climbing plants) on fences and façades of building along sidewalks.

4.4 Optimize the Spatial Composition of Urban Green Spaces

Recent findings also showed that spatial characteristics of urban green spaces may affect public health. Huang Qiuyun et al.[60] examined the impact of grasslands, woodlands, and impervious paved areas with virtual reality, pointing out that grasslands relieve stress more efficiently. Payam Tabrizian et al.[61] assessed the restoration potential of different landscape compositions and configurations through the immersive virtual technology and found that mixed forests, sparse forests and grasslands, and deciduous tree species performed the best, while buildings and impervious paved areas showed negative impacts. Recent empirical research by Deng Li et al.[62] suggested that landscapes with natural forest morphology and water features may be the best physical and psychological recovery environment. In response, urban planners should figure out the rational configuration of “grey” and “green” spaces—the “grey” ones for physical and social activities and “green” ones to relieve stress.

4.5 Construct a Network Pattern of Urban Green Spaces

A network pattern of urban green spaces and park systems is suggested for urban planning and design. For one thing, the network featured like the “Emerald Necklace” holds high accessibility which encourages outdoor activities; linear recreational green spaces (e.g. greenways) connecting various green spaces attract citizens to travel on foot or by bicycle, which means

作为纽带连接各个绿地斑块，能够在最大程度上鼓励居民选择步行、骑行等慢行交通出行方式，从而提升体力活动水平。另一方面，网络状的绿地结构有利于城市生态系统的稳定性[63]，从而促进城市绿地生态系统调节功能的充分发挥。例如，余兆武等人[64]指出理想状态下多等级的正六边形网络状绿地空间格局能够最大程度地降低城市热岛效应，进而减少中暑等病状的发生。

4.6 降低城市绿地对人群健康的消极影响

健康导向下的实践研究还应密切关注对城市绿地所产生的消极影响的回应，如城市绿地植被传粉所导致的过敏性疾病等。据统计，全球有30%～40%的人口正在遭受过敏性疾病的困扰，其中很大一部分病因即源自植物花粉过敏[65]。因此，城市规划设计中应明确城市树种的选择标准，以控制使用某些会大量传播花粉的物种数量。

5 结论

本文以城市绿地促进人群健康的作用途径为切入点，从鼓励体力活动、缓解精神压力、促进社会凝聚力和提供生态调节／支持服务4个层面构建了理论研究框架，并借此提出健康导向下的城市绿地系统规划应对策略。未来研究在进一步深入探索城市绿地对人群健康影响的潜在途径的同时，还应注重城市绿地的健康实践，提出更多面向提升人群生理、心理和社会健康的规划设计应对策略。如通过绿地的组成（绿地植被种类、绿地中的水体、活动设施等）与配置（绿地的类型、大小、形状等）对人群健康实施“主动式”干预，让有限的城市绿地发挥更大的健康效益。**LAF**

more physical activities. For another thing, the network pattern is conducive to the stability of the urban ecosystem[63] that could give full play to regulating services. For instance, Yu Zhaowu et al.[64] suggested that the urban green spaces spatial pattern in a hierarchical hexagonal structure can ideally mitigate the urban thermal environment, and thus reduce the incidence of heat-related illnesses.

4.6 Reduce the Negative Impacts of Urban Green Spaces on Public Health

Strategies respond to urban green spaces' negative impacts on public health also need more discussion. For instance, 30% to 40% of the world's population are suffering from allergic diseases, most of which are caused by pollen allergies[65]. Therefore, in urban planning and design, criteria should be set for urban tree species selection to minimize species that produce lots of pollen.

5 Conclusion

Based on the impact mechanism of urban green spaces in promoting public health, this article builds a theoretical research framework from 4 aspects: physical activity encouragement, stress management, social cohesion enhancement, ecosystem regulating / supporting services provision, and further proposes a new pathway to health-oriented urban green space system planning. Future discussion should make further efforts in exploring the potential impact mechanism and focus on planning practices that employ more strategies to improve the physical, psychological, and social health of citizens. For instance, "proactive" interventions should be implemented to exert more health benefits with limited urban green spaces by optimizing its composition (e.g. vegetation types, water bodies, and activity facilities) and configuration (e.g. types, size, and shape). **LAF**

REFERENCES

[1] Hartig, T., Mitchell, R., De Vries, S., & Frumkin, H. (2014). Nature and Health. Annual Review of Public Health, (35), 207-228. doi:10.1146/annurev-publhealth-032013-182443

[2] Akpinar, A., Barbosa-Leiker, C., & Brooks, K. R. (2016). Does green space matter? Exploring relationships between green space type and health indicators. Urban Forestry and Urban Greening, (20), 407-418. http://dx.doi.org/10.1016/j.ufug.2016.10.013

[3] Yao, Y., & Li, S. (2018). Review on Research of Urban Green Space Based on Public Health. Chinese Landscape Architecture, 34(1), 118-124. doi:10.3969/j.issn.1000-6664.2018.01.029

[4] European Commission. (2015). Towards an EU Research and Innovation Policy Agenda for Nature-Based Solutions and Re-Naturing Cities: Final Report of the Horizon 2020 Expert Group on 'Nature-Based Solutions and Re-Naturing Cities'(full version). Directorate-General for Research and Innovation—Climate Action, Environment, Resource Efficiency and Raw Materials. Retrieved from http://publications.europa.eu/resource/cellar/fb117980-d5aa-46df-8edc-af367cddc202.0001.04/DOC_2

[5] Liu, J., Lin, T., Zhao, Y., Lin, M., Xing, L., Li, X., ... Ye, H. (2019). Research Progress on Nature-Based Solutions towards Urban Sustainable Development. Acta Ecologica Sinica, 39(16), 6040-6050. doi:10.5846/stxb201812042648

[6] Li, X., Zhang, Y., Mu, H. & Zhang, R. (2020). Vision and mission: Landscape architecture in response to public health. Landscape Architecture, 27(4), 91-94. doi:10.14085/j.fjyl.2020.04.0091.04

[7] Zhang, J., Yu, Z., Zhao, B., Sun, R., & Vejre, H. (2020). Links between green space and public health: A bibliometric review of global research trends and future prospects from 1901 to 2019. Environmental Research Letters, 15(6). Advance online publication. https://doi.org/10.1088/1748-9326/ab7f64

[8] Clancy, J., & Ryan, C. (2015). The role of biophilic design in landscape architecture for health and well-being. Landscape Architecture Frontiers, 3(1), 54-61.

[9] Tan, S., Yang, C., Li, L., & Zhang, L. (2020). Park environment influences on health restoration review. Chinese Landscape Architecture, 36(2), 53-58. doi:10.19775/j.cla.2020.02.0053

[10] Vujcic, M., Tomicevic-Dubljevic, J., Grbic, M., Lecic-Tosevski, D., Vukovic, O., & Toskovic, O. (2017). Nature-based solution for improving mental health and well-being in urban areas. Environmental Research, (158), 385-392. http://dx.doi.org/10.1016/j.envres.2017.06.030

[11] Van den Bosch, M., & Sang, Å. O. (2017). Urban natural environments as nature-based solutions for improved public health—A systematic review of reviews. Environmental Research, (5), 373-384. https://doi.org/10.1016/j.jth.2017.05.230

[12] Jiang, B., Zhang, T., & Sullivan, W. C. (2015). Healthy cities: Mechanisms and research questions regarding the impacts of urban green landscapes on public health and well-being. Landscape Architecture Frontiers, 3(1), 24-36.

[13] Gan, J., Yang, W., & Wang, L. (2020). Spatial characteristics of urban green space under different health impact pathways. Landscape Architecture, 27(4), 95-100. doi:10.14085/j.fjyl.2020.04.0095.06
[14] Lai, H., Flies, E. J., Weinstein, P., & Woodward, A. (2019). The impact of green space and biodiversity on health: Synthesis and systematic review. Frontiers in Ecology and the Environment, 17(7), 383-390. doi:10.1002/fee.2077
[15] Chang, C. -Y., & Tang, I. -C. (2015). Connecting healthy urban ecology with human health. Landscape Architecture Frontiers, 3(1), 45-54.
[16] World Health Organization. (2000). WHO remains firmly committed to the principles set out in the preamble to the Constitution. Retrieved from https://www.who.int/about/who-we-are/constitution
[17] Gascon, M., Triguero-Mas, M., Martínez, D., Dadvand, P., Rojas-Rueda, D., Plasència, A., & Nieuwenhuijsen, M. J. (2016). Residential green spaces and mortality: A systematic review. Environment International, (86), 60-67. http://dx.doi.org/10.1016/j.envint.2015.10.013
[18] Van den Berg, M., Wendel-Vos, W., Van Poppel, M., Kemper, H., Mechelen, M., & Maas, J. (2015). Health benefits of green spaces in the living environment: A systematic review of epidemiological studies. Urban Forestry and Urban Greening, 14(4), 806-816. http://dx.doi.org/doi:10.1016/j.ufug.2015.07.008
[19] De Vries, S., Ten Have, M., Van Dorsselaer, S., Van Wezep, M., Hermans, T., & De Graaf, R. (2016). Local availability of green and blue space and prevalence of common mental disorders in the Netherlands. BJPsych Open, 2(6), 366-372. doi:10.1192/bjpo.bp.115.002469
[20] Roe, J., & Aspinall, P. (2011). The restorative outcomes of forest school and conventional school in young people with good and poor behaviour. Urban Forestry and Urban Greening, 10(3), 205-212. doi:10.1016/j.ufug.2011.03.003
[21] Cohen-Cline, H., Turkheimer, E., & Duncan, G. E. (2015). Access to green space, physical activity and mental health: A twin study. Journal of Epidemiol Community Health, 69(6), 523-529. doi:10.1136/jech-2014-204667
[22] Ulrich, R. S. (1984). View through a window may influence recovery. Science, (224), 420-423.
[23] Kaplan, S. (1995). The Restorative Benefits of Nature: Toward an Integrative Framework. Journal of Environmental Psychology, (15), 169-182.
[24] Tan, S., & Li, J. (2009). Restoration and stress relief benefits of urban park and green space. Chinese Landscape Architecture, (6), 79-82. doi:10.3969/j.issn.1000-6664.2009.06.020
[25] Berman, M. G., Kross, E., Krpan, K. M., Askren, M. K., Burson, A., Deldin, P. J., ... Jonides, J. (2012). Interacting with nature improves cognition and affect for individuals with depression. Journal of Affective Disorders, 140(3), 300-305. doi:10.1016/j.jad.2012.03.012
[26] Wells, N. M. (2000). At home with nature: Effects of "greenness" on children's cognitive functioning. Environment and Behavior, 32(6), 775-795.
[27] Sullivan, W. C. (2015). A significant but under-appreciated benefit of landscape architecture: Supporting people's capacity to pay attention. Landscape Architecture Frontiers, 3(1), 36-44.
[28] Kahn, P. H., & Kellert, S. R. (2002). Children and Nature: Psychological, Sociocultural, and Evolutionary Investigations. Cambridge: The MIT Press.
[29] Orban, E., Sutcliffe, R., Dragano, N., Jöckel, K. H., & Moebus, S. (2017). Residential surrounding greenness, self-rated health and interrelations with aspects of neighborhood environment and social relations. Journal of Urban Health, 94(2), 158-169. doi:10.1007/s11524-016-0112-3
[30] O'Brien, L., Burls, A., Townsend, M., & Ebden, M. (2011). Volunteering in nature as a way of enabling people to reintegrate into society. Perspectives in Public Health, 131(2), 71-81. doi:10.1177/1757913910384048
[31] Jennings, V., & Bamkole, O. (2019). The relationship between social cohesion and urban green space: An avenue for health promotion. International Journal of Environmental Research and Public Health, 16(3), 452-466. doi:10.3390/ijerph16030452
[32] Cariñanos, P., & Casares-Porcel, M. (2011). Urban green zones and related pollen allergy: A review. Some guidelines for designing spaces with low allergy impact. Landscape and Urban Planning, 101(3), 205-214. doi:10.1016/j.landurbplan.2011.03.006
[33] Löhmus, M., & Balbus J. (2015). Making green infrastructure healthier infrastructure. Infection Ecology and Epidemiology, 5(1), 1-11. http://dx.doi.org/10.3402/iee.v5.30082
[34] Bortolini, L., Cividino, S. R. S., Gubiani, R., Cecchini, M., Delfanti, L. M. P., & Colantoni, A. (2016). Urban green spaces activities: A preparatory groundwork for a safety management system. Journal of Safety Research, (56), 75-82. http://dx.doi.org/10.1016/j.jsr.2015.12.004
[35] Bratman, G. N., Anderson, C. B., Berman, M. G., Cochran, B., De Vries, S., Flanders, J., ... Daily, G. C. (2019). Nature and mental health: An ecosystem service perspective. Science Advances, 5(7), 1-14. doi:10.1126/sciadv.aax0903
[36] Labib, S. M., Lindley, S., & Huck, J. J. (2020). Spatial dimensions of the influence of urban green-blue spaces on human health: A systematic review. Environmental Research, (180), 108869. https://doi.org/10.1016/j.envres.2019.108869
[37] Dadvand, P., Bartoll, X., Basagaña, X., Dalmau-Bueno, A., Martinez, D., Ambros, A., ... Nieuwenhuijsen, M. J. (2016). Green spaces and general health: Roles of mental health status, social support, and physical activity. Environment International, (91), 161-167. http://dx.doi.org/10.1016/j.envint.2016.02.029
[38] Zhang, J., Cheng, Y., Wei, W., & Zhao, B. (2019). Evaluating Spatial Disparity of Access to Public Parks in Gated and Open Communities with an Improved G2SFCA Model. Sustainability, 11(21), 5910. doi:10.3390/su11215910
[39] Yu, Y., Wang, X., & Lu, S. (2019). Promoting healthy urban landscape: The impact of green space on physical activity. Chinese Landscape Architecture, 35(10), 67-71. doi:10.19775/j.cla.2019.10.0067
[40] Heinen, E., Van Wee, B., & Maat, K. (2010). Commuting by bicycle: An overview of the literature. Transport Reviews, 30(1), 59-96. doi:10.1080/01441640903187001
[41] Grigsby-Toussaint, D. S., Turi, K. N., Krupa, M., Williams, N. J., Pandi-Perumal, S. K., & Jean-Louis, G. (2015). Sleep insufficiency and the natural environment: Results from the US behavioral risk factor surveillance system survey. Preventive Medicine, (78), 78-84. http://dx.doi.org/10.1016/j.ypmed.2015.07.011
[42] Aspinall, P., Mavros, P., Coyne, R., & Roe, J. (2015). The urban brain: Analysing outdoor physical activity with mobile EEG. Brtish Journal of Sports Medicine. 49(4), 272-276. doi:10.1136/bjsports-2012-091877
[43] Hammen, C. (2005). Stress and depression. Annual Review Clinical Psychology, (1), 293-319. doi:10.1146/annurev.clinpsy.1.102803.143938
[44] Bratman, G. N., Hamilton, J. P., Hahn, K. S., Daily, G. C., & Gross, G. G. (2015). Nature experience reduces rumination and subgenual prefrontal cortex activation. Proceedings of the National Academy of Sciences, 112(28), 8567-8572. https://doi.org/10.1073/pnas.1510459112
[45] Liu, Y., Zhang, F., Liu, Y., Li, Z., & Wu, F. (2017). The effect of neighbourhood social ties on migrants' subjective wellbeing in Chinese cities. Habitat International, (66), 86-94. http://dx.doi.org/10.1016/j.habitatint.2017.05.011
[46] Cattell, V., Dines, N., Gesler, W., & Curtis, S. (2008). Mingling, observing, and lingering: Everyday public spaces and their implications for well-being and social relations. Health and Place, 14(3), 544-561. doi:10.1016/j.healthplace.2007.10.007
[47] Kuo, F. E., Sullivan, W. C., Coley, R. L., & Brunson, L. (1998). Fertile Ground for Community: Inner-City Neighborhood Common Spaces. American Journal of Community Psychology, 26(6), 823-851. https://doi.org/10.1023/A:1022294028903
[48] Jackson, L. E., Daniel, J., McCorkle, B., Sears, A., & Bush, K. F. (2013). Linking ecosystem services and human health: The Eco-Health Relationship Browser. International Journal of Public Health, 58(5), 747-755. doi:10.1007/s00038-013-0482-1
[49] De Jesus Crespo, R., & Fulford, R. (2018). Eco-Health linkages: Assessing the role of ecosystem goods and services on human health using causal criteria analysis. International Journal of Public Health, 63(1), 81-92. https://doi.org/10.1007/s00038-017-1020-3
[50] Ruokolainen, L., Fyhrquist, N., & Haahtela, T. (2016). The rich and the poor: Environmental biodiversity protecting from allergy. Current Opinion in Allergy and Clinical Immunology, 16(5), 421-426. doi:10.1097/ACI.0000000000000304
[51] Coppel, G., & Wüstemann, H. (2017). The impact of urban green space on health in Berlin, Germany: Empirical findings and implications for urban planning. Landscape and Urban Planning, (167), 410-418. http://dx.doi.org/10.1016/j.landurbplan.2017.06.015
[52] Zhang, J., & Zhao, B. (2018). Location and layout optimization of urban parks based on accessibility. Journal of Nanjing Forestry University (Natural Sciences Edition), 42(6), 151-158. doi:10.3969/j. issn. 1000-2006.201710022
[53] Zhang, J., Wei, W., Cheng, Y., & Zhao, B. (2019). Study on site selection of small and medium-sized city parks based on GIS suitability evaluation. Journal of Nanjing Forestry University (Natural Sciences Edition), 43(1), 171-178. doi:10.3969/j.issn.1000-2006.201810036
[54] Schipperijn, J., Ekholm, O., Stigsdotter, U. K., Toftager, M., Bentsen, P., Kamper-Jørgensen, F., & Randrup, T. B. (2010). Factors influencing the use of green space: Results from a Danish national representative survey. Landscape and Urban Planning, 95(3), 130-137. https://doi.org/https://doi.org/10.1016/j.landurbplan.2009.12.010
[55] Annerstedt, M., Östergren, P. -O., Björk, J., Grahn, P., Skärbäck, E., & Währborg, P. (2012). Green qualities in the neighbourhood and mental health–results from a longitudinal cohort study in Southern Sweden. BMC Public Health, 12(1), 337. https://doi.org/https://doi.org/10.1186/1471-2458-12-337
[56] Triguero-Mas, M., Dadvand, P., Cirach, M., Martínez, D., Medina, A., Mompart, A., ... Nieuwenhuijsen, M. J. (2015). Natural outdoor environments and mental and physical health: Relationships and mechanisms. Environment International, (77), 35-41. https://doi.org/10.1016/j.envint.2015.01.012
[57] Grazuleviciene, R., Dedele, A., Danileviciute, A., Vencloviene, J. Grazulevicius, T. Andrusaityte, S., ... Nieuwenhuijsen, M. J. (2014). The influence of proximity to city parks on blood pressure in early pregnancy. International Journal of Environmental Research and Public Health, 11(3), 2958-2972. doi:10.3390/ijerph110302958
[58] Barnes, M. R., Donahue, M. L., Keeler, B. L., Shorb, C. M., Mohtadi, T. Z., & Shelby, L. J. (2018). Characterizing Nature and Participant Experience in Studies of Nature Exposure for Positive Mental health, An Integrative Review. Frontiers in Psychology, (9), 2617. doi:10.3389/fpsyg.2018.02617
[59] Ma, M., & Cai, Z. (2016). Research on health and urban green open space—Health benefits and design strategy. Chinese Landscape Architecture, 32(11), 66-70.
[60] Huang, Q., Yang, M., Jane H. A., Li, S., & Bauer, N. (2020). Trees, grass, or concrete? The effects of different types of environments on stress reduction. Landscape and Urban Planning, (193). Advance online publication. https://doi.org/10.1016/j.landurbplan.2019.103654
[61] Tabrizian, P., Baran, P. K., Van Berke, D., Mitasova, H., & Meentemeyer, R. (2020). Modeling restorative potential of urban environments by coupling viewscape analysis of lidar data with experiments in immersive virtual environments. Landscape and Urban Planning, (195). Advance online publication. https://doi.org/10.1016/j.landurbplan.2019.103704
[62] Deng, L., Li, X., Luo, H., Fu, E. -K., Ma, J., Sun, L. -X., ... Jia, Y. (2020). Empirical study of landscape types, landscape elements and landscape components of the urban park promoting physiological and psychological restoration. Urban Forestry and Urban Greening, (48). Advance online publication. https://doi.org/10.1016/j.ufug.2019.126488
[63] Liu, B., & Wang, P. (2010). Green Space Ecological Network Planning: Evolution and Research Frontier in China. Chinese Landscape Architecture, (3), 1-5. doi:10.3969/j.issn.1000-6664.2010.03.002
[64] Yu, Z., Fryd, O., Sun, R., Jørgensen, G., Yang, G., Özdil, N. C., & Vejre, H. (2020). Where and how to cool? An idealized urban thermal security pattern model. Landscape Ecology. Advance online publication. https://doi.org/10.1007/s10980-020-00982-1
[65] Cariñanos, P., Casares-Porcel, M., & Quesada-Rubio, J. M. (2014). Estimating the allergenic potential of urban green spaces: A case-study in Granada, Spain. Landscape and Urban Planning, (123), 134-144. http://dx.doi.org/10.1016/j.landurbplan.2013.12.009

本文引用格式 / PLEASE CITE THIS ARTICLE AS

Xie, Y., Nolf, C., Dong, N., Dai, D., & Zhang, D. (2020). Taipu Canal as a Regional Spine: A Prototypical Approach to Territorial Planning. Landscape Architecture Frontiers, 8(4), 114-125. https://doi.org/10.15302/J-LAF-1-040019

https://doi.org/10.15302/J-LAF-1-040019　收稿时间 RECEIVED DATE / 2020-08-25　中图分类号 / TU984　文献标识码 / B

区域“脊柱”太浦河：基于原型设计的国土空间规划补充途径

TAIPU CANAL AS A REGIONAL SPINE: A PROTOTYPICAL APPROACH TO TERRITORIAL PLANNING

摘要

2018年以来，长江三角洲区域一体化发展上升为国家战略，以加强该区域城市间的协作，但目前开放空间的保护与规划途径以定量评价为主，依然沿用自上而下的控制性规划导则。太浦河流经上海、苏州和杭州之间的区域绿心，目前主要发挥工程功能。本设计研究项目提出将太浦河升级为串联公民生活的轴线，制定新的区域发展框架，并使其串联沿线多样化的开放空间、生态系统和历史水乡古镇。项目采用了跨尺度的“地情－原型”方法，整合样本图绘、类型学研究和实验场地的原型设计探索，并将其贯穿于各个尺度，以评估如何将原型设计策略归纳为系统性的规划导则，并在区域尺度进行统一实施。本文总结的这种原型设计途径为中国自上而下的国土空间规划体系提供了适当补充，以更好地应对愈加复杂的场地条件和更大尺度的空间规划需求。

关键词

原型；设计研究；景观特征；景观基础设施；国土空间规划；长江三角洲一体化；江南公园

ABSTRACT

Since 2018, the integrated regional development of the Yangtze River Delta has been subjected as a national strategy to intensify the interconnection between its cities. However, the questions of open space conservation and planning have so far remained essentially quantitative and strongly informed by regulatory and top-down principles. Focusing on the vast green heart between Shanghai, Suzhou, and Hangzhou, this design-driven research project hypothesizes that Taipu Canal can be upgraded from its current technical role into a civic spine that frames new developments and articulates the rich diversity of open spaces, ecosystems, historic water towns and villages. The research adopts a cross-scale method of "contextual prototypes" that combines sampling, typological classification, and prototypical design explorations in pilot projects. A reflective phase zooms out to critically assess how these prototypical strategies can be systemized as structuring principles at the regional scale. The conclusion of the article discusses how this prototypical approach offers an opportunity to inductively complement the top-down Chinese territorial planning system, which needs to cope with increasingly complex conditions and vaster scales.

KEYWORDS

Prototype; Research-by-Design; Landscape Characteristics; Landscape Infrastructure; Territorial Planning; Yangtze River Delta Integration; Jiangnan Park

谢雨婷
浙江大学园林研究所讲师，浙江大学－西交利物浦大学联合江南实验室负责人，慕尼黑工业大学中国城市景观实验室负责人

克里斯蒂安 · 诺尔夫*
西交利物浦大学城市规划与设计系副教授、城市设计硕士项目负责人，浙江大学－西交利物浦大学联合江南实验室负责人

董楠楠
同济大学建筑与城市规划学院院长助理、建成环境技术中心副主任、景观学系副教授

戴代新
同济大学建筑与城市规划学院景观学系副教授，注册规划师，一级注册建筑师，教育部生态化城市设计国际合作联合实验室景观空间分实验中心主任

张斗
美国景观设计师协会会员、美国注册景观设计师、LEED AP BD+C及SITES资格认证专业人士，Sasaki设计事务所高级主管及上海办公室总监

XIE Yuting
Lecturer at the Institute of Landscape Architecture of Zhejiang University; Director of Jiangnan Lab; Director of China Urban Landscape Lab at Technical University of Munich

Christian NOLF
Associate Professor and Program Director of the MSc Urban Design in the Department of Urban Planning and Design at Xi'an Jiaotong Liverpool University; Director of Jiangnan Lab

DONG Nannan
Dean Assistant, Deputy Director of the Built Environment Technology Center, and Associate Professor of Department of Landscape Studies, College of Architecture and Urban Planning (CAUP), Tongji University

DAI Daixin
Associate Professor of College of Architecture and Urban Planning (CAUP), Tongji University; Registered Planner; National 1st Class Registered Architect; Director of Landscape Space Sub-experimental Center of the Joint Laboratory of International Cooperation on Eco-urban Design of the Ministry of Education

ZHANG Dou
ASLA, PLA, LEED AP BD+C, SITES AP; Senior Associate and Director of Shanghai Office, Sasaki

*通讯作者
地址：江苏省苏州市工业园区仁爱路西交利物浦大学北校区建筑环境楼EB412
邮编：215123
邮箱：Christian.Nolf@xjtlu.edu.cn

基金项目
江苏省科技计划项目“苏州水资源综合管理的空间影响研究”（编号：BK20151244）
西交利物浦大学科研发展基金项目“长三角都市圈基于空间整合的水资源管理研究”（编号：RDF 14-03-23）
浙江省教育厅一般科研项目“基于圩田景观评价的蓝绿基础设施构建研究——以嘉兴市为例”（编号：188310-542126/031）
中央高校基本科研业务费专项资金项目“浙北平原地区乡村景观特征及其演变研究”（编号：2019QNA6023）
浙江大学教育基金会孙筱祥风景园林教育基金项目“江南公园：大都市景观区域设计”（编号：317000-11103/001）
国家自然基金委外国青年学者研究基金项目“空间规划与水体治理在城市化地区的应用——中国长江三角洲与欧洲斯海尔德－马士河－莱茵河的对比研究”（编号：51550110235）

RESEARCH FUNDS
Exploring the Spatial Implications of Integrated Water Management in the Suzhou Metropolitan Area, Jiangsu Province Program of Science and Technology (No. BK20151244)
Towards Spatially Integrated Water Resource Management in the Yangtze River Delta Metropolis, The Research Development Fund of Xi'an Jiaotong-Liverpool University (No. RDF 14-03-23)
Structuring Blue-Green Infrastructure Based on Polder Landscape Assessment: A Jiaxing Case, General Scientific Research Projects of Zhejiang Provincial Education Department (No. 188310-542126/031)
Research on the Characteristics and Evolution of Rural Landscape in North Zhejiang Plain, Fundamental Research Funds for the Central Universities (No. 2019QNA6023)
Jiangnan Park: Designing a Metropolitan Landscape, Zhejiang University Education Foundation—Sun Xiaoxiang Landscape Architecture Education Fund (No. 317000-11103/001)
Integrating Spatial Planning and Water Management in Urbanised Deltas: A Comparison of Instruments in the Yangtze (CN) and Scheldt-Meuse-Rhine (EU) River Delta Regions, Young International Scientist Program of the National Science Foundation of China (No. 51550110235)

编辑 王胤瑜　**翻译** 肖杰　王胤瑜　谢雨婷
EDITED BY WANG Yinyu　**TRANSLATED BY** XIAO Jie　WANG Yinyu　XIE Yuting

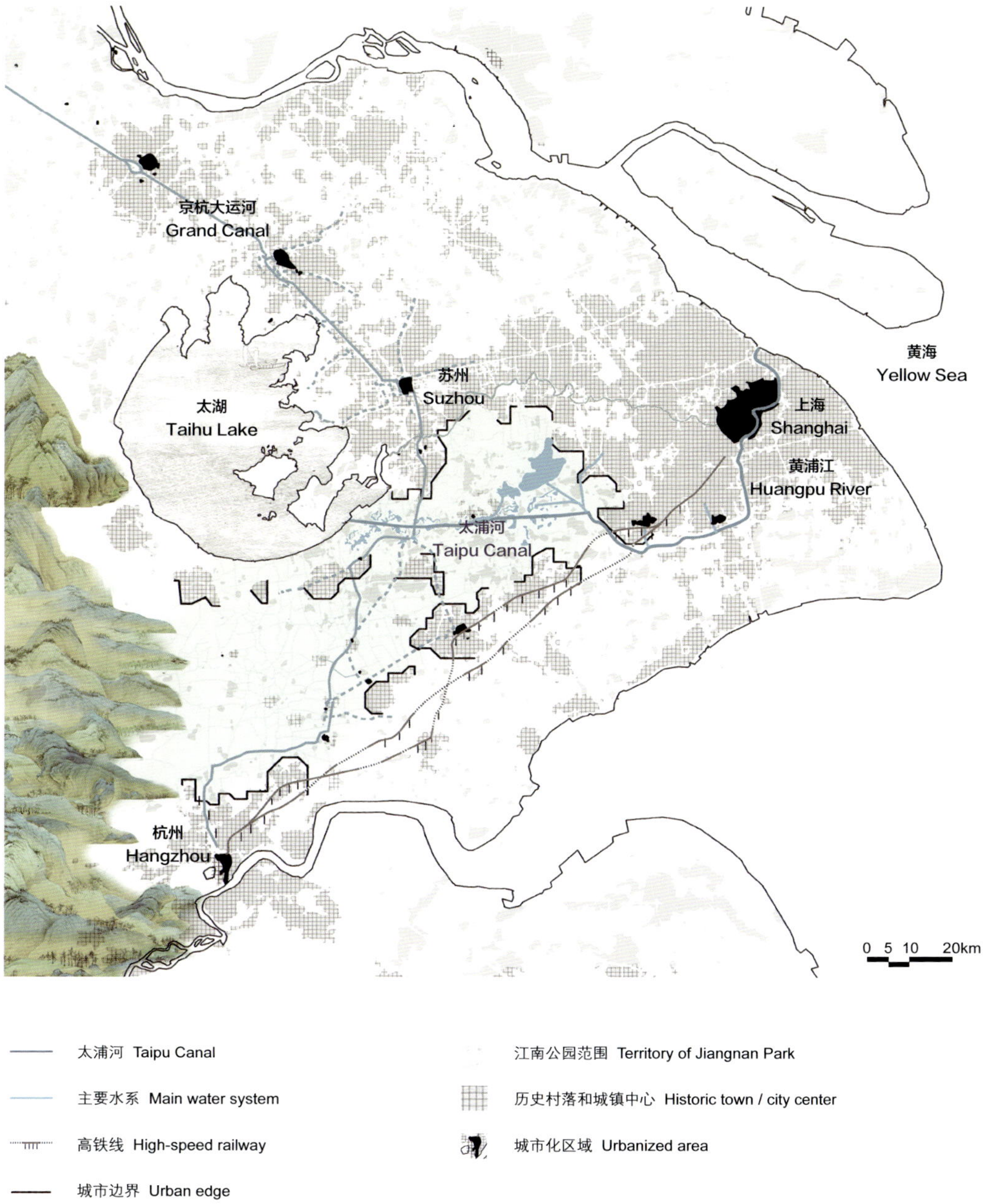

© Xie Yuting, Christian Nolf, Han Mengyi

1

1. 太浦河衔接太湖与上海的黄浦江，横跨了高速城镇化进程中的长三角巨型城市区下游地带。

1. The Taipu Canal connects Taihu Lake to the Huangpu River in Shanghai across the lower reaches of the rapidly urbanizing Yangtze River Delta megacity region.

1 背景和挑战

1.1 如何整合长江三角洲一体化规划中的开放空间？

为更好地协调上海、浙江、江苏和安徽巨型城市区的空间与经济发展，中共中央国务院于2019年发布了《长江三角洲区域一体化发展规划纲要》，该规划最初旨在调整区域交通、能源和城市服务的尺度[1]，后逐渐将开放空间纳入规划范畴。同年发布的《长三角生态绿色一体化发展示范区总体方案》提出了与开放空间相关的具体目标[2]，主要关注生态空间和永久基本农田的保护问题，但依然停留在定量描述和指标化层面。2020年6月，示范区国土空间总体规划方案发布[3]，明确了蓝绿开放空间的比例及风景道路、绿道和蓝道系统的长度和整体结构。尽管这是国内首个跨省域国土空间规划，具有里程碑意义，但其依然以功能区划为目标，沿用自上而下的控制性规划原则，忽略了这一生态和历史敏感地区的复杂性。

本项目从江南公园[4]的视角重新审视了这片区域，将上海、苏州和杭州之间的三角地带视为长江三角洲（下文简称“长三角”）巨型城市区的生态文化“绿心”，尝试通过由设计驱动的跨尺度方法，实现自上而下的控制性功能区划手段与地方性解决方案的衔接。

1.2 为什么将太浦河定位为区域脊柱？

新建绿道网络，或赋予既有线性景观或基础设施新的空间功能，从而将其纳入公园系统，是整合碎片化开放空间的有效策略之一[5][6]。其中，最著名的案例包括美国波士顿的翡翠项链公园、德国的埃姆歇公园，以及荷兰的新荷兰水线项目[7][8]。重组后的开放空间不仅能更好地发挥生态廊道和网络的作用[9]，亦有助于增强区域社会文化凝聚力。线性公园系统在空间和功能层面将孤立的场地联系起来，有效提高了居民的归属感，并通过与一个地方或区域建立有形的空间关系形成地方认同感[7]。对于游客来说，线性系统能够带来全新的序列性游赏体验，使其感受到一个区域的连贯性和多样性[10]。

太浦河是一条全长57km的排水渠，起于太湖、止于上海，横跨太湖流域生态敏感性较高的圩区（图1）。该运河于1958年开始分阶段修建，1995年竣工，发挥着重要的防洪、排水和灌溉功能，并于2016年开始成为上海大都市区的淡水供给通道。太浦河虽然只承担工程功能且可达性较差（图2），但由于河道平直、空间跨度较大，因此依然是该地区的主要空间参照物之一。近期的示范区国土空间总体规划方案将太浦河定位为主要生态廊道，进一步凸显了其战略意义。

本文介绍的设计研究项目“太浦河Studio 2020”①假设太浦河能够引导江南公园绿心区域的一体化开发，并从两个层面对该地区进行重塑：在沿河道方向，运河可从当前的排水渠升级为生态游憩轴线，连接各类开放空间及生态系统；在跨河道方向，运河可将开放空间网络和水乡古镇串联起来，构建新的城市发展格局。

① 太浦河Studio 2020隶属于江南公园系列项目，由江南实验室负责人克里斯蒂安·诺尔夫副教授（西交利物浦大学城市规划与设计系）和谢雨婷博士（浙江大学园林研究所）主导，并与董楠楠副教授、戴代新副教授（同济大学建筑与城市规划学院景观学系）和来自Sasaki设计事务所的张斗共同合作完成。

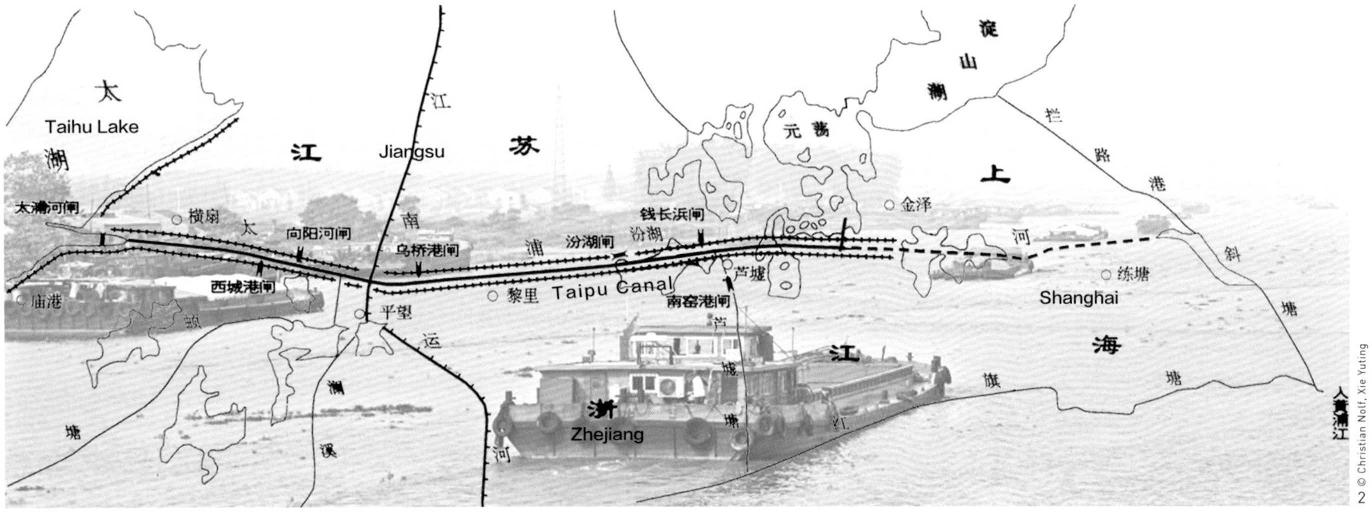

2. 太浦河于1958～1995年间分阶段修建，除水利与交通用途外，自2016年起还承担了向上海供应淡水的功能。沿河的工程缓冲带降低了河道可达性，并造成了两岸地区空间上的割裂。（历史地图来源：参考文献[11]）

2. Built in several phases from 1958 to 1995, the Taipu Canal combines the hydraulic functions of drainage, transport and, since 2016, the supply of fresh water to Shanghai. Poorly accessible and bordered by technical buffers, the canal is currently impacting the region as a spatial divide (Historic map source: Ref. [11]).

1.3 如何塑造复杂的异质性景观?

值得注意的是，长三角地区的开放空间并非一片白板。经过数百年的高强度开发，这里聚集了大量人口，有着从圩田演变而来的各类景观。受地形和历史条件影响，这些景观的特征也不一而同[12]。其中，太浦河是一个特例，其直线形态与周边景观的有机肌理格格不入。不同于自公元7世纪以来持续影响着江南地区发展的京杭大运河[13]，太浦河未能推动沿线地区的发展，反而宛如异质性景观中的一道伤痕，将原有的城镇群、湖泊和林地割裂开来。

近期的示范区国土空间规划针对太浦河生态廊道提出了一系列环境治理和生态修复措施，但仍未考虑河流沿线的景观异质性。规划根据太浦河沿线的圩田景观基底划定了4个生态区（大湖区、淺港区、湖荡区与河网区）[3]，但针对不同景观类型及其生态空间的解决方案仍然

表1：跨尺度的原型设计方法
Table 1: Overview of the cross-scale prototypical method

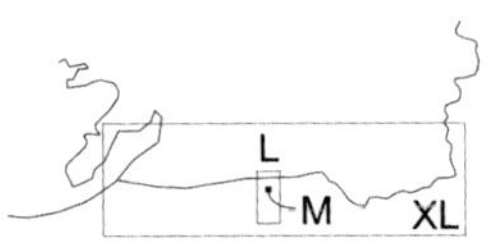	分析 关注内容 **Analysis** what we look at	诠释 具体行动 **Interpretation** what we do	设计 产出成果 **Design** what we produce
XL（100km） 尺度：区域 XL (100 km) Region	景观特征及系统 Landscape characteristics and systems	识别典型的空间条件 Identify typical spatial conditions	区域尺度的规划目标 （连续性、一致性、认同感） Regional scale intentions (continuity, cohesion, identity)
L（5km×10km） 尺度：纵断面 L (5 km × 10 km) Transects	历史演变研究＋对现有规划和项目的评价 Historical evolution + critical review of existing plans and projects	探索如何激活特色景观（子）系统以强化太浦河的空间塑造作用 Explore how characteristic landscape (sub)systems can be activated to enhance the structuring role of the Taipu Canal	景观途径主导的策略性框架规划 Landscape-based strategic framework plan
M（1km×1km） 尺度：项目 M (1 km × 1 km) Projects	典型地情／要素的详细分析 Detail of a typical context / element	详细的设计措施 Detail design interventions	针对典型地情／要素的原型项目 A prototypical project for a typical context / element
回溯L尺度和XL尺度 Back to L and XL Scales	区域内的其他类似场地 Other comparable conditions at the regional scale	验证原型项目／策略在其他类似场地中的适用性 Verify the applicability of the prototypical projects / strategies in other comparable contexts	区域尺度的系列规划设计导则 A set of design and planning principles at the regional scale

3. 根据江南公园的5个维度对太浦河进行专题分析。

3. Thematic analysis of the Taipu Canal at the XL scale according to the five dimensions of Jiangnan Park.

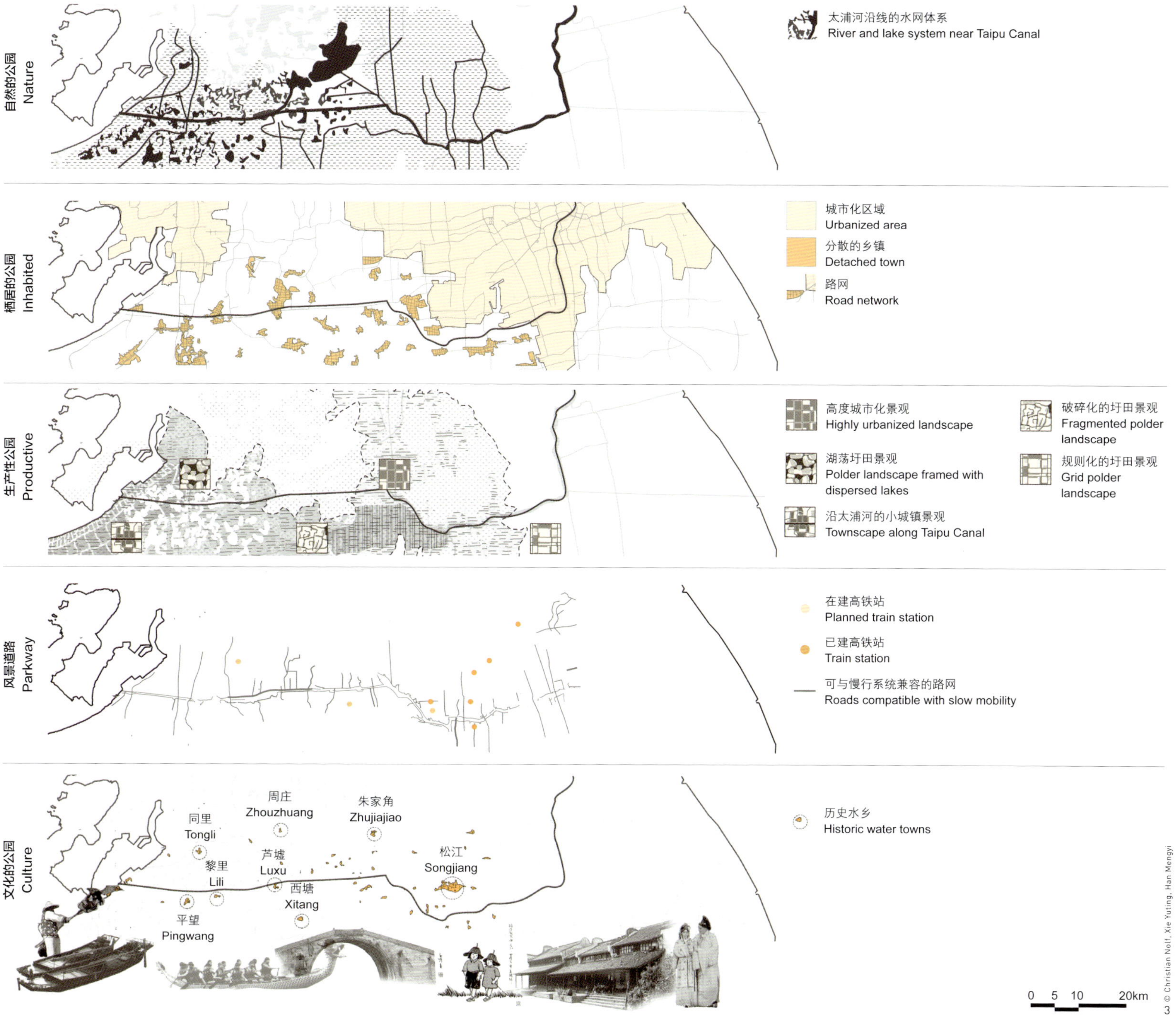

缺失。因此，将太浦河打造为区域“脊柱”不能局限于单一的空间方案，而应实现沿岸景观在连续性与多样性之间，以及维持一致性与应对异质性之间的平衡。

2 方法：太浦河地情–原型设计

鉴于自上而下的规划方式通常会带来将复杂地域问题简化的风险[14][15]，本项目采用了跨尺度的“地情–原型”方法来把握长三角地区的高度复杂性。“地情”旨在反映对地域特征的细致理解，“原型”则强调通过生成实验性的解决方案，创建补充通用控制性规划的设计途径。为此，本项目综合运用样本图绘、类型学研究和设计探索手段，从XL、L和M三个互补的尺度对区域进行解读、展现和设计（表1）。

包括建筑学、城市规划、景观生态学和地理学在内的多个空间学科均需要将复杂的环境解构为一系列典型的构成元素（或类型），进而通过原型概念探索重组这些元素的可能性[11][16]-[22]。这套方法常被用于空间规划和管理领域，以制定兼顾景观多样性保护和土地资源可持续利用的策略[23]-[25]。在景观管理与研究中，将复杂、多变的景观归纳为不同的类型或空间单元有助于更好地解读景观[19][26][27]。

2.1 XL尺度

XL尺度的研究区域长达100km，覆盖太浦河全线，包括其流入黄浦江的河段。为了从区域尺度评估太浦河塑造空间的潜力，项目团队通过查阅历史档案和地图、卫星影像、数据集和规划资料，并结合江南公园的五大主题[4]，从多个维度对太浦河进行了图绘并提出了相应的策略（图3）：

自然的公园：提升太浦河沿岸缓冲带的生物多样性，修复和连接破碎的蓝绿生态网络，从而打造生态轴线。

栖居的公园：将太浦河从民用基础设施转型为串联公民生活的基础设施，将水利设施（如水闸和桥梁等）和废弃的滨水岸线改造为公共空间，以凸显水乡的地域特色。

生产性公园：作为淡水输送渠道和交通基础设施，太浦河串联着各类生产性景观，可以将其升级为可支持短链物流经济模式的本地资源供应基地。

风景道路：太浦河将太湖和上海市中心联系起来，但太浦河及其支流的沿岸空间尚未得到有效利用。可将这些空间开发为连接火车站和港口的非机动车交通网络，实现多式联运。

文化的公园：太浦河与京杭大运河在江南地区交汇，可作为连通沿线知名与不知名水乡的文化纽带，并可在地标性场所举办多种大型文化活动。

2.2 L尺度

将景观特征、基础设施系统和XL尺度专题分析结果汇总为一张综合性概念图，以体现太浦河沿线的典型空间特征（图4）。从每种典型空间选取5km×10km的纵断面样本区域，研究其历史演变、地方特征及当前所面临的环境和发展挑战（图5），并描述每个纵断面的景观格局、基础设施与城镇形态之间的复杂关系。为展示该区域空间的视觉特征，项目运用中国传统地图中平立面相结合的绘图方法，并对该区域的典型迁移方式、建筑、基础设施和景观4类常见元素进行了提取和描绘（图6）。

根据L尺度分析而制定的设计策略探讨了如何通过优化太浦河与周边地区的空间关系来解决每个纵断面样本地区发展所面临的挑战。这种基于尺度调节的规划途径能够将既有开发活动与规划预期的转型有效整合为统一的行动方案，适用于水资源管理、环境保护、后工业更新和城市发展等多个方面。

2.3 M尺度

框架规划提出的策略在1km×1km的原型项目场地得到了验证，并

4. 综合性概念图上标示了太浦河沿线不同的典型空间特征。

4. Synthetic interpretive mapping identifying the different typical spatial conditions crossed by the canal.

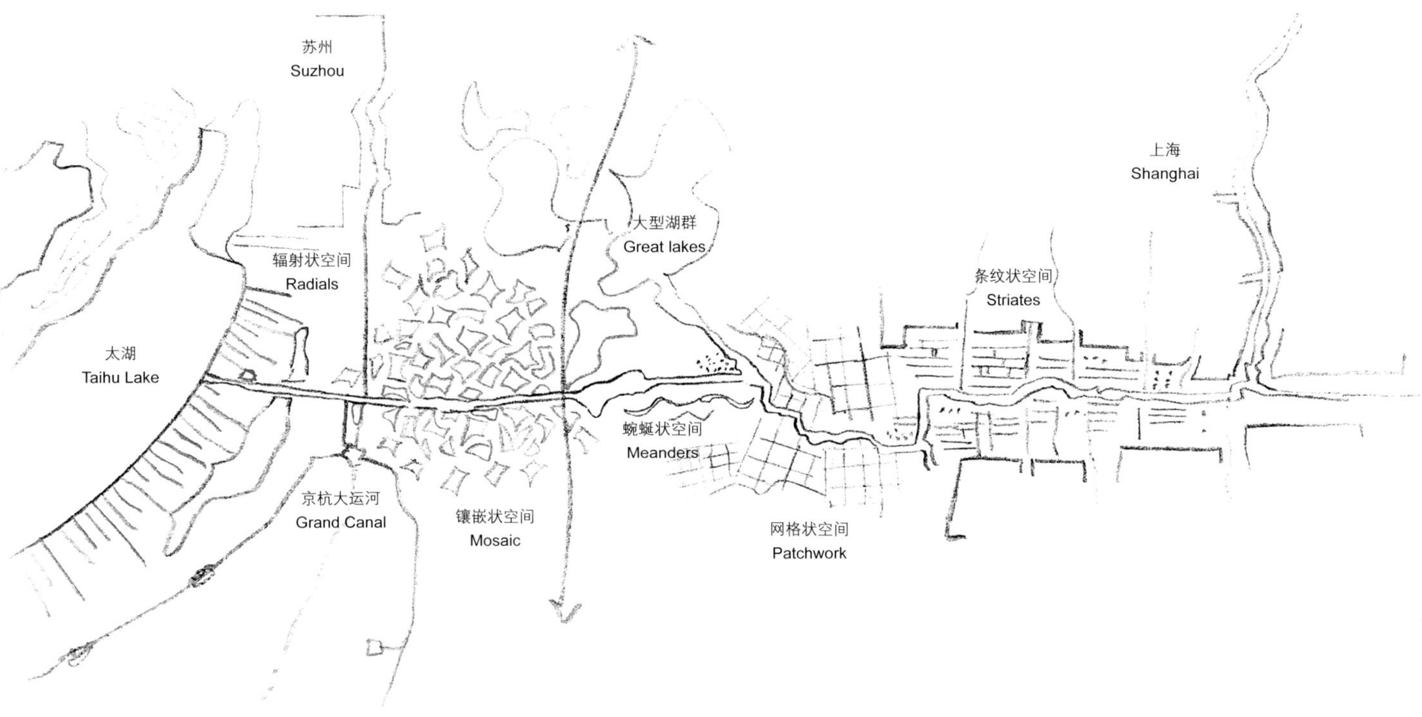

衍生出更为详细的设计方案（图7）。这一尺度主要针对场地内的某一典型元素（如一条支流、一座典型村庄或一类基础设施）提出具体的实施策略，并探讨对潜在利益相关方的影响。

2.4 尺度回溯：推导规划导则

最后，项目回溯到L尺度和XL尺度，在区域尺度重新定位这些原型项目以及相应的场地策略。通过识别太浦河沿线其他具有相似特征的场地，可以评估将原型设计策略归纳为系统性规划导则并优化整个区域结构的可能性。在太浦河项目中，对6个纵断面的对比分析表明，整个区域普遍面临运河沿岸生物多样性低、去工业化，以及由水路运输衰落和现代道路系统割裂导致的公共空间网络破碎等挑战。这些原型项目的比较结果也强调了不同场地面临的共同机遇，例如可通过改造跨河道方向的废弃空间、运河支流及道路基础设施来提高太浦河沿线地区的空间连贯性。在策略层面，6个原型项目均体现了将农业生产、生态修复、风景道路建设和水资源管理等多部门项目议程整合为统一的空间规划的可能性。

3 结论与讨论：将原型设计作为国土空间规划的补充途径

项目运用基于原型设计的跨尺度规划方法，探索了太浦河在长三角区域绿心塑造空间的潜力，并为示范区自上而下的国土空间规划模式提供了补充路径。该方法将宏观尺度的多维度主题分析和中观尺度的原型项目相结合，推导系统性的规划导则来提高开放空间和生态系统的多样性、串联水乡古镇及塑造城市开发新格局。此外，该规划方法不仅适用于长三角这一特定的地理环境，也为其他地区国土空间规划的完善提供了参考，帮助更好地应对愈加复杂的场地条件和更大尺度的空间规划需求。下文试图通过解答以下问题，对这一设计研究项目的成果进行讨论。

（1）示范区国土空间规划存在哪些不足？

近期发布的示范区国土空间规划是跨省域国土空间规划实践的里程碑，为长三角一体化发展添加了生态、绿色的维度。尽管该国土空间规划尝试了跨省级行政主体之间的协作，但仍未脱离基于定量评价手段、自上而下的传统规划模式，无法灵活应对该地区的多样性、复杂性和动态性。根据景观特征将该地区的国土空间分为4类，代表了在规划思路上的突破，但对不同景观类型采用同一的评价方法仍会催生“一刀切”、同质化的规划方案。此外，人性化视角在示范区国土空间规划中也有所缺失。

（2）基于原型设计的规划途径如何弥补上述不足？

项目采用了包含样本分析、景观元素、系统及特征分类、基于原型的设计实践等过程的复杂规划途径，初步解读了太浦河流域的复杂性，并对研究区域进行了从宏观规划到微观设计再回到宏观的双向研究推导。项目在尺度回溯阶段将基于地情的设计策略和原型项目重置于区域语境中进行评估和比较，发现了在一体化规划中整合不同部门项目和议程时所面临的共同挑战和机遇。这种“从特殊到一般”的规划原则推导过程可从三方面完善现行的国土空间规划手段：

首先，这一规划途径提供了人性化尺度的视角，丰富了国土空间的描绘方式。示范区现有的各类规划忽视了空间质量，而该项目则通过将区域概观与具体的场地印象相结合，对国土空间进行度量，从而确定合理的规划设计尺度。其次，该途径考虑了国土空间的复杂性。自上而下的区域规划手段往往忽略地方特征，功能区规划容易导致国土空间的割裂。而跨尺度的原型设计途径充分尊重了当地的独特性，并提供了多维度的视角，通过整合跨部门的项目，进一步维持或强化国土空间的复杂性。最后，该途径提高了规划的可操作性。地情—原型方法可基于真实地情推进策略的可行性论证，亦有助于调动潜在的利益相关方和可利用资源。因此，这种方法能够有效协调各部门的项目议程，共同协作、形成统一的规划目标并付诸实施。**LAF**

致谢

感谢弗洛伦斯·万诺贝克和韩孟怡为本项目提供的研究支持。

项目信息

项目地址： 中国江苏省、浙江省、上海市
项目长度： 100km
项目指导： Christian Nolf、谢雨婷、董楠楠、戴代新、张斗
项目团队： 徐雯雯、张悦、陈琳、应佳欣、吴雪琳、朱泽宇、厉超、王星儿、陈雨聪、王君妍、包纪元、郭梦阳（浙江大学）；赵易秋、潘丽君、徐元、吕玉言、罗雯雯、蔡奇峰、李晓威（西交利物浦大学）；曹阳、侯昭薇、王佳菲、赵双睿、冯婧婕、丛楷昕、欧阳慕莹、汪方心怡、朱雯、陈奕、江卉卿（同济大学）
客座点评： Kelly Shannon（比利时鲁汶大学）、Lee Parks（AECOM）、刘伟（长三角生态绿色一体化发展示范区总体方案执行委员会生态规划建筑办公室）
设计时间： 2020年3～6月

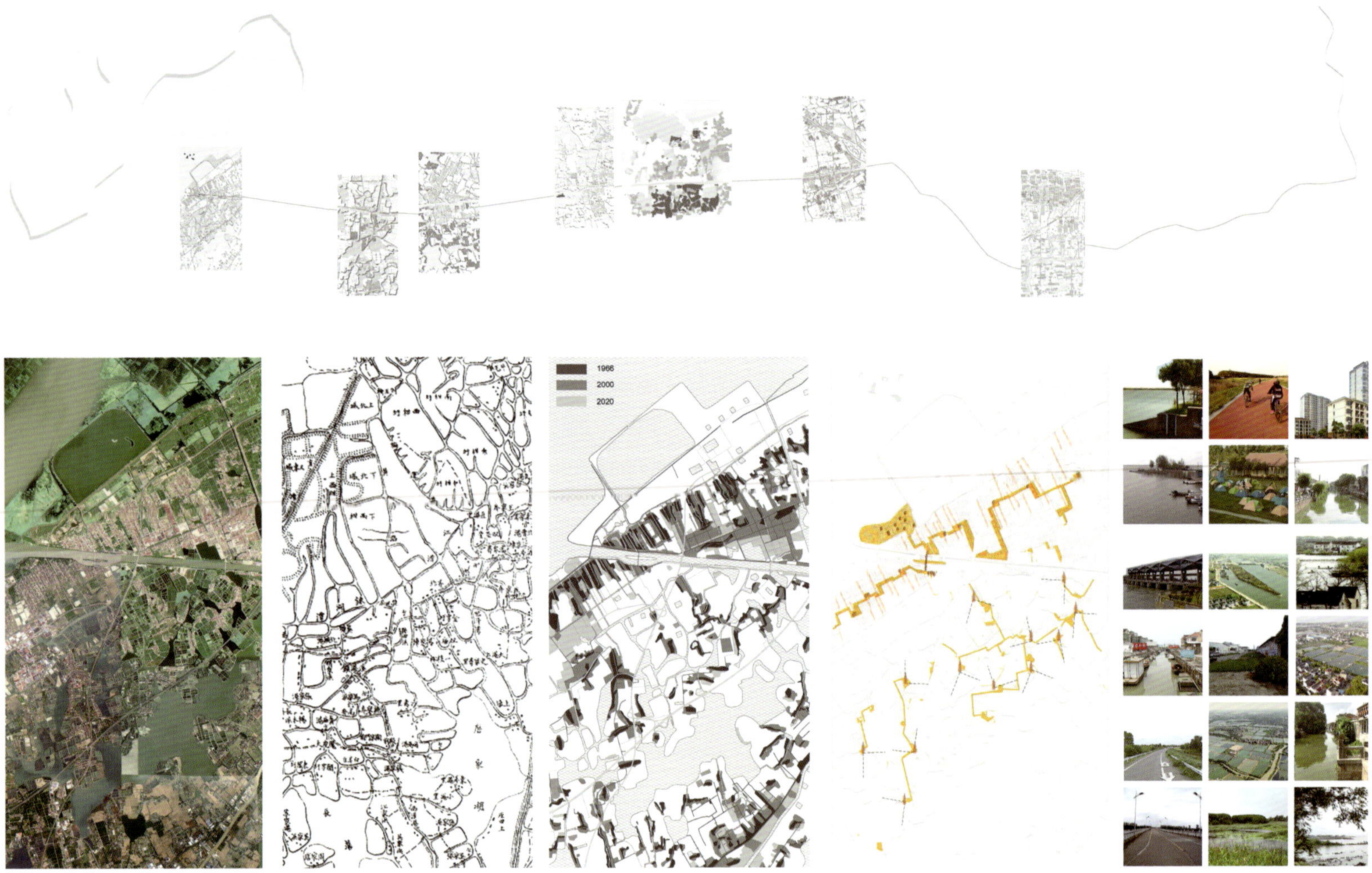

© Luo Wenwen, Xu Yuan, Christian Nolf, Xie Yuting, Taipu Canal Studio 2020

5-1

5. L尺度纵断面：对每个纵断面进行历史分析、空间特征解读以及现有规划评价，并制定策略性规划框架（图5-1）。图5-2为放大后的纵断面1，展示了如何将位于建成区夹缝内的开放空间作为公共花园，并将水闸及其所在的小岛改造为公园，从而改善淥港圩田景观与太浦河道之间的消极空间关系（历史地图来源：参考文献[28]）。

5. L scale transects: for each transect, the historical analysis, the interpretation of local characteristics, and the critical review of existing plans lead to the formulation of a strategic framework plan (Fig. 5-1). The zoom on Transect 1 (Fig. 5-2) illustrates how the accidental relationship between the radial Lougang polder landscape and the intrusive canal can be re-articulated by the requalification of interstitial open spaces in collective gardens, and by the reclamation of the sluice island as a public park (Historic map source: Ref. [28]).

1 Context and Challenges

1.1 How to Consolidate the Open Space of the Yangtze River Delta Integration Plan?

Responding to the urgent need to coordinate the spatial and economic development of the megacity region spanning across Shanghai and the three provinces of Zhejiang, Jiangsu, and Anhui, in 2019, the Central Committee and the State Council launched the Yangtze River Delta (YRD) Integration Plan. Primarily driven by the “re-scaling” at a regional level of transportation, energy, and urban services[1], the YRD integration plan has gradually included environmental ambitions. In 2019, the Overall Plan for the Demonstration Zone for Integrated Ecological and Green Development in the YRD incorporated specific objectives related to open space[2]. However, focused on the preservation of ecological space and permanent prime farmland, these objectives remained limited to quantitative prescriptions and quotas. In June 2020, a more precise plan for the demonstration zone was published[3], specifying the proportion of green and blue open space, as well as the length and overall structure of a parkway, greenway, and blue waterway system. Even though this plan marks a milestone as the first cross-provincial territorial plan in China, the planning approach remains strongly informed by regulatory, top-down, and functional zoning principles that tend to overlook the complexity of this ecologically and historically sensitive area.

The project introduced in this article explores the same area, but from the perspective of Jiangnan Park[4], a territorial vision that regards the vast triangular region between Shanghai, Suzhou, and Hangzhou as the ecological and cultural “green

① Taipu Canal Studio 2020 is a part of the Jiangnan Park project and is directed by the joint-initiative of the Jiangnan Lab, promoted by Associate Professor Christian Nolf (Department of Urban Planning and Design, Xi'an Jiaotong-Liverpool University) and Dr. Xie Yuting (Institute of Landscape Architecture, Zhejiang University). This joint studio was developed in cooperation with Associate Professor Dong Nannan and Associate Professor Dai Daixin (Department of Landscape Studies, College of Architecture and Urban Planning, Tongji University), as well as with Zhang Dou from Sasaki.

heart" of the YRD megacity region. It investigates how cross-scale and design-driven approaches can bridge the gap between current top-down regulatory zoning approaches and local site-specific solutions.

1.2 Why Considering the Taipu Canal as a Regional Spine?

An evident strategy to consolidate fragmented open spaces is to re-articulate them in a park system[5]. This can be achieved by introducing new webs of greenways[6], or by conferring a new structuring role to an existing linear landscape or infrastructural element. The re-articulation strategy along an existing linear element has been most famously illustrated in the Emerald Necklace in Boston, USA, the Emscher Park in Germany, and the New Dutch Waterline in the Netherlands[7][8]. The reweaving of open spaces does not only strengthen their role as ecological corridors and networks[9]; it can also contribute to the socio-cultural cohesion of a region. By connecting isolated places physically and functionally, a linear park system can reinforce the sense of belonging of the residents and establish a local identity through tangible relationships to the place or a region[7]. Likewise, for the visitors, an articulating linear system can open up new sequential perspectives that reveal the coherence and diversity of a region[10].

The Taipu Canal is a 57-kilometer-long drainage channel linking Taihu Lake to Shanghai across the ecological sensitive polder areas of Taihu Basin (Fig. 1). Excavated in different phases from 1958 to 1995, the Taipu Canal has played an important role in flood control, drainage, irrigation, and since 2016, supply of fresh water to the Shanghai metropolitan area. Despite its purely technical function and limited accessibility (Fig. 2), the canal by default stands out as a main spatial referent in the region because of its straight route and majestic scale. Its strategic importance has been further comforted by the recent territorial planning of the demonstration zone that designates it as a main ecological corridor.

Taipu Canal Studio 2020①, a design-driven research project, hypothesizes that the Taipu Canal can guide the spatial development of the vast green heart of Jiangnan Park as a cohesive entity, and can (re)articulate the region in two directions: longitudinally, the canal can be upgraded from its current drainage function into an ecological and recreational spine that links the rich diversity of open spaces and ecosystems; transversally, the canal can interweave the network of open spaces, connect historic water towns and villages, and frame new urban developments.

1.3 How to Articulate a Complex Heterogeneous Landscape?

It is important to note that the YRD's open space is anything but empty. Densely populated and intensively exploited for several centuries, the area is characterized by a multiplicity of typical landscapes that all derive from polder structures, but with variations linked to distinct topographical conditions and historical evolutions[12]. Interestingly, the Taipu Canal remains an exception in this complex and historically charged context. Designed as a straight line to drain water, the Taipu Canal contrasts drastically with the organic and cellular patterns of its surrounding landscapes. At the difference with the Grand Canal that conditioned the development of the Jiangnan region since the early 7th century[13], the relatively recent Taipu Canal has not generated development along its route. Bordering the backside of modest towns, splitting lakes in two, or crossing patches of forests, the Taipu Canal still appears as an incision across a juxtaposition of heterogeneous landscapes.

In the recent official territorial plan for the zone, the environmental governance and ecological restoration solutions for the Taipu Canal as an ecological corridor are homogenous from east to west. Even though four ecological zones along the Taipu have been framed according to the underneath polder landscape structures (Great Lakes, Lougang, Hudang, and River Network Zones)[3], specific design solutions for different landscape types and their ecological spaces are still missing. The project presented in this article considers that the requalification of the Taipu Canal as a regional spine cannot be limited to a

© Luo Wenwen, Christian Nolf, Xie Yuting, Taipu Canal Studio 2020
5-2

single spatial solution along its entire route. A balance must be found between continuity and variations, between maintaining a certain consistency and responding contextually to the diversity of the landscapes crossed.

2 Method: Contextual Prototypes for the Taipu Canal

In order to grasp the rich complexity of this vast territory and to avoid the risks of approximation and simplification often associated with top-down planning approaches[14][15], this project adopts a cross-scale method of "contextual prototypes." "Contextual" aims to reflect a sensitive understanding of the territory; "Prototype" expresses the ambition to generate pilot solutions that inaugurate alternative approaches to the generic statutory planning praxis. To these ends, a combination of sampling, typological classification, and design exploration techniques are used to read, represent, and design the territory at three complementary scales: XL, L, and M scale.

The process of deconstructing complex environments into a set of typical constitutive elements (or typologies) and exploring their transformative capacity through prototypes has been applied in several spatial disciplines, ranging from architecture, urbanism, landscape ecology to geography[11][16]-[22]. It is particularly relevant in the field of spatial planning and management to support strategies that combine conservation of landscape diversity with sustainable use of land resources[23]-[25]. The complex, variable landscapes could be interpreted and communicated better when described and classified into types or spatial units in landscape management and research[19][26][27].

2.1 XL Scale

The analysis at the XL scale defined a 100-kilometer-long study area that covers the entire length of the Taipu Canal, including the section where it flows into the Huangpu River. In order to assess the structuring potential of the canal at the regional scale, the team reviewed historical archives and maps, satellite images, datasets, and plans to draw up a multidimensional portrait of the canal territory according to the five themes of Jiangnan Park[4] (Fig. 3):

Park for Nature: to become an ecological spine, the canal can have its currently monoculture buffers upgraded into biodiverse fringes and hence reweave the disrupted blue-green ecological networks.

Inhabited Park: to make the canal evolve from a civil into a civic infrastructure, the numerous hydraulic engineering elements (sluices, bridges, etc.) and abandoned waterfront margins can be reclaimed as public spaces, and thus contribute to strengthening the regional identity of the water towns and villages.

Productive Park: as a conveyor of fresh water and transport infrastructure crossing diverse productive landscapes, the canal can be enhanced as a provider of locally produced resources supporting short circular economic models.

Parkways: the Taipu Canal offers a direct connection between Taihu Lake and the heart of Shanghai. The underutilized technical banks of the canal and its tributaries can be reclaimed to form a continuous and multimodal soft mobility

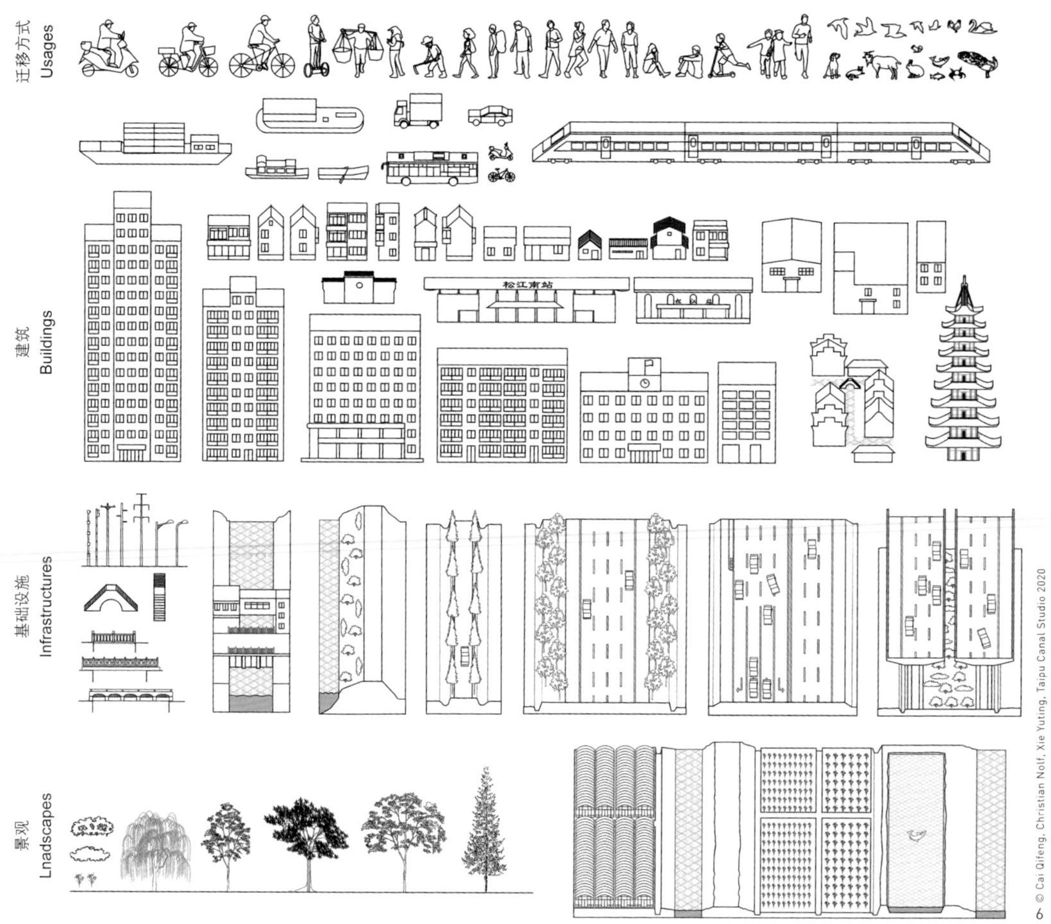

6. 区域典型元素的工具箱

6. Toolbox of typical elements found in the region.

network connected to several train stations and ports.

Cultural Park: as the perpendicular counterpart of the Grand Canal in the Jiangnan region, the Taipu Canal can support multiple cultural circuits linking the constellation of well-known and less-known water towns and villages, while also hosting major cultural events in emblematic sites.

2.2 L Scale

The landscape characteristics, the infrastructural systems, and the results of the thematic analyses at the XL scale were summarized in a synthetic interpretative map that identifies a set of typical spatial conditions crossed by the canal (Fig. 4). For each typical condition, a representative transect of 5 km × 10 km was sampled and examined in terms of historical evolution, local characteristics, and current environmental and developmental challenges (Fig. 5). The complex relationships between landscape pattern, infrastructures, and forms of urbanization of each transect were described. In order to capture the visual identity of the region, the local characteristics were represented using a traditional Chinese mapping technique combining plan and elevation. A toolbox of common elements found in the region were featured and classified into four categories of typical usages, buildings, infrastructures, and landscapes (Fig. 6).

On the basis of this analysis at the L scale, contextual design strategies were imagined, exploring in each transect how an enhanced relationship between the Taipu Canal and its surrounding could contribute to addressing local development challenges. This rescaling approach provides a framework that integrates and aligns ongoing and planned transformations—for water management, environmental protection, post-industrial requalification, and urban development—toward a coherent agenda.

2.3 M Scale

The strategies of the framework plans were then tested in concrete prototypical projects in 1 km × 1 km sites (Fig. 7). By focusing on a characteristic element (e.g., a tributary, a typical village, an infrastructural element), this level of detail helped visualizing how the strategies can be implemented on the ground and which stakeholders are potentially impacted.

2.4 Zoom out: Inducing Structuring Principles

The last phase zoomed out to position the site-specific strategies and prototypical projects in a wider regional context at the L and XL scales. By identifying similar conditions in other sites along the canal, this zoom-out exercise hence assessed the capacity of prototypical strategies to be systemized as structuring principles at the regional scale. In the case of the Taipu Canal, the comparison of the six transects highlighted several common challenges, such as the limited biodiversity of the canal fringes, the process of deindustrialization, and the fragmentation of public space networks due to the decline of water transport and the divisive impact of the road system. The comparison of prototypical projects also highlighted common opportunities, such as the potential of transversal marginal spaces, tributaries, and road infrastructures to restore the spatial cohesion of the areas crossed by the Taipu Canal. In terms of strategy, finally, the six prototypical projects highlighted the possibilities of combining sectoral programs and agendas of agriculture, ecological restoration, parkways, water management etc. in integrative spatial projects.

3 Conclusion and Discussion: Toward a Prototypical Approach to Territorial Planning

Developed to assess the potential structuring role of the Taipu Canal as a regional spine in the green heart of the YRD, the cross-scale prototypical approach presented in this article offers a useful alternative to the top-down method applied in the recent territorial planning for the demonstration zone. Combining a multidimensional thematic analysis at the large scale and pilot projects at the medium scale, it aims to identify systemic principles to articulate the rich diversity of open spaces and ecosystems, link historic water towns and villages, and frame new urban developments. In addition, it can be argued that beyond the specific geographic context of the YRD, this approach also offers possibilities to complement the regulatory territorial planning for other territories, which has to cope with increasingly complex conditions and vaster scales. The authors try to discuss the outcomes of the research-by-design project in line with the following research questions.

(1) What is lacking in the territorial planning for the demonstration zone?

The very recently released territorial planning for the demonstration zone in the YRD marks a milestone in two senses: it scales-up the planning scope across provincial territories; it adds an ecological and green dimension to the YRD integration plan. Even though this territorial plan is exemplary of cross-provincial coordination, it still applies quantitative and top-down principles inherited from past planning practices. It remains too rigid to respond in an adaptive manner to the diversity, complexity and dynamics of this area.

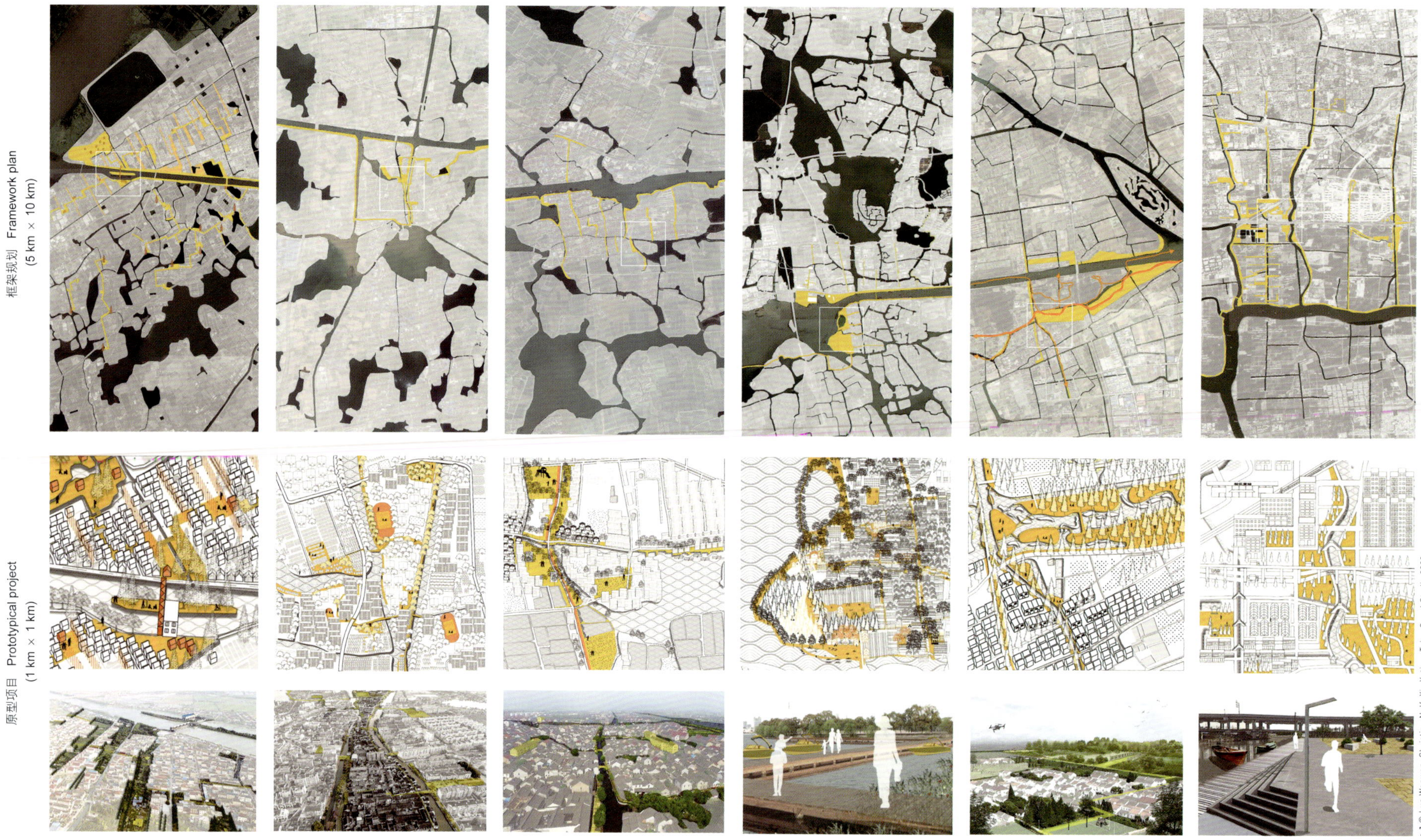

© Luo Wenwen, Christian Nolf, Xie Yuting, Taipu Canal Studio 2020

7

The decomposition of the territory into four types of landscape characteristics represents an appreciable progress. However, these different landscapes are evaluated according to a single assessment method, which entails risks of generating simplified and homogeneous planning solutions. Finally, human perspective is missing in the official territorial plan.

(2) How could this prototypical approach complement it?

The project presented in this article is a preliminary attempt to grasp the complexity of the vast Taipu Canal territory. To this end, it uses a comprehensive approach, comprising a process of sampling, classification of typical elements, systems and characteristics, as well as prototypical design explorations. This process iterates in scales from the general large scale to the details and back. The zoom out phase positions the site-specific strategies and prototypical projects in a wider regional context. The repositioning and comparison of prototypical projects highlight the common challenges and opportunities to combine sectoral programs and agendas in integrative plans. This inductive process, which reasons from the specific to the general to define structuring principles, complements territorial planning in three ways:

First, it enriches the description of the territory with a human-sized perspective. The combination of the regional

7. 使用相同的表现手法和元素对比不同纵断面的策略性框架规划与原型项目，揭示了太浦河沿线多样化的空间特征，同时发现了不同场地面临的共同挑战与机遇。

7. Facilitated by the use of common representation modes and elements, the comparison of strategic framework plans and prototypical projects for the different transects reveals the rich diversity of conditions encountered along the Taipu Canal, but also some recurring challenges and opportunities.

overview with phenomenological impressions on the ground makes it possible to capture space qualities that are invisible in plan; it also takes the measure of the territory and helps to define appropriate scales of planning and intervention. Second, it acknowledges the complexity of territories. Too often, top-down regional planning approaches are limited, by ease and by inadvertence of local specificities, to zoning plans that separate functions and thereby disintegrate territories into sterile fragments. Based on distinct characteristics of places, the cross-scale prototypical approach provides multiple perspectives on space that hence makes it possible to envisage the combination of different programs that maintain or reinforce the complexity of territories. Third, it supplements planning with an operative dimension. The contextual prototype method not only provides in-field insights on the physical feasibility of implementing a strategy; it also identifies which stakeholders would be impacted and which resources could potentially be mobilized. As such, the method can contribute to aligning agendas and forming coalitions to converge and operationalize planning objectives. **LAF**

ACKNOWLEDGEMENT

This studio work benefited from the research support from Florence Vannoorbeeck and Han Mengyi.

PROJECT INFORMATION

LOCATION: Jiangsu and Zhejiang Province and Shanghai City, China
AREA (LENGTH): 100 km
STUDIO INSTRUCTORS: Christian Nolf, Xie Yuting, Dong Nannan, Dai Daixin, Zhang Dou
STUDIO TEAM: Xu Wenwen, Zhang Yue, Chen Lin, Ying Jiaxin, Wu Xuelin, Zhu Zeyu, Li Chao, Wang Xinger, Chen Yucong, Wang Junyan, Bao Jiyuan, Guo Mengyang (Zhejiang University); Zhao Yiqiu, Pan Lijun, Xu Yuan, Lyu Yuyan, Luo Wenwen, Cai Qifeng, Li Xiaowei (Xi'an Jiaotong-Liverpool University); Cao Yang, Hou Zhaowei, Wang Jiafei, Zhao Shuangrui, Feng Jingjie, Cong Kaixin, Ouyang Muying, Wang Fangxinyi, Zhu Wen, Chen Yi, Jiang Huiqing (Tongji University)
GUEST CRITICS: Kelly Shannon (KU Leuven), Lee Parks (AECOM), Liu Wei (Office of Ecology, Planning & Construction, Executive Committee of Yangtze River Delta Ecological Green Integrated Development Demonstration Zone)
DESIGN PERIOD: March to June, 2020

REFERENCES

[1] Central People's Government of the People's Republic of China. (2019, December 1). Outline of the integrated regional development of the Yangtze River Delta. Retrieved from http://www.gov.cn/zhengce/2019-12/01/content_5457442.htm
[2] National Development and Reform Commission. (2019, October 26). The overall plan to build a demonstration zone for integrated ecological and green development in the Yangtze River Delta region (Report No. 1686). Retrieved from http://www.gov.cn/xinwen/2019-11/19/5453512/files/1ea2d01619194ceeadbd0160215ffb66.pdf
[3] Department of Natural Resources of Zhejiang Province. (2020, June 18). Masterplan of territorial spatial planning for the demonstration zone for integrated ecological and green development in the Yangtze River Delta (2019-2035). Retrieved from http://zrzyt.zj.gov.cn/art/2020/6/18/art_1289924_47444338.html
[4] Nolf, C., & Xie, Y. (2020). Positioning regional design in Chinese territorial spatial planning: An exploratory project in the Yangtze River Delta megacity region. Landscape Architecture Frontiers, 8(1), 92-107. https://doi.org/10.15302/J-LAF-1-030010
[5] Maruani, T., & Amit-Cohen, I. (2007). Open space planning models: A review of approaches and methods. Landscape and urban planning, 81(1-2), 1-13. https://doi.org/10.1016/j.landurbplan.2007.01.003
[6] Liu, Z., Lin, Y., De Meulder, B., & Wang, S. (2019). Can greenways perform as a new planning strategy in the Pearl River Delta, China? Landscape and Urban Planning, (187), 81-95. https://doi.org/10.1016/j.landurbplan.2019.03.012
[7] Nijhuis, S., & Jauslin, D. (2015). Urban landscape infrastructures: Designing operative landscape structures for the built environment. Designing operative landscape structures for the built environment. Research in Urbanism Series, 3(1), 13-34. https://doi.org/10.7480/rius.3.874
[8] Verschuure-Stuip, G. (2020). Hold the Line: The transformation of the New Dutch Waterline and the Future Possibilities of Heritage. In C. Hein (Ed.), Adaptive Strategies for Water Heritage (pp.250-269). Cham: Springer. https://doi.org/10.1007/978-3-030-00268-8_13
[9] Dramstad, W. E., Olson, J. D., & Forman, R. T. T. (1996). Landscape ecology principles in landscape architecture and land-use planning. Washington: Island Press.
[10] Shannon, K., & Smets, M. (2010). The landscape of contemporary infrastructure. Rotterdam: NAi Publishers.
[11] Local Chronicles Compilation Committee of Jiangsu Province. (2001). Water Conservancy Chronicles of Jiangsu Province. Nanjing: Jiangsu Ancient Books Publishing House.
[12] Xie, Y. (2017). Restructuring cultural landscapes in metropolitan areas: A typological approach to permanent forms and green blue infrastructure in the Yangtze River Delta region in China (Doctoral dissertation). Technical University of Munich, Munich. Retrieved from https://mediatum.ub.tum.de/?id=1378536
[13] Vannoorbeeck, F., Nolf, C., & Wang, Z. (2019). The Grand Canal in Jiangnan: Origin and development of a multifunctional infrastructure. Plan, Magazine of the International Society of City and Regional Planners (ISOCARP), (9), 26-33.
[14] Secchi, B. (1992). Urbanistica Descrittiva [Descriptive Urbanism]. Casabella, (588), 22-23.
[15] Corner, J. (1999). The Agency of Mapping. Speculation, Critique, and Invention. In D. Cosgrove (Ed.), Mappings (pp.213-252). London: Reaktion Books.
[16] Rossi, A. (1984). The architecture of the city. Cambridge, MA: MIT Press.
[17] Cataldi, G., Maffei, G. L., & Vaccaro, P. (2002). Saverio Muratori and the Italian school of planning typology. Urban Morphology, 6(1), 3-14.
[18] Whitehand, J. W. R. (2001). British urban morphology: The Conzenion tradition. Urban Morphology, 5(2), 103-109.
[19] Simensen, T., Halvorsen, R., & Erikstad, L. (2018). Methods for landscape characterisation and mapping: A systematic review. Land use policy, 75(2018), 557-569. https://doi.org/10.1016/j.landusepol.2018.04.022
[20] Steenbergen, C. (2008). Composing landscapes: analysis, typology and experiments for design. Switzerland: Birkhäuser.
[21] Viganò, P. (1999). La città elementare [The Elementary City]. Milano: Skira.
[22] Notteboom, B. (2017). Stories, methods and systems: Bureau Bas Smets and the urban landscape. Narrating Urban Landscapes, (98), 103-108. Retrieved from https://www.oasejournal.nl/en/Issues/98/Storiesmethodsandsystems
[23] Wascher, D. M. (2005). European landscape character areas: Typologies, cartography and indicators for the assessment of sustainable landscapes. Wageningen: Landscape Europe. Retrieved from https://library.wur.nl/WebQuery/wurpubs/fulltext/1778
[24] Kim, K. -H., & Pauleit, S. (2007). Landscape character, biodiversity and land use planning: The case of Kwangju City Region, South Korea. Land Use Policy, 24(2007), 264-274. https://doi.org/10.1016/j.landusepol.2005.12.001
[25] Hazeu, G. W., Metzger, M. J., Mücher, C. A., Perez-Soba, M., Renetzeder, C. H., & Andersen, E. (2011). European environmental stratifications and typologies: An overview. Agriculture, Ecosystems and Environment, 142(1-2), 29-39. https://doi.org/10.1016/j.agee.2010.01.009
[26] Antrop, M., & Van Eetvelde, V. (2017). Landscape perspectives: The holistic nature of landscape. Dordrecht, the Netherlands: Springer.
[27] Bunce, R. G. H., Barr, C. J., Clarke, R. T.,Howard, D. C., & Lane, A. M. (1996). Land classification for strategic ecological survey. Journal of Environmental Management, 47(1), 37-60. https://doi.org/10.1006/jema.1996.0034
[28] Sokuryobu, R. (1986). 1:50,000 Map Collection of Mainland China, Vol.1. Tokyo: Kagaku Shoin.

本文引用格式 / PLEASE CITE THIS ARTICLE AS

Rong, H. H., Yang, J., & Qian, W. J. (2020). Enabling Participatory Actions in Community Design and Management: A Collective Intelligent Digital Platform in Ang Sila, Thailand. Landscape Architecture Frontiers, 8(4), 126-139. https://doi.org/10.15302/J-LAF-1-040017

促进社区设计和管理中的参与性行动：泰国昂西拉地区集体智能数字平台

ENABLING PARTICIPATORY ACTIONS IN COMMUNITY DESIGN AND MANAGEMENT: A COLLECTIVE INTELLIGENT DIGITAL PLATFORM IN ANG SILA, THAILAND

https://doi.org/10.15302/J-LAF-1-040017 收稿时间 RECEIVED DATE / 2020-05-24 中图分类号 / TU986, TP3 文献标识码 / B

戎航
麻省理工学院建筑和城市设计与研究专业硕士，CIVIS设计与咨询公司创始人、合伙人，哥伦比亚大学规划系博士候选人

杨竣程
麻省理工学院建筑和城市设计与研究专业硕士，CIVIS设计与咨询公司合伙人

钱经纬
康奈尔大学建筑学学士，CIVIS设计与咨询公司数字化设计师

Helena H. RONG*
MIT SMArchS Urbanism; Founder and Partner of CIVIS Design and Advisory; PhD Candidate in Urban Planning at Columbia University

YANG Juncheng
MIT SMArchS Urbanism; Partner of CIVIS Design and Advisory

William Jingwei QIAN
Bachelor of Architecture in Cornell University; Computational Designer of CIVIS Design and Advisory

*Corresponding Author
Address: 77 Massachusetts Avenue, Cambridge MA 02139, USA
Email: hrong@mit.edu

摘要

过去10年间，随着数据收集、计算机技术及可视化方法的发展，“可持续智慧城市”这一旨在运用数字技术解决各类城市问题的新兴概念逐渐得到推广。然而，早期的方法忽略了公众参与决策过程的重要性，导致社会个体与专家权威之间信息不对称，弱势群体的代理权日益萎缩。本文介绍了由研究团队所设计的“共同设计昂西拉”（CoDAS）这一公民参与数字平台和工作流程：这个工具可以促进民众和专家权威在项目的各个阶段中持续沟通。通过让众多利益相关者作为共同创作者参与到设计过程之中，CoDAS可以提高不同群体之间的沟通效率，并实现设计和开发结果的公平及项目建成后使用阶段的公共资源管理。研究团队就泰国一个历史悠久的渔村——昂西拉附近的一处新开发项目展开了场地设计实验，对这一构想进行了验证。

关键词

集体智慧；城市设计；城市治理；社区营造；可持续智慧城市；社区平台；数字应用

ABSTRACT

Advancements in data collection, computing, and visualization methods have given rise to a new form of urban concept over the last decade: the smart sustainable city which tackles various urban challenges with digital technologies. However, earlier approaches omit the importance of citizens' involvement in decision-making processes, which leads to an imbalanced information asymmetry between individuals and authorities and an increasingly reduced agency for the vulnerable. In this article, a tool and process was proposed which integrates the voices of evolving self-organizing entities to solve collective action challenges: Named as CoDAS (Co-Design Ang Sila), it is a digital platform which facilitates continuous communication between citizens and authorities during different development phases of a given project. By including a large number of stakeholders to participate in the co-design process as co-creators, CoDAS aims to improve communication efficiency while achieving equitable outcomes in design and development, along with post-occupancy common resource management. To test this hypothesis, a site design experiment was conducted on a site near a historical fishing village of Ang Sila, Thailand.

KEYWORDS

Collective Intelligence; Urban Design; Urban Governance; Community Building; Smart Sustainable City; Community Platform; Digital Application

编辑 田乐 **翻译** 田乐 戎航
EDITED BY Tina TIAN **TRANSLATED BY** Tina TIAN Helena H. RONG

1 项目背景

过去10年间，为了解决各类城市问题，数字技术不断创新，“可持续智慧城市”概念也得到日益推广。国际电信联盟将“可持续智慧城市”（smart sustainable city）定义为“利用信息和通信技术等手段提高生活品质、城市运营和服务效率，以及竞争力，同时确保其满足当代人和子孙后代在经济、社会、环境，以及文化方面的需求的创新城市”[1]。然而，在智慧城市的建设过程中，由于公民对决策过程的理解和参与不足， 民众与政府之间的信息不对等问题日益加剧。在自然资

源丰富、主要依靠外部投资拉动经济快速发展的地区，开发建设的成本往往很高，且存在当地居民收益不均的问题。此外，公民参与的缺失也使得社区居民与团体利益相关者之间难以建立信任，长远来看，共享资源的最佳管理框架和方法也将无法实现。针对这些问题，英国建筑师杰森·波默罗伊提出了“智慧城市2.0”（一种最新的规划设计策略）的构想，通过借助相关技术，使公民能够有机会参与设计和规划过程[2]。这一策略强调跨领域协作以及切实理解公众意见的必要性。

根据教育学家理查德·阿德勒和朱迪·戈金的定义，“公民参与”（citizen engagement）是指“公民为了改善他人的生活条件或帮助营建社区的未来而参与社区生活的方式”[3]。雪莉·阿尔斯坦的“公民参与阶梯”理论为城市规划实践提供了一种启发式框架，该框架包含8个与“公民决定最终产品的权力”[4]相对应的梯级。本文着眼于公民参与和共同创造，提出了一种能够汇集多个不断发展的自组织机构的意见的工具和表达途径，以促进开发过程的公平、公正。首先，本文介绍了由研究团队所设计的“共同设计昂西拉”（CoDAS）这一公民参与数字平台，该平台可以在项目开发的不同阶段中引导并促进民众与政府 / 专家（如建筑师、开发商、政府和管理公司等）之间的持续沟通。其次，通过让众多利益相关者作为共同创作者参与到共同设计过程之中，CoDAS可以提高不同群体之间的沟通效率，并实现设计和开发结果的公平及项目建成后使用阶段的公共资源管理。

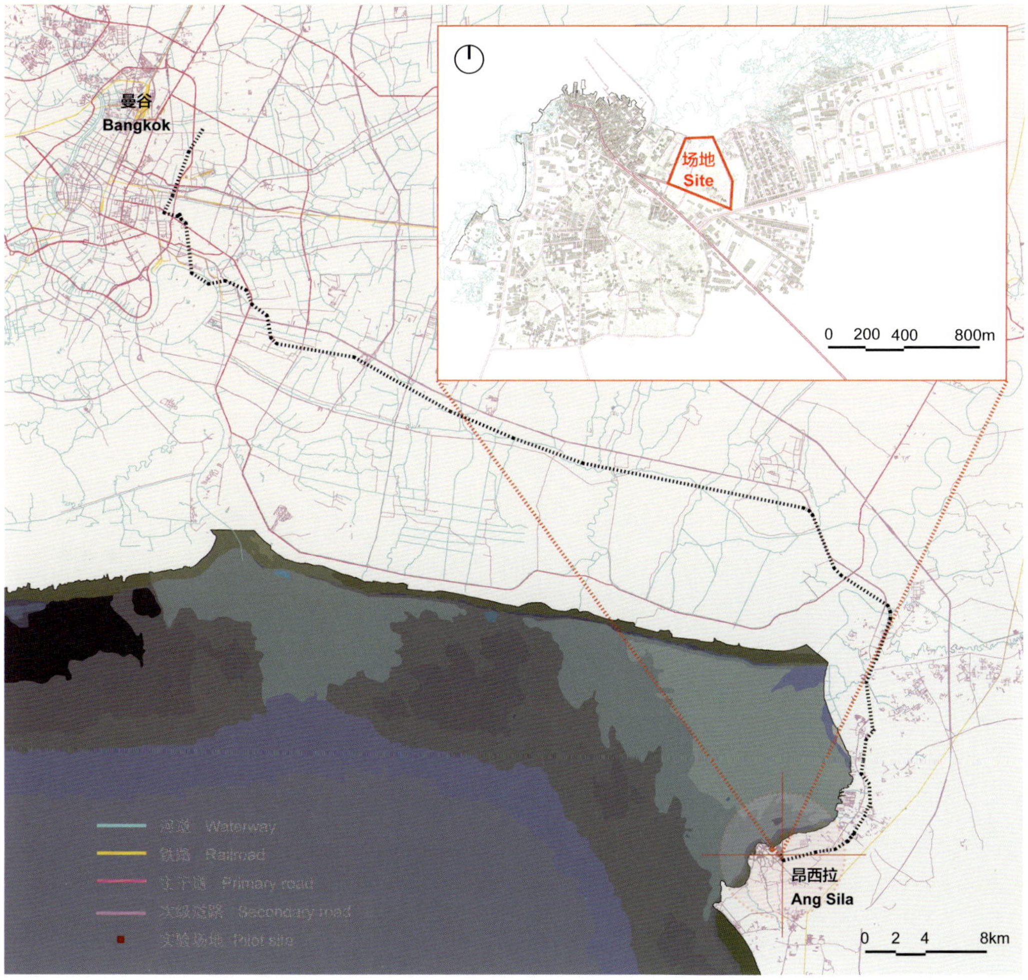

© Helena Rong, CIVIS Design and Advisory

1

1. 场地区位图：昂西拉与曼谷相距91km。

1. Location map of the pilot site showing Ang Sila's relation to Bangkok (91 km apart).

本研究旨在探究以下问题：

1）数字参与如何改变市民或终端用户在城市规划和设计决策过程中的作用?

2）在开发前设计和使用后管理阶段中，哪些数字工具可以促进不同参与者之间的沟通?

3）如何借助公众意见数据，通过设计邻接空间、共享空间和多功能建筑来协调不同社会群体的利益?

研究团队以泰国昂西拉地区为试点，对这一工具的有效性进行了测试。昂西拉是一个隶属于旅游胜地春武里府的小渔村，位于曼谷东南方向约91km处（图1）。试点地区西侧毗邻泰国历史最悠久的捕鱼区之一，而东侧为茂密的红树林区。春武里府目前有意开展适合当地环境的新型物联网基础设施建设项目。随着旅游业的发展，春武里府所面临的挑战在于：如何在无差别旅游业开发的威胁下保护当地的本土文化和生态特征（如红树林），同时满足不断增长的游客需求，并公平分配新型经济带来的收入。

试点场地是一片面积约14hm^{2}的待开发空地，泰国本土开发商计划将这里开发成一个充满活力的、满足多代际需求且具有多元文化特色的混合社区，并修建游客酒店、当地居民住房、海鲜市场、餐馆、共享工作空间和老年社区中心等设施。该地段复杂的人口结构与错综的文化背景使设计问题变得既有趣又富有挑战性：设计需要协调盈利性发展商机与地域特征保护之间的冲突。场地的开发计划最初由香港建筑设计团队主导，但其毫无特色的常规商业化设计方案并未回应当地的文化背景。2019年，开发商委托来自曼谷的CHAT建筑设计事务所对该项目进行重新设计。基于社区参与对保持当地特色原真性的重要性，开发商和CHAT建筑设计事务所意在探索研究本地文化的方法并研发创新性数字化解决方案，以提升当地的可持续性。

在这种情况下，一个能够将公众意见引入决策过程的工具将通过利用公众的集体智慧为专业人员的分析提供意见参考，这将使项目设计大受裨益。此外，在由外部资本推动的如此大规模的开发过程中，公众参与将有助于规避利益分配不均问题。

该项目分阶段进行：第一阶段和第二阶段分别为前期设计和规划阶段，其中包括背景研究和红树林的生态修复；第三阶段引入海鲜市场和购物街的设计；第四阶段引入当地餐馆；第五阶段引入酒店和其他社区功能，并对开发项目进行收尾。本文将展示如何在整个项目中将CoDAS用作参与工具，以及在项目完成后如何将之用作社区数字平台来维护社区中的社会和经济关系——这一工具有助于界定公民和其他利益相关者在复杂社会环境中的角色、职能定位、价值观和行为规范。

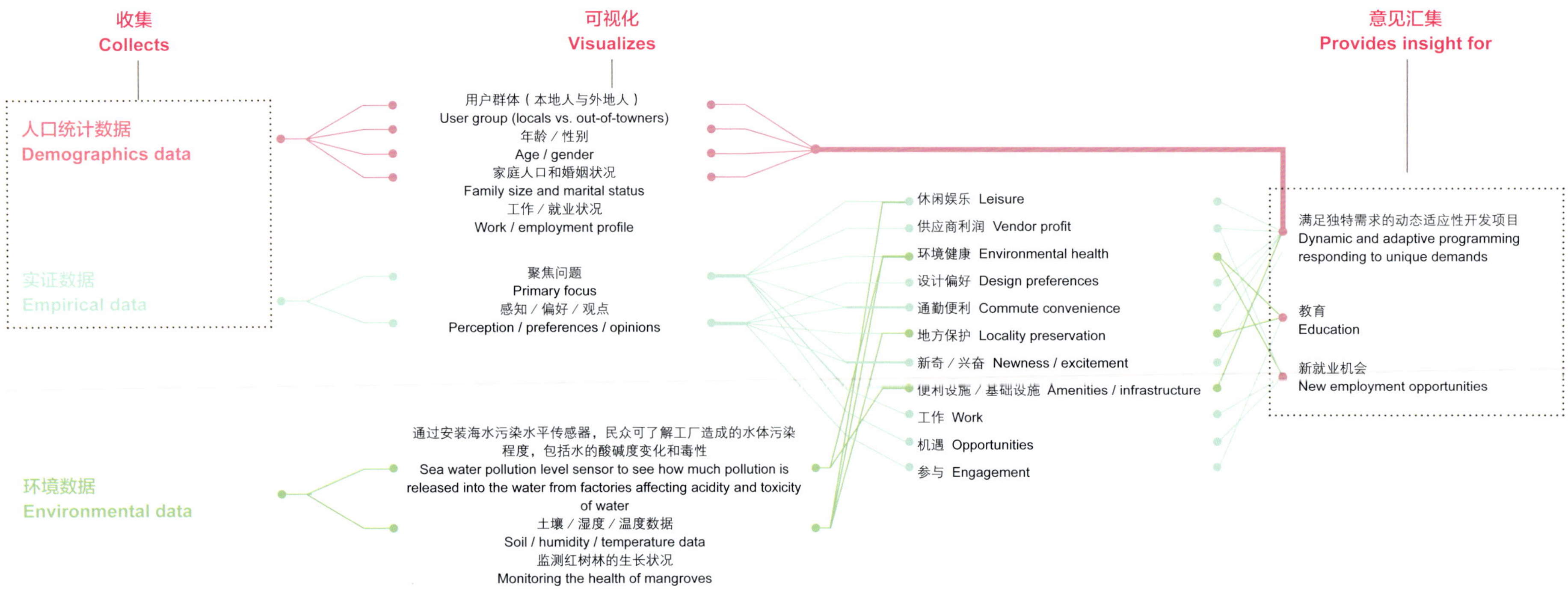

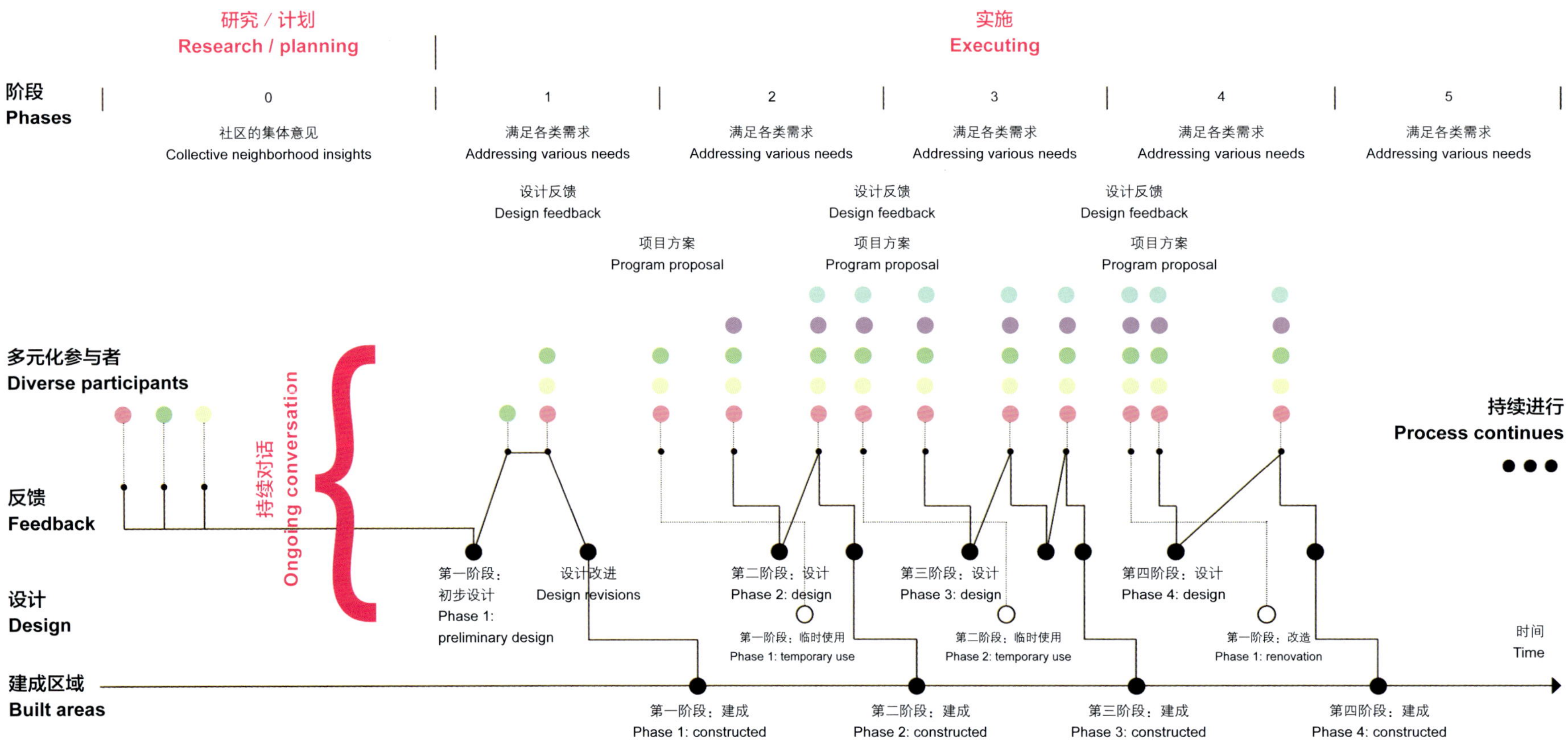

© CIVIS Design and Advisory
2

① 《参与式唐人街》由艾默生学院参与实验室、大都会区规划委员会、亚洲社区发展公司和莫西兰软件公司于2010年联合开发。

② 《我的社区》由Mojang电子游戏公司、微软和联合国人居署于2012年联合开发。

2 实例研究

研究团队对过去10年间全球范围内出现的数个关注公众参与的数字平台和应用程序进行了调研。本文将重点介绍一些对推动公众参与做出突出贡献的成功案例。

早期的公众参与数字工具着重理论方法上的创新。2010年推出的《参与式唐人街》实验性多人电子游戏①旨在使波士顿唐人街的居民通过社区会议的方式参与当地的总体规划工作。在游戏的虚拟世界中，48位参与者通过扮演各式各样的职能角色，从不同角度思考唐人街的未来发展规划。该项目使社区有机会评估唐人街的当前发展情况并确定其未来发展的优先事项。

另一个游戏化的公众参与工具范例是于2012年推出的《我的社区》②，通过将该模块植入广受欢迎的视频游戏《我的世界》，可提高社区民众对公共空间规划的参与度。社区居民通过在游戏中建模来表达他们的想法，并将之可视化。这种3D游戏环境可以让人们在快速推演和分享创意的过程中以一种经济、便捷的方法将自己的各种想法可视化。

与强调创新过程的工具不同，创建于2011年的数字平台“街区未来”旨在让政府机构、开发商和公民组织参与到项目的开发过程中来；街区未来为各类用户提供了全面的工具包，为活动和规划类项目的进一步完善提供了长期的技术支持。

在学术研究领域，由约翰内斯·穆勒率领的新加坡—苏黎世联邦理工学院中心未来城市实验室发起了一个公民参与领域的新研究分支——公民设计科学。公民设计科学将借助信息和通信技术收集而来的众包意见和观点与快速城市分析工具包相结合。该工具包是一个适用于项目初期的网页界面应用程序，用户可以在3D环境中改变一小部分可移动对象的几何布局[5]。然而，如何使程序中高度简化的3D设计工具更具指导性，以及如何使程序覆盖各个年龄层用户等问题仍有待进一步研究和改进。

3 设计方法论与策略

3.1 CoDAS：实时地理空间信息平台

CoDAS是一个社区层面的开放平台，它将现实生活中面对面的亲密人际关系与具有规模化和即时性特点的在线网络结合起来。作为一个实时地理空间信息平台，CoDAS将开发规划方案可能带来的变化在平台上予以即时展示，并吸引那些自愿参与社区建设和集体决策的昂西拉当地居民加入开发和设计的过程中，使他们可以保障自身在当地社区发展中的权利，而不再被动地接受外部资本的决策。在使用后阶段，该平台除了跟踪并记录现有共享资源的使用情况外，还可以通过培育各种生活类或商业类志愿团体来加强居民间的联系，这也将有助于居民获得餐饮业、海产品加工、市场推广、电商、环境保护等方面的额外收入。这些团体与社区个体居民间可以通过竞争或合作的方式共同享用本地资源。目前，这些活动的组织形式仍较为随意，主要依靠居民口口相传或在一些社交媒体平台上发布信息。CoDAS通过提供一个从整体层面审视社区的视角，来促进社区内不同事务的互联与协调，从这个意义上讲，该平台可以使包括团体和个人的不同利益相关者之间就各种问题进行持续对话，从而实现集体决策、协作和监督（图2）。

2. 作为一种数字工具，CoDAS为开发商、设计师和民众个人提供了一个建言献策的对话平台；在从预设计到规划再到使用后的不同阶段，CoDAS可以维持各个利益相关方之间的持续对话。这一平台可以将收集到的民意进行数字可视化，从而实现对昂西拉社区的“情绪普查”。

2. CoDAS, as a tool, is an interface between developers, designers, and individuals, inviting contributions from large amounts of audience; as a process, CoDAS supports a continuous conversation between different stakeholders, from pre-design / planning to post-occupancy. The platform collects digital overlay of personal narratives and perceptions, creating an emotional census of Ang Sila neighborhoods.

作为一个实验性项目，CoDAS可向当地政府、社区组织或物业管理公司提供“平台型服务”（PaaS）。CoDAS当前阶段的主要任务包括：1）鼓励公众参与开发和设计过程；2）在社区层面实现信息的开放获取；3）促进转型中的偏远社区的商业发展。

3.2 设计实验

通过实地调研，研究团队依照使用者特点归纳出了5类用户（图3）：

1）昂西拉当地商人（如渔民和售卖当地特色手工艺品的摊贩），他们主要关心商机拓展与当地环境保护；

2）本地回头客：居住在周边封闭式社区中，却只有很少休闲选择的中产阶级；

3）关注生态保护和公众教育的环保主义者；

4）来自曼谷的外乡游客，他们通常希望在良好的自然环境中享受悠闲的周末时光；

5）热爱冒险或想要获得原汁原味旅行体验的外国游客，包括穷游的学生旅行者、寻求度假胜地的退休外国游客，以及打算长期旅居的远程办公族。

根据2019年3月进行的场地走访调研结果及CHAT建筑设计事务所对当地人口进行的统计研究，研究团队按年龄、婚姻状况、收入等级，以及兴趣和目标的不同，对潜在用户群体进行了预测。该实验性设计项目有助于评估如何通过协调不同使用群体的意见来推动当地的设计与开发过程，其目标是创建可满足并协调不同使用需求的功能空间，以便将当地的特色、生活习惯和文化与新兴旅游业相融合。

整套系统分为数字平台和实体空间两个部分，可在开发人员、设计师和当地居民之间建立一个交流界面，邀请民众参与设计和开发过程。这种类似“情绪普查”的方法可以叠加每一个个体对于社区的理解和感知，汇集并展现不同的意见，从而服务于昂西拉地区的开发与设计决策。

最近的一项研究发现，泰国的社交媒体渗透率非常高——Youtube、Facebook、LINE、Instagram和Twitter的使用率分别达到了97.1%、96.6%、95.8%、56.0%和27.6%[6]——泰国民众已在这些社交平台上形成了活跃的在线社群。昂西拉当地人非常关心也愿意投身于社区事务（如愿意接受面对面采访），因此像CoDAS这样的数字平台将有助于促进当前公众参与的积极态势，尤其是那些小型社区的事务讨论活动。

在项目的初始阶段，研究团队需要在场地的主要公共场所内安置

3. 研究团队依照人口统计特征将使用者分为了5类：昂西拉当地商人、本地回头客、环保主义者、外乡游客和外国游客。

3. Generalization of on-site demographics into 5 user groups: local Ang Sila merchants, local repeat clientele, environmentalists, out-of-town Thai travelers, and foreign tourists.

若干个信息亭，以向公众展示CoDAS项目计划，为游客或不习惯使用电子设备的人们介绍相关信息（图4）。而下载了CoDAS移动应用程序的社区居民则通过CoDAS的聊天机器人接收调查问卷或社区公告等通知，了解关于开发项目各个阶段的最新资讯。用户可以通过文本、媒体或投票的方式提交回复。这一开源的网络平台可以定位众包信息，并将关键信息以可视化的形式推送给建筑师和开发商，同时支持项目的动态跟踪。当用户首次连接CoDAS聊天机器人时，CoDAS将以匿名的方式采集用户基本信息，包括地点、访问频率、年龄段和家庭人数等。此类数据将用于生成某项议题的用户群体地理空间分布。网络信息中心会记录总参与人次，支持特定用户群体和年龄段用户的信息筛选，同时支持用户查看项目所处阶段与实时进展，浏览过往的调查问题及公告，并了解新闻动态、民众的热点议题、情绪分析和投票结果（图5）。

该项目的设计过程会不断地进行迭代，在这一过程中，从潜在用户群体收集来的公共反馈意见可以帮助建筑师在不同的开发阶段完善设计想法。在研究阶段，CoDAS设置了若干问题来收集现有“热点地区”的信息，以获知当地居民的偏好和习惯，这些众包信息可以帮助专家了解当地居民对现有公共场所的感知情况（图6）。例如，在第一阶段红树林修复期间，CoDAS不仅对现有的社区活动进行宣传，还招募社区成员加入到造林工作中。在第二阶段，在设立功能空间之前，社区可以根据市民的投票和反馈意见在闲置地块上组织临时性活动（图7）。第三阶段引入了第一批建筑项目，包括海鲜市场和特色购物街。CoDAS聊天机器人会询问社区居民是否有意愿进行商业经营，以及他们喜欢的商业类型（图8）。根据收到的积极反馈意见，建筑设计方案增加了更多类型的功能空间，如共享办公空间、教育中心和有机超市（图9）。社区居民的进一步反馈使设计师能够了解潜在用户的特定习惯和需求，从而对设计进行调整。在第四阶段，场地引入了新的餐饮业商户。基于CoDAS对社区居民饮食偏好的调查，场地选择性地引入了一些品牌商户，以保护本地商铺免受外来大型连锁店的冲击（图10）。设计的最后阶段通过采纳多元化的公众意见，在场地内增设了新的功能空间，包括观景台、雕塑公园、码头餐厅和托儿所（图11）。

尽管目前本实验采用的数据和信息都是假设的，但研究团队仍可以通过与在Instagram和Twitter等社交媒体平台上发布的内容（如有关本地居民偏好和习惯的内容）相互参照，来确保假设的合理性。

4 使用后案例研究

城市发展和设计不会随着项目的落成而告终。对于昂西拉等新兴城乡地区而言，公共资源（公共空间、设施和自然资源）的管理与使用将一直是一个关键问题。本项目思考的另一个问题是：能否将开发与设计阶段中公众参与的热情延续到使用后管理过程中？随着当地居民、开发商、市政机构、社会团体等利益相关方被串联在一起，CoDAS有助于在开发项目投入使用后继续维持这些或合作或竞争或错综的互动关系。

在使用后阶段，CoDAS将作为社区的信息基础设施，服务于社区未来的长期规划和管理。当地利益相关方可以利用这一数字平台，随着规划和设计工作的推进，建立起彼此间的相互关系。例如，致力于红树林保护的当地居民可以成立生态保护团体；海鲜市场的租户和业主可以成立海鲜产业委员会，以组织开展季节限定促销活动；酒店和

© CIVIS Design and Advisory

4. 初始阶段：在主要的公共场所放置信息亭，以便公众了解开发项目和CoDAS计划的相关内容。

4. Initial intervention: placing information kiosk stations in key public spaces to begin informing the public about the development project and the CoDAS initiative.

短期出租屋业主也可以建立行业协会，以协调旅游业相关问题。除了个体间的互动外，这些自组织群体之间也会出于利益而形成合作或竞争关系。

为了应对这种动态且复杂的环境，CoDAS需要设计完整的数字化工具包，并规范用户的交互流程。但这项工作难度巨大，因此研究团队利用假想用户群体来推演符合当地实际情况的场景，从而制定假设条件、预测问题，并探寻可能的解决方案。昂西拉独特的场地条件为本次实验项目提供了一个复杂但相对封闭的测试环境（图14~16）。

5 讨论与回顾

CoDAS是一个拥有宏大目标的实验性项目，试图将短期的参与式规划设计与长期的使用后社区管理这两个城市发展过程的重要环节结合起来。其基本逻辑相对简单，即从鼓励当地利益相关者的公众参与，到提供定制的应用工具包来实现长远的社区共治。在前期，该工具包通过为设计师提供有价值的公众意见来优化设计方案；通过全程参与设计过程，研究团队在这一框架下积累了大量设计经验，使他们能够提出更为精准的调查问题，以便收集对于具体设计决策具有实际指导意义的反馈意见。值得一提的是，CoDAS提出的解决方案摒弃了满足所有需求的幻想，而是提供了一种能够促进多方对话的透明合作机制，有助于发现那些未知的或被忽略的关键问题。该研究提出的方法和工具在城市数据收集、公众参与、微型场地研究，以及利用众包数据了解不同用户需求并优化设计方法等方面进行了创新。就诸多层面而言，该工具重新定义了专业人士与普通民众之间的“代理权”概念，以一种务实的态度，将设计视为一种动态的（而并非依靠单方面决策的）、有据可循的（而非全然主观的）实践过程。

同时，在使用后管理过程中，CoDAS作为一种信息基础设施，可以长期促进并维持物理空间与社会网络之间的信息交换。不同实体之间的正式合作伙伴机制和非正式联系网络将会对商业生态及社区未来发展产生重大影响。两者分别代表了两种社交结构，即“社会”（基于正式组织架构之间的合作关系）与“社群”（基于参与者之间的非正式联结）。在动态的经济发展过程中，这两种结构既互相平衡也互相促进，为地区发展创造适宜的制度性环境[7]。

CoDAS强化了当地利益相关者之间的社交网络，以应对在现代城市中实现公共资源公平管理的挑战。当社区的开发建设依赖严格的专业权威（无论是具有一定专业知识的开发商或建筑师、地方政府机构，还是社区委员会）时，信息不对称可能会导致代理权问题，即执行代理人在代表社区时会带有自己的主观偏见。此外，如果社区中的多元化利益相关者彼此信任度低且信息获取不平等，那么社区会经常在共享资源（包括公共空间、共享设施、共享第三方服务等）管理中遇到落实不力的问题。针对信息不对称和社会信任危机的问题，CoDAS鼓励个人积极了解社区计划，并就设计和规划进展等议题提供反馈意见。

CoDAS并不认为当地利益相关者经过长期的互动后会为了实现利

益最大化而达成合作。毫无疑问，不同的个人和群体都会面临利益冲突问题。然而，当人们在公共空间使用问题上存在个体利益冲突时，这种利益冲突也会体现在物理空间上。从长远来看，人们将不得不通过协商的方式，共同决定如何使用共享空间，而这需要制定对于各方而言都可接受的方案——从这个意义上讲，CoDAS需要在处理不同类型的社会关系时保持中立。

但是，这件看似简单的事情却需要大量的工作，其中，CoDAS的设计和试点项目的启动尤为困难。首先，尽管现场走访调研表明诸如Facebook之类的社交软件在昂西拉的老年人口中非常流行，但研究团队仍担心对他们来说，CoDAS的移动端和网页端界面可能会存在操作困难。因此，团队需要与当地社区合作，开展在线或现场操作教学。其次，尽管信息亭的设计目标是为社区居民提供一个离线界面，从而减少潜在的数字鸿沟，但信息亭位置的选择仍有可能造成某些特定人群的使用不便。在开发过程中，尤其是开发初期，仍需同时展开工作坊等其他线下的社区参与活动。第三，研究团队还担心，在当地居民组建志愿团体后，用户体验可能不符合他们过去习惯的互动方式，这将需要对CoDAS的功能进行现场测试和迭代更新。最后，作为PaaS项目，CoDAS必须获得地方当局的批准并与现有的公共及私人组织合作。除了拥有可靠的本地合作伙伴外，项目的启动还需要付出巨大的努力，并能够预见所在地区的政治和社会阻碍。在当前阶段，CoDAS仍是基于诸多假设的实验性项目，研究团队将在条件允许时对其进行验证和调整。未来，研究团队将尝试与开发商和建筑师联合研发在线平台，以在适当时机将CoDAS引入昂西拉地区的各个社区并收集两大类信息：1）现场使用数据，如众包热点、实时活动、个人评论，以及志愿团体的注册信息；2）对当前产品原型的评价反馈。考虑到未来将CoDAS应用于其他环境下的可能性，这两类数据对于CoDAS短期的迭代更新和长期的改进完善而言都非常关键。

互联网并非单纯通过数据收集和统计均值来汇集人类的智慧，而是通过"一种聚合版本控制的新的开源模式来邀请所有代理进行相互编辑，从而获得社区的集体知识——在某种形式的指导下，可以自由无限制地进行实践"[8]。这种集体知识的聚合概念概括了马里奥·卡波尔所引用的亚当·斯密的"看不见的手"或"众人之手"，从而将个人利己主义转化为集体智慧[8]。本项目并非旨在研究互联网城市，而是研究一种可以由个体使用者塑造的城市。**LAF**

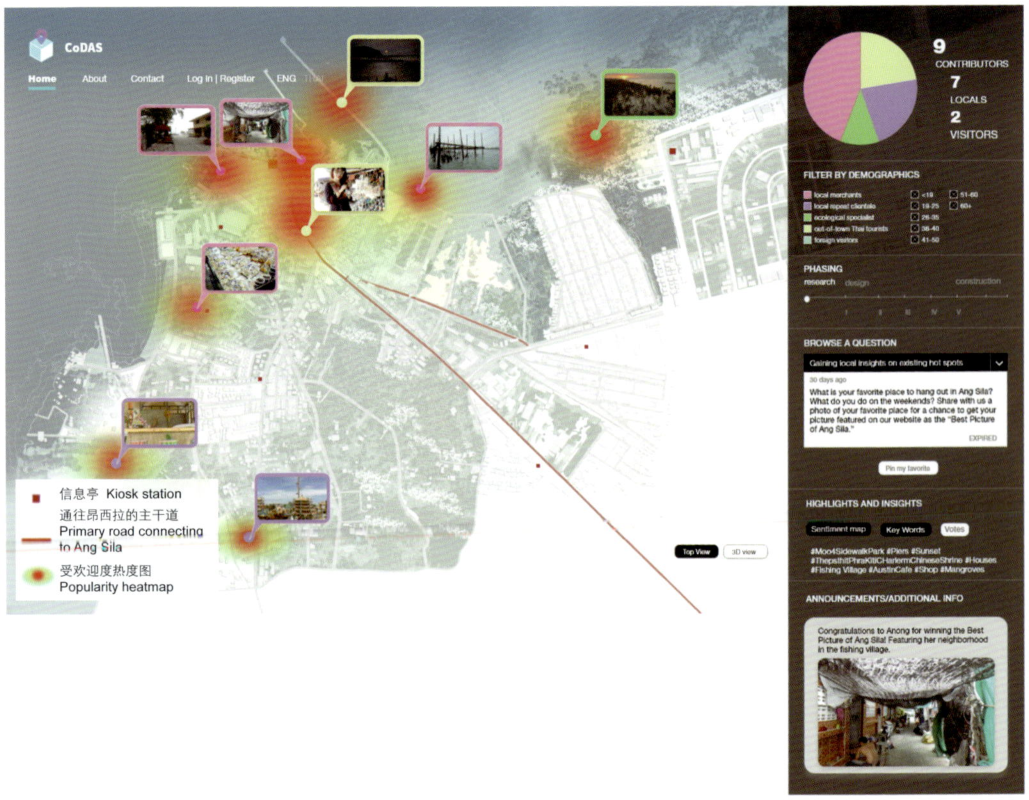

© Helena Rong, CIVIS Design and Advisory 5

© Helena Rong, CIVIS Design and Advisory 6

项目信息

项目地址：泰国昂西拉地区
项目面积：14hm^2
首席设计师：戎航
设计团队：杨竣程、钱经纬
研究时间：2019~2020年

5. 调研阶段：通过收集现有“热点”相关信息来获知当地居民的偏好和习惯，使得专家权威可以透过这些众包数据来了解当地人对现有公共场所的感知情况。
6. 第一开发阶段：在红树林修复期间，CoDAS不仅可对现有的社区活动进行宣传，还可招募社区成员加入到造林工作中。
7. 第二开发阶段：在设立功能空间之前，社区可以根据市民的投票和反馈意见在闲置地块上组织临时性活动。

5. Research Phase: a questionnaire is deployed to gather information about the existing "hot spots" to gain local insights on preferences and habits, demonstrating how crowd-sourced data can help authorities understand local perception of existing public spaces.
6. Development Phases I: CoDAS helps with broadcasting a community activity opportunity and recruits members of the community to participate into the process of mangrove reforestation.
7. Development Phase II: prior to the introduction of architectural programs, vacant plots host temporary events based on votes and suggestions of the citizens.

© Helena Rong, CIVIS Design and Advisory

7

1 Introduction

The last decade witnessed a tremendous trend in harnessing innovative digital technologies to respond to myriad urban challenges, with an effort to optimize the city under the smart sustainable city concept. Defined by the International Telecommunication Union, a smart sustainable city is an "innovative city that uses information and communication technologies and other means to improve quality of life, efficiency of urban operation and services, and competitiveness, while ensuring that it meets the needs of present and future generations with respect to economic, social, and environmental as well as cultural aspects"[1]. However, what is missing from these discussions is citizens' perception and involvement in the decision-making processes, which leads to an increasing information asymmetry between individuals and authorities. At locations with abundant natural resources and rapid economic development driven by external investment, the development process is often highly costly, and people are unevenly benefited. Further, the lack of civic engagement prevents the communities from fostering trust between individuals and group stakeholders, hindering optimal management framework and methodology for shared resources in the long run. Countering to this, Smart Cities 2.0, a very recent strategy presented by British architect Jason Pomeroy, suggests an alternative approach which emphasizes human-centered technologies and possibilities of engaging citizens in the design and planning process[2]. Such an approach outlines a people-oriented vision driven by a cross-sectoral coalition which recognizes the need for understanding public opinions in an enabling environment.

Civic engagement refers to scholars in Education Richard Adler and Judy Goggin's definition of "the ways in which citizens participate in the life of a community in order to improve conditions for others or to help shape the community's future"[3]. In the field of urban planning, Sherry Arnstein's "ladder of citizen participation" provides a heuristic device for structuring her argument as 8 rungs corresponding "citizens' power in determining the end product"[4]. This article, by focusing on citizen engagement and co-creation, proposes a tool and formulation which integrates the voices of evolving self-organizing entities to advance an equitable development process. First, this article introduces CoDAS (Co-Design Ang Sila) as a citizen engagement digital platform which mediates and facilitates continuous communication between citizens and authorities such as architects, developers, government, and management companies during different phases of a given project. Second, by including a large number of stakeholders to participate in the co-design process as co-creators, CoDAS aims to improve communication efficiency between different groups while achieving equitable outcomes in design and development, along with post-occupancy common resource management.

This research investigates the following questions:

1) How is digital participation changing the role citizens or end-users play in the decision-making processes of urban planning and design?

2) What digital tools can facilitate the interaction between different actors in pre-development design and post-occupancy management?

3) How to use public opinion data to negotiate various interests of different social groups by designing spatial adjacencies, shared spaces, and hybrid programming?

To validate the effectiveness of the proposed methodology, the hypothesis was tested in Ang Sila, Thailand. Ang Sila is a small fishing village located in the touristic province of Chonburi that is 91 km southeast of Bangkok (Fig. 1). The pilot plot is adjacent to one of the oldest fishing neighborhoods in Thailand to the west and rich mangrove forests to the east, currently welcoming novel IoT infrastructure initiatives to engage with its local context. As Chonburi develops in tourism, the challenge lies in preserving vernacular cultural and ecological features (mangrove forests) of the site under the threat of generic tourism development, accommodating new needs of serving increasing visitors and distributing equitably the wealth generated from new economy.

This site is a 35-acre vacant land to be developed by a Thailand-based developer into a vibrant and hybrid, multi-generational and multicultural community featuring programs such as hotels for tourists, housing for locals, a seafood market, restaurants, co-working spaces, and a senior center. The site's intricate demographic structure and complex cultural heritage renders the design problem both interesting and difficult: the tension between lucrative development opportunities and preservation of regional locality challenges the design to negotiate and cater to the needs of opposite interests. The site was initially designed by a Hong Kong architectural team with a conventional plan for commercial projects, which led to a generic proposal insensitive to local cultural context. In 2019, the developer appointed CHAT Architects. Understanding the importance of engaging the community in order to preserve authenticity of local characteristics, the developer and CHAT Architects seek ways to research local cultures and experiment with innovative digital

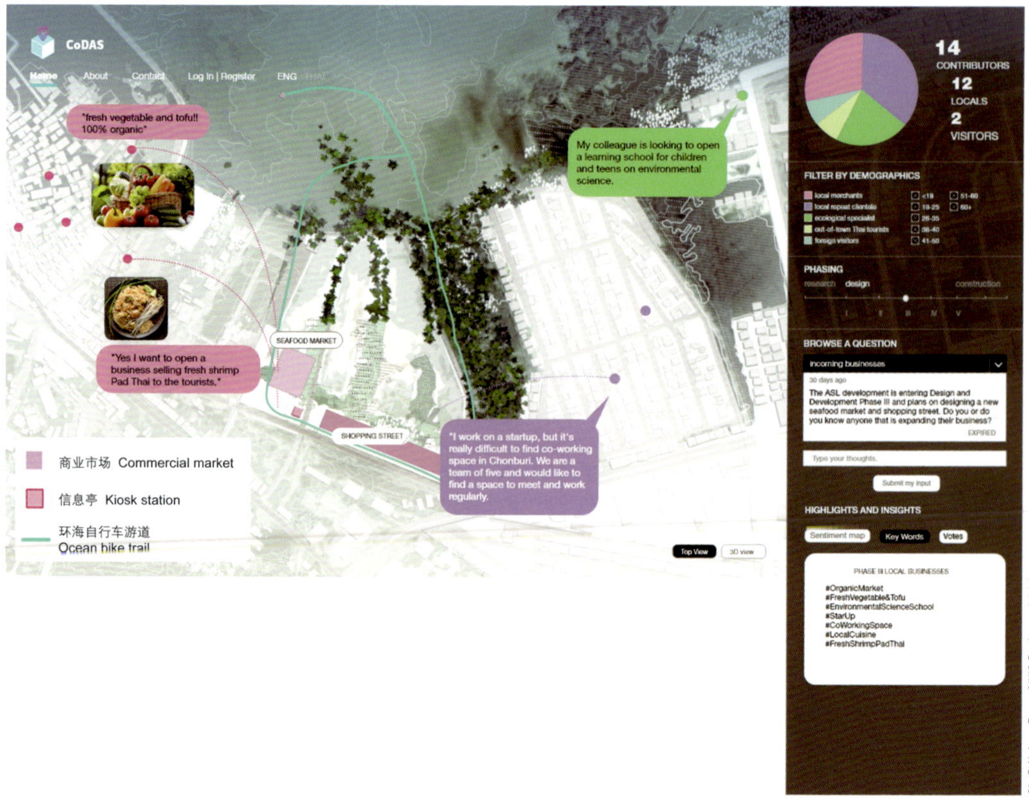

8 © Helena Rong, CIVIS Design and Advisory

9 © Helena Rong, CIVIS Design and Advisory

① Participatory Chinatown was launched in 2010 by Emerson College Engagement Lab in collaboration with the Metropolitan Area Planning Council, the Asia Community Development Corporation, and Muzzy Lane Software.

② Block by Block was launched in 2012 by Mojang, Microsoft, and UN-Habitat.

solutions for a greater sustainability.

In this context, a tool which helps channel public input into decision-making process could tremendously benefit the project by engaging the collective wisdom of the public to provide analytical insights for the professionals. In addition, public participation may help avoid unequal distribution of the benefits brought by the development and secure indigenous residents' rights in Ang Sila during such a massive process initiated by external capitals.

The project occurs in phased development: the first and second phases are pre-design and planning, which involve contextual research and ecological restoration of the mangrove forests; the third phase introduces design of a seafood market and shopping street; the fourth phase welcomes local restaurants; the fifth phase brings in hotels and additional community programs and concludes the development project. This article will demonstrate how CoDAS can be used as an engagement tool throughout the project and how it can remain useful as a community digital platform after project completion to maintain social and economic relations in the community, creating complex social structures that help define roles, positions, values, and norms for citizens and other stakeholders.

2 Case Studies

The research team surveyed a number of digital platforms and applications that focus on public engagement in the past decade and highlighted several projects that are making successful impact on public engagement across the globe.

Early attempts in public engagement through digital tools emphasized on methodological innovations. Participatory Chinatown, launched as an experiment in 2010, is a multiplayer video game① which engages residents of the Boston Chinatown in the master planning process through community meetings. In the virtual world, 48 participants assumed the role of fictional characters in Chinatown to consider future planning from different viewpoints. The project gives the community a chance to assess recent growth about Chinatown and determine priorities for its future.

Another example of gamified participatory tool is Block by Block②, launched in 2012, which attempts to enhance community engagement in public space planning through the popular video game Minecraft. Neighborhood residents were asked to express and visualize their ideas through modeling in the gaming environment. The 3D game environment provides a cost-effective way for people to visualize their ideas in a format designed for rapid iteration and idea sharing.

Different from tools which emphasize innovative processes, Neighborland, founded in 2011, is a digital platform that aims to engage government agencies, developers, and civic organizations on a project basis. With a comprehensive toolkit for typical engagement tasks in planning, Neighborland provides technical support for recurring events and planning projects in the long run.

In academic literature, a new branch of research conducted at Singapore-ETH Centre Future Cities Laboratory led by Johannes Müller expands from the field of citizen engagement to a novel approach termed "Citizen Design Science." The Citizen Design Science approach combines crowd-sourced opinions and thoughts by citizens through information and communication technology with active design tools the team has developed called the Quick Urban Analysis Kit (qua-kit). This is an early-stage web-based application where users can directly manipulate 3D moveable objects and modify geometric layouts, although only minimally[5]. However, unresolved challenges, such as the instructiveness of the highly reductive 3D designs and technological accessibility for different age groups, require further research and improvements.

3 Design Methodology and Strategies

3.1 CoDAS: A Real-Time Geospatial Information Platform

CoDAS is a community-level open platform that combines the scale and instantaneous connectivity of an online network with the kinship created through face-to-face interactions. As a real-time geospatial information platform, CoDAS visualizes proposed changes during development, and engages community residents who are willing to voluntarily contribute to community building and collective decision-making. The tool incentivizes Ang Sila residents to participate into the development and design processes to ensure their own rights to Ang Sila, instead of accepting passively the outcomes determined by external capitals. In the post-occupancy stage, besides keeping track of current usage of existing shared resources, the platform may connect residents by fostering voluntary groups on various life- or business-related subjects also which could help residents generate supplemental income: food tasting, seafood production, marketing, online business, and environmental preservation. These groups along with individuals may compete over or collaborate in the use of local resources. These activities are currently organized haphazardly among residents via either word of mouth or across several social media platforms. CoDAS will allow for interconnections and unification of different matters within the community by providing a holistic view of the community. In that sense, the platform facilitates a

8. 第三开发阶段：通过CoDAS聊天机器人询问社区居民商业经营及业务类型的意愿，从而了解餐馆和海鲜市场的潜在租户的需求。

9. 第三开发阶段：来自社区的反馈使设计师能够了解潜在用户的习惯和需求，并相应地调整设计，在市场中加入居住单元，并建立与有机蔬果园直接连接的超市。

8. Development Phase III: CoDAS ChatBot asks the community whether they seek to open a business and the type of business they prefer, researching the needs of potential tenants of restaurants and seafood market.

9. Development Phase III: feedback from the community allows the designer to understand latent habits and needs, and adjust the design accordingly to include living units in the market and relocate the supermarket to connect with the organic gardens.

continuous conversation between different stakeholder groups and individuals on various issues, enabling collective decision-making, collaboration, and supervision (Fig. 2).

As a pilot project, CoDAS is a subscription-based Platform as a Service (PaaS) employed by local government, community organizations, or property management companies. The key missions of CoDAS at the current stage are 1) to encourage public participation during development and design; 2) to realize the open access to information at the community-level; and 3) to facilitate business creations for remote yet transforming communities.

3.2 Design Experiment

From the field survey, the research team learned that demographics on the site can be generalized into five types of users (Fig. 3):

1) Local Ang Sila merchants, such as fishermen and vendors who sell local crafts primarily concerned with business opportunities and locality preservation;

2) Local repeat clientele: middle-class living in gated communities in surrounding neighborhoods with few options for leisure;

3) Environmentalists who concern with ecological preservation and public education;

4) Out-of-town Thai traveling from Bangkok who seek a relaxing weekend stay;

5) Foreign tourists who prioritize adventure and an authentic travel experience, ranging from budget college student travelers to retired foreign tourists seeking a resort vacation, to digital nomads intending to stay for longer periods of time.

Based on these insights from the on-site surveys and interviews conducted in March, 2019, as well as thorough demographic research conducted by CHAT Architects, the research team speculates potential user groups by age, marital status, income bracket with a diverse mix of interests and goals. The hypothetical design project can evaluate how design and development benefit from negotiating the voices of different perspectives. The project's goal is to create programs and spaces that accommodate and negotiate different needs and integrate local narratives, habits, and cultures into the newly developed tourism.

Consisting of both digital and physical components, the tool creates an interface between developers, designers, and residents, and invites contributions from a broad audience on the site to participate in the design and development process. It is a means to create an emotional census of Ang Sila neighborhoods and a digital overlay of people's individual narratives and perceptions,

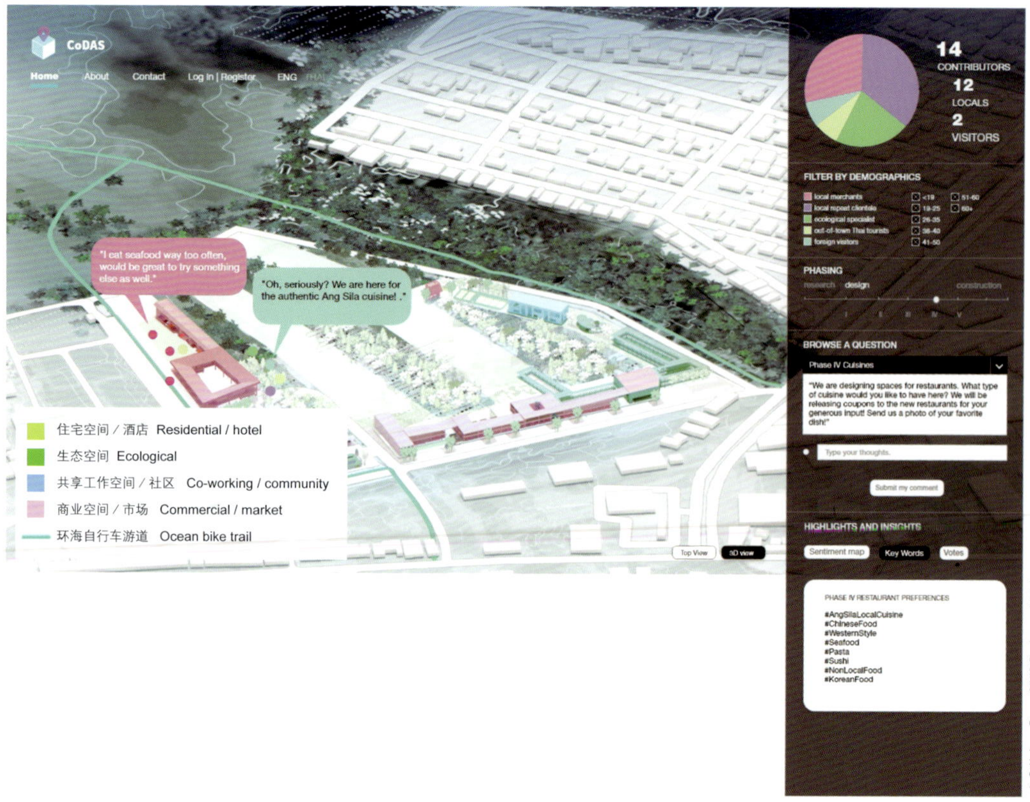

© Helena Rong, CIVIS Design and Advisory

10

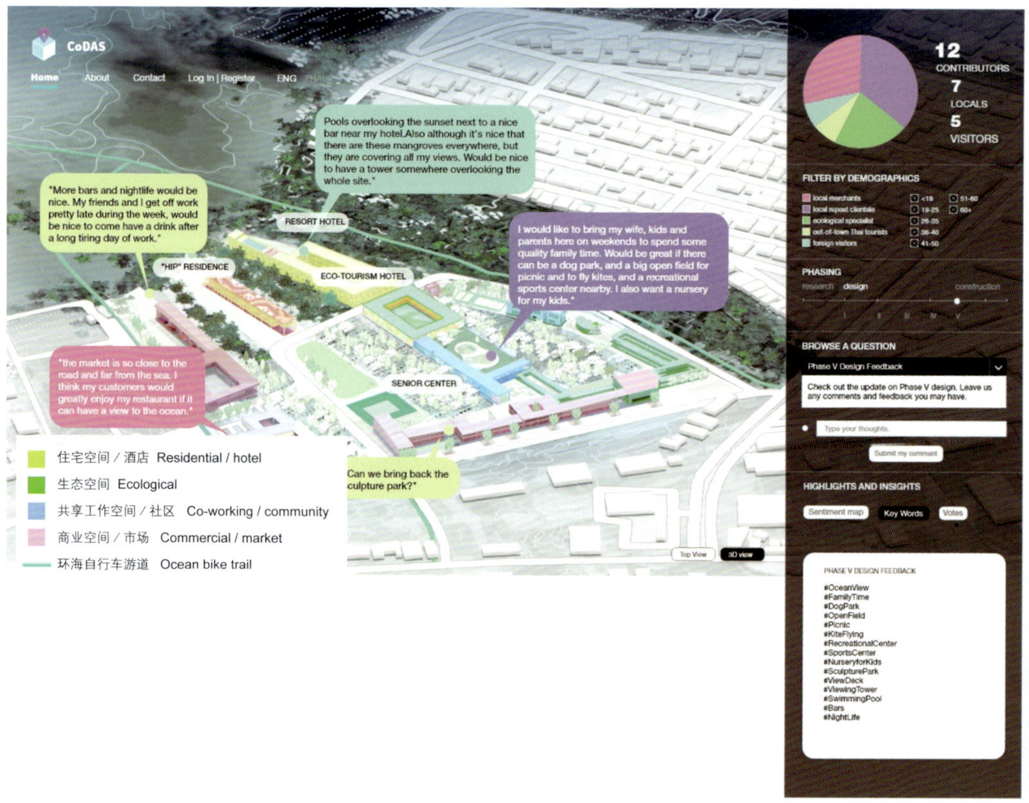

© Helena Rong, CIVIS Design and Advisory

11

10. 第四开发阶段：项目基于CoDAS对社区居民饮食偏好的调查，引入了一批品牌租户入驻场地。
11. 第五开发阶段：通过采纳社区居民对于设计的反馈意见，在场地内增设了新的功能空间，包括观景台、雕塑公园、码头餐厅和托儿所。

10. Development Phase IV: CoDAS solicits cuisine preferences from the local community to provide an alternative way of recruiting anchor tenants.
11. Development Phase V: community input further diversifies the mixed use and programming to include a viewing deck, a sculpture park, a pier restaurant, and a nursery.

providing granular neighborhood insights which assist with design decision-making.

A recent study finds that social media penetration in Thailand is extremely high, where Internet users actively form online communities on platforms such as Youtube (97.1%), Facebook (96.6%), LINE (95.8%), Instagram (56.0%), and Twitter (27.6%)[6]. Ang Sila locals' willingness to participate in traditional community engagement processes (e.g. in-person interview) is high and a digital platform like CoDAS will help facilitate existing activities such as discussing local matters within smaller communities.

Initially, several information kiosk stations are introduced to key public spaces on site to begin informing the public about the project and the CoDAS initiative, providing information for visitors or people who are not digitally connected (Fig. 4). Community members connect with the CoDAS mobile app, and receive a notification from the CoDAS ChatBot whenever a survey question is deployed or an announcement is made, to stay virtually connected with the project at each stage. Users respond to these questions in the form of text, media, or votes. The open-source web platform geospatially locates the crowd-sourced information and visualizes key information for the architects and developer, and tracks changes of the project overtime. When the users initially connect with the CoDAS ChatBot, the platform collects users' basic information through an anonymized survey, including locality, frequency of visit, age bracket, and family size. Such data are mapped onto the web interface, displaying geospatial distribution of interest of different user groups. The web dashboard keeps a tally of total number of participants, allows filtering of information based on different group and age bracket, displays the phasing of the project, allows for the browsing of other survey questions, and shows highlights, key concerns, sentiment analyses, and voting results (Fig. 5).

The design process is an iterative process in which public feedback collected from potential user groups helps the architects refine design proposals at each development phase. During the research phase, questions are deployed to gather information about existing "hot spots" to gain local insights on preferences and habits (Fig. 6), demonstrating how crowd-sourced information can help authorities understand local perception of existing public spaces. During the mangrove restoration in Phases I, CoDAS helps with broadcasting a community activity opportunity and recruits community members to participate in the reforestation process. During Phase II, prior to the introduction of architectural programs, vacant plots host temporary events based on votes and feedback of the citizens (Fig. 7). Phase III introduces the first architectural programs: a fish market and a featured shopping street. CoDAS ChatBot asks the community members whether they seek to open a business and the type of business they prefer (Fig. 8). As a result of the active input, the programming has covered more typologies of spaces, such as co-working spaces, an education center, and an organic supermarket (Fig. 9). Further feedback from the community allows the designers to understand latent habits and needs, adjusting the design accordingly to specific needs. During Phase IV, the site welcomes new restaurant tenants. CoDAS solicits local community's cuisine preferences to provide an alternative in recruiting anchor tenants and protecting local businesses from intrusions of larger chains (Fig. 10). During the final stage of design, community input further diversifies the mixed use and programming and includes a viewing deck, a sculpture park, a pier restaurant, and a nursery (Fig. 11).

Although data and information used in this experiment are currently based on speculation, the research team is able to cross-reference their assumptions (e.g. local insights on preferences and habits) with contents found on social media platforms such as Instagram and Twitter.

4 Post-Occupancy Case Study

Projects of urban development and design do not permanently end with the completion of construction. Post-occupancy management of shared resources—public spaces, facilities, and natural resources—remains critical for emerging urban-rural areas like Ang Sila. Is it possible to extend the enthusiasm of participation into the process of post-occupancy management? By bringing together local stakeholders into the participatory design process, be it residents, developers, municipal institutions, or social groups, CoDAS helps foster sophisticated interactions—collaboration, competition, and conflict, all of which will continue when the project is physically completed.

In the post-occupancy stage, the use of CoDAS is extended into long-term community planning and management. The platform will serve as an informational infrastructure and a digital tool for local stakeholders to build upon their relationships developed during the planning and design phases. For instance, local residents who are passionate about preserving mangroves may form a local alliance that takes charge of management; vendors and business owners at the seafood market may organize a seafood business committee that hosts seasonal events to improve sales; hotel and short-term rental housing owners might have their own association that addresses issues pertinent to tourism. Besides interactions among individuals, it is also possible to speculate these self-organized groups may collaborate or compete with each other for different interests.

Responding to such a dynamic, complex social context requires CoDAS to invent carefully designed digital toolkits and user-interaction processes. However, understanding the difficulty of designing tools and processes for speculated post-occupancy tasks, speculative potential user groups are introduced to construct context-specific scenarios to help develop the hypotheses, questions, and solutions. The variety of characters and unique site conditions of Ang Sila provide a complex but contained testing environment (Fig. 14 ~ 16).

5 Discussion and Review

CoDAS is an ambitious experimental project that attempts to join two distinctive components of urban development: participatory design (short-term) and post-occupancy community management (long-term). The underlying logic is simplistic—from encouraging participation of local stakeholders to providing tailored toolkits and procedures that foster long-term collaboration and supervision. On the one hand, the tool benefits the design process by providing designers with valuable public insights to improve proposed solutions. Positioned as a designer and running through the design process using this framework, the research team is able to ask better design questions for each decision-making. The system by no means guarantees a utopic outcome which satisfies all observed needs, but rather provides a device to facilitate conversations in a transparent and collaborative way, leading to better design questions which have been previously unknown or overlooked. The proposed methodology and tool innovates in data collection, community engagement, micro-scale site research, and utilizing crowd-sourced data to optimize a design by negotiating user needs. In many ways, this approach equalizes and redistributes the notion of agency of the agents and patients from prior professional beliefs and broadens a pragmatic understanding of design as a dynamic and conscious practice.

On the other hand, within post-occupancy management procedures, CoDAS functions as a digital infrastructure that facilitates the information exchange between the existing physical and social networks to build and sustain long-term relationships. The quality of formal partnerships and informal networks among these entities may place significant impacts upon the existing business ecology as well as its future development of communities. The two represent two forms of social integration—society (based on the "bridging" between formal partnerships) and community (based on the informal "bonding" among participants). The two balance, check, and improve each other in the dynamic process of economic development, constructing the institutional environment for development[7].

Empowering the social networks among local stakeholders, CoDAS responds to the challenges in achieving equitable management of public resources in the contemporary urban realm. When a community relies on a heavy-handed professional authority, be it trained developers or architects, a local government institution or a community committee, informational asymmetry may easily lead to the agency problem where the executive agents prioritize their own biased opinions while representing the community. Meanwhile, communities that engage with diverse stakeholders yet with weak trust and unequal access to information are frequently faced with collective action problems in the management of shared resources—including public space, shared facilities, and third-party shared services. Seeking remedies for informational asymmetry and weak social trust, CoDAS incentivizes individuals to actively learn about community initiatives and provide feedback on matters such as design and planning updates.

CoDAS does not take for granted that local stakeholders, after a long-period of interaction, would collaborate to maximize their interests. There is no doubt that individuals and groups with different interests are faced with conflicts of interests. However, when individuals have mutually exclusive plans for the use of these types of spaces, spaces become a physical representation of conflict of interest. In the long run, people will have to confront and negotiate with each other to collectively decide the use of the shared spaces. There needs to be an acceptable plan for all the stakeholders involved. In that sense, CoDAS remains neutral when it needs to deal with different types of social connections.

However, building upon the simplistic logic requires a significant amount of work, particularly the difficulties of

© CIVIS Design and Advisory

12

12. 使用后阶段：公共活动的计划与组织。CoDAS包含“活动管理”和“即时通讯”功能模块。通过活动管理功能模块，使用者能够自主发起不同类型的公共或个人活动。此外，CoDAS的“智能助手”功能模块可以帮助用户迅速完成活动注册及相关手续的办理，尤其是那些在特定公共空间举行的活动。

12. Post-occupancy: public event planning and organizing. CoDAS integrates "event manager" and "message" to work hand in hand. Through the event manager, the users will be able to initiate events in different categories. In addition, intelligent bot modules are also designed to expedite the event registration process, especially with those that require designated public spaces.

13. 使用后阶段：公众投票。推动以数据认知为基础的、经由指导的公民参与是CoDAS的核心目标。CoDAS平台上的各个部分皆引入了“投票”功能模块，每个用户都可以便捷、平等地发起公众投票——小到跑步路线，大到公共基础设施的建设。此外，每个用户都能够浏览当前或过去的公开投票结果。

14. 使用后阶段：物联网（IoT）。CoDAS为城市传感器提供了网络基础设施，可供市民查看实时数据及变化趋势。用户可以通过CoDAS的IoT平台订阅特定活动的传感器，并进行个性化的设备配置。采集到的数据将经过充分处理并用于优化迭代。

13. Post-occupancy: public voting. Informed, data-empowered civic participation is the core value of CoDAS. Voting module is integrated into every part of CoDAS platform structure. Everyone will be able to initiate a public voting ranging from running routes and public infrastructure development in an easy and equal way. Also, everyone will be able to browse active / archived public voting sessions.

14. Post-Occupancy: Internet of Things (IoT). CoDAS provides network infrastructures for urban sensors that provide community members with real time data and record based trend analysis. CoDAS's IoT platform enables the users to subscribe to specific active public sensors and they will be able to set up their own devices as well. The data will be processed adequately for optimization iterations.

© CIVIS Design and Advisory

13

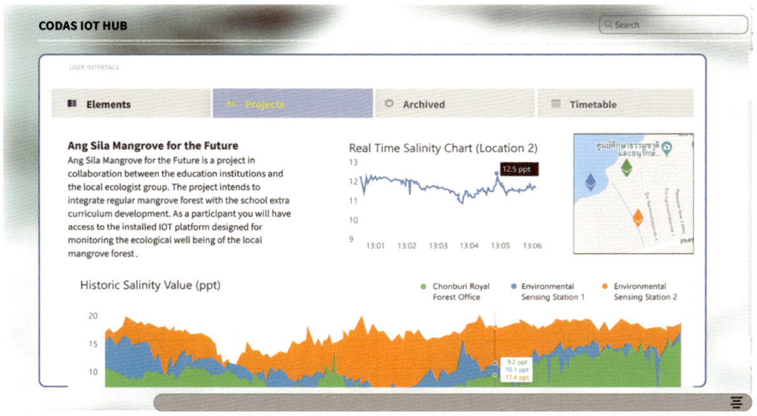

© CIVIS Design and Advisory

14

designing CoDAS and launching a pilot. First, although on-site interviews suggest that digital software, such as Facebook, is popular among aged populations in Ang Sila, the research team worry that the interface of CoDAS (both mobile and web page) might not be technologically friendly for every individual. Such a challenge requires the team to collaborate with local communities to launch online or on-site learning sessions. Second, although kiosk stations are designed to provide an offline interface with the community which helps reduce potential digital divide, the location selection may still have bias towards certain demographics. Additional in-person community engagement activities such as workshops will be carried out during the development process, especially at the very beginning. Third, the team are also concerned that, when local residents are forming voluntary groups, the user experience might not correspond intuitively to the way people interact in the past. This would require on-site testing and upgrades of CoDAS' functions. Last, as a PaaS project, it is imperative for CoDAS to acquire approvals from local authorities and collaborate with existing public and private organizations. Besides having reliable local partners, launching the project still requires a tremendous amount of effort and should anticipate political and social challenges in the region. For the current stage, CoDAS remains as an experimental project based on a number of assumptions made during the design process, which will be verified and adjusted when it comes with the opportunity for on-site testing. For the next step, the team intends to work with the developer and architects to launch the online platform, looking for a chance to introduce the project to the local communities of Ang Sila. In that way, two groups of information will be collected: 1) on-site usage data, such as crowd-sourced interest spots, real-time activities, individual reviews, and registration of voluntary groups; and 2) reviews of the current prototype. Both sets of data will provide critical inputs for short-term upgrades and long-term modifications, especially considering the possibility to implement CoDAS in different contexts.

The Internet empowers wisdom of crowds not through mere data collection and statistical mean-finding, but through "a new, open-ended mode of 'aggregatory' versioning, where the collective knowledge of a community is garnered by inviting all agents to edit one another—in theory, ad libitum atque ad infinitum [and] in practice, under the stewardship of some form of curation"[8]. This aggregation of collective knowledge summates to what Mario Carpo refers to as Adam Smith's "invisible hand" or "style of many hands," which transfers individual egoism into a collective wisdom[8]. This project studies not what an Internet city looks like, but a user-generated city. **LAF**

PROJECT INFORMATION

LOCATION: Ang Sila, Thailand
AREA (SIZE): 35 acres
CHIEF DESIGNER: Helena H. Rong
PROJECT TEAM: Yang Juncheng, William Jingwei Qian
RESEARCH PERIOD: 2019 ~ 2020

REFERENCES

[1] Kondepudi, S. N., Ramanarayanan, V., Jain, A., Singh, G. N., Agarwal, N., Kumar, R., ... Menon, M. (2014). Smart sustainable cities: An analysis of definitions. Geneva: The ITU-T Focus Group on Smart Sustainable Cities.

[2] Pomeroy, J. (2017). Smart Cities 2.0. Retrieved from https://www.jasonpomeroy.sg/copy-of-smart-cities-2-0

[3] Adler, R. P., & Goggin, J. (2005). What do We Mean by "Civic Engagement"?. Journal of Transformative Education, 3(3), 236-253. doi:10.1177/1541344605276792

[4] Arnstein, S. R. (1969). A Ladder of Citizen Participation. Journal of the American Institute of Planners, 35(4), 216-224. https://doi.org/10.1080/01944366908977225

[5] Office of Policy and Strategic Affairs, Electronic Transactions Development Agency, Ministry of Digital Economy and Society. (2018). Thailand Internet User Profile 2017. Bangkok: Electronic Transactions Development Agency.

[6] Mueller, J., Lu, H., Chirkin, A., Klein, B., & Schmitt, G. (2018). Citizen Design Science: A strategy for crowd-creative urban design. Cities, (72), 181-188. http://dx.doi.org/10.1016/j.cities.2017.08.018

[7] Storper, M. (2005). Society, Community, and Economic Development. Studies in Comparative International Development, 39(4), 30-57.

[8] Carpo, M. (2013). Digital indeterminism: The new Digital commons and the dissolution of architectural authorship. In P. Lorenzo-Eiroa & A. Sprecher (Eds.), Architecture in Formation: On the Nature of Information in Digital Architecture (pp. 47-51). London: Routledge.

本文引用格式 / PLEASE CITE THIS ARTICLE AS

Steiner, H., Winston, R., Oabel, A., & Grimm, A. (2020). Curbing Sediment: A Prototyping Process to Explore How to Capture Road Pollutants in Stormwater Events via Curb and Apron Redesign. Landscape Architecture Frontiers, 8(4), 140-149. https://doi.org/10.15302/J-LAF-1-040018

https://doi.org/10.15302/J-LAF-1-040018　收稿时间 RECEIVED DATE / 2020-07-08　中图分类号 / TU992, TV122+.1, P349　文献标识码 / B

路缘沉积：
利用原型思维过程探究如何通过路缘及路肩设计截留暴雨中的路面污染物

CURBING SEDIMENT: A PROTOTYPING PROCESS TO EXPLORE HOW TO CAPTURE ROAD POLLUTANTS IN STORMWATER EVENTS VIA CURB AND APRON REDESIGN

哈丽娜·斯坦纳
俄亥俄州立大学诺尔顿建筑学院景观系助理教授

瑞恩·温斯顿
俄亥俄州立大学食品、农业与生物工程系及土木工程、环境与测量工程系助理教授

艾薇·欧贝尔
俄亥俄州立大学诺尔顿建筑学院景观系本科生

亚力克·格林姆
俄亥俄州立大学环境与自然资源学院本科生

Halina STEINER*
Assistant Professor at Landscape Architecture Section, Knowlton School of Architecture, Ohio State University

Ryan WINSTON
Assistant Professor at Department of Food, Agricultural, and Biological Engineering, and Civil, Environmental, and Geodetic Engineering, Ohio State University

Avee OABEL
Undergraduate Student at Landscape Architecture Section, Knowlton School of Architecture, Ohio State University

Alec GRIMM
Undergraduate Student at School of Environment and Natural Resources, Ohio State University

*Corresponding Author
Address: 1279 City Park Ave., Columbus, OH 43206, USA
Email: steiner.298@osu.edu

摘要

路缘的设计简单明了：路缘本身为雨水提供了输送途径，促使水和污染物由街道汇入河道。路面上存积着各种沉积物，包括草坪肥料中的营养物质、细菌、病毒、杀虫剂、金属元素，以及各种油和油脂。当暴雨发生时，这些物质会在未经处理的情况下被冲入雨水管道，而后排入河道，进而影响水质乃至整个生态系统。那么，如何通过提升路缘设计标准来产生更大的系统性影响？

如果重新设计路缘，使其可以像磁石一样吸附雨水中的污染物，则将打破路缘固有的设计标准。2019年夏，一支跨学科研究团队在俄亥俄州立大学对标准混凝土路缘及路肩的替代方案进行了测试。该团队使用迭代设计过程在路缘和路肩表面增加了不同的图案和凹槽，并使用全尺寸模型测试了模拟暴雨事件，收集了相关数据以评估21种替代设计方案的表现。结果表明，新的路缘及路肩组合设计方案可以有效地在道路上拦截污染物，避免其进一步危害水体及水生生态系统。

关键词

基础设施；水文学；雨洪；路缘；沉积物；城市设计

ABSTRACT

The design of a curb is straight forward. The curb itself provides a conveyance of stormwater, facilitating the movement of water and pollutants from the street into waterways. Pollutants such as sediment, nutrients from lawn fertilizers, bacteria, viruses, pesticides, metals, and petroleum by-products accumulate on the road surface and are released during storm events, carried to storm drains, and deposited into waterways, often without treatment. Once pollutants enter the waterways they impact the ecosystem and affect water quality. How can discrete standards—like a curb—be leveraged to have larger systemic impacts?

The redesign of the curb to perform as a magnet for pollutants can challenge this design standard. During the summer of 2019, the interdisciplinary research team tested alternatives to the standard concrete curb and apron at Ohio State University. The team used an iterative design process to add patterning and crenellations to the face of the curb and apron. Using full scale models to test simulated storm events, the team collected data to evaluate the performance of 21 alternative designs. The results suggest the new combined curb and apron designs can abstract pollutants from roadways before they are detrimental to water bodies and aquatic ecosystems.

KEYWORDS

Infrastructure; Hydrology; Stormwater; Curb; Sediment; Urban Design

编辑 田晓劼　**翻译** 田晓劼　王胤瑜　李慧彦
EDITED BY TIAN Xiaojie　**TRANSLATED BY** TIAN Xiaojie　WANG Yinyu　LI Huiyan

1 引言

纵横交错的道路形成了不断扩张的沥青路网。根据美国联邦公路管理局公布的数据，全美国的沥青公路总长度约为670万公里[1]，它们主要由各城市和各州政府进行维护，对于促进人员流动和货物流通至关重要[1]，也是经济生活的必要基础。然而，路面上也存积着各种污染物，包括沉积物、草坪肥料中的营养物质、细菌、病毒、杀虫

© Halina Steiner, Ryan Winston
1

剂、金属元素、塑料微粒、融雪剂，以及各种油和油脂[2]。当暴雨发生时，这些物质会在未经处理的情况下，经混凝土路缘／排水沟／路肩被冲入雨水管道，而后排入河道[2]，进而影响水质乃至整个生态系统。但是，水体中的塑料微粒等污染物清除起来非常困难，那么，是否可以通过街道设计的创新来解决这一问题？用于排水的路缘和排水沟能否发挥其他作用？

当代的街道、人行道及路缘／排水沟／路肩系统的设计已沿用了数个世纪，就连路缘坡道这样简单的创新性设计也直到1945年才在密歇根州卡拉马祖市首次引入（以帮助坐轮椅的退伍军人便利出行）[3]，这一设计后来也为骑行、推婴儿车和携带行李箱的行人提供了便利。然而，这一设计并未迅速普及，直到1992年路缘坡道才被写入《美国残疾人法案》，成为人行道建造的法定规范之一[4]。近些年来，与绿色基础设施有关的道路设计创新不断涌现。早在20世纪90年代初，马里兰州乔治王子郡就采用了路缘切口引导水流进入生态草沟[5]。近年来这一技术被广泛应用于那些未能达到《清洁水法》规定的水质标准的美国城市，并引发了设计的迭代与提升——从试点或原型性探索项目逐步转向制定新的设计标准。生态草沟可以在降雨高峰期有效降低雨水流量，同时过滤污染物，但沉积物和垃圾可能使生态草沟堵塞而丧失过滤能力。由美国环境保护署签发的《接收公路与停车场径流的绿色基础设施运行与维护技术备忘录》指出，施工活动、受侵蚀的裸露土壤（植被稀少区域），以及冬季路面覆砂是城市径流中常见的沉积物来源，并进一步解释了沉积物如何在不透水地表堆积，并在流向生态草沟的过程中堵塞排水口及土壤空隙，阻碍植物根系呼吸[6]。那么，如何利用路缘这一常见的道路元素截留尚未进入河道的污染物，从而改善流域健康？

2 设计过程

2.1 原型开发前

原型开发过程需要考量诸多因素。设计团队首先与俄亥俄州立大学模拟创新与建模中心合作，探索了数字模拟模型的使用。数字模型可用于流体动力学计算，能够比物理模型更精确地模拟沉积物粒度和暴雨事件，它能对单个路缘横截面进行测试，而无法分析连续的路缘表面。由于尚不具备开发一套连续路缘表面数字模型所需的运算技

1. 通过小型样本测试探索不同的铣刀钻头尺寸、图案密度和铣削深度，是了解数控雕刻机优势和局限性的关键起始步骤。
2. 首轮测试中某一方形路缘设计的定格照片

1. Small scale sample tests explored different router bit sizes, pattern densities, and depths, which was a critical first step to understand the opportunities and constraints of the CNC Mill.
2. A still photograph of the first-round test for a square curb configuration

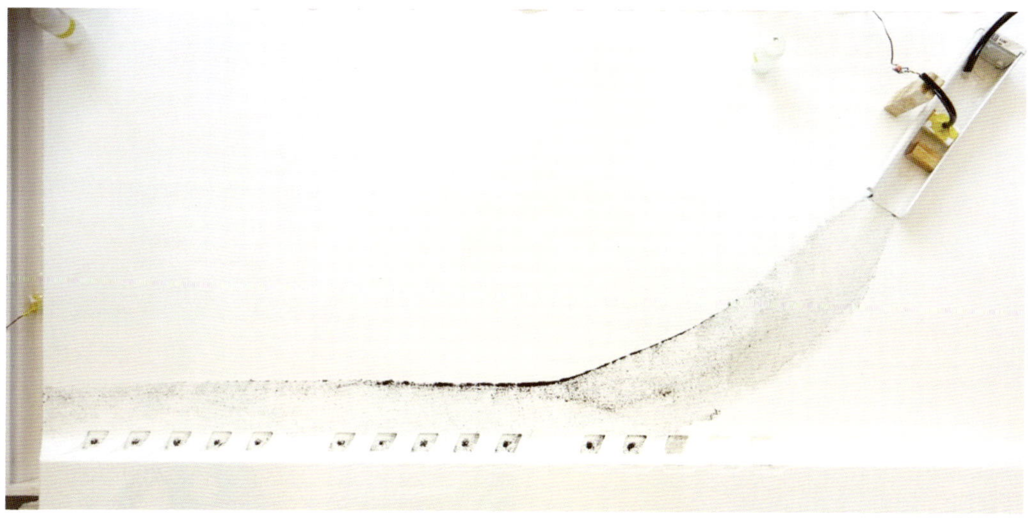

© Halina Steiner, Ryan Winston
2

术，团队未对数字模型展开进一步研究。

团队最终选择使用物理模型进行设计验证测试，并根据已有的原型设计技术及水文挟沙水流建模方法来确定物理模型的制作方法。其中，俄亥俄州立大学副教授杰克·博斯韦尔在关于浮动混凝土容器的研究中，在校内的MAT／FAB实验室运用数控雕刻技术制作聚苯乙烯泡沫模具，上油之后再用密度小于水的浮式混凝土浇铸成可支撑植物生长的容器，以对抗伊利湖中的藻华[7]。毕业于俄亥俄州立大学的吴浩文（音译）也使用数控铣床和聚苯乙烯泡沫制作了赛欧托河模型，该模型采用乳胶漆进行防水，并将水墨混合物泵入水体，以研究河水的流动轨迹。弗吉尼亚大学副教授布雷恩·戴维斯和宾夕法尼亚大学助理教授肖恩·伯克霍尔德在“未来健康港口”项目中亦融入了建模技术。他们通过将计算机建模与在明尼苏达大学圣安东尼瀑布实验室进行的物理建模进行结合，研发了一种可用于探究五大湖中潜在沉积物流动的方法。[8]上述项目从多个角度为本研究提供了启发与借鉴。

2.2 制作过程

本次研究选用的聚苯乙烯泡沫型材尺寸为1.2m × 2.4m × 0.2m，适宜制作全比例模型，可清晰显示并准确模拟出沉积物的截留过程；轻盈的材质也使得型材与成品模型的存储、制造和运输较为便捷。此外，经过热丝切割及数控雕刻的泡沫表面纹理也与混凝土十分相似。

为了制作路缘模型，首先要将1.2m × 2.4m × 0.2m的聚苯乙烯泡沫型材块制成标准道路剖面。团队最初采用数控铣床铣削轮廓，大约耗费4小时才将一块型材泡沫铣削成一个不带路缘和路肩图案的街道截面。为了最大程度地缩短制作时间，团队最终使用了一台热丝长度为2.4m的热丝切割机来制作基本公路断面，包括高15.24cm的路缘和横向坡度为1.5%的1m宽路面；为适应某些路缘的特殊形态，路缘高度可降至11.4~12.7cm。由于制作15.24cm高的路缘时，镂铣机刀头与路缘模型的顶部会产生碰撞，导致设备与模型损坏，故研究先用Rhino三维建模软件对路缘和路肩进行数字建模，然后在RhinoCAM插件中模拟铣削迭代过程以映射刀具轨迹，并预测可能出现的刀具碰撞或与原始Rhino模型的不符之处。数字模拟完成后将生成一个5轴G代码，将其输入昂思路5轴数控铣床中，即可在热丝切割机加工过的基础路缘剖面上雕刻路肩和路缘图案。由于图案和凹槽受限于数控刀具的尺寸，本次研究使用了一系列直径为6.3~25mm的平口和球面刀具。模型一端被铣削成45° 角的锥形，以将水流导入测试台末端的路缘排水沟，用于检测水质。最后，清除模型上的泡沫边角料，并涂上一层环保乳胶底漆，以起到防水作用。

在设计路肩图案时，团队从路面现有元素的形态中获得了灵感。盲道铺装单元由高5.08 ± 0.51mm、直径3.5cm的平顶圆形凸起组成，提示有视力障碍的行人前方有十字路口。团队采用了相似的尺寸设计了最初的点状路肩图案，并在后续迭代中设计了相似尺寸的凹槽，以提高路面的步行友好性，确保行人和骑行者的安全。

3 © Halina Steiner, Ryan Winston

4 © Halina Steiner, Ryan Winston

3. 如图所示的点状图案以盲道铺装为灵感。
4. 不同斜线图案沿线条走向的凹陷深度不同。
5. 波浪式斜线图案的转弯处截留了更多沉积物。
6. 平行于路缘的直线图案在靠近路面的一端截留了更多沉积物。

3. Tactile pavement was the inspiration for the dot- pattern.
4. The base of the diagonal lines varied in depth along the run of each line.
5. The diagonal squiggle pattern noticeably collected more sediment where the lines turned to change direction.
6. Line pattern parallel to the curb collected more sediment closer to the road surface.

2.3 原型设计过程

设计过程具有迭代性，每个阶段的设计都是基于上一轮测试的数据和观察结果。1:1全尺寸模型充分呈现了设计方案的真实效果。在进行测试之前，团队先将模型放置在人行道和街道旁以实地观察实际比例，从而了解其在景观中的尺度和视觉效果。

首轮测试仅对单独改变路缘面或路肩表面设计进行考察。在铣削全尺寸模型之前，团队测试了不同的铣削密度和深度以了解雕刻机的作业极限（图1）。团队对每种路缘或路肩改造方案分别进行测试，以便了解其单独运作的情况，以及二者最佳的组合方案。测试将一种人工合成的雨水混合物倾倒在模型路面上，使之流经路肩或路缘上的图案凹槽，整个过程持续8分钟。测试完成后，用肉眼观察沉积物淤积情况，并测量排出水体的浊度降低量（水的清澈度表征之一）及总悬浮固体物（TSS）减少量，以评估设计效果。

这一轮轮测试选定了圆形、方形和三角形三种路缘面凹槽设计。图2所示的方形路缘凹槽可截留的沉积物明显多于其他设计，因此研究团队在此基础上进行进一步探索。在路肩设计的测试中，团队采用重复利用模型的方式测试了不同密度的点状、直线及水波形图案，即首先铣削出图案密度最低的模型，测试后再次铣削，以增加图案的密度（图3~6），并根据模型水流入口和出口的浊度传感器读数来评估不同设计的截污效果。结果证明，直线形设计的截污效率最高；通过改变直线的角度及路径形态（波浪斜线、梳齿状、网格状）等来增加截留沉积物的表面积，进而降低雨水流速。

进一步测试的对象为单独截污效果最佳的路缘和路肩组合设计，主要考察路肩向路缘凹槽体转移沉积物的能力。在若干次迭代设计中，团队不断改变路缘凹槽的间距和尺寸、路肩凹槽的连接方式，以及路肩图案的排列方式和间距，并发现当路肩凹槽与路缘面凹槽相连时组合设计的效果更好，且以此三种组合为最佳：网格状路肩和7.62cm宽的方形路缘凹槽，各组凹槽之间间隔7.62cm（图7）；线形路肩和5.08cm宽的方形路缘凹槽，凹槽每隔45cm有15.24cm的间隙（图8）；以及梳齿状路肩和等距分布的5cm宽的方形路缘凹槽（图9）。

2.4 模拟暴雨测试

原型测试在俄亥俄州立大学的MAT / FAB实验室中进行。实体装备包括一端连接着乙烯塑料排水沟的1.2m × 2.4m的试验台、1.2m × 2.4m × 0.2m的聚苯乙烯泡沫型材块、两个约117L的手提式塑料桶、一台工业搅拌机、一台秤、从当地获取的土壤、沙子、数个采样瓶、两个配有模拟浊度传感器的Arduino微控制器、一台iPad、一台GoPro Hero 6数码摄像机、三台笔记本电脑，以及一部索尼a7RII数码相机。将经过铣削并做过防水处理的泡沫块放置在试验台上，在其上方悬挂数码摄像机和数码相机。摄像机用于记录整个测试过程，相机每隔10秒拍摄一张照片。测试开始时，在塑料桶内倒入70~80kg的水，并将当地土壤和沙子以6:4或7:3的比例进行混合，以模拟雨水。为确保在模拟暴雨事件全过程中“雨水”的沉积物浓度一致，需用搅拌机使土壤和沙子混合物均匀地分散在水中，并由放置在桶底的潜水泵泵至模型表面，模型入水口处的浊度传感器将记录其水质变化情况。在每轮测试中，模拟雨水将在模型表面自由流动8分钟，随后流入装有第二个传感器的排水沟，经出水口排至第二个桶内，最后将出水口桶中的水及进水口桶中剩余的水进行称重。在每轮测试中，每隔2分钟在进水口和出水口用采样瓶随机采样一次。

本次研究对21种路缘和路肩设计进行了测试，并对每个设计进行了三次重复测试（图10）。对每次测试后残留在模型表面的泥沙进行测定可得出每个设计的有效泥沙截留量（图11）。之后对三个截留量

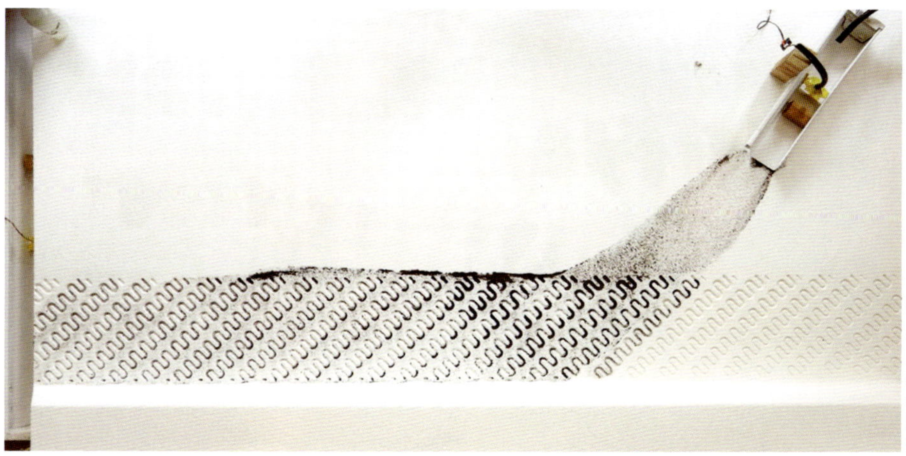

5 © Halina Steiner, Ryan Winston

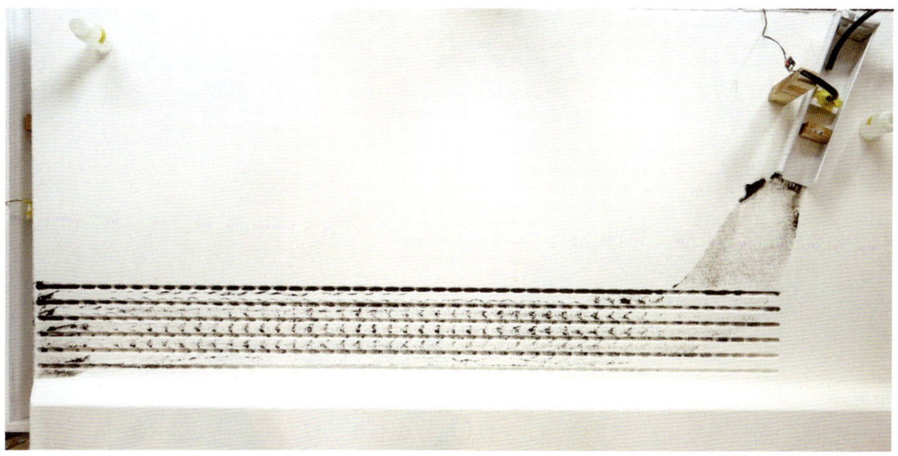

6 © Halina Steiner, Ryan Winston

© Halina Steiner, Ryan Winston
7

© Halina Steiner, Ryan Winston
8

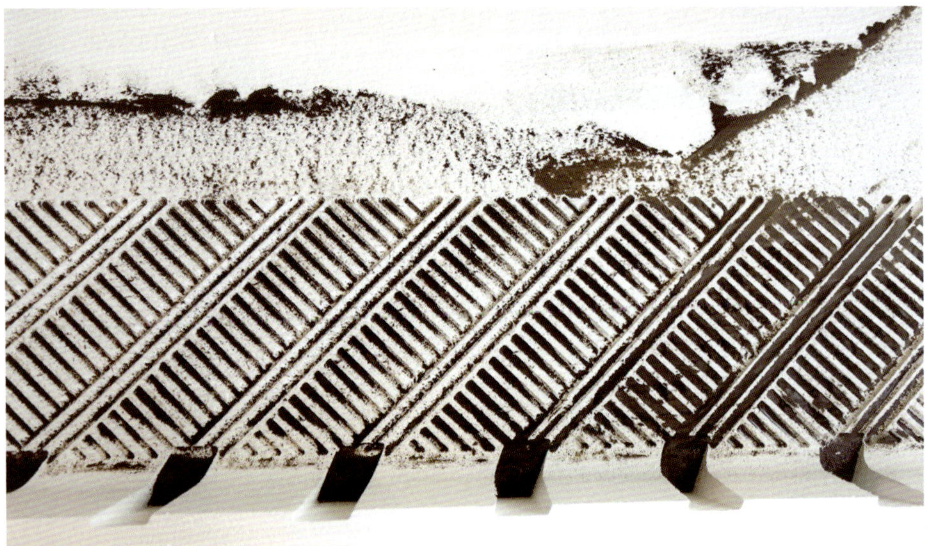

© Halina Steiner, Ryan Winston
9

7. 网格状路肩与方形路缘凹槽
8. 15.24cm间隔的斜线路肩与方形路缘凹槽
9. 梳齿状路肩与方形路缘凹槽

7. Cross hatch apron with square curb crenellations
8. Diagonal line apron at 6" gap with square curb crenellations
9. The prototype model of comb apron with square curb crenellations

最大的设计再进行1~7轮模拟暴雨测试，逐轮增加模拟雨水中的沉积物量，以确定设计的最大截留量及截留时间。

2.5 研究发现

团队在测试过程中采取了三种方式进行数据收集：一是通过相机和摄像机收集可视化数据；二是对采样瓶和出水口桶中水体的清澈度进行肉眼评估；三是在俄亥俄州立大学雨洪管理项目实验室中对随机样本进行TSS和粒度分布分析，并将结果与测试期间获得的传感器实时数据进行对比（表1）。

团队对每项设计的沉积物数据进行了收集和分析，发现同时改造路缘和路肩的组合设计比仅改造路缘或路肩的设计效果更好。据美国国家污染物排放削减体系规定，俄亥俄州雨水的排放标准要求TSS降低量不得低于80%，本研究提出的8种组合设计中有7种达到或超过了这一要求（图12）。

3 结论

通过对21种设计原型进行测试，“路缘沉积”研究表明，对路缘和路肩的设计标准进行重新设定是提升路面污染物截留水平的可行选择。这些新型设计可与绿色基础设施相结合，以减少污染物造成的堵塞，也可以单独应用于路面。本研究提出的设计方案占地面积小，适用于种植大树和人行道狭窄的路面，其图案也可根据商业改造区或城市特定的美学、水文或其他环境条件进行定制，且使用常见的街道清洁设备即可完成日常维护。

尽管如此，在受控环境中进行测试也存在一定的局限性。下一阶段的设计将进行现场测试，对可能影响设计效果的多种时空参数（如雨水水质）进行进一步校准和调整，届时设计将被置于不同的暴雨强度和不同的径流流速条件下，同时承受车辆、自行车和行人日常使用的磨损测试。这将有助于进一步制定最佳维护方法及所需的维护频率，从而优化设计。生态草沟的推广案例已经证明，场地尺度的小型干预设计即可改善区域水质；“路缘沉积”项目则从设计标准的角度引发当前设计实践的思考：单个设计元素能否发挥更大的作用？原型测试是回答这个问题的第一步，而景观设计师则可能是设计出具有多重功能且美观的城市元素的最佳人选。**LAF**

项目信息

测试地点： 美国俄亥俄州哥伦比亚市俄亥俄州立大学MAT / FAB实验室
项目资助： 俄亥俄州立大学工程学院暑期研究项目（启动资金来自Ryan Winston及Halina Steiner）
设计团队： Halina Steiner、Ryan Winston、Avee Oabel、Alec Grimm
设计时间： 2019年2月至今
测试设计： 2019年5~8月

1 Introduction

Roads crisscross the landscape forming an ever-expanding network of asphalt. According to the Federal Highway Administration, this network comprises 6.7 million kilometers of road in the United States[1]. They are the system of public space primarily maintained by cities and states and critical in facilitating movement of people and goods within cities[1]. They are a vehicle for connection and an integral component of USA economy. However, this network also acts as a magnet for pollutants, such as sediments, nutrients from lawn fertilizers, bacteria, viruses, pesticides, metals, microplastics, deicing salt, and oil and grease[2]. Pollutants accumulate on the road surface and are washed off during storm events, carried to storm drains via concrete curbs / gutters / aprons, and deposited into waterways often without treatment[2]. Once pollutants enter the waterways, they negatively impact the water quality and even the ecosystem, while the removal of pollutants, such as microplastics, is challenging. How can innovations in street design work to remedy this problem? Curbs and gutters are designed to move water, but can they do more?

The design of a street, sidewalk, and the curb / gutter / apron system has maintained a relative stasis for centuries. For example, innovations as simple as curb ramps were first introduced in 1945 in Kalamazoo, Michigan to aid veterans in wheelchairs[3]. Benefits of the curb ramp then extend to cyclists, strollers, and suitcases. Yet adoption was slow, curb ramps were not made a legal requirement of sidewalks until 1992, as part of the Americans with Disabilities Act[4]. Recently, it has seen increasing innovations primarily tied to green infrastructure. Curb cuts allow water to flow into bioswales and were first used in the early 1990s at the Prince George's County, Maryland[5]. However, the recent adoption of this technology is largely driven by U.S. cities failing to meet the Environmental Protection Agency's (EPA) water quality standards set by the Clean Water Act. As a result, the large-scale implementation and development of bioswales has led to iteration and improvement of designs as they move from pilot- or prototype-scale projects to new design standards. Bioswales are useful and effective in reducing stormwater flow at peak hours and filtering pollutants. Sediment and trash impair the ability of bioswales to function properly as they may cause clogging and failure to filter. In EPA's Operation and Maintenance of Green Infrastructure Receiving Runoff from Roads and Parking Lots Technical Memorandum, construction activities, bare soil (i.e. poorly vegetated area) erosion, and winter sand application are cited as common sources of sediment in urban runoff. The EPA further explains how sediments accumulate on impervious surfaces and, when routed to bioswales, build up at inlets, clog soil, and smother plants[6]. How can we leverage the curb, a commonplace design in urban areas, to collect pollutants before they enter the waterways and in so doing improve the health of watersheds?

2 Design Process

2.1 Pre-prototype Process

Many factors were considered in the prototype process. The team initially explored the use of digital simulation models in partnership with the Ohio State University (OSU) Simulation Innovation and Modeling Center. Digital model allows for fluid dynamical computation with a greater specificity of sediment size and storm events than a physical model, and is able to test one cross section of the curb, rather than a continuous curb face. Advanced computing would be necessary to develop a digital model of a continuous curb face, and the computational technology required to develop such a model was not available. So digital model was not further researched.

Then, the team chose physical testing to address the proof of concept goal, and examined prototyping techniques and hydrological sediment flow modeling. In the research on floating concrete vessels, Jake Boswell, associate professor at OSU, used CNC router to create EPS foam molds in the OSU MAT / FAB Lab, then coated them with oil and cast with floating concrete that is less dense than water. The vessels provide a structure for plant life that can aid in combating algal blooms in Lake Erie[7]. Wu Haowen, a former graduate student at OSU, fabricated a model of the Scioto River also using the CNC mill and EPS foam. The model was waterproofed with latex paint, a mixture of water and ink was pumped through the water to study river flow. Brain Davis, Associate Professor at University of Virginia, and Sean Burkholder, Assistant Professor at University of Pennsylvania, have integrated modeling into their project Healthy Port Futures. Through physical modeling, conducted at the St. Anthony Falls Lab at the University of Minnesota, coupled with computational modeling, they have developed a methodology to understand potential sediment flows in the Great Lakes.[8] Facets of each of these projects informed or were integrated into the current Curbing Sediment research.

2.2 Fabrication Process

EPS foam was chosen for modeling due to its appropriate stock size, lightweight nature, and surface textural property. The 1.2 m × 2.4 m × 0.2 m EPS stock size allows the team to create full scale models, clearly showing and accurately simulating

© Halina Steiner, Ryan Winston

10

sediment capture. The foam's light weight makes the stocks and models easy for transporting from storage to the various stages of fabrication and testing. The surface texture of EPS foam becomes similar to concrete once cut with the hot wire and passed through the CNC router.

To create the curb models, the stock pieces of EPS foam were cut down to a standard road profile. The team originally milled this profile using the CNC mill. The CNC mill took approximately 4 hours to mill the stock foam into a street section model with no curb or apron patterns. To minimize fabrication time, a 2.4-meter hot wire cutter was used to cut the stock pieces into basic curb and road profiles consisting of a 15.24-centimeter-high curb and a 1-meter-wide roadway with a 1.5% cross slope. To fit the geometry of some curb designs, the curb height would be reduced to 11.4 ~ 12.7 cm. However, fully modeling a 15.24-centimeter curb would cause colliding damage of both the router bits and the top of the curb model, thus Rhino 3D Modeling software was used to create digital models of curb and apron alterations. The physical process of milling these iterations was then digitally simulated in RhinoCAM to map tool paths and predict potential tool collisions or inconsistencies from the original Rhino model. After simulating the models in RhinoCAM, a 5-axis G-code was created and exported to an Onsrud 5-Axis CNC Router for milling apron and curb patterns on the basic curb profiles from the hot wire cutter. The patterns and crenellations were limited to the sizes of CNC tools available: a series of flat and ball tools ranging from 6.3 ~ 25 mm in diameter were used. One end of the model was milled to taper at a 45° angle to direct water into the curb gutter at the end of the testing table, which was used to assess water quality downstream of the crenellations. Finally, the curb models were cleared of excess EPS foam and painted with a layer of latex primer to prevent the models from absorbing water during tests.

When designing apron patterns, the team took inspiration from the dimensions of elements already present on roadways. Tactile paving units, made up of truncated flat-topped domes (5.08 ± 0.51 mm in height and 3.5 cm in diameter), are used to signal an upcoming intersection to pedestrians with visual impairments. The team used similar dimensions for the initial "dot" apron patterns. Design iterations featured similarly-scaled crenellations to ensure walkability and maintain safety of pedestrians and cyclists.

2.3 Prototype Design Process

The design process was iterative, with each phase built on the

10. 多轮测试的定格照片
11. 测试后模型上留下的水和沉积物

10. Stills from each round of testing
11. Water and sediment left on the model after test

© Halina Steiner, Ryan Winston

11

data and observations from the previous round of testing. The 1:1 prototyping helped the team understand how the proposed designs would look at full scale. Before testing, the team placed models next to a sidewalk and a street for additional insights about scale and visibility in the landscape.

The first designs tested were limited to alterations of either the curb face or the apron surface. Before full scale models were milled, the team tested different densities and depths to understand the limits of the routers (Fig. 1). The team tested the curb and apron modifications respectively to better understand how they function alone and how they may be incorporated best to become a system. The testing process involved 8-minute trials during which a synthetic stormwater mixture was pumped across the patterned crenellations in the apron or curb. After testing, designs were evaluated based on visual observations in sediment accumulation, measured turbidity reduction (i.e., a measure of water clarity), and total suspended solids (TSS) reduction.

The first round of testing focused on 3 curb face modifications: rounded, square, and triangular crenellations.

表1：在TSS和浊度降低方面表现良好的组合设计
Table 1: Combined designs that perform well in TSS and turbidity reduction

设计类型 **Design type**	测试次数 **Number of trials**	进水口TSS平均浓度（mg/L） **Average TSS at inlet (mg/L)**	出水口TSS平均浓度（mg/L） **Average TSS at outlet (mg/L)**	TSS平均减少量（%） **Average reduction in TSS (%)**	进水口浊度平均水平（NTU） **Average turbidity at inlet (NTU)**	出水口浊度平均水平（NTU） **Average turbidity at outlet (NTU)**	浊度平均降低量（%） **Average reduction in turbidity (%)**
网格状路肩与方形路缘凹槽 Cross hatch apron with square curb crenellations	7	1,717	212	87	1,402	1,044	22
15.24cm间隔的斜线路肩与方形路缘凹槽 Diagonal line apron at 6" gap with square curb crenellations	4	1,262	150	87	1,249	541	61
梳齿状路肩与方形路缘凹槽 Comb apron with square curb crenellations	4	829	142	82	1,189	752	42
花式斜线路肩与方形路缘 Squiggles apron with square curb crenellations	3	1,440	129	89	995	324	66
P+P方形路缘凹槽 P + P square curb crenellations	3	839	104	87	818	394	53
水波形路肩与方形路缘凹槽 Zigzag apron with square curb crenellations	3	920	145	84	938	1,085	42
网格状路肩与反向方形路缘凹槽 Cross hatch apron with inverted square curb crenellations	3	842	117	84	1,239	552	55
交替水波形路肩与方形路缘凹槽 Alt zigzag apron with square curb crenellations	3	642	163	72	947	236	76

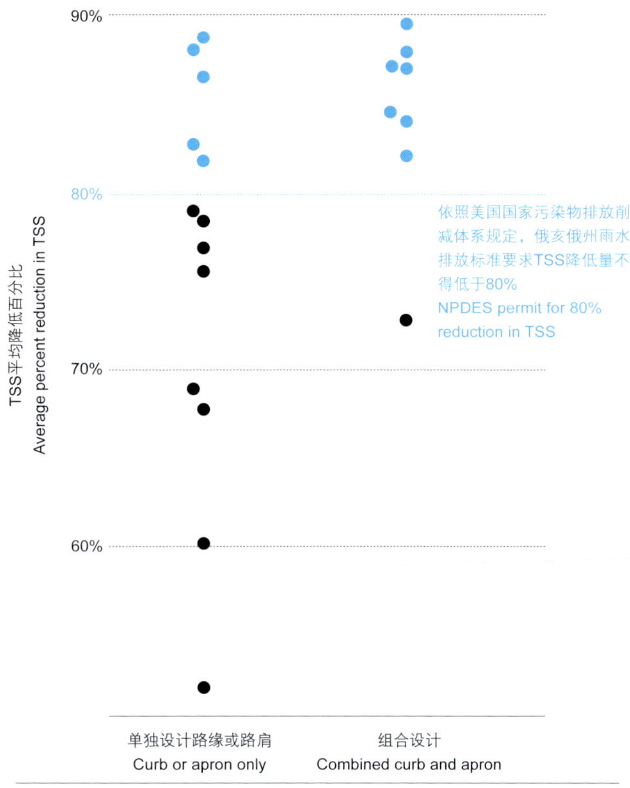

© Halina Steiner, Ryan Winston

12

12. 单独设计路缘或路肩与组合设计中TSS浓度降低百分比的分布

12. Distribution of percentage reduction in TSS concentrations for independent or combined designs of curb and apron

The square crenellation noticeably outperformed the other modifications in terms of sediment trapping and was selected for further development (Fig. 2). For apron design modifications, the team initially tested dot, line, and zigzag patterns at varying densities. This was achieved by reuse of models, first milling a lower density then re-milling the model to increase the density of the design (Fig. 3 ~ 6). The team evaluated each design using data from the turbidity sensors located at the inlet and outlet of the model. Among the 3 initial patterns, the line design was proved to be the most effective in sediment capture and chosen for further development. Variations on the line design were focused on providing additional surface area for sediment capture and slowing the velocity of the stormwater. This included altering the angle of the line, making the line path into combs, squiggles, and cross-hatches among others.

Further testing focused on designs combining the best performing curb and apron modifications, evaluating the apron's ability to convey sediments into curb extrusions. Iterations altered the spacing and sizing of curb crenellations, the way apron crenellations connected, and the placement and spacing of apron patterns. Then better performances were observed when connected apron crenellations were connected to curb extrusions, and the most effective 3 combinations were: the cross hatch apron with 7.62 cm square curb crenellations with 7.62 cm spacing between each curb crenellation (Fig. 7), the line apron with 5.08 cm square curb crenellations with 15.24 cm gaps every 45 cm (Fig. 8), and the "comb" apron design with 5 cm square curb crenellations with uniform spacing (Fig. 9).

2.4 Simulated Stormwater Tests

The prototypes were tested at the OSU MAT / FAB Lab. The physical setup included a 1.2 m × 2.4 m platform with a vinyl gutter attached to one end, 1.2 m × 2.4 m × 0.2 m stock pieces of EPS foam, two 31-gallon tote plastic tubs, an industrial mixer, scale, native soil, sand, sampler bottles, 2 Arduino microcontrollers with analog turbidity sensors, an iPad, GoPro Hero 6, three laptops, and a Sony a7RII. Milled and sealed foam pieces were placed on the platform with the GoPro Hero 6 and Sony a7RII suspended above them. The GoPro recorded video of the tests and the camera took still images every 10 seconds. The testing began with weighing approximately 70 ~ 80 kg of water into the tote plastic tubs. A mixture of roughly 60% ~ 70% native soil and 30% ~ 40% sand was added to the water to simulate stormwater. The mixer dispersed the soil and sand mixture uniformly in the tub, ensuring simulated sediment concentrations were consistent throughout the simulated storm event. A submersible pump, placed at the bottom of the tub, conveyed the water onto the surface of the model. A turbidity sensor was placed to gather data at the pumped simulated stormwater inlet. Simulated stormwater moved freely over the surface of the model during each 8-minute test. The water then flowed into the gutter where the second sensor was located and finally into the outlet tub. Outlet water in the tub was weighted as well as any remaining water in the inlet tub. During the tests grab samples were taken at the inlet and outlet at 2-minute intervals with the sampler bottles.

21 curb and apron designs were tested. Each design was tested in triplicate in succession (Fig. 10). Sediment from each test was left on the model's surface to determine how much sediment each design could effectively capture (Fig. 11). The 3 most successful designs received 1 ~ 7 rounds of additional simulated storm events, each with increased volumes of sediment to determine the failure modes and timing.

2.5 Findings

Data was collected via 3 means. Visual data were collected with the camera and GoPro during the tests. Additionally, the team could visually assess water clarity in grab sample bottles and outlet tub water. Grab samples were tested in the lab at the OSU Stormwater Management Program for TSS and particle size distribution. Sensor data were reviewed during the tests and further analysis was conducted to compare findings with grab sample data (Table 1).

Sediment data analyses were conducted for all designs tested. The results showed that designs with both curb and apron modifications performed better than those with only a curb or an apron modification. According to an 80% reduction in TSS for discharged stormwater management in Ohio required by the National Pollution Discharge Elimination System (NPDES) permit program, 7 of the 8 combined curb and apron designs met this standard (Fig. 12).

3 Conclusion

Prototype testing of 21 designs in Curbing Sediment proved that redesigning curb and apron standards can be a viable option to collect pollutants on roadways. These new designs can be used in concert with green infrastructure to reduce clogging or independently on roadways as a feasible alternative to the existing standards for curb and apron design with small footprint, mature trees, and narrow sidewalks. Custom patterns could be developed for Business Improvement Districts or by municipalities to adapt to specific aesthetic, hydrologic, and / or other physical conditions. Regular maintenance of curb and apron designs can be performed by street cleaning machines already in use.

However, testing in a controlled environment has its limits. The next phase of design will include field testing. This will allow the team to further calibrate and adjust the designs to temporally and spatially varied parameters which might affect the performance of Curbing Sediment, including rainfall and stormwater quality. By exposing the designs to varied storm events and flow rates, and regular use by vehicles, cyclists, and pedestrians, this will help with the analysis of best maintenance methods and required frequency of maintenance to optimize Curbing Sediment. Bioswales have proven that small-site-scale interventions deployed at a regional scale can improve water quality. Curbing Sediment leverages the design standard to question current design practices: Can each element do more? Prototype testing is the first step in answering this question and landscape architects may be best suited to design productive and beautiful alternatives. **LAF**

PROJECT INFORMATION

TESTING LOCATION: MAT / FAB Lab at Ohio State University, Columbus, Ohio, USA
FUNDED BY: College of Engineering Summer Research Program, Ohio State University (Start-up funds from Ryan Winston and Halina Steiner)
DESIGN TEAM: Halina Steiner, Ryan Winston, Avee Oabel, Alec Grimm
DESIGN PERIOD: Since February, 2019
TESTING PERIOD: May ~ August, 2019

REFERENCES

[1] U.S. Department of Transportation: Federal Highway Administration. (2018, August 23). Public Road Length - 2017, Miles by Ownership. Retrieved from https://www.fhwa.dot.gov/policyinformation/statistics/2017/hm10.cfm
[2] Rasmussen, T. J., & Schmidt, H. C. (2009, December). Stormwater Runoff: What it is and why it is important in Johnson County, Kansas. Retrieved from https://pubs.usgs.gov/fs/2009/3103/pdf/FS2009-3103.pdf
[3] Brown, S. (1999). The Curb Ramps of Kalamazoo: Discovering Our Unrecorded History. Disability Studies Quarterly, 19(3), 203-205.
[4] The Civil Rights Division of the U.S. Department of Justice. (2016). Curb Ramps and Pedestrian Crossings under Title II of the ADA. Retrieved from https://www.ada.gov/pcatoolkit/ch6_toolkit.pdf
[5] James, W. (1994). Current Practices in Modelling the Management of Stormwater. Boca Raton: CRC Press.
[6] United States Environmental Protection Agency. (2016, September). Operation and Maintenance of Green Infrastructure Receiving Runoff from Roads and Parking Lots. Retrieved from https://www.epa.gov/sites/production/files/2016-11/documents/final_gi_maintenance_508.pdf
[7] Knowlton School of Architecture of Ohio State University. (2017, October 26). Landscape Architecture Faculty/Student Design Collaboration Leads to Possible Patent. Retrieved from https://knowlton.osu.edu/news/2018/10/landscape-facultystudent-design-collaboration-leads-possible-patent
[8] Healthy Port Futures. (n.d.). Methodology. Retrieved from http://healthyportfutures.com/methodology/#_edn2

探索与过程

不同以往的时间

专栏编辑

陆小璇

香港大学建筑学系园境建筑学部助理教授

https://doi.org/10.15302/J-LAF-1-050024 收稿时间 RECEIVED DATE / 2020-08-24 中图分类号 / TU984 文献标识码 / C

本文引用格式 / PLEASE CITE THIS ARTICLE AS

Lu, X. (2020). It Is Different This Time. Landscape Architecture Frontiers, 8(4), 150-151. https://doi.org/10.15302/J-LAF-1-050024

在设计过程中，景观设计师积极地探索两种时间——顺应自然流动的时间与映射人为活动的时间——之间交叠的边界。正因存在于景观与时间之间的微妙联系，我们的时间概念随着人类群体对环境影响的规模和强度的变化而不断演化与拓展。在18世纪末和19世纪初，一种由汉弗莱·雷普顿所推动的景观表达创新，充分运用了线性的时间概念。雷普顿在其职业生涯中共制作了100多本景观“红皮书”，并在其中使用了叠合“改造前”与“改造后”景观图绘的方法以说明他对场地改造的建议。一个半世纪后，于1969年出版的两本书在20世纪推动景观设计学科发展的多样化议题和思辩中脱颖而出。这两本书都通过周期性和延续性的时间概念来理解景观，指出景观设计学不仅是关于空间更是关于时间的学科。在《设计结合自然》一书中，伊恩·麦克哈格以科学为出发点重新定位了人类对环境的干预，即从开发和耗竭转向对自然规则和过程的响应。[1]在《RSVP循环：人们在环境中的创造过程》一书中，劳伦斯·哈普林以艺术为出发点，将其视作一种能够使人类的创造力参与自然系统的节奏、关系和自发性的设计途径。[2]

雷普顿、麦克哈格和哈普林对存在于时间理解与设计哲学二者之间关系的思考，回应了其各自所处的文化、社会和政治环境。同样，近期对于二者之间关系的新理念也是对“人类世”这一地质学新纪元的回应：自进入人类世以来，人类已成为地球的主要地质力量；其影响如此普遍而深远，以至于推动人类自身及其所栖身的地球真正进入了“未知领域”。这场全球性危机以人为驱动的变化——从生态系统的构成到大气和海洋的地质化学变化——为主要特征，要求我们重新考虑人类与时间之间在地质、生态和生理层面的关系。本期的两个项目分别侧重于中国海南填海造地的生物修复及美国洛杉矶油田的修复和再利用。它们在各自探寻人类与其他生命共存的原型设计过程中，开启了透过自然过程所理解的时间与透过人为干预所理解的时间之间的新对话。

在《响应式生物修复：规范海南沿海开发的不确定性、评价及调和》一文中，郭小曼探寻了一种用以评估和缓解由疏浚和填海造地所造成的负面生态和社会影响的设计原型，并特别讨论了如何修复珊瑚礁以保护沿海地区免受风暴潮和波浪冲刷的影响。郭小曼以位于海南省儋州市北岸的面积达780hm^{2}的人工群岛“海花岛”为例，指出存在于该项目环境影响评估过程中的漏洞，以及人工干扰后生态修复措施的缺乏，并提出了可应用于疏浚前和疏浚期的“牡蛎–海草–珊瑚滤床系统”，以解决上述问题。该项目的亮点是为海花岛工程重新设定了2005~2025年的项目进度表，综合考虑了生态、法律、科学和经济过程中的时间因素，并强调了工程所面临的风险、不确定性和偶然性，以挑战填海造地开发模式中利益至上的论调。

在《大地舞台：面向未来的废弃土地修复》一文中，安娜·科尔尼瓦和厄尔玛克·图兰里分享了一种后工业景观再生原型的推导过程。该原型一方面旨在提高公众对资源枯竭和人为气候变化的认识，另一方面为未来从化石燃料到可再生能源的必然转变奠定基础。该项目的试验场是美国最大的连片城市油田，即位于洛杉矶的面积达4km^{2}的英格尔伍德油田。在该项目中，科尔尼瓦和图兰里以舞蹈编导来隐喻对空间秩序与格局的设计，并使用“大地舞台”的概念来描述景观再生规划及其实施过程，即通过妥善安排人类和非人类主体在场地上的活动，持续推动场地内的空间建构、资源分配与功能区重置。该项目对场地现有结构、材料和地形的再利用并非出于怀旧的意图，而是为了促生过去、现在和未来之间的关键性互动。在这一框架下，公众不断变化的需求及景观修复再生技术的发展将主导未来场地功能更替的速度和规模。

两篇文章的作者都在各自提出的协调、修复和再生过程中强调并利用了时间的力量。这两个案例以“节奏”“过程”“序列”“进化”等时间概念来描述人类世的景观设计，并指出其在本质上同时具有社会性、自然性和时间性。**LAF**

EXPERIMENTS & PROCESSES

IT IS DIFFERENT THIS TIME

COLUMN HOST

LU Xiaoxuan

Assistant Professor of Landscape Architecture at the University of Hong Kong

In the design process, landscape designers actively navigate the overlapping boundaries between time as ordained by nature and time as understood in the context of human activities. This relation between time and the landscape makes our conception of time necessarily evolve and broaden along with the scale and intensity of our collective environmental impacts. One of the innovations in landscape representation spearheaded by Humphry Repton at the end of the eighteenth and beginning of the nineteenth centuries described a linear notion of time. Over the course of his career, Repton produced over 100 of celebrated "Red Books" in which he employed the device of "before and after" drawings using overlays to illustrate how his proposals would transform his prospective clients' estates. A century and a half later in 1969, two books captured the diverse intellectual themes and debates that advanced the discipline of Landscape Architecture over the twentieth century. Both books understood landscapes with cyclical and continuous conceptions of time, reinterpreting landscape design very much as a temporal and spatial discipline. In *Design with Nature*, Ian McHarg used scientific knowledge as the starting point of his quest to re-orientate our environmental interventions away from exploitation and depletion, toward responsiveness to the landscape's natural patterns and processes.[1] In *The RSVP Cycles: Creative Processes in the Human Environment*, Lawrence Halprin explored art as a way to develop design methods that could allow human creativity to engage with the rhythms, relationships, and spontaneity of natural systems.[2]

Repton, McHarg, and Halprin's musings on the relationship between human's understanding of time and design philosophy were responsive to their respective cultural, social, and political contexts. Recently, new concepts of this relationship have emerged as we enter the Anthropocene, increasingly recognized as a geological epoch where humanity has become a dominant planetary geophysical force so pervasive and profound that human impacts are now propelling us and our planet into what is truly terra incognita. This global crisis, characterized by human-driven changes ranging from the makeup of ecosystems to the geochemistry of the atmosphere and the ocean, requires us to reconsider our geological, ecological, and physiological relationships with time. Focusing on the bioremediation of coastal land reclamation in Hainan, China and the remediation and repurposing of an oil field in Los Angeles, U.S., respectively, the two projects featured in this issue provoke new conversations about time as understood in terms of natural processes and time in terms of human intervention, prototyping for the coexistence of human and non-human.

In Responsive Bioremediation: Regulating the Uncertainty, Assessment, and Negotiation for Coastal Developments in Hainan, China, Kwok Siu Man explores design prototypes that could evaluate and mediate the negative ecological and social effects of dredging and land reclamation, particularly the degradation of coral reefs that protect coastal regions from storm surges and erosion. Taking Ocean Flower Island, a 780-hectare artificial archipelago located at Danzhou on the north coast of Hainan as an exemplar, Kwok highlights the dilemmas that vex the project's environmental impact assessment process and the deficiencies of the ecological restoration measures in place. With this in mind, she proposes an "oyster-seagrass-coral filtration bed system" to be implemented before and during the dredging process. The highlight of her project is a revised project timeline from 2005 to 2025. By overlapping the temporal scales of ecological, legal, scientific, and economic processes, and foregrounding the risks, uncertainties, and contingencies of such a project, Kwok challenges the profit-driven narrative that land reclamation is a quick, cheap and reliable way to establish open land for development.

In Earth Choreographer: Remediating Obsolete Grounds of the Future, Anna Korneeva and Irmak Turanli share with us the rationale behind the development of a post-industrial landscape rehabilitation prototype designed to raise public awareness about resource depletion and anthropogenic climate change, and to set the stage for the foreseeable transition from fossil fuel to renewable energy generation. The testing ground for this project is the 400-hectare Inglewood Oil Field in Los Angeles, the largest contiguous urban oil field in the U.S. Using the metaphor of dance which organizes movements to create order and pattern, Korneeva and Turanli use the term "Earth Choreographer" to describe the planning and implementation of rehabilitative processes whereby the ground is constantly constructed, reconfigured, and reterritorialized by the strategic organization of movement of human and non-human agencies. Instead of looking nostalgically to the past, the re-appropriation of existing structures, materials, and topographies facilitates critical engagements between past, present, and future. In this context, the speed and scale of new programs are determined by the ever-changing needs of the public as well as the evolution of remediation technologies.

Both articles recognize and deploy the power of time in their respective negotiation, remediation, and rehabilitation processes. In both cases, landscape design in the Anthropocene is described in terms of time using concepts such as "rhythm," "process," "sequence," and " evolution," and is understood to be simultaneously social, natural, and temporal in nature . **LAF**

REFERENCES

[1] McHarg, I. L. (1969). Design with Nature. New York: American Museum of Natural History.

[2] Halprin, L. (1969). The RSVP Cycles: Creative Processes in the Human Environment. New York: George Braziller, Inc.

本文引用格式 / PLEASE CITE THIS ARTICLE AS

Kwok, S. M. (2020). Responsive Bioremediation: Regulating the Uncertainty, Assessment, and Negotiation for Coastal Developments in Hainan, China. Landscape Architecture Frontiers, 8(4), 152-163. https://doi.org/10.15302/J-LAF-1-050022

https://doi.org/10.15302/J-LAF-1-050022 收稿时间 RECEIVED DATE / 2020-07-08 中图分类号 / X37, X5, X820.3, U616 文献标识码 / B

响应式生物修复：规范海南沿海开发的不确定性、评价及调和

RESPONSIVE BIOREMEDIATION: REGULATING THE UNCERTAINTY, ASSESSMENT, AND NEGOTIATION FOR COASTAL DEVELOPMENTS IN HAINAN, CHINA

郭小曼*
粤港澳大湾区生态与景观联盟秘书长

KWOK Siu Man
Secretary General, Guangdong-Hong Kong-Macau Greater Bay Area Ecology and Landscape Alliance (GBAELA)

*通讯作者
地址：中国香港铜锣湾告士打道262号中粮大厦11楼
邮编：999077
邮箱：mandykwok@gbaela.org

摘要

填海造地和疏浚活动会损害海洋和沿海生态。本研究理性分析了获批的环境影响评价中存在的冲突点，包括对沿海和海洋生境所受直接及间接影响的忽视，环评流程中的漏洞，以及海洋环境修复方案的缺陷，旨在使利益相关者更好地了解填海造地对海洋和沿海生态系统造成的直接及间接影响，以促使其遵循合理的环评流程，并实施响应式海洋生物修复方案。研究以中国海南海花岛为例，通过在疏浚之前及过程中应用响应式牡蛎－海草－珊瑚滤床系统，使周边海域的水浊度和悬沙浓度保持在珊瑚礁的耐受范围之内。

关键词

填海造地；疏浚；环境影响评价；海洋生物修复；响应式原型；牡蛎－海草－珊瑚滤床系统

ABSTRACT

Land reclamation and dredging have a damaging effect on marine and coastal ecology. This study rationally analyzes the conflicts in the approved environmental impact assessment (EIA), including the negligence of the direct and indirect effects on coastal and marine habitats, the short circuit of the EIA procedures among stakeholders, and the insufficient marine environmental restoration schemes. This study also promotes awareness among the stakeholders so they will understand the direct and indirect effects of land reclamation on marine and coastal ecosystems, as well as the indications if they follow the EIA procedures, and implement a responsive marine bioremediation before and during the dredging process. By taking the Ocean Flower Island in Hainan, China as an example, this study applied the responsive oyster-seagrass-coral filtration bed system before and during the dredging process to maintain the water turbidity and suspended sediment concentration below the tolerance limits of the coral reefs in the adjacent areas.

KEYWORDS

Land Reclamation; Dredging; Environmental Impact Assessment; Marine Bioremediation; Responsive Prototype; Oyster-Seagrass-Coral Filtration Bed System

编辑 田晓劼 **翻译** 李慧彦 田晓劼
EDITED BY TIAN Xiaojie **TRANSLATED BY** LI Huiyan TIAN Xiaojie

1 背景

相关统计显示，21世纪全球填海造地活动愈演愈烈。自2006年以来，中国海南填海造地面积不断扩大，并于2013年达到峰值（1 351.77km^2）[1]。2010年，中央政府宣布将海南定位为“国际旅游岛”[2]，开发商随即开始在其沿海区域竞相圈地、填海造地，以期通过这种快速且相对廉价的方式获得绝佳海景。然而，研究发现海南的珊瑚礁覆盖率已从20世纪80年代的70%下降至21世纪10年代的10%左右[3]，这与愈演愈烈的填海活动及随之而来的渔业及疏浚工程等人类干扰密切相关。

治理不力是海南珊瑚礁栖息地消失的主要原因。保护体系、流程及相关法律法规未被严格贯彻执行，不完善的环境影响评价（下文简称“环评”）体系，以及科学知识的匮乏又致使疏浚活动对于珊瑚礁保护区的影响被低估。由于海南沿海及海洋环境遭到严重破坏，中央政府在对海南进行了数月的环境监察后，于2017年12月叫停了所有填海造地项目[4]。

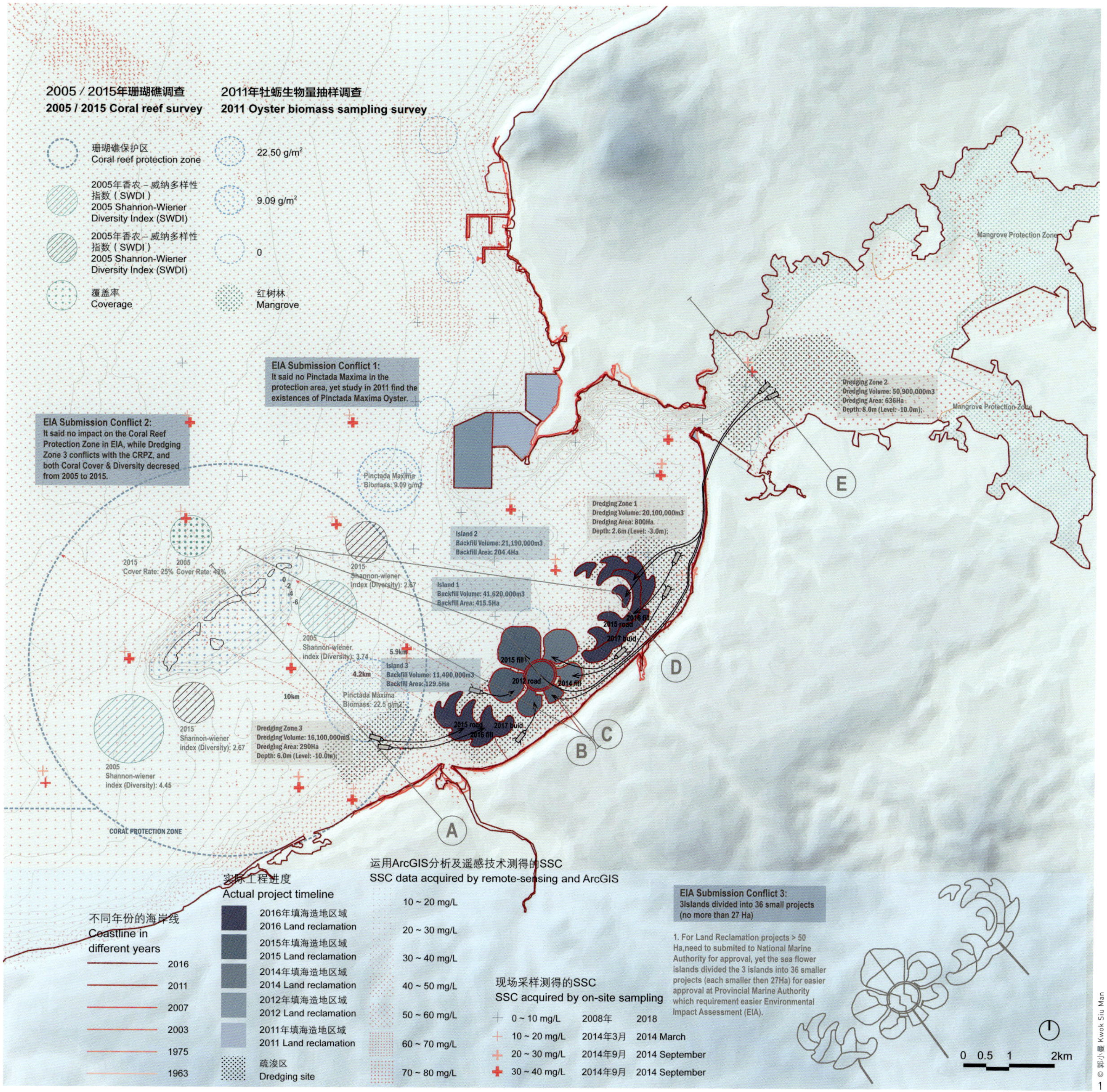

© 郭小曼 Kwok Siu Man

1

1. 填海造地及疏浚活动给海花岛周边海域造成的影响，以及海花岛环评报告与其他研究结果间存在的矛盾冲突。

1. A map of land reclamation and dredging impacts around Ocean Flower Island with conflicts in EIA report

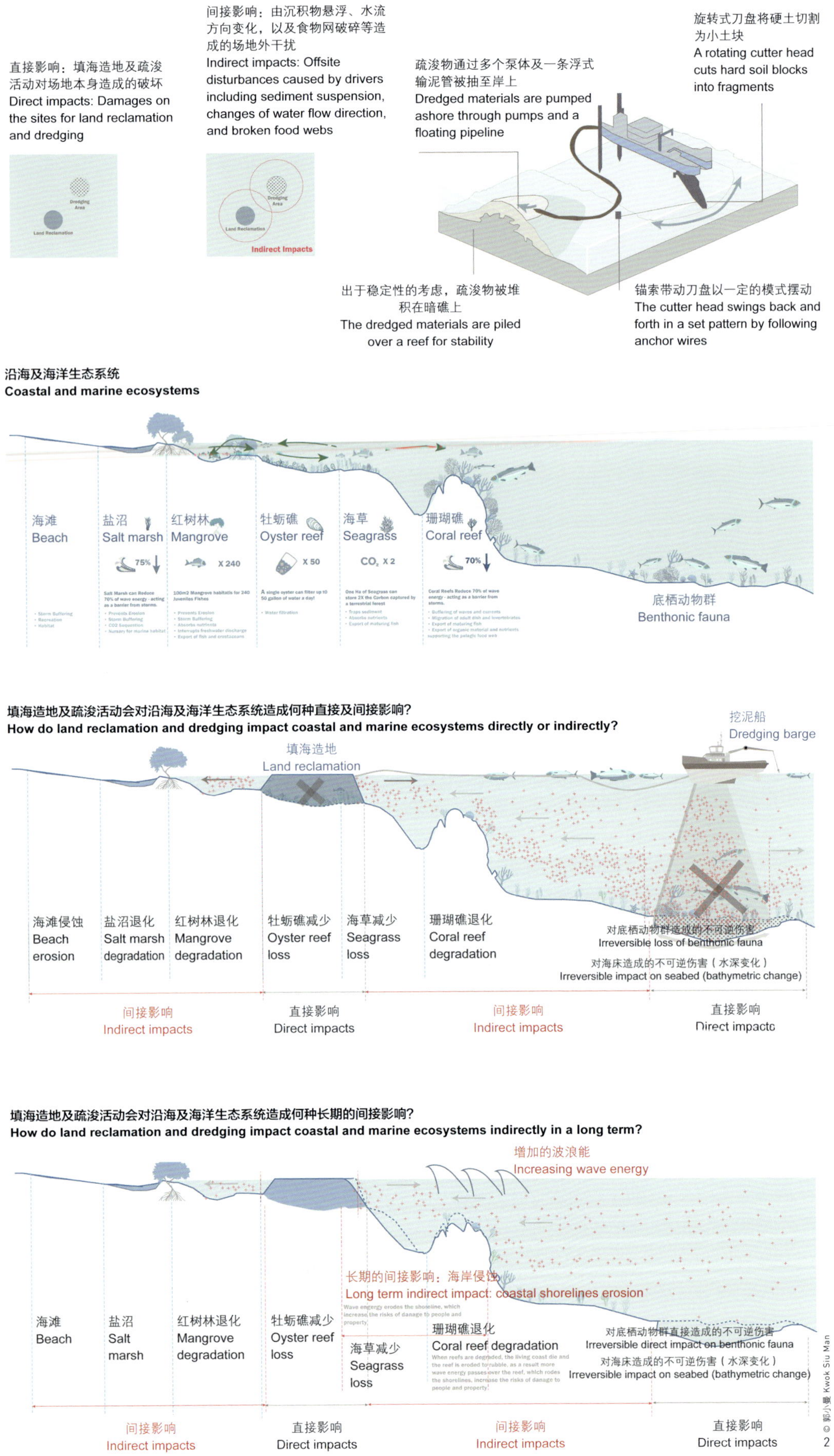

2

2 提案

一个健康的沿海及海洋生态系统应由不同的海洋生境组成，包括渔场、珊瑚礁、海草、牡蛎场、红树林和盐沼，各生境之间相互提供生态系统服务。疏浚和填海活动会对海洋生态系统造成不可逆转的损失以及生境退化，直接导致底栖动物群死亡及海床变化，并使海水悬沙浓度（SSC）增加，间接引起珊瑚退化。由于间接影响的测算需要较长时间，因此中国的许多环评项目都将其略过，或仅以简单笼统的陈述代替量化评价。长此以往，珊瑚礁自身的退化将导致其消浪能力不断下降，无法阻挡波浪能对海岸线的侵蚀，使人类的生命和财产安全面临风险。然而，疏浚过程导致的SSC上升也为滤食性动物牡蛎增加了食物来源。这一生物修复过程可用于缓解填海造地带来的问题。

通过研究多种海洋生存环境以及牡蛎和海草的生物修复作用，并对牡蛎滤床、海草滤床、牡蛎–海草滤床原型进行测试后，本研究提出了牡蛎–海草–珊瑚滤床系统，以保护珊瑚礁，降低波浪对沿海地区的冲刷。在疏浚之前及疏浚过程中，采用本研究设计的滤床系统并严格遵循EIA流程，可使水浊度和SSC维持在低水平（10mg/L），为珊瑚的健康生长提供理想的水环境，进而改善珊瑚生境。

3 模拟设计

本课题的研究区域"海花岛"位于海南省儋州市北岸，是一个于2012年9月开工建造的面积约为780hm^{2}的人工群岛，包含三个从附近的海床上挖泥填海而成的独立小岛（海花岛1~3号）。研究首先深入分析了已获批的环评报告中的信息与学术论文中发表的海洋生境数据之间存在的冲突。除评价程序本身存在的漏洞以及不当操作之外，研究进一步确定了4项主要冲突点（图1，2）。

冲突点1：环评报告对2011~2012年以及填海造地施工期内的保护区情况进行了评价对比，称在2011年未发现大珠母贝（*Pinctada maxima*），但该物种曾出现在2011年进行的一项研究中[5]。

冲突点2：已获批的环评报告称，疏浚活动对珊瑚礁保护区没有影响，但此前有研究指出，疏浚三区对该区域造成了影响，致使珊瑚的覆盖率及多样性在2005~2015年间不断降低[6]。

冲突点3：国家规定，对于50hm^{2}以上的填海造地项目，其环评报告及所有项目计划书都要上报至国家层面进行审批，审批时间较长且可能会被驳回[7]。因此，该项目被划分为36个小项目，以便尽快、顺利通过审批[8]。

冲突点4：海花岛环评报告显示，2008年其周边海域的SSC小于珊瑚健康生长的理想水浊度阈值10mg/L。在2015年的报告中，两次现场抽样结果显示，海花岛区域在2014年3月和9月的SSC范围分别为10~20mg/L和20~40mg/L。然而，其他众多研究结果表明，疏浚区的SSC普遍不低于100mg/L。

基于由重量分析法确定的总固体悬浮物水平与浊度计读数之

2. 填海造地及疏浚活动对海洋生态系统造成的直接及间接影响
3. 与疏浚区距离不等的采样点的SSC水平

2. Direct and indirect impacts of land reclamation and dredging on marine ecosystem
3. SSC of sample sites at different distances from dredging site

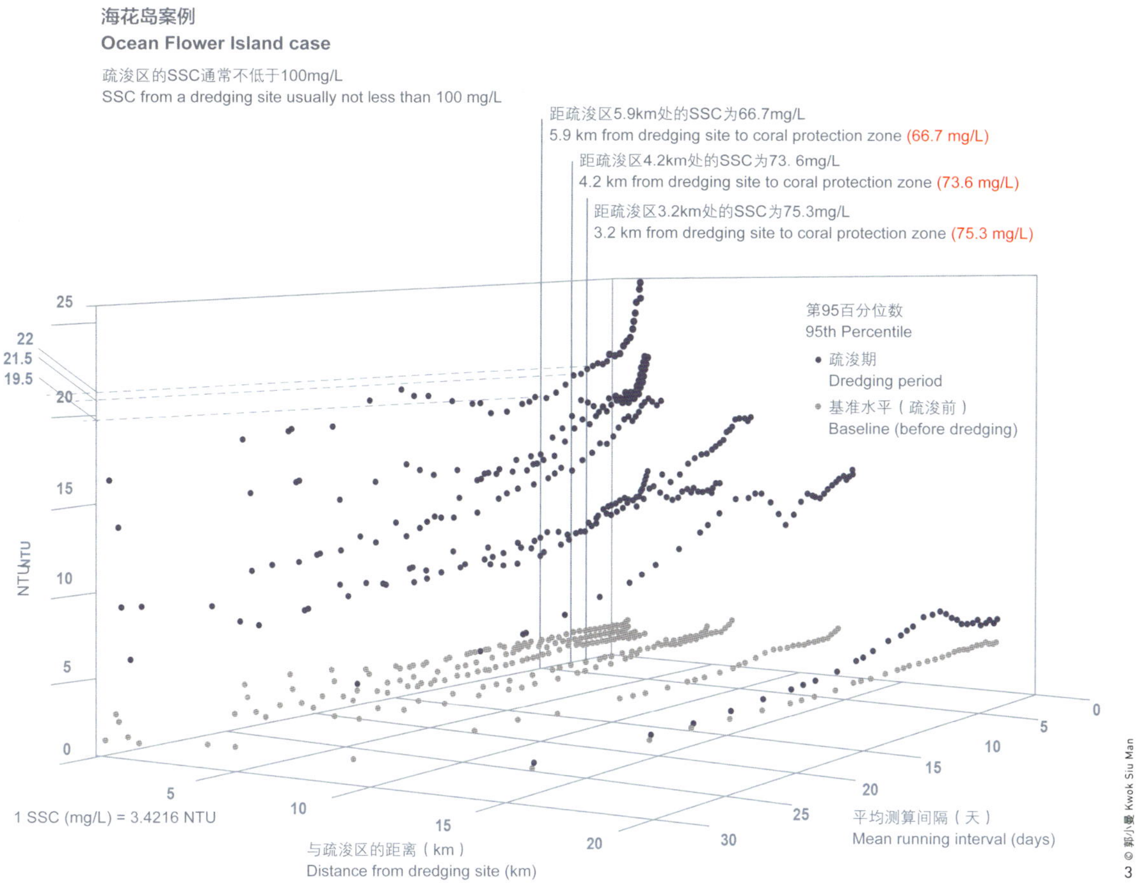

比，比浊法浊度单位（NTU）数据可以通过换算系数转换为SSC（1 SSC=3.4216 NTU）。本研究将海花岛疏浚区的SSC设为100mg/L，距离疏浚区越远，SSC越低。对位于疏浚区和珊瑚保护区之间的三个地点（分别距疏浚区3.2km、4.2km及5.9km）进行采样，测得其SSC分别为75.3mg/L、73.6mg/L和66.7mg/L，均为经大量研究证实的珊瑚部分致死浓度（图3）。此前的一项研究将珊瑚生长的SSC耐受水平分为三个等级并规定了相应阈值：10mg/L级，珊瑚可存活；20mg/L级，珊瑚部分死亡；以及100mg/L级，珊瑚全部死亡[9]。

环评报告除了与其他研究结果存在冲突外，亦忽略了疏浚和填海造地所带来的间接影响。在报告中，此类影响被理所当然地认为难以测量，但多项研究已成功评价出了与疏浚区距离不等的采样点的SSC水平[10]-[12]，并证实这些疏浚区所带来的间接影响严重威胁着珊瑚生境。

4 设计策略

4.1 滤床原型

为了解决上述冲突，本研究通过详细调研生物修复过程、各种海洋生境的维持条件（表1），以及可在疏浚和填海造地之前及施工期间进行的生产—修复周期与培育过程（图4~6），提出了一项设计策略——利用牡蛎的滤食习性，将其与海草一起制成过滤层来防止珊瑚退化，从而降低波浪能，保护沿海区域。

本研究开发了三种滤床原型（图4~6）。这些滤床的过滤阈值不同，可设置在海花岛填海造地及疏浚区附近的不同水深处（图7，8）。

原型一为牡蛎滤床，可布置在水深为1~3m、SSC为10~100mg/L的位置。一只成年牡蛎每天可过滤$0.2m^3$的水，而一个30m×120m的牡蛎滤床单元可容纳36万只牡蛎，其过滤速率可满足被一艘疏浚速率为3 000m^3/小时（即72 000m^3/天）的挖泥船所影响的水体的净化需要。

原型二为海草滤床，可布置在水深为1~15m、SSC为10~20mg/L的位置。一个30m×120m的滤床单元可容纳72万株海草。

原型三为牡蛎—海草滤床，可布置在水位为1~15m、SSC为10~100mg/L的位置。一个尺寸为30m×120m的牡蛎—海草滤床单元可容纳36万只牡蛎和72万株海草。

4.2 响应式生物修复设计

对于初始SSC水平为100mg/L的疏浚区，使用响应式牡蛎滤床可将SSC降至30mg/L；继续使用响应式牡蛎—海草滤床后，SSC将进一步

表1：牡蛎－海草－珊瑚栖息地生存条件
Table 1: Living conditions of oyster-seagrass-coral habitat

过滤目标 Filtration target	水深 Water depth	生命周期 Life cycle	生长条件 Growing conditions	数量 Quantity	成功案例 Successful cases
一只牡蛎一天可过滤0.19m³的水体。牡蛎直径为100~115mm An Oyster can daily filter 0.19 m³ water. Oyster size：100 ~ 115 mm	潮间带与潮下带，水深约为1~3m Intertidal and sub-tidal zones with water depth of around 1 ~ 3 m	2~6周培育，2~3年成熟，3年后进入繁殖期 2 ~ 6 weeks for nursery; 2 ~ 3 years to be mature; reproductive prime at 3 years of age	温度0~4℃，微咸水环境 Temperature between 0 ~ 4 ℃; Brackish water	0.4hm²可培育出750 000只牡蛎 One acre can produce 750,000 Oysters	大湾区河口：360hm²的生物滤床每4天可将整个河口的水体过滤一次 Great Bay estuary: 360-hectare filtration bed can filter the entire estuary every 4 days
海草可过滤浅水 Seagrass can filter shallow water	多数海草生长在水深1~15m的水域，最深可生长于58m处。 Many seagrass species live in depths of 1 ~ 15 m, but the deepest-growing one has been found at a depth of 58 m.	大约6年 Approximately 6 years	温度10~16℃，清澈、富含营养的低波浪能浅水域 Temperature between 10 ~ 16 ℃; Clear, shallow, nutrient-rich, and low-energy water	0.4hm²可培育出近30 000株海草 One acre can produce nearly 30,000 seagrass trace sediments	海草滤床能截留沉积物以降低SSC Seagrass filtration bed can reduce SSC by trapping sediments
珊瑚能够降低波浪能，进而避免海岸线侵蚀 Coral reef can reduce wave energy to protect coastline from erosion	水深为2~6m Water depth of 2 ~ 6 m	8~14个月培育（从1~2cm的断枝培育成直径6~9cm的幼年珊瑚） 8 ~ 14 months for nursery (from 1 ~ 2 cm fragments to 6 ~ 9 cm in diameter)	温度23~29℃ Temperature between 23 ~ 29 ℃	珊瑚礁能够降低70%的波浪能 Coral reef can reduce wave energy by 70%	菲律宾、日本富士市、马尔代夫 The Philippines, Fuji, Japan, and Maldives

下降至10mg/L，达到适宜珊瑚生存的水平。不过，一些意外事件或过度疏浚可能会导致过滤系统崩溃，本研究为此进一步设计了具有多重阈值的牡蛎—海草—珊瑚系统，以响应不同的水质条件：当SSC超过10mg/L时，珊瑚首先停止正常生长；当SSC超过30mg/L时，海草停止正常生长；SSC超过100mg/L，牡蛎则会停止滤食，闭合外壳。

牡蛎—海草—珊瑚响应系统可通过远程闭路电视（CCTV）进行监控。如果牡蛎壳张开，则该牡蛎正在进行滤食；如果牡蛎壳闭合，则说明SSC超过了100mg/L。在后一种情况下，海洋管理部门可责令疏浚方停止作业并接受检查。同样，如果海草生长状况不佳，则说明SSC可能超过了30mg/L（图9）。

另一种响应式设计是在珊瑚礁附近培育珊瑚，通过观察珊瑚的生长情况评价水质是否达到了珊瑚的健康生存标准。珊瑚养殖者收割珊瑚后，放在养殖盘或珊瑚树上培育幼珊瑚，并通过远程水下CCTV进行监控，如果珊瑚在数月内生长良好，则说明水质达标，珊瑚将会被转移至原来的生境，以增加原生境的珊瑚覆盖率；若珊瑚死亡，疏浚作业则会被叫停并接受检查（图10）。

综上，通过对填海造地的环评程序进行微调并融合生物修复方案，本研究提出了一个新的海花岛施工时间表（图11），其表明如果在疏浚前和疏浚期间妥善使用响应式牡蛎—海草—珊瑚滤床进行生物修复并严格遵循环评流程，海花岛1号填海造地和地面建设的开工时间将分别至少推迟5年和8年。

5 结论

在疏浚过程中采用响应式牡蛎—海草—珊瑚滤床系统作为生物修复手段并遵循合理的环评流程可以有效保护并改善海洋生境，但在实施环评流程以及在不同利益相关方之间进行协调的时间成本也将显著增加。本研究提出的修复设计方案均基于理想状态，实际施工中的突发事件或各种延迟都会影响项目进度。在这种情况下，鉴于开发时间成本高、生物修复投入大，利益相关者在决定填海造地前必定会进行谨慎权衡，因为这与他们快速获取廉价土地的初衷相矛盾。然而，无论时间成本如何，响应式生物修复设计对生态系统而言都是具有价值的——这些生物修复原型可用于净化任何高SSC水体，从而改善海洋生态。

人类活动影响着生态系统和生态环境，而生态系统的崩溃将会威胁到人类的生命和财产安全。生态系统所包含的种类丰富的生境为其赋予了生命力，使其成为城市建设中活跃而复杂的主体，在物理和生物层面与各种先进生物技术、治理活动、公共政策和土地动态变化发生关联。本研究探讨了牡蛎—海草—珊瑚生境体系所提供的生态系统服务及其作用机制。该系统所展现出的水体净化能力表明其在海洋和沿海保护方面均具备响应性、适应性及有效性，是一种全新的创造性生物修复途径，证明了“解决自然问题最终需借助自然之力”。**LAF**

致谢

本文为作者在香港大学攻读景观设计硕士课程期间开展的研究。作者感谢其论文导师艾希莉・斯科特・凯利的支持和指导，皮埃尔・比朗格尔教授和王爱民先生对课题提出的宝贵意见和反馈，以及助理教授陆小璇的帮助。

1 Background

Statistics shows that land reclamation activities are increasing worldwide in the 21st century. The land reclamation areas in Hainan, China are rising since 2006 and eventually reached the peak at 1,351.77 km^2 in 2013[1]. After the central government declared Hainan as an International Tourism Island in 2010[2], developers rushed to occupy the coastal area because land reclamation is a fast and cheap way to obtain excellent sea view lands. However, research findings showed that the percentage of local coral reef cover decreased from 70% in the 1980s to nearly 10% in the 2010s[3]. Such dramatic shrinking is closely related to the increasing land reclamation, as well as the following human activities like fisheries and dredging.

The loss of coral reef habitats in Hainan is caused by governance failure. Conservation structures, processes, regulations, and laws are bypassed by stakeholders. The effect of dredging on coral reef protection zone is underestimated due to the insufficient environment impact assessment (EIA) and lack of scientific knowledge. In December 2017, all land reclamation projects were paused after months of environmental inspection by the central government in Hainan due to the serious coastal and marine environmental damages[4].

2 Proposition

A healthy coastal and marine ecosystem consists of different marine habitats, including fisheries, coral reefs, seagrasses, oyster beds, mangroves, and salt marshes, which provide ecosystem services to each other. Dredging and land reclamation activities cause irreversible loss and habitat degradation to marine ecosystems. The direct effects include the irreversible loss of benthonic fauna and changes in the seabed, and the indirect one, which can be attributed to the increasing suspended sediment concentration (SSC), causes coral degradation. Given that it takes long to measure the latter, many EIAs in China exclude this part or just provide a simple and general statement without quantification assessments. In the long term, the wave reduction ability of degraded coral reefs will decline. As a result, increased wave energy passes over the reef, which causes shoreline erosion and increases the risks of damage to people's lives and properties. On the other hand, the increasing SSC caused by the dredging process can serve as a positive source for oysters as filter feeders, which is an ecological solution to land reclamation through the bioremediation process.

By examining the different marine living conditions and

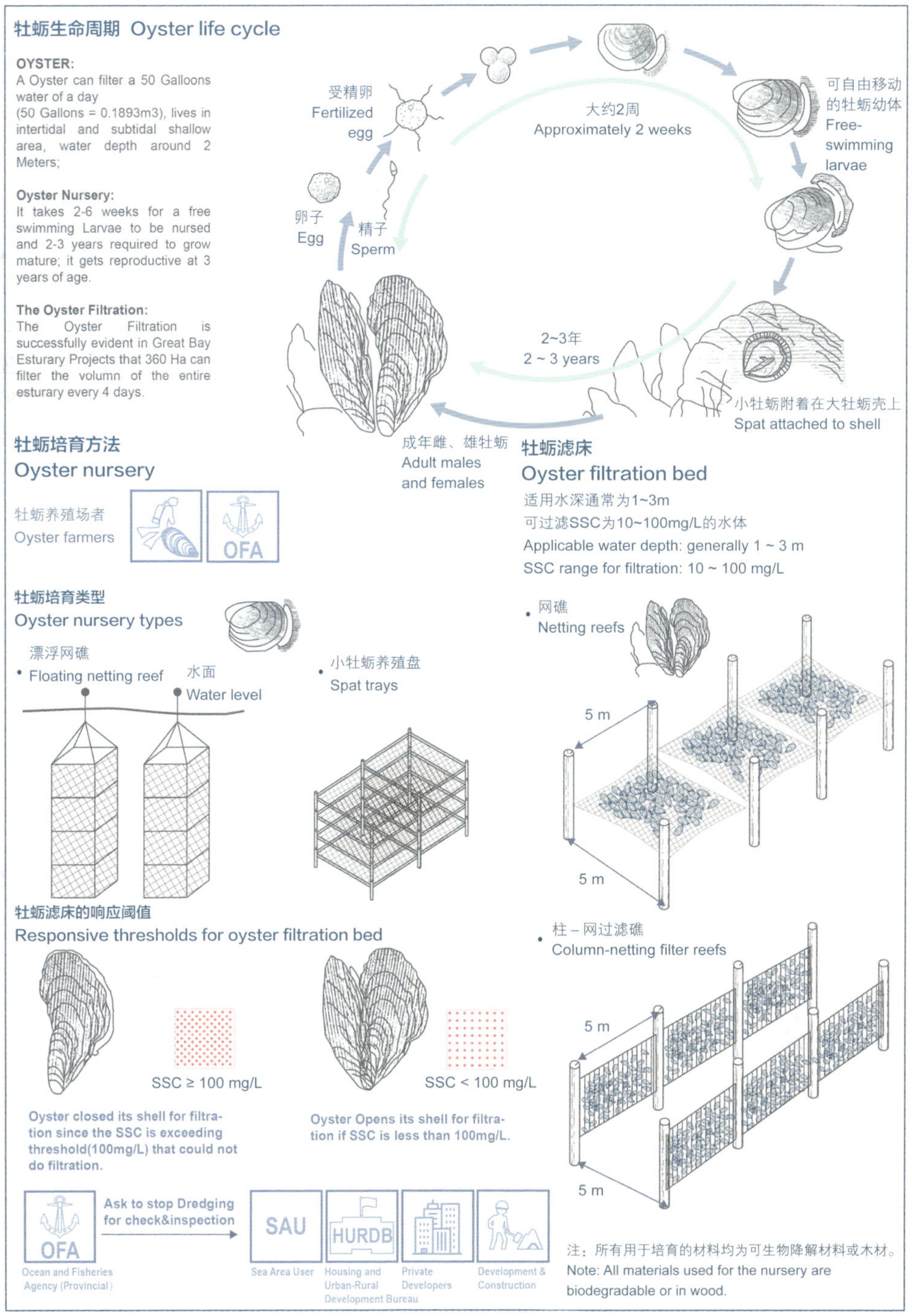

4 © 郭小曼 Kwok Siu Man

4. 牡蛎的生命周期、培育方法及滤床设计

4. Life cycle, nursery, and filtration bed design of oysters

bioremediation that oysters and seagrass provide, and testing the prototypes of oyster filtration bed, seagrass filtration bed, and oyster-seagrass filtration bed, the oyster-seagrass-coral filtration bed system is proposed in this study to protect the coral reef and consequently reduce wave energy and protect the coastal area. Adopting the designed filtration bed system before and during the dredging process and strictly following the EIA procedures can maintain the water turbidity and the SSC at a low level (10 mg/L), thereby providing an ideal living water condition for the healthy growth of corals and enhancing their habitats.

3 Speculation

The study area is the Ocean Flower Island, a 780-hectare artificial archipelago located at the north coast of Danzhou in Hainan. The island consists of three independent islets (Ocean Flower Islet 1 ~ 3), which were reclaimed by dredging from the nearby seabed since September, 2012. The study started with a thorough analysis of the conflicts between the information declared in the approved EIA and the marine habitat data published in research papers. In addition to the short circuit and misconduct of EIA procedures, four other major conflicts were identified (Fig. 1, 2).

Conflict 1: No *Pinctada maxima* was reported in 2011 in the protection area in EIA which evaluated and compared the coastal ecology in 2011 ~ 2012 and during the land reclamation and dredging, but a study conducted in 2011 found this oyster species in the region[5].

Conflict 2: The approved EIA claimed that the dredging activities have no effect on the coral reef protection zone, but a previous study stated that Dredging Zone 3 affected this zone and the coral coverage and diversity decreased from 2005 to 2015[6].

Conflict 3: As the central government requires, the EIA and all project proposals of land reclamation projects covering more than 50 hectares should be approved at the national level, which may take a long time and be rejected[7]. Therefore, the project was divided into 36 small projects to obtain approval quickly and easily[8].

Conflict 4: The Ocean Flower Island EIA report showed that the SSC around the island in 2008 was less than 10 mg/L (the threshold of an ideal water turbidity for the healthy growth of corals). In the EIA conducted in 2015, a two site-sample survey showed that the SSC range in March and September 2014 was 10 ~ 20 mg/L and 20 ~ 40 mg/L, respectively. However, the results were inconsistent with the findings of numerous studies,

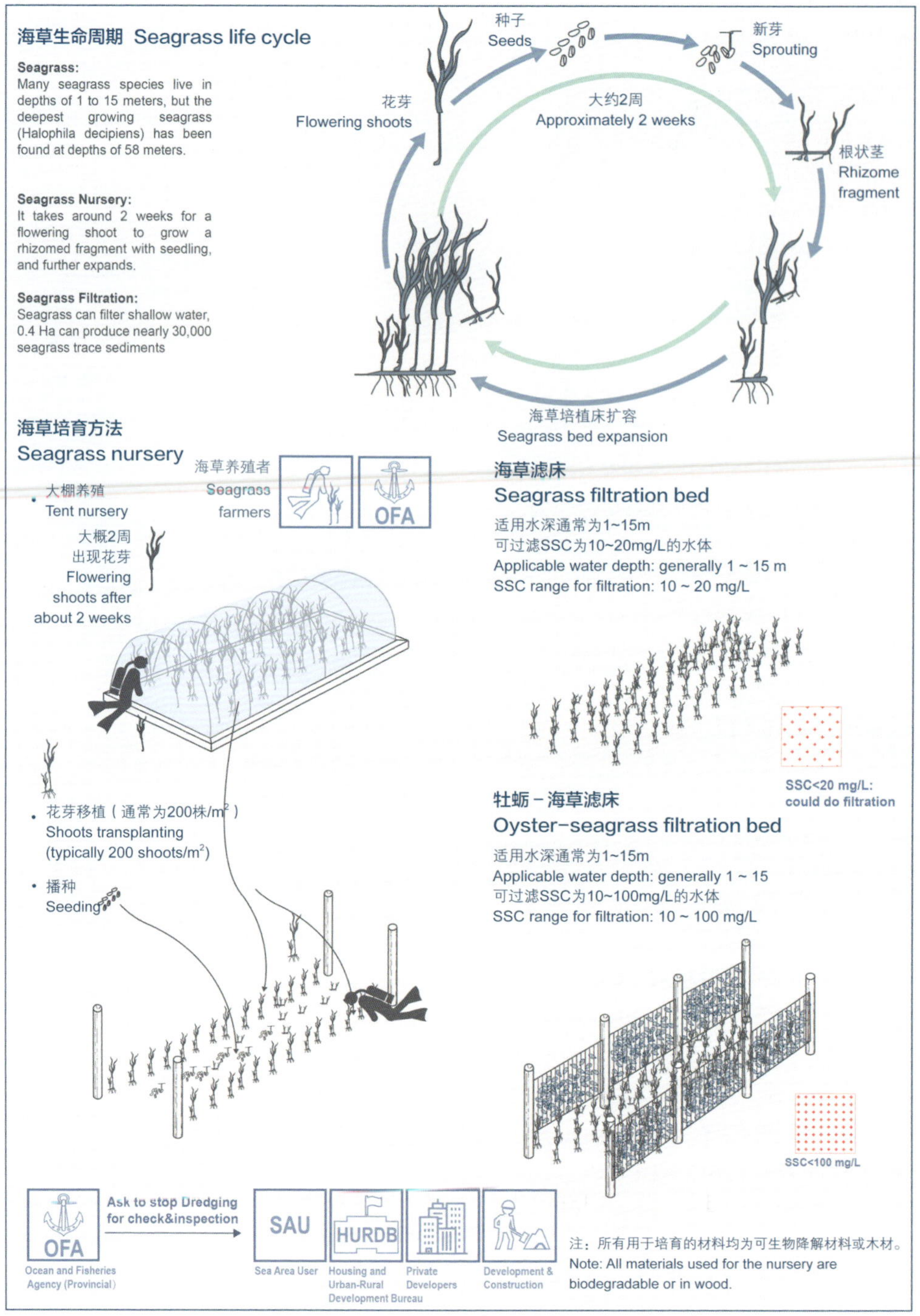

5 © 郭小曼 Kwok Siu Man

5. 海草的生命周期、培育方法及滤床设计

5. Life cycle, nursery, and filtration bed design of seagrasses

which argued that the SSC of a dredging site is generally not less than 100 mg/L.

The nephelometric turbidity unit (NTU) data can be converted into SSCs (mg/L) by applying site-specific algorithms (conversion factors) based on gravimetrically determined total suspended solid levels versus nephelometer readings (1 SSC = 3.4216 NTU). The SSC of the dredging site in the Ocean Flower Island was set as 100 mg/L, which negatively correlates with the distance to the island. Three locations with distances of 3.2 km, 4.2 km, and 5.9 km, respectively from the dredging site to the coral protection zone were sampled, and their SSC levels were 75.3, 73.6, and 66.7 mg/L, all of which can cause partial coral mortality according to many studies (Fig. 3). A previous research categorized the SSC tolerance levels and critical thresholds for coral growth into three: 1) level where corals survive (10 mg/L), 2) level where corals face partial mortality (20 mg/L); and 3) level where corals die (100 mg/L)[9].

Aside from the conflicts with other research findings, the indirect effects of dredging and land reclamation sites were also disregarded in the EIA report. Such effects are assumed to be immeasurable in EIA, but several studies were able to evaluate the SSC levels at different distances from the dredging site[10]~[12]. The findings revealed that the indirect effects of these sites pose serious threats to coral habitats.

4 Design Strategy

4.1 Filtration Bed Prototypes

The design strategy, which aims to address the abovementioned conflicts, is based on the detailed investigation of the bioremediation process, living conditions of various marine habitats (Table 1), and life cycle and nursery processes for production and remediation, which are conducted before and during the dredging and land reclamation operations (Fig. 4 ~ 6). This strategy intends to utilize the filtration function of oysters by combining their filtration layers with seagrasses to protect corals from degradation and consequently reduce wave energy and safeguard the coastal areas.

Three filtration bed prototypes are developed (Fig. 4 ~ 6). These beds can be set adjacent to land reclamation and dredging sites in Ocean Flower Island at different locations with distinctive water depths and filtration thresholds (Fig. 7, 8).

Prototype 1 is an oyster filtration bed, which can be deployed at locations with water depth of 1 ~ 3 m and SSC of 10 ~ 100 mg/L. An adult oyster can filter 0.2 m^3 water per day, and an oyster filtration bed unit with a size of 30 m by 120 m can contain 360,000 oysters and therefore facilitate full

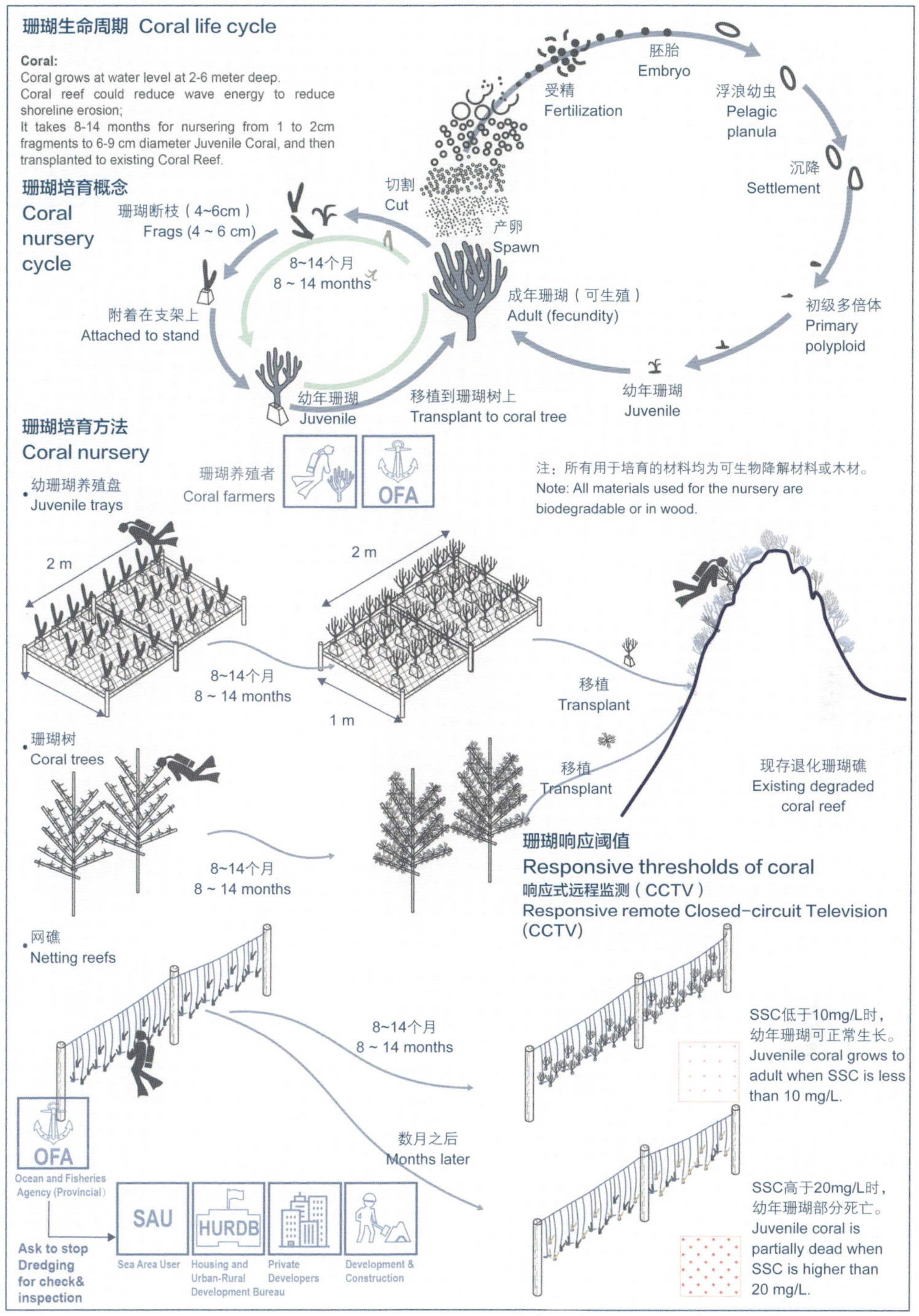

© 郭小雯 Kwok Siu Man
6

6. 珊瑚的生命周期、培育方式及响应机制

6. Life cycle, nursery, and response mechanism of corals

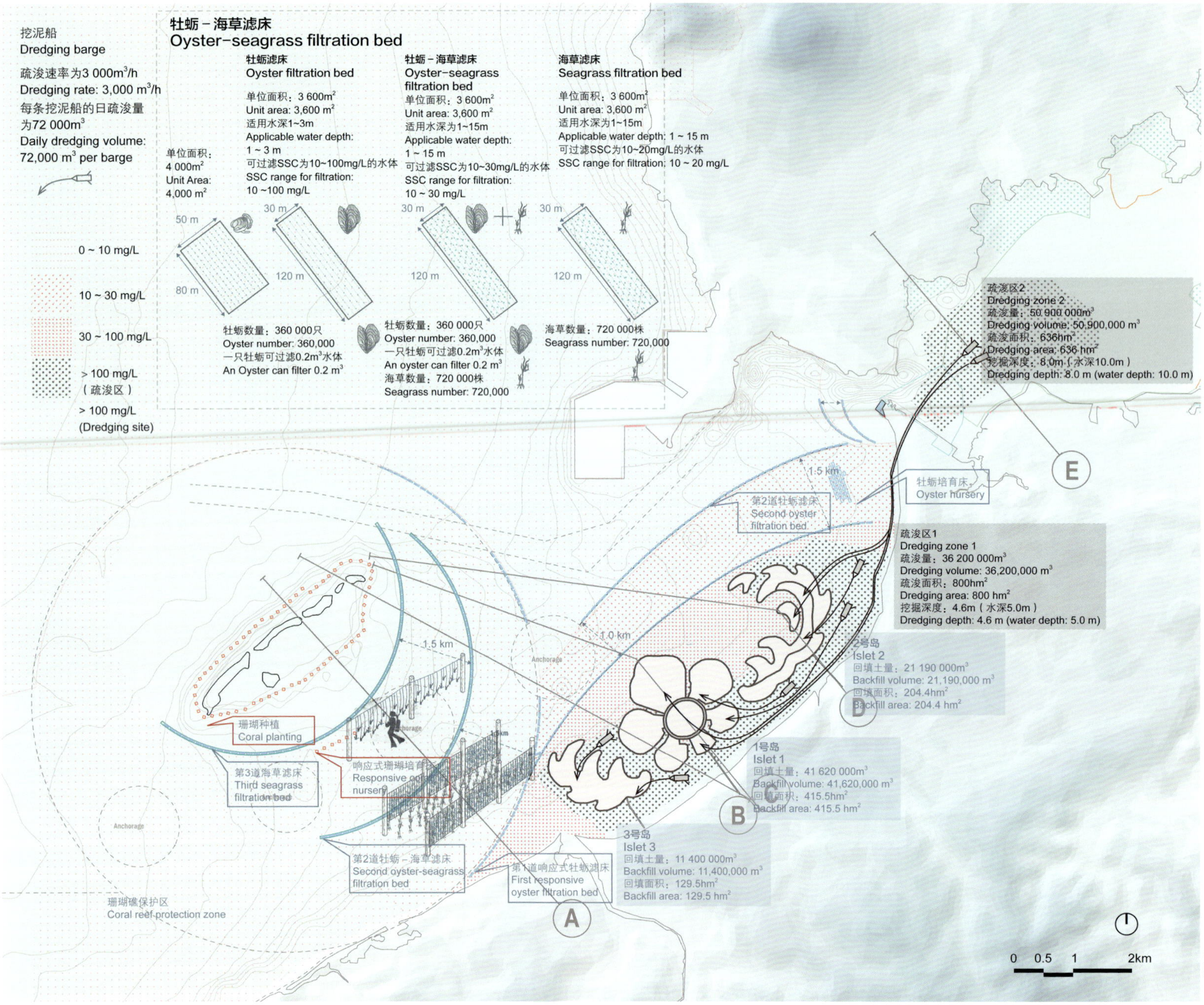

© 郭小曼 Kwok Siu Man
7

7. 海花岛生物修复措施应用布局

7. The layout of bioremediation layers for Ocean Flower Island project

filtration at a dredging rate at 3,000 m^3 per hour (i.e. 72,000 m^3 per barge per day).

Prototype 2 is a seagrass filtration bed, which can be deployed at locations with water depth of 1 ~ 15 m and SSC of 10 ~ 20 mg/L. The size of the seagrass filtration bed unit, which contains 720,000 seagrasses, is 30 m by 120 m.

Prototype 3 is an oyster-seagrass filtration bed, which can be deployed at locations with water level and SSC of 1 ~ 15 m and 10 ~ 100 mg/L, respectively. An oyster-seagrass filtration bed unit contains 360,000 oysters and 720,000 seagrasses with a size of 30 m by 120 m.

4.2 Responsive Bioremediation Design

For a dredging site with an initial SSC level of 100 mg/L, the application of the first responsive oyster filtration bed can reduce the SSC to 30 mg/L. After the second responsive oyster-seagrass filtration bed is used, the SSC level will further decline to 10 mg/L. However, contingencies or over-dredging events can cause the system to break

8. 生物修复措施布局横剖面透视图

8. A sectional perspective of bioremediation layers

down. To address such drawbacks, the oyster-seagrass-coral system is designed to respond to their corresponding physical conditions. Oysters will stop the filtration and close their shells if the SSC exceeds 100 mg/L, and seagrasses and corals will not mature if the water quality is below the normal thresholds (30 mg/L for seagrasses and 10 mg/L for corals).

The responsive oyster-seagrass-coral system can be monitored using Remote Closed-circuit Television (CCTV). If an oyster shell is opened, the oyster is performing filtration; otherwise, the SSC is higher than 100 mg/L. In the latter case, the dredging party might be instructed by the marine authority to stop for inspection. Similarly, if the seagrasses are not growing well, the SSC may be higher than 30 mg/L (Fig. 9).

The coral nursery is another responsive design that is implemented near the coral reef to assess if the water quality exceeds the healthy living threshold. Coral farmers cut the corals and nurse the juvenile on a tray or a coral tree. If the coral exhibits excellent growth during the months monitored by the remote underwater CCTV, the water quality is considered good and the coral will be transferred to the original coral habitat to increase the coral coverage. If the coral dies, the dredging activities will be stopped for inspection (Fig. 10).

Finally, a new project timeline for Ocean Flower Island is proposed, which incorporates a slightly revised land reclamation EIA procedure and adopts bioremediation programs (Fig. 11). The timeline indicates that the start of the land reclamation and ground-level construction of Ocean Flower Islet 1 will be delayed for at least 5 and 8 years, respectively, if the bioremediation process for the responsive oyster-seagrass-coral filtration bed runs smoothly before and during the dredging process and the EIA procedure is followed properly.

5 Conclusion

Adopting the responsive oyster-seagrass-coral filtration bed system as a bioremediation design and following the EIA procedures for the dredging process to maintain or enhance marine habitats, it takes years of longer time in the process for the assessment and negotiation among different stakeholders in the land reclamation and dredging process. The time cost is extremely high, and everything is counted in an ideal situation. The contingencies or delays in the project will prolong the project timeline. Under such situations, the stakeholders must carefully think before making decisions regarding land reclamation, because high time costs and bioremediation inputs contradict their original intention to obtain land in a fast and cheap way. Regardless of the time cost, the responsive bioremediation design is valuable to the ecosystem. The bioremediation prototypes can be used in any water body with high SSC levels to perform filtration and enhance the marine ecology.

Human activities affect the ecosystem and the ecology.

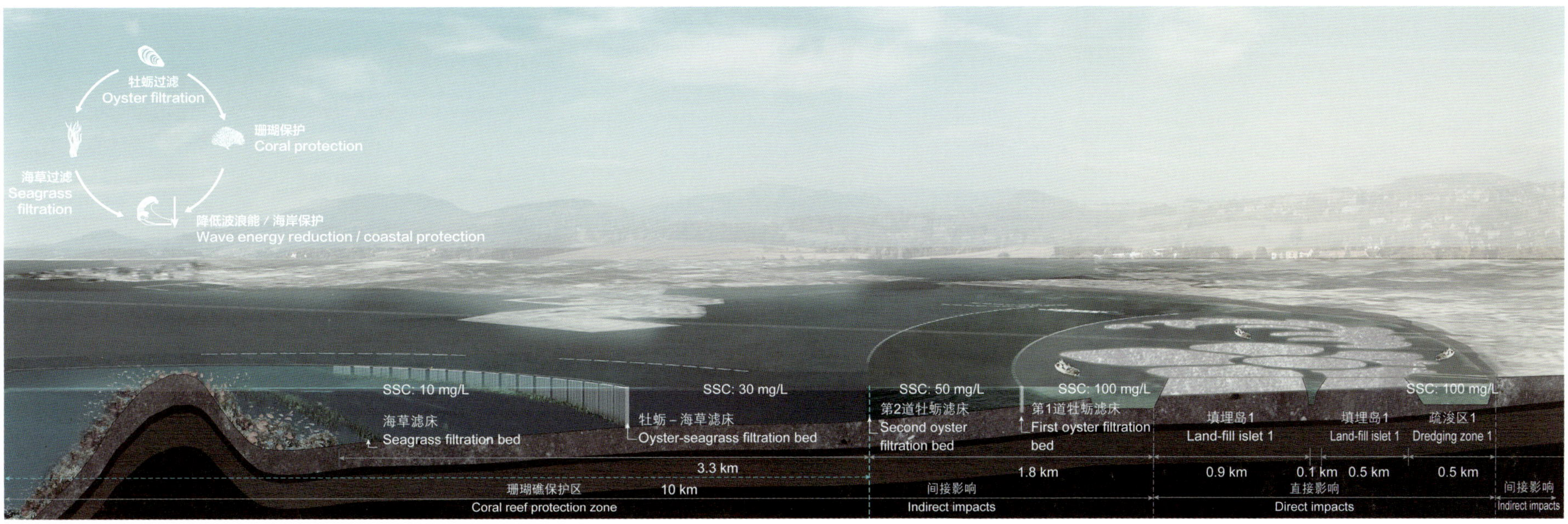

8

The collapse of the ecosystem poses risks to human lives and properties. The ecosystem is interrelated with different habitats to be a generating force, an active though complicated agent in the structuring of the city, and an agent that physically, biologically, and constructively engages in the various advanced biotechnologies, governances, public policies, and land dynamics. This study discusses the functions of the oyster-seagrass-coral habitat in their ecosystems, including their services and mechanisms. The filtration capacity of this system manifests a new and creative form of bioremediation practices, which are responsive, adaptive, and effective for marine and coastal protection, implying the concept that "design with nature, solve nature with nature." **LAF**

ACKNOWLEDGMENTS

This study was conducted under the Master in Landscape Architecture program at the University of Hong Kong. The author would like to thank her thesis supervisor, Ashley Scott Kelly, for his heartfelt support and guidance. Grateful acknowledgments are also dedicated to Professor Pierre Bélanger and Mr. Aimin Wang for their valuable comments and feedback on this project, and Assistant Professor Lu Xiaoxuan for her kind help.

9. 响应式牡蛎—海草—珊瑚滤床

9. Responsive oyster-seagrass-coral filtration bed

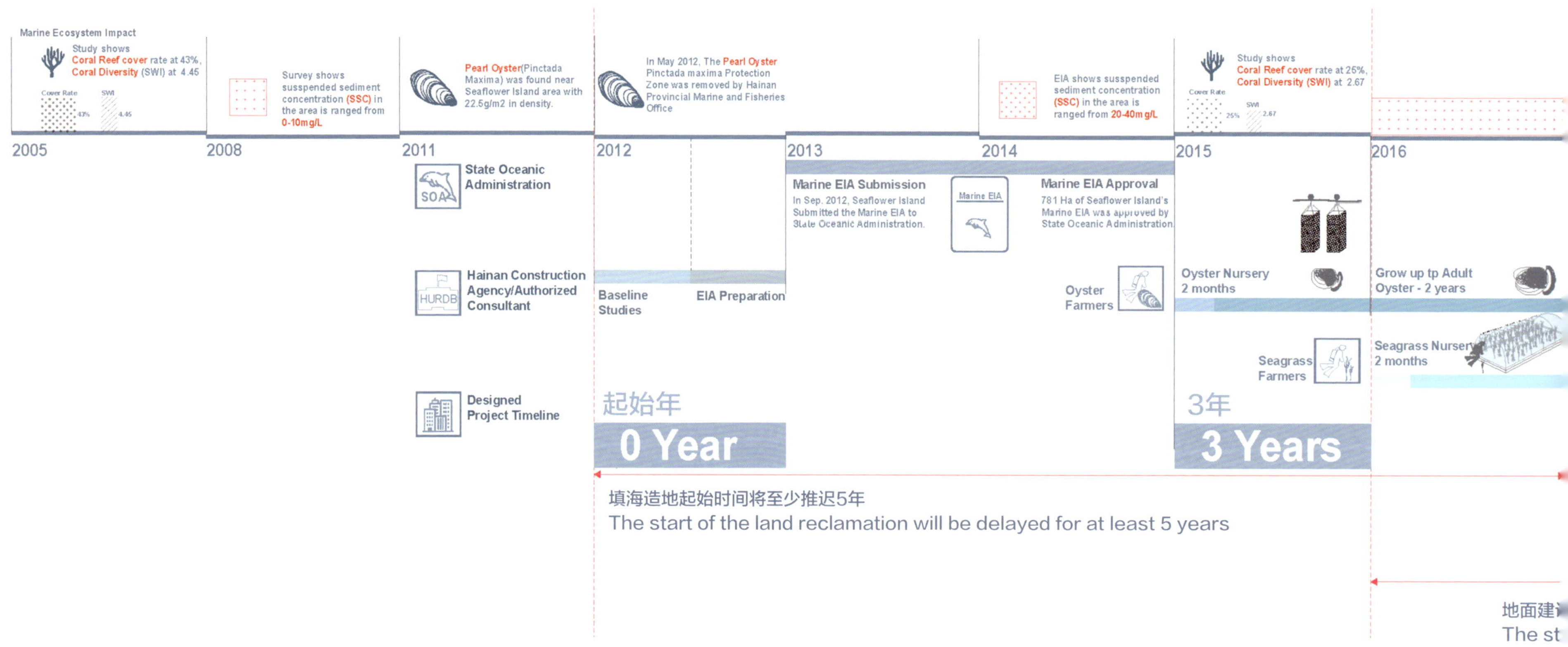

© 郭小曼 Kwok Siu Man

10

10. 响应式珊瑚培育
11. 新提出的海花岛工程进度表

10. Responsive coral nursery
11. The proposed timeline for Ocean Flower Island project

REFERENCES

[1] Wang, Y., Wang, T., & Fu, S. (2015). Discussion on the Current Situation and Management Countermeasures of Land Reclamation in Hainan Province. Ocean Development and management, (8), 56-59.

[2] The Central People's Government of the People's Republic of China. (2010, January 4). Several Opinions from the State Council on Construction and Development of Hainan International Tourism Island. Retrieved from http://www.gov.cn/zwgk/2010-01/04/content_1502531.htm

[3] Hughes, T. P., Huang, H., & Young, M. A. L. (2013). The Wicked Problem of China's Disappearing Coral Reefs. Conservation Biology, 27(2), 261-269. doi:10.1111/j.1523-1739.2012.01957.x

[4] Zhao, X., & Zhou, C. (2017, December 23). Hainan Authorities Colluded with Developer to Break Environmental Rules. Retrieved from http://china.caixin.com/2017-12-23/101188882.html

[5] Wang, X., Chen, Z., & Huang, Z. (2016). Preliminary Analysis of Pinctada Maxima in Nature Reserves along Coastal Area in the Northern South China Sea. South China Fisheries Science, (2), 110-115. doi:10.3969/j.issn.2095-0780.2016.02.016

[6] Huang, H., You, F., Lian, J., Zhang, C., Yang, J., Li, X., ... Dong, Z. (2012). Composition and Distribution of Hermatypic Coral in the North Western Sea Area of Hainan Island. Marine Sciences, (9), 64-74.

[7] Law of the People's Republic of China on the Management of Sea Areas Use. (2001). Article 18. Retrieved from http://www.law-lib.com/law/law_view.asp?id=16434

[8] Li, X. (2018, August 10). Hainan Rectified Several Illegal Reclamation Projects and Strictly Controlled Reclamation. Retrieved from http://finance.sina.com.cn/roll/2018-08-10/doc-ihhnunsq6084268.shtml

[9] Erftemeijer, P. L. A., Riegl, B., Hoeksema, B. W., & Todd, P. A. (2012). Environmental Impacts of Dredging and Other Sediment Disturbances on Corals: A Review. Marine Pollution Bulletin, 64(9), 1737-1765. doi:10.1016/j.marpolbul.2012.05.008

[10] Lenzen. M., Murray, S. A., Korte, B., & Dey, C. (2003). Environmental Impact Assessment Including Indirect Effects—A Case Study Using Input-Output Analysis. Environmental Impact Assessment Review, 23(3), 263-282. doi:10.1016/S0195-9255(02)00104-X

[11] Jones, R., Bessell-Browne, P., Fisher, R. P., Klonowski, W. M., & Slivkoff, M. (2016). Assessing the Impacts of Sediments from Dredging on Corals. Marine Pollution Bulletin, 102(1), 9-29. doi:10.1016/j.marpolbul.2015.10.049

[12] Maclaren, V., & Whitney, J. B. (1985). New Directions in Environmental Impact Assessment in Canada. Toronto: Methuen Publications.

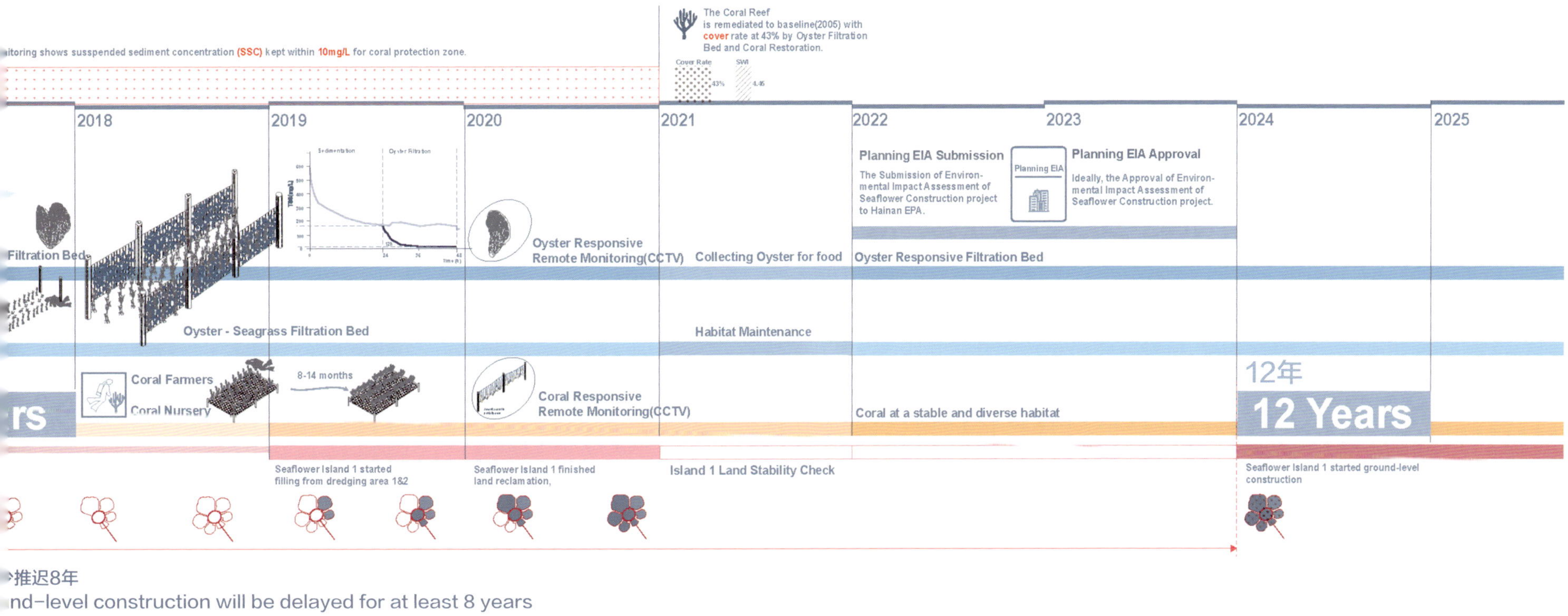

© 郭小曼 Kwok Siu Man

11

本文引用格式 / PLEASE CITE THIS ARTICLE AS

Korneeva, A., & Turanli, I. (2020). Earth Choreographer: Remediating Obsolete Grounds of the Future. Landscape Architecture Frontiers, 8(4), 164-173. https://doi.org/10.15302/J-LAF-1-050023

大地舞台：面向未来的废弃土地修复

EARTH CHOREOGRAPHER: REMEDIATING OBSOLETE GROUNDS OF THE FUTURE

https://doi.org/10.15302/J-LAF-1-050023 收稿时间 RECEIVED DATE / 2020-08-02 中图分类号 / TU984 文献标识码 / B

安娜 · 科尔尼瓦
雪城大学建筑学院建筑学学士

厄尔玛克 · 图兰里
雪城大学建筑学院建筑学学士

Anna KORNEEVA*
Bachelor of Architecture at School of Architecture, Syracuse University

Irmak TURANLI
Bachelor of Architecture at School of Architecture, Syracuse University

*Corresponding Author
Address: 276 Clifton Pl, Brooklyn, NY, 11216, USA
Email: akorneev@syr.edu

摘要

作为一种设计方法，“大地舞台”聚焦于废弃油田景观的规划设计与功能重构。本文所介绍的项目以此方法命名，探讨了废弃工业用地修复和再利用的迫切需求与机遇，以在未来几十年间——乃至工业用地达到预期使用年限后——不断发掘土地的开发潜力，制定相应的预景，并在设计过程中保留场地和景观曾遭受破坏的痕迹。在技术不断发展、自然资源危机日益加剧的背景下，本文回答了以下问题：1）生产性景观的“一手保护，一手重建”意味着什么？2）如何描绘一个不断被机械重塑的地平面，以及随之变化的人类与非人类活动区域的边界？3）一片不断自我消解和重建的场地是什么样？

该项目采用动态设计方法提出了2025~2080年的若干预景设计，使场地能够根据不断变化的使用者需求和利益取向持续发展，回应气候变化和资源枯竭危机，为废弃景观的改造和复兴提供原型参考。

关键词

石油开采；废弃景观；修复；再利用；原型；夯土

ABSTRACT

Earth Choreographer is a design methodology that focuses on choreographing, scoring, and de-territorializing the landscape of an obsolete oil field. The project introduced in this article, titled Earth Choreographer, explores the imperatives and opportunities in remediation and repurposing of obsolete industrial sites, aiming to continuously investigate the potential of the land and possible scenarios over decades—even when the intended life cycle of the industrial site is over. It presents a design process that recognizes the ruination of the ground and the landscape. By acknowledging the evolving technologies and ever-increasing preoccupation with natural resources, it answers the following questions: 1) What happens when a productive landscape is sought to be both partially preserved and recreated? 2) How to represent a ground plane that is being constantly reconfigured by machines with ever-changing boundaries of spaces for human and non-human occupation? And 3) what does a site that constantly erases and reconstructs itself look like?

With several scenarios from 2025 to 2080, this project acts as a prototype for inhabiting obsolete landscapes by addressing climate change and depletion of resources. Its dynamic design methodology allows the site to constantly evolve and change over time based on the needs and interests of its occupiers.

KEYWORDS

Oil Extraction; Obsolete Landscape; Remediation; Repurposing; Prototype; Rammed Earth

编辑 王胤瑜 **翻译** 李慧彦 王胤瑜
EDITED BY WANG Yinyu **TRANSLATED BY** LI Huiyan WANG Yinyu

1 废弃

化石燃料产业是全世界最主要的能源制造者之一，但由于自然资源的日趋枯竭和化石燃料对气候变化的负面影响，未来人类将逐渐降低对这一产业的依赖。对于许多工业场地而言，生产活动的结束即意味着它们将面临被遗弃的境遇[1]。随着技术的不断进步、相关监管和环境政策的日益完善，以及关注自然资源的共识越发广泛，建筑师们不断致力于改造废弃的后工业场地，以使其重获新生。“大地舞台”项目首先研究了那些一达到预期使用寿命即被改作他用的工业用地，并将不同类型的废弃设施——如水塔、储气罐、地下矿坑隧道、油罐及防空洞等——整理汇编，以便分析比较改造后的场地用途。结果表明，大多数废弃工业设施及场所都被改造成了娱乐休闲设施[2]。然而，此类改造方式无法解决当代的环境问题，而且这些一成不变的设计和项目也终将废弃。本项目意在打破这种先例，提出可应对持续变化的动态设计方案。

2 选址

随后，项目选取位于加利福尼亚州洛杉矶市中心的美国最大连片城市油田——英格尔伍德油田为设计场地（图1）。该油田发现于1924年，于同年投入开采，至今已产油近4亿桶。油田按照传统方式开采，即在钻井平台上安装独立的抽油机，整个场地完全开放、一览无遗，场地附近还有许多住宅、学校和休闲公园。如今，油田占地约4km²，共有1 601座油井，其中696座仍在运转，但这处油田很快可能因石油枯竭而停产[3]。于是，“大地舞台”提出了针对废弃后的英格尔伍德油田的修复方案。加利福尼亚州曾是美国最大的石油产地之一，但其石油工业一直在走下坡路，因此英格尔伍德油田将不是唯一面临此种命运的油田[4]（图2）。面对越来越多的废弃油田，本项目可作为一种修复原型，帮助应对气候变化和资源枯竭等环境问题。

1

1. 加利福尼亚州洛杉矶市的油井分布

1. The distribution of oil wells in Los Angeles, California

3 核心问题

为了制定场地修复方案，项目首先调研了石油生产过程对场地造成的影响，即分析石油生产造成的土壤毒化与污染情况，并确定这些有害物质的分布（图3）。截至2020年，场地上仍有相当多的废弃油井未被妥善封顶[4]。由于这些油井可能会向土壤中释放毒素，项目提出采用物理、生物和化学的综合性方法净化土壤，并封闭油井（图4）。

上述工作的重要目的之一是解决土壤资源（包括已挖出的土方和未经开挖的土壤）有限这一难题。因此，项目提出将场地上的既有土方加工成夯土，可作为主要建筑材料。采用“随挖随填”的方法，可就地加工钻探油井时产生的多余土方，无需从他处获取建筑材料（图4）。

在基于土地现状明确了现有景观的改造优先级之后，笔者提出项目应该在灵活适应现有场地的同时，响应气候变化和资源枯竭危机，并决定将场地打造为一个服务于美国国家航空航天局，以及特斯拉和欧特克等未来科技公司的试验场，为化石燃料等有限资源的替代品研发提供支持（图5）。

试验场将提供多种配套工作空间，如用于装配和实体建模的创客工厂，以及空中交通模拟实验室。这些空间的规模和形式可根据公司需要量身定制，并依循被石油生产活动塑造的地表而建，以纪念场地的原始景观及其变迁。

4 预景

在未来数十年间，现有油田将逐渐荒废，闲置土地不断增多，由此可逐步重构油田景观，并不断推广这种新的改造模式。本次研究采用时间—情境设计方法模拟了一系列针对废弃场地的动态响应，以展示在人类及非人类主体的共同作用下，场地如何通过建造永久性构筑物、资源重组，以及重置功能区划实现持续的重构。

笔者用基于未来特定时间和地点的若干切片来展示设计策略，并逐一细化这些预景，用不同类型的线条代表每个切片中的地形、地理和时间信息。未来每一个新的发展阶段都会引入新线条，表示新的主体开始发挥作用。首个预景设定于2025年，重构活动将首先从远离石油生产区、人口最为稠密的已封闭油井区开始（图6）。

2030年，设计重点将转移到现状炼油厂附近的试验场。虽然最终整个场地都将被改造，但部分已达到设计使用年限的能源基础设施仍将按原貌保留下来，以强调过去和未来的并存。项目意在正面展示场地上废弃石油基础设施留下的痕迹，而场地修复的实现不仅需要情怀，更需要新技术的多管齐下。

鉴于油田的使用主体将不断变化，这一过程离不开多种机器人、无人机和机械的参与，以及人类和非人类主体的共同作用。不同主体将分组承担不同的任务，合作建造试验场。

到2040年，既有的休闲公园和生产性景观将在场地内共存（图7）。项目提出在紧邻现有石油基础设施的地方建造一座更具可持续性的能

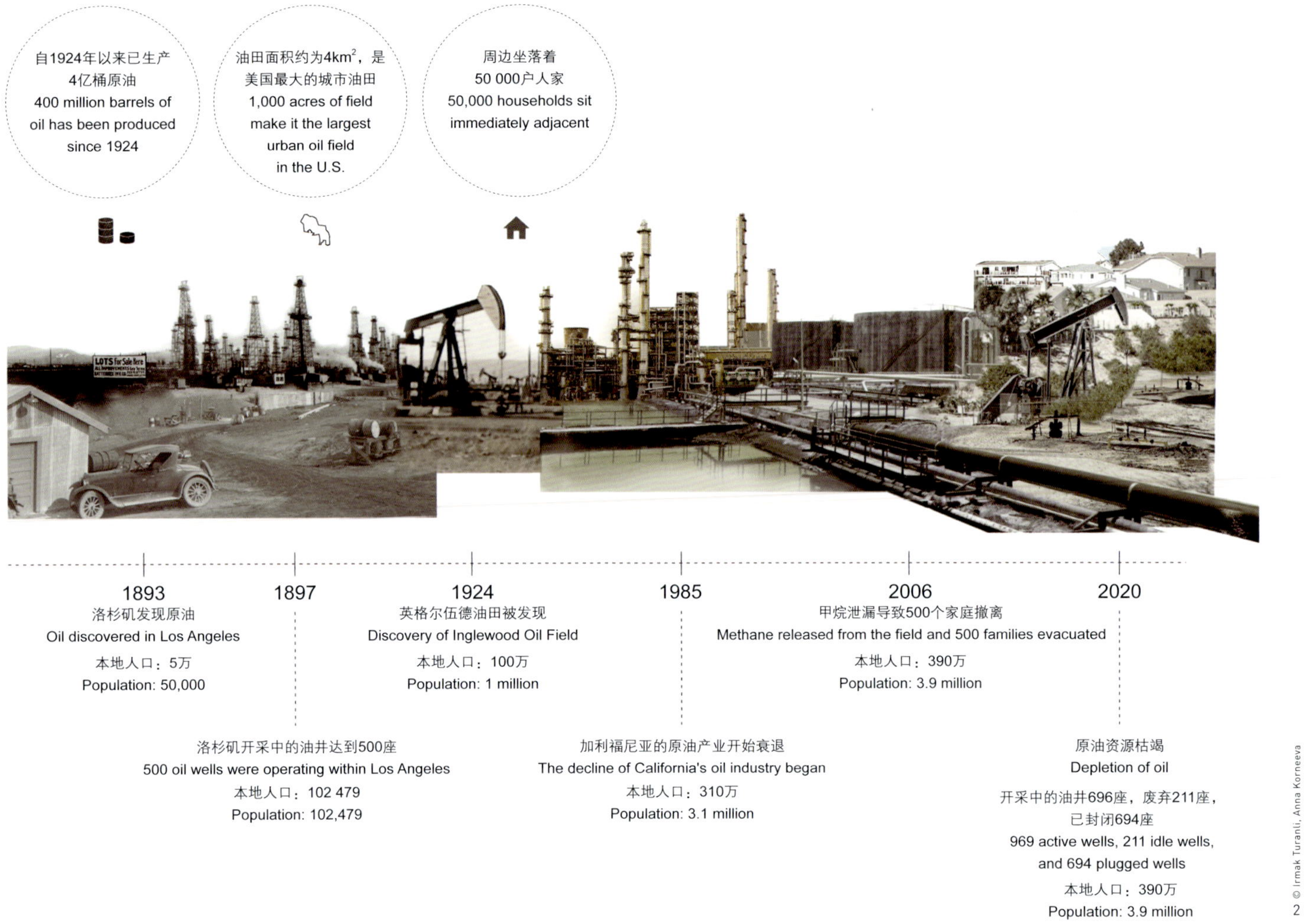

2. 英格尔伍德油田发展历程

2. A timeline showing the development of Inglewood Oil Field's Oil Production

源生产设施，以在新、旧能源生产设施之间形成对比。

在地面上，富有活力的休闲公园和重工业建设场地比邻而立。这促使团队进一步思考如何妥善处理两者之间的边界，从而确保人类活动与非人类主体的施工作业互不干扰（图8）。

项目将地面作为协调地上和地下能源生产的媒介：在地上安装太阳能能源装置并设计一个可将健身脚踏车产生的动能转化为电能的健身房，地下则是废弃石油基础设施的遗迹。在本项目中，原本隐于地下的传统能源基础设施通过图绘形式得以展现，并在大地表面与未来的能源生产模式碰撞交汇，形成鲜明的对比。

到2060年，参与项目建设的人类劳动力数量有望大幅减少（图9）。随着机器人和人工智能技术的发展，原本由人类主导的工作将逐步由机器人承担，大部分人力将转而从事无人机和机器人的维护工作，并对机器人进行编程与分组，使其可以利用夯土建造构筑物[5]。这一转变不仅可解决本项目中建筑工人稀缺的问题，也为整个建造行业面临的人力资源短缺提供了解决方案，展现了建造场景下人类与非人类主体之间的新型互动关系（图10）。

2080年，项目将关注场地邻近城市的区域，此处的建筑形式设计应使试验场的一部分对场地外的公众可见，使未来科技公司的工作在一定程度上得到监督。

5 原型

虽然洛杉矶当前仍然是美国最大的产油城市，但其石油工业已然走向衰落，大片油田的废弃将成为必然。本项目为此类场地的复兴提供了一个原型范例，展示了利用废弃景观的新方式（图11）。

“大地舞台”项目深受动态设计方法论的影响，可根据场地使用者的需求与利益取向，随时间推移不断变化。该项目通过时间—情境设计方法展示了废弃场地的动态未来，是一种可从根本上修复并重构废弃景观功能的关键性途径。**LAF**

3. 英格尔伍德油田毒化土壤分布图

3. The map of soil toxicity for Inglewood Oil Field

1 The Obsolescence

Although fossil fuel industries are some of the largest energy producers in the world, the dependency on these industries is expected to decrease because of the depletion of natural resources and their negative effects on climate change. As the activities on the industrial sites will come to an end, many sites will soon become obsolete[1]. With evolving technologies, more complex regulatory and environmental policies and ever-increasing preoccupation with natural resources, architects have been designing new lives for obsolete post-industrial sites. This project, Earth Choreographer, began with the investigation of those industrial sites that are used outside of their original purpose once they reach the end of the intended life cycle. To analyze and compare them, a catalog of obsolete industrial facility types was produced to show the new programs deployed at post-industrial sites. The catalog included water towers, gasometers, tunnels of underground coal mines, oil tanks, air raid shelters and more. Most of these sites were repurposed for recreation and pleasure purposes[2]. Such uses fail to embrace contemporary environmental issues and their static, non-flexible designs and programs are also bound to eventually become obsolete. Therefore, the project is focused on a dynamic design that is constantly in flux as opposed to previously seen static examples.

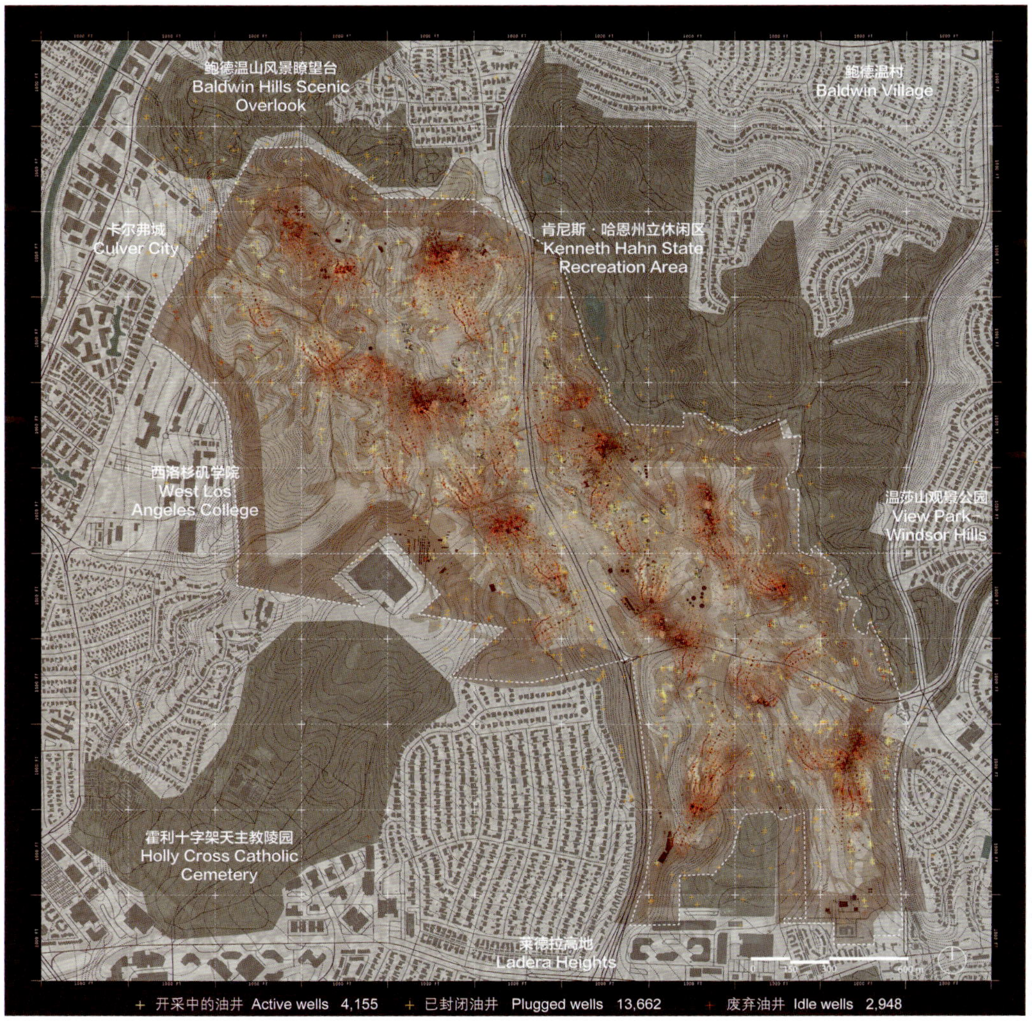

© Irmak Turanli, Anna Korneeva

3

2 The Location

After investigating various obsolete precedents, Inglewood Oil Field, the largest contiguous urban oil field in the U.S. located in the center of Los Angeles, California (Fig. 1), was selected. Discovered in 1924 and in continuous production ever since, it has produced almost 400 million barrels of oil. The oil field is visually entirely open to the public, and it was developed in the traditional manner of individual pump jacks on drilling pads. There are many homes, schools, and recreational parks adjacent to the oil field. Today, the oil field covers approximately 1,000 acres and there are a total of 1,601 wells, 696 of which are still active. However, it is now reaching the end of its lifetime as the oil in the field is almost depleted[3]. The project proposes Inglewood Oil Field's remediation once its oil extraction comes to an end. Although California used to be one of the biggest oil producers in the U.S., its oil industry has been in decline and therefore Inglewood Oil Field will not be the only field that is reaching its intended life cycle[4] (Fig. 2). Earth Choreographer acts as a prototype for the remediation of an increasing number of obsolete oil fields by addressing climate change and depletion of resources.

3 The Parameters

In order to choreograph the remediation of the site, the existing land conditions and materials created by the oil production process were investigated. Firstly, the toxicity and the contamination of the soil were analyzed and located (Fig. 3). As of 2020, there are a significant number of idle wells on the site that are not yet properly capped[4]. As they might be emitting toxins to the soil, a combination of physical, biological, and chemical strategies were deployed in order to decontaminate the soil and plug the well (Fig. 4).

An important goal of such work was to acknowledge and address the finite supply of the earth resources in terms of both extracted and raw materials. Therefore, Earth Choreographer used already extracted soil on the site and converted it into rammed earth which is intended to be the primary construction material. For this purpose, the "cut and fill" method was deployed to directly turn extracted excess soil from the drilling sites of oil wells into rammed earth as construction materials, instead of bringing new soil from elsewhere (Fig. 4).

After analyzing the existing land conditions and determining the priorities while working with the existing landscape, it was concluded that the project should be flexible to adapt to the existing site conditions while responding to climate change and depletion of resources. The project is intended to be an experimental testing ground targeted for future technology institutes and companies such as NASA, Tesla, and Autodesk which work on new technologies as substitutes for fossil fuels and other resources in depletion (Fig. 5).

The testing ground will be designed to include various programs for these companies, such as makerspaces for fabrication and mock-ups, and simulation labs for air mobility. Their scales and forms will vary depending on the type of space the companies need, and follow the existing topography which has been already altered and traced by the oil production industry, giving tribute to the original landscape and its alterations.

4. 土壤修复流程框架

4. Soil remediation framework

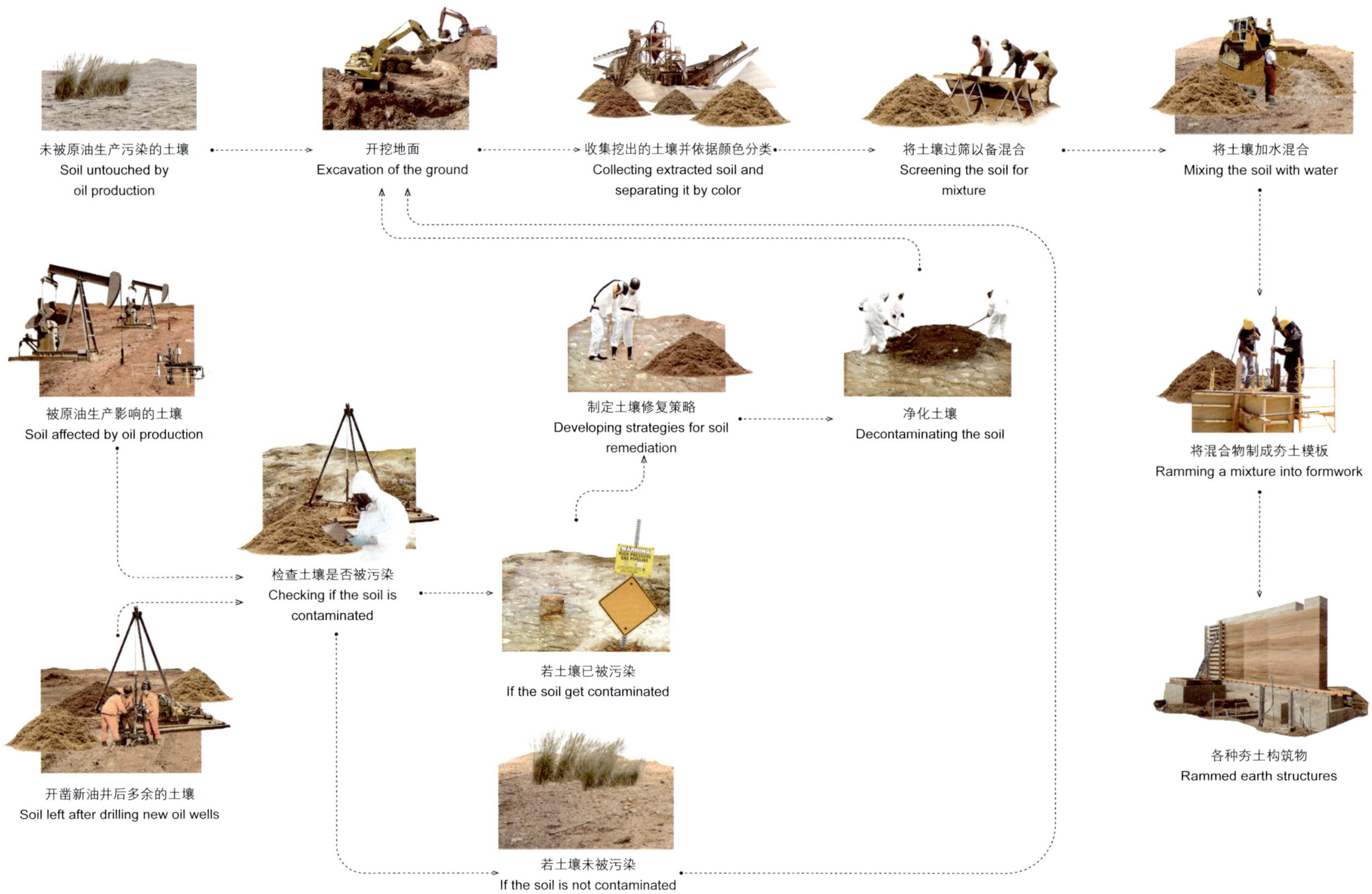

4 © Irmak Turanli, Anna Korneeva

5. 2030年预景下的场地透视图

5. A perspective of the scenario in 2030

5 © Irmak Turanli, Anna Korneeva

4 The Choreography

This project proposes a constant reconfiguration of the oil field's landscape which will be reclaimed parcel by parcel as it becomes available, and continue growing and extending in phases over the coming decades. Therefore, Earth Choreographer exemplifies a temporal-situational design methodology to simulate a kinetic response to obsolete sites, which presents the ideas of continuous reformatting through permanent construction, reconfiguration, and de-territorialization of the ground by human and non-human agencies.

The proposed choreography of the site was shown as frames picked from certain times and locations. Layers of lines in each frame represent the topographic, geographic, and temporal mechanical information. With each phase new lines are introduced to represent the new actors starting to play out in this process. Starting in 2025, the speculation for choreographing the earth will begin from the most populated areas of capped wells, farthest from the active ones (Fig. 6).

In 2030, the focus will be relocated to the testing ground close to the existing oil refinery. Although the whole site will be reclaimed, some energy infrastructures for oil production will remain untouched even after they reach the end of intended life cycle. By suggesting such a remediation strategy, the juxtaposition between the past and the future was emphasized. This was intended to reveal the traces left by obsolete oil infrastructures on the site, arguing that reclamation of the site can be achieved through radical technological juxtapositions without having to be nostalgic.

As the oil field is permanently choreographed for its changing occupiers, a variety of robots, drones, and machines will contribute to this process. Both human and non-human actors will work on the site. The actors are choreographed according to the specific tasks they are assigned to, working collaboratively towards constructing the testing ground.

As the focus moves to 2040, the site will be a juxtaposition of the existing recreational park and the productive landscape (Fig. 7). A more sustainable energy production facility adjacent to the existing oil infrastructure is proposed, creating a tension between old and new energy production facilities.

Above the ground, there is the juxtaposition between the active recreational park and the heavy industrial construction site. This leads to further investigation about how to deal with the boundary of public active spaces in close proximity to construction sites and how to sustain a boundary between human and non-human actors (Fig. 8).

The ground will become the medium for negotiating the energy production above and below the ground. Above, solar energy will be harnessed and electric power will be generated by the kinetic energy of the stationary bikes in a gym, while below the traces of the obsolete oil infrastructure can be observed. These traces of past and future energy sources will collide and entangle at the surface of the Earth. This collision is exposed by revealing invisible infrastructure through the graphic representation used throughout this project.

By the year of 2060, Earth Choreographer expects to have fewer people involved in the construction field (Fig. 9). With the

6. 2025年预景下的场地鸟瞰图

6. A bird's eye view of the scenario in 2025

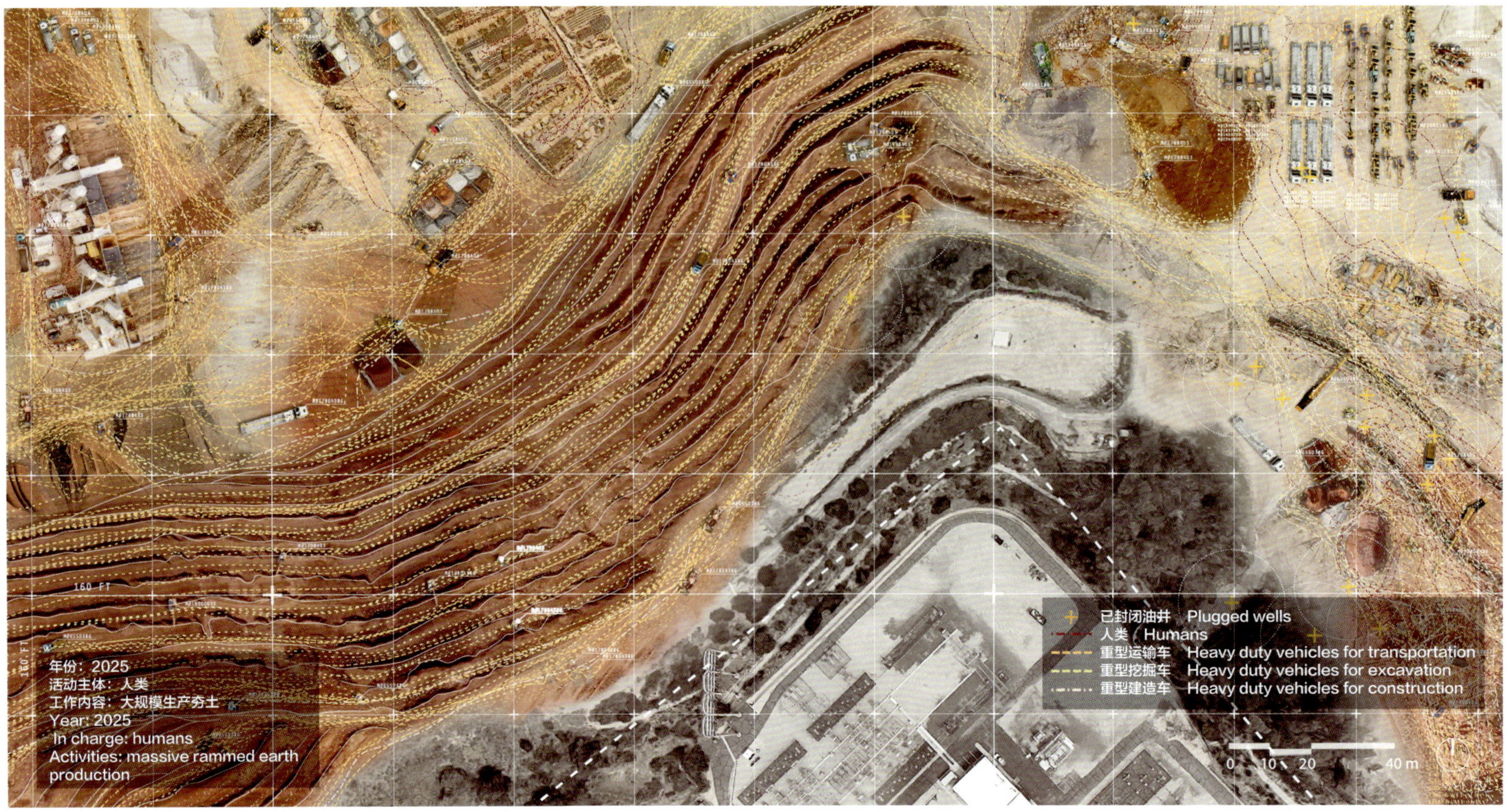

6 © Irmak Turanli, Anna Korneeva

7. 2040年预景下的场地鸟瞰图
8. 2040年预景下的场地透视图

7. A bird's eye view of the scenario in 2040
8. A perspective of the scenario in 2040

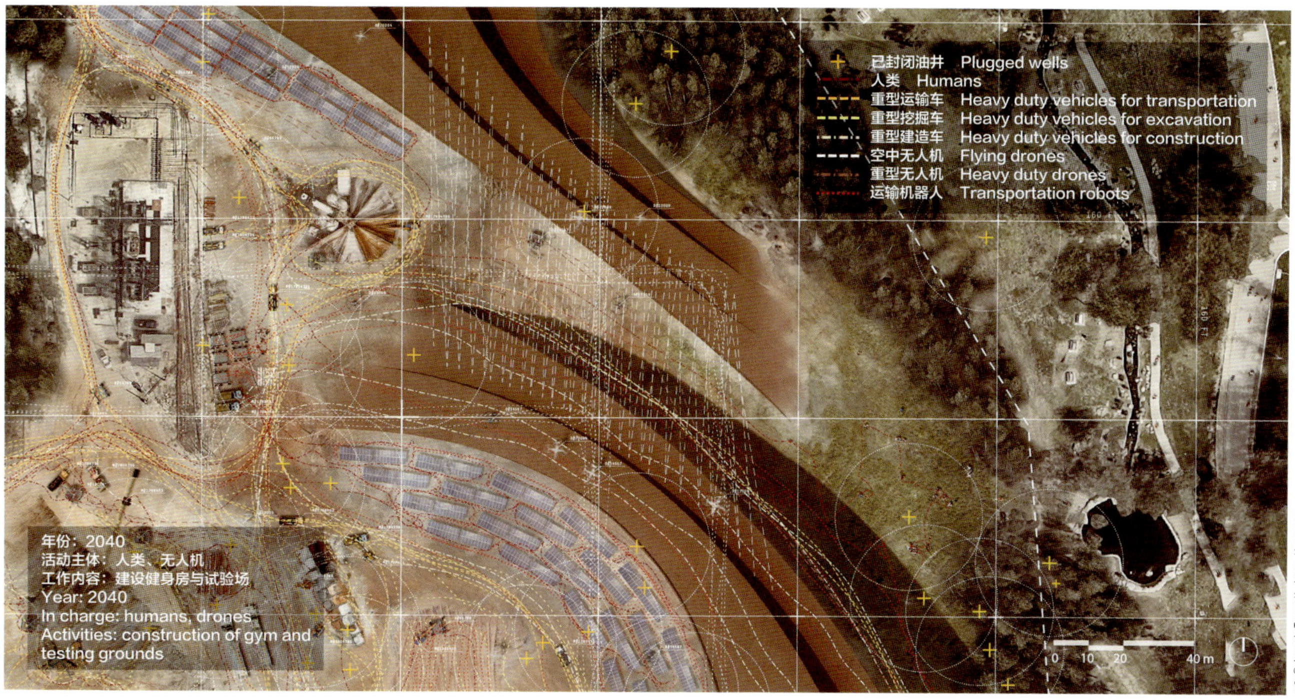

7

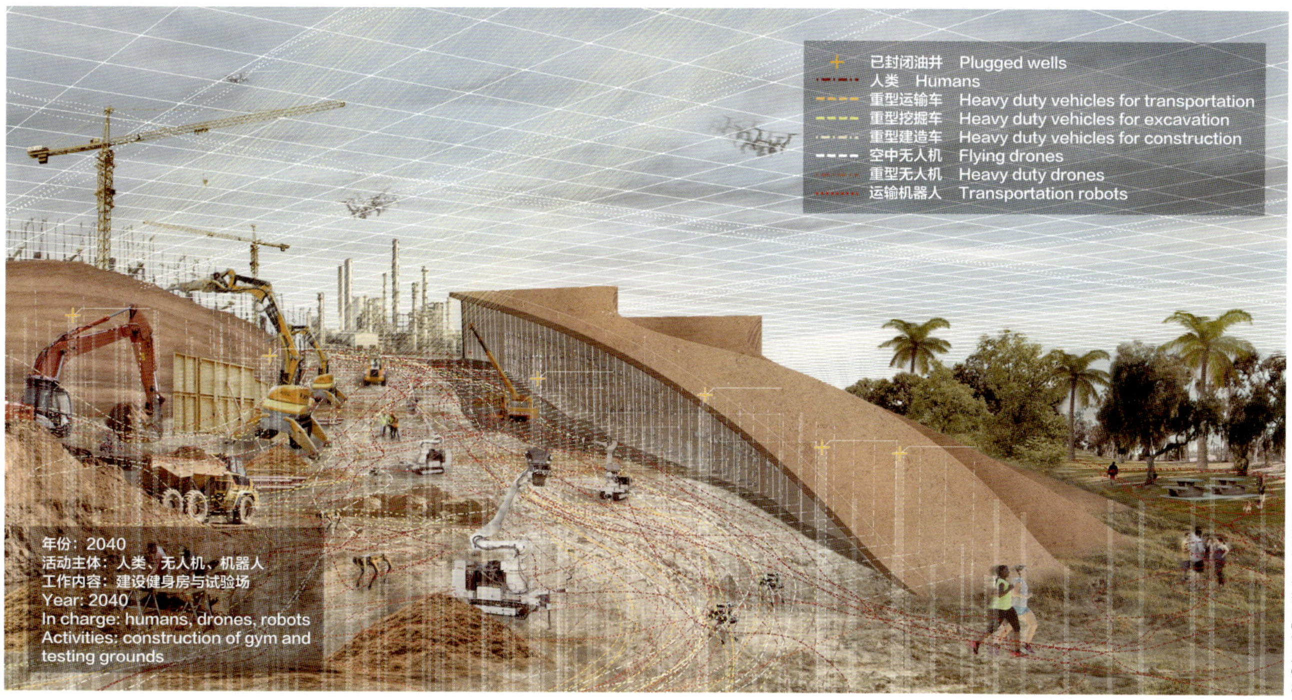

8

evolving robotic and AI technologies, there will be a shift from human labor to robotics in the construction industry. Most of the human labor will be shifted towards maintaining drones and robots which will be programmed to work in teams to build structures using rammed earth[5]. This shift can address the scarcity of human labors in this project and in the construction industry, showing how new relationships and interactions between human and non-human will be choreographed in the construction site (Fig. 10).

In 2080, the focus will be shifted to the area adjacent to the city fabric, where the building form is designed to allow the testing ground to be partially exposed to the public.This allows

© Irmak Turanli, Anna Korneeva
9

© Irmak Turanli, Anna Korneeva
10

9. 2060年预景下的场地鸟瞰图
10. 2060年预景下的场地透视图

9. A bird's eye view of the scenario in 2060
10. A perspective of the scenario in 2060

the work of the future technology companies to be transparent to a certain extent.

5 The Prototype

Although Los Angeles remains as the largest urban oil field in the US, currently its oil industry is in decline and will ultimately result in an abundance of obsolete sites. This project is meant to be a prototype for those sites by exemplifying new ways of inhabiting obsolete landscapes of the future (Fig. 11).

Earth Choreographer is heavily influenced by a dynamic design methodology and acts as a prototype by constantly evolving and changing over time based on the needs and interests of its occupiers. By emphasizing a temporal-situational

11. 2080年预景下的场地轴测剖面图

11. An isometric section of the scenario in 2080

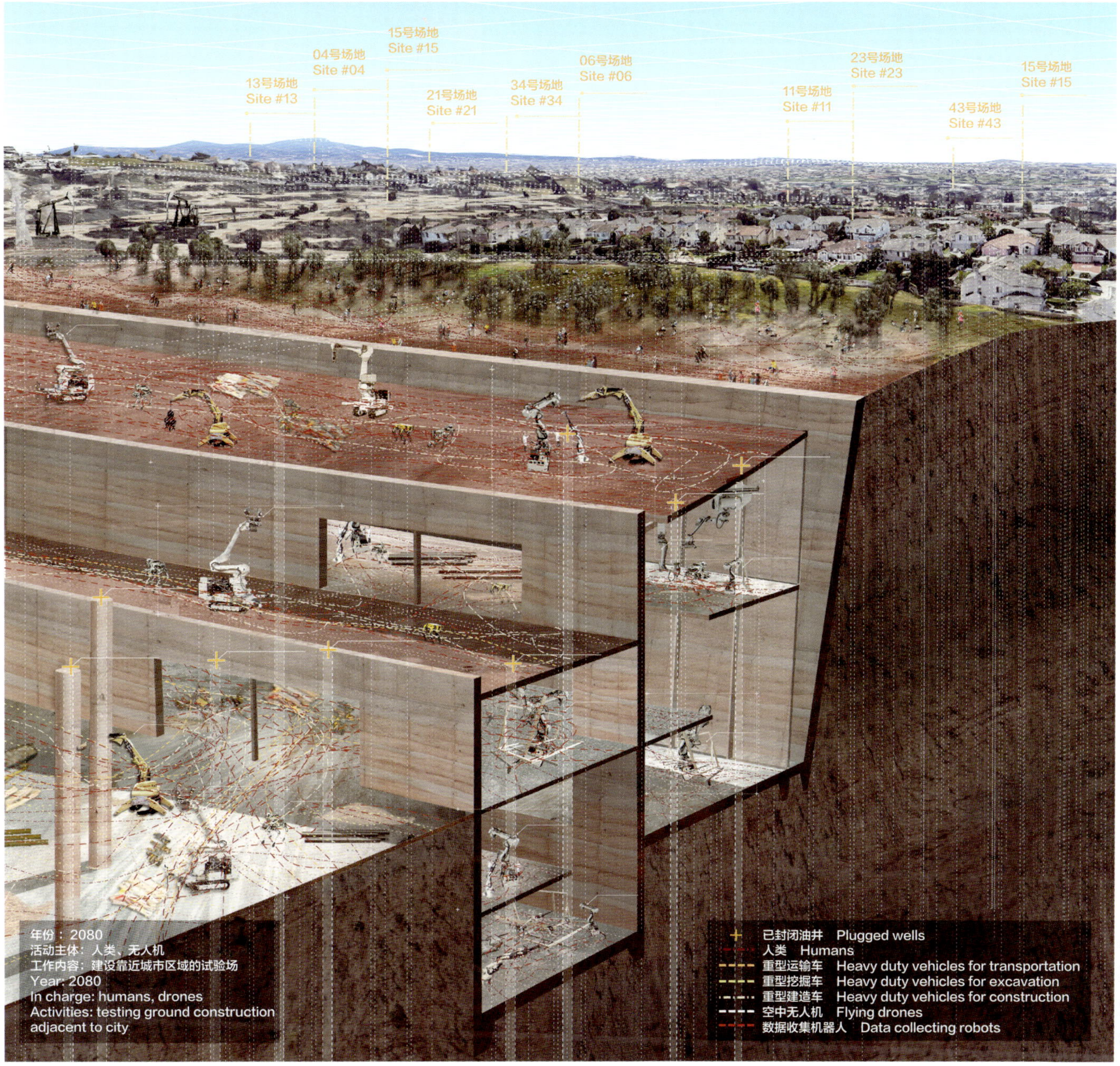

11

design methodology, it seeks to bring a kinetic response to obsolete sites, providing a pivotal speculation for radically remediating and reprogramming obsolete landscapes of the future. **LAF**

REFERENCES

[1] McGlashen, A. (2020, April 14). Oil Market Woes Raise Concerns that More Wells Will Be 'Orphaned'. Retrieved from https://www.audubon.org/news/oil-market-woes-raise-concerns-more-wells-will-be-orphaned

[2] McKenna, J. (2018, December 21). Abandoned Mines Could Become the Farms of the Future. Retrieved from https://www.weforum.org/agenda/2018/12/abandoned-mines-could-become-the-farms-of-the-future/

[3] Norimitsu, O. (2014, July 7). A California Oil Field Yields Another Prized Commodity. Retrieved from https://www.nytimes.com/2014/07/08/us/california-drought-chevron-oil-field-water-irrigation.html

[4] Olalde, M., & Menezes, R. (2020, February 6). The Toxic Legacy of Old Oil Wells: California's Multibillion-Dollar Problem. Retrieved from https://www.latimes.com/projects/california-oil-well-drilling-idle-cleanup/

[5] Markoff, J. (2012, August 18). Skilled Work, Without the Worker. Retrieved from https://cn.nytimes.com/business/20121022/c22applesix/en-us/.

贵阳 远洋 · 万和世家

E P O E T I C D W E L L I N G
WWW.GZ-SPI.COM

广亩项目实景：
成都｜德商 & 朗诗·麓湖熙华天玺

（图片：深圳福田记忆公园实景）

L&A 奥雅
TANG SHAN LA-VONDERLAND SHADOW PLAY PARK
唐 山 皮 影 主 题 乐 园
L&A DESIGN
TO CREATE A BETTER ENVIRONMENT
奥雅设计 创造更美好的人居环境
唐山皮影主题乐园是奥雅设计、洛嘉儿童共同打造的以创意设计为先导的EPC项目。乐园的设计理念——“舞动的皮影，行进的唐山”和“最古老的动漫、最时尚的皮影”，是对唐山文化的全新诠释，也是对皮影非物质文化遗产的传承与发展。唐山皮影主题乐园是洛嘉儿童对于非物质文化遗产的新尝试，是探索实践非物质文化遗产活化的一条切实可行的新路径，洛嘉儿童是其全部无动力设施的供应商，从策划、规划、设计、研发、建造、安装、投产、运营全程参与。
因为乐园，因为快乐、爱上唐山这座城。唐山皮影乐园集家庭式游玩、研学、拓展为一体，以其趣味性、教育性、科技性、挑战性荣获2020第四届ELA国际景观大奖年度十大景观、2019第四届REARD全球地产设计大奖旅游类景观银奖。
奥雅设计于2001年在改革开放前沿深圳蛇口创立，公司前身为1999年在香港成立的奥雅园境师事务所。经过近二十年的引领发展，奥雅设计以景观规划设计为基础，逐渐发展成为新型城镇化土地开发及综合文旅开发的大型文创机构。目前以深圳为总部，在全国各地设有18家分子公司，拥有由1200余位行业精英组成的国际化专业团队。
深圳南山蛇口兴华路南海意库5号楼3层 / 4层404 T 0755 26826690 F 0755 26826694 E sz@aoya-hk.com W www.aoya-hk.com
城乡规划 URBAN-RURAL PLANNING
开发策划 DEVELOPMENT STRATEGY
城市设计 URBAN DESIGN
文创旅游 CULTURAL TOURISM
景观设计 LANDSCAPE ARCHITECTURE
招商运营 INVESTMENT AND OPERATION
建筑设计 ARCHITECTURE
公共艺术 PUBLIC ART
生态规划 ECOLOGICAL PLANNING
品牌运营 BRANDING & MEDIA
广告 / AD

北京“千荷泻露”大桥

西安城市生态公园

“时空的扭转”景观盒

景观盒位于北京市大兴区
内部空间约 30m²
整体采用轻质高强的 FRP 复合材料
与内部钢结构一体成型
外部呈三角曲面形
利用未来概念造型体现时空的扭转
代表大兴永兴河生态恢复的华丽转身

设计单位：土人设计

北京“千荷泻露”大桥

北京“千荷泄露”大桥位于通州中心商务区
全长 210m
主体为钢拱结构
外部自由曲面封护造型采用复合材料夹心芯板
面积约 9000 ㎡
景观步道如同四条白色飘带穿在八片荷瓣中间
呈现“千荷泻露”的唯美造型

设计单位：北京市政设计院

重庆龙湖两江长滩原麓示范区入口

重庆龙湖两江长滩原麓示范区
位于重庆两江新区龙兴镇
入口处的弧形曲面大门长 37m
由复合材料组装而成
形态优美
气势磅礴

设计单位：重庆纬图景观

秦皇岛红飘带公园

秦皇岛红飘带公园位于河北省秦皇岛市
2006 年竣工
园中座椅全长约 600m
首创集观赏、照明、科普和休憩功能于一体的
复合材料景观制品
2007 年荣获美国景观设计师协会景观设计大奖
2008 年荣获国际建筑奖

设计单位：土人设计